Saudi Capital Market

International Banking and Finance Law Series

VOLUME 31

Series Editors

Professor Joseph Norton, Professor Ross Buckley and Professor Douglas Arner.

Subjects

Topical issues in international banking and financial services law, such as regulatory responses to the global financial crisis or regulation of alternative investment funds.

Objective & Readership

To provide authoritative analysis of trends and complex subjects for academics, regulators and practitioners involved in international banking and financial services law.

The titles published in this series are listed at the end of this volume.

Saudi Capital Market

Developments and Challenges

Bader Alkhaldi

Wolters Kluwer

Published by:
Kluwer Law International B.V.
PO Box 316
2400 AH Alphen aan den Rijn
The Netherlands
Website: www.wklawbusiness.com

Sold and distributed in North, Central and South America by:
Wolters Kluwer Legal & Regulatory U.S.
7201 McKinney Circle
Frederick, MD 21704
United States of America
Email: customer.service@wolterskluwer.com

Sold and distributed in all other countries by:
Turpin Distribution Services Ltd
Stratton Business Park
Pegasus Drive, Biggleswade
Bedfordshire SG18 8TQ
United Kingdom
Email: kluwerlaw@turpin-distribution.com

ISBN 978-90-411-8351-4

e-Book: ISBN 978-90-411-8352-1
web-PDF: ISBN 978-90-411-8353-8

I dedicate this book to my parents, Norah and Abdulaziz,
to my wife, Mashael, and to my children Sultan and Danah.

Table of Contents

Preface

The recent oil price collapse, and its immediate and long-term impact on the world economy, has cast light on the Saudi Arabian economy, which is the largest in the Middle East and North Africa ("MENA") region and the 19th largest in the world. Saudi Arabia's importance is more than economic: the Kingdom is also home to the two Holy Mosques and some 30 million people. Thus, the Kingdom should consider its reaction to the oil price collapse in order to create a more modernized and sustainable future for its people.

But, the transformation of the traditional commodity-based economy of the Kingdom of Saudi Arabia (KSA) to a "modern" economy poses a substantial challenge for the country. To achieve this objective, diversifying the economy with an eye towards long-term sustainability will be required. This would include meaningful central planning that would serve as an effective roadmap. Also desirable would be a leadership role for the government in international organizations such as the Gulf Cooperation Council, the World Trade Organization (WTO), and the G20. The *Vision 2030* plan embodies many of these goals.

Part of the modernization process will be to develop a robust capital market that is based on transparency and fairness. This effort suffered a significant setback in the Saudi stock market crash in 2006 ("Crash of 2006"), which exposed serious flaws in the capital market's overall structure. Active membership in international organizations like the International Organization of Securities Commissions ("IOSCO") is an important part of the recovery and movement towards a modern capital market.

Moreover, there are serious questions about the dispute resolution system in Saudi Arabia in dealing with financial matters. Shari'ah law, the law of the land in the Kingdom, is not all encompassing. In fact, some components of a modern economy would appear to violate Islamic law, at least to some extent. To deal with this shortcoming, the Kingdom has come to rely on quasi-judicial committees, including the Committee for Resolution of Securities Disputes ("CRSD"). The CRSD has ascertainable ties to the Capital Market Authority ("CMA"), financially and administratively. This dependence arguably renders the CRSD unconstitutional, a matter that will need to be dealt with.

There should also be market disclosure requirements that are consistent with international standards. Such rules are necessary to promote confidence in an equitable capital market, thus increasing investment and diversifying the economy. The foundation is largely in place, thanks to the Capital Market Law of 2003 ("CML") and some other regulations, but violators are not apprehended, prosecuted, and punished in a manner that contributes to market fairness.

There are similar challenges facing insider-trading laws. While there is a prohibition in place, to date, there are only five cases from the CRSD that interpret the law's provisions, and the jurisprudence that does exist is not consistent. Other problematic issues include the investing public's lack of awareness of insider-trading laws, anemic penalties that do not effectively deter wrongdoing, and lackluster enforcement of the laws. This system for dealing with insider trading stands in stark contrast to the one in the United States, which features a multilayer approach to the disposition of these matters, along with an effective whistleblower program that significantly aids the prosecution of insider-trading cases.

Considering these challenges, this book will focus on three substantive areas related to the Saudi transformation: (i) the roles of economic planning and a capital market in economic modernization; (ii) the level of transparency and fairness in the capital market; and (iii) appropriate judicial and administrative authorities.

The central proposition being presented in this book is that in order for Saudi Arabia to have a modern, sustainable, and well-functioning economy, it must have a strong capital market. In doing so, it is important for the government, the CMA, the CRSD, and Saudi law-policy makers to focus on and to develop various approaches: (i) to educate investors and the general public about illegal activities in the capital market; (ii) to increase the penalties for securities law violations; and (iii) to take full advantage of the enforcement provisions that are in place.

This book should contribute to an advancement and better understanding of the new CML and its related regulations, especially the laws related to disclosure, nonpublic information, and insider trading.

Acknowledgments

I would like to express my thanks to Professor Joseph J. Norton at Southern Methodist University for his continued and unlimited support, consistent guidance, invaluable comments, and ongoing encouragement during my studies and researches at Southern Methodist University. I am honored and privileged to have had the opportunity to work and search under his supervision.

Moreover, I would like to express my thanks and appreciation to the Supervisory Committee at Southern Methodist University for their time and constructive feedback including Professor Joseph J. Norton, Primary Faculty Member; Professor Marc I. Steinberg, Second Internal Faculty Member; and Dr. Ramy El Borai, External Expert Member.

I also would like to express my thanks to Dean Marin Camp, the Assistant Dean for Graduate and International Programs at Southern Methodist University, for his support, advice, and kind efforts to eliminate any obstacles that I have faced during my study at SMU.

Furthermore, I wish to thank Mr. Adel Gabani, the Secretary-General of the Committees for the Resolution of Securities Disputes, for his generous support, help, and encouragement. Mr Gabani offered me valuable insight into the Committee's interworking which greatly enhanced the final product.

Many thanks go to the Dean of the SMU Dedman School of Law, Jennifer Collins, to the Admission office staff, especially Ms Bobbye Heine, the Assistant Director for Graduate Legal Programs, to librarians in SMU's Underwood Law Library, and to all of the faculty members at Dedman School of Law for their support and help at all times.

Special thanks go to my parents, brothers, and sisters for their love and support. Also, many, many thanks go to my dear wife, Mashael, for her support and patience during my research.

List of Abbreviations

1934 Act	U.S. Securities Exchange Act 1934
ACRSD	Appeal Committee for the Resolution of Securities Disputes
Ajwa Co.	Ajwa Company
Amiantit	Saudi Arabian Amiantit Company
BCL	Saudi Banking Control Law
BIPP	Bureau of Investigation and Public Prosecution
Bishah	Bishah Agricultural Development Company
CFI	Capital Finance International
CGR	Corporate Governance Regulations
CMA	Capital Market Authority
CML	Capital Market Law
CRSD	Committee for the Resolution of Securities Disputes
CSBD	Committee for the Settlement of Banking Disputes
CSDR	Committee for Securities Dispute Resolution
CTU	Central Trading Units
Dodd-Frank Act	Dodd-Frank Wall Street Reform and Consumer Protection Act
DOJ	U.S. Department of Justice
EMDE	Emerging Market and Developing Economy
EMU	European Monetary Union
ESIS	Electronic Securities Information System
FDI	Foreign Direct Investment
FSB	Financial Stability Board
G-20	Group of Twenty
GATT	General Agreement on Tariffs and Trade
GCC	Cooperation Council for the Arab States of the Gulf
GDP	Gross Domestic Product

IMF	International Monetary Fund
IODS	International Ongoing Disclosure Standards
IOSCO	International Organization of Securities Commissions
IPF	Investor Protection Fund
IPO	Initial Public Offering
IRALC	Instructions for Regulating Announcements of Listed Companies in the Saudi Capital Market
ITSA	Insider Trading Sanction Act
ITSFEA	Insider Trading and Securities Fraud Enforcement Act
KSA	Kingdom of Saudi Arabia
LR	Listing Rules
MCR	Market Conducts Regulations
MD&A	Management's Discussion and Analysis of Financial Condition and Results of Operations
MENA	Middle East and North Africa
MFN	Most Favored Nation
MMOU	Multilateral Memorandum of Understanding
MOU	Memorandum of Understanding
NCBs	National Central Banks
NTP	National Transformation Program
OPEC	Organization of the Petroleum Exporting Countries
OSR	Offers of Securities Regulations
OTC	Over-the-counter
OWB	Office of the Whistleblower
QAC	Qassim Agriculture Company
RICO	Racketeer Influenced Corrupt Organization Act
S&P	Standard & Poor
SAGIA	Saudi Arabian General Investment Authority
SAIF	Saudi Arabian Investment Fund
SAMA	Saudi Arabian Monetary Agency
SAR	Saudi Riyal
SEC	U.S. Securities and Exchange Commission
SHC	Saudi Hotels Company
SIFIs	Systematically Important Financial Institutions
SMEs	Small and Medium-Sized Enterprises
SOCAL	Standard Oil Company of California
SOCPA	Saudi Organization for Certified Public Accountants
SSRC	Saudi Share Registration Company

STC	Saudi Telecom Company
Tadawul	Saudi Stock Exchange
TASI	Tadawul All Share Index
The Charter	Cooperation Council Charter
TPC	Turkish Petroleum Company
U.S.	United States
USTR	United States Trade Representative's
WTO	World Trade Organization

Introduction

The Saudi Arabian economy has expanded significantly over the past several decades, especially with the increased foreign investment that is now possible. Now, Saudi Arabia is the largest economy in the Middle East/North Africa ("MENA") region, the 19th largest in the world, and a member of the G-20 (Leaders) Group. Thus, the Saudi economy has a significant impact on its neighbors clustered around the Arabian Gulf and across the world. The nation is also culturally important to the world's two billion Muslims, due to the presence of the Two Holy Mosques in Mecca and Medina.

The capital market is one of the key bellwethers in a country's economy, because it combines so many economic forces: consumer confidence, investor assets, short-term and long-term economic outlook, the relative financial stability of companies and corporations, government economic policies, and so on. All these items come together to drive the market up or down, so any assessment of Saudi Arabia's economic past, present and future must include a detailed analysis of Tadawul, the Kingdom's stock market.

In Saudi Arabia, this journey begins with the modern Kingdom's beginning in 1932. For much of its history, many international observers have viewed the Kingdom as simply another oil emirate. And, in the past, such opinions may have been more or less valid. But because of a series of Five-Year Plans and the revolutionary *Vision 2030* plan, both of which stress privatization, domestic, and foreign investment are becoming much more important to the Saudi economy. The Saudi Stock Exchange ("Tadawul"), which has been a rather closed and secretive market since its inception, should develop as well, and the latest trends indicate that such growth is happening.

Growth hardly ever occurs on a smooth linear path, and Tadawul's development is no exception to this general rule. The worldwide investment bubble in the mid 2000s had a rather profound impact in Saudi Arabia, partially because the market lacked fundamental guarantees of transparency and fairness. These ingredients are essential for a healthy capital market. Despite the setback, which included a near-debilitating stock market crash, the Kingdom showed its determination to move forward. This book examines the 2006 Crash in considerable detail. The end result is that the Kingdom's forward-thinking attitude paid dividends in the crash's aftermath, is still paying dividends today, and it appears that this trend will continue into tomorrow as Tadawul assumes a prominent place in the plan to reshape the economy.

Conflicts are inevitable in any investment marketplace, and the decision-maker created the quasi-judicial Committee for the Resolution of Securities Disputes to intervene in these matters, mostly because the more traditional *Shari'ah* courts, which have general jurisdiction in civil cases, have been either unwilling or unable to resolve these disputes. There are some serious questions about the Committee for the Resolution of Securities Disputes' ("CRSD") constitutionality and place in the dispute resolution system, even in the wake of the 2007 Judiciary Law, and these questions should be addressed if the market is to flourish from both an economic and political standpoint.

The 2003 Capital Market Law (CML), and the Capital Market Authority (CMA) that this law created, established clearer rules in this area as a stepping-stone to effective dispute resolution, particularly in some sectors. Disclosure is a key element in market fairness, because if all investors are not on a level playing field, potential new participants will take their money elsewhere. The CML has enacted disclosure laws that are largely in line with international standards, and it is up to the CMA to enforce these laws in a consistent, fair, and evenhanded manner that is also completely transparent. Part of this book examines the historical contributions of the disclosure laws to promote the level of disclosure and transparency in the Saudi capital market, as well as ongoing efforts to protect investors and uphold the integrity of the capital market.

Insider trading is a closely related matter, and in this area, the issues may be more societal than political. Many citizens do not think insider trading is wrong, do not know it is illegal, or do not believe that it is a serious infraction. The weak and rather poorly defined laws in this sector reflect society's attitude, as does the lack of vigorous enforcement. To correct these deficiencies, a whistleblower program and some other reforms may give insider trading more of a social stigma, creating a ripple effect that will bring about harsher laws and tighter enforcement. This book critically examines the law and procedure of insider trading in Saudi Arabia, and makes some suggestions for improving the processes and laws. One such improvement should come by borrowing the "Whistleblower Program" from the United States (U.S.). Indeed, comparing Saudi laws with the insider-trading laws in the U.S. and elsewhere may open up a treasure trove of information that policy-makers can use in their efforts to reshape the economy.

The story is not over yet, and Tadawul has an important role to play in *Vision 2030* and the Kingdom's economic future. A transparent and fair capital market that welcomes investors and effectively monitors activity is within reach, and this economic pillar would make a tremendous difference in everyday Saudi life well into the future.

CHAPTER 1

The Backdrop: Transformation of the Traditional Commodity-Based Economy of the Kingdom of Saudi Arabia

SUMMARY

Since the Kingdom's foundation in 1932, petroleum and other energy-related industries have dominated the country's economy. Petroleum revenue accounts for about 90 % of the Saudi Gross Domestic Product, but given the recent radical decline in oil prices, and its adverse impact on Saudi Arabia's budget, this foundation appears to be unsteady, at best. Now, Saudi Arabia should take a risk that will certainly alter the future of millions. The time to begin these changes should be now, given the current economic climate and the immediate uncertainty it presents. Moreover, a petroleum-based economy does not appear to be sustainable in the short or long term, and gradual and sustained changes are in order.

The first step is to lay the proper foundation in a market economy that is based on private ownership. Since a market economy is primarily built on private property and capital investment, the State should continue to encourage the privatization and investment-friendly environment that are already in place.

Effective long-range planning is essential, and a Five-Year Plan can provide an effective roadmap to economic diversity and stability. This vision should include enhancing the participation in the GCC, WTO, G-20, and other similar regional and international organizations. The next logical step after the Five-Year Plans is a plan to redesign the economy, and the bold new *Vision 2030* is such a plan. The Deputy Crown Prince Mohammed bin Salman hopes to broaden the economic base, make the government more ambitious, and create a more positive social environment.

The government has made a firm commitment to update its laws and diversify the economy. With this commitment in place, and with a concerted effort to change, it is possible to overcome the challenges of globalization.

This chapter explores how intentional change can make a positive difference to Saudi Arabia and its people. Only by becoming globalized can Saudi Arabia be a truly developed nation, and have a place among the world's economic and political elite.

§1.01 INTRODUCTION

Long before the first drop of oil was drilled out of the Saudi Arabian desert, people gravitated towards the area that is now known as The Kingdom of Saudi Arabia (KSA). Until the nineteenth century, the Arabian Peninsula largely consisted of loosely organized tribes. At about that time, Muhammed bin Abdul Wahab and Muhammed Bin Saud established the First Saudi State, which soon controlled most of modern-day Saudi Arabia. After a brief war with the Ottoman Turks, the Al-Saud family established the Second Saudi State in 1824, followed by the Second Ottoman War and the proclamation of the Third Saudi State in 1902. Thereafter, Al-Saud incorporated the remaining independent tribes into the KSA, which was proclaimed in 1932.[1] Oil was discovered shortly thereafter, in 1938.[2]

The early desert nomads have largely been replaced by urban dwellers, thanks largely to the efforts of Abdul Aziz, the first King of Saudi Arabia in 1932. Especially during those earliest days, he probably had little idea that the Kingdom would one day grow into one of the world's most influential economic powers.[3] Yet, just over eighty years later, Saudi Arabia stands on the cusp of fulfilling that role. What, if anything, is holding the Kingdom back?

The answer to this question lies first in the internal workings of Saudi Arabia's economy, and then in an analysis of the Kingdom's moves towards globalization. By understanding the former, it becomes clear why the latter has occurred in "fits and starts," at best. As mentioned above, the appearance of the Third Saudi State roughly coincided with the discovery of oil, so it is understandable that the early economy was almost totally dependent on petroleum exploration and production. The vast quantities of petroleum that were, and still are, pooled beneath the ground necessarily means that oil represents a significant portion of the economy's present and future. But, as the Kingdom grew and the price of oil became increasingly unstable, it became apparent that structural changes had to take place. As a result, the government has made a concerted effort to develop nonpetroleum sectors and to diversify the economy. For this effort to fully bear fruit, there must be a free exchange of ideas, goods, and money across international borders.

---

1. *See* Daniel Yergin, *The Prize, the Epic Quest For Oil, Money, And Power*, Simon & Schuster, New York (1992); James Wynbrandt, *A Brief History of Saudi Arabia 191* (Facts On File, 2nd ed. 2010); Royal Embassy of Saudi Arabia in Washington, DC, *History*, (Nov. 7, 2015), http://www.saudiembassy.net/about/country-information/history/.
2. In 1938, commercial quantities of oil were discovered. This well, Dammam No. 7, near Dhahran in the Eastern Province of the Kingdom of Saudi Arabia, was the first to strike oil. *See* Wynbrandt, *supra* n. 1, at 191.
3. *Cf.* International Monetary Fund, *World Economic and Financial Surveys-Regional Economic Outlook: Middle East and Central Asia* (Oct. 15, 2015) (reporting that Saudi Arabia could be bankrupt in 2020, principally as a result of the recent decline in oil prices).

This new idea had to come as a shock to many in Saudi Arabia. Those who were accustomed to only looking underground for oil now had to look across both the Arabian Gulf and the Red Sea. It is thus little surprise that forging a political and economic "partnership" with other neighboring Muslim countries has been hard enough: relationships with non-Muslim countries have been more trying.

That is not to say that these relationships have been a disaster. Changes within the Saudi economy have paved the way for better relationships with other Gulf States, as well as other countries, in the increasingly small globe that we all share. To be sure, that road has had a lot of potholes, and more of the same lies ahead. The Kingdom's ability, and willingness, to persevere through these difficulties and keep its eye on the ultimate goal (becoming a developed country) has fueled its efforts thus far, and will continue to do so in the future.

In recent times, the Saudi State has made a decision to integrate with the rest of the world, because that is where the future lies.[4] In order for Saudi Arabia to arrive where it has determined to go, some structural and philosophical changes should be made. Indeed, those changes are already in progress. The reforms are not random and spontaneous, but rather planned and purposeful.[5] More of these changes need to happen.

This chapter provides an overview of the Saudi economy and its development over the past eight decades, beginning with King Abdulaziz's groundwork and ending with *Vision 2030*'s plans. More specifically, it addresses the Saudi government's role in reforming and modernizing the economy. Additionally, it discusses Saudi Arabia's movement towards regional and global economic and financial relevance.

§1.02 THE SAUDI ECONOMY AND ITS DEVELOPMENT

The modern Saudi Arabia economy bears little resemblance to the now-ancient realm of King Abdul Aziz. That economy looked to basic agriculture and subsistence farming as its primary revenue bases. The KSA has evolved over the years. These developments are identified and discussed in this chapter.

Change is a slow process in a traditional society.[6] To avoid cultural and societal shock, reforms in a conservative society are usually introduced incrementally and according to a set plan and timetable. The Saudi government recognizes this, and has introduced reforms that, step-by-step, are moving Saudi Arabia towards "globalization."[7]

Petroleum is the "800-pound gorilla" of the Saudi economy. Saudi Arabia's proven oil reserves stood at a staggering 266.58 billion barrels at the end of 2014. The

4. For example., the Kingdom's participation in the GCC, WTO, and G-20 are discussed hereinafter.
5. *See* II[B] (The Case for Central Planning and Five-Year Plans).
6. *See* Garth N. Jones, Strategies and Tactics of Planned Organizational Change: Case Examples in the Modernization Process of Traditional Societies, 24 Hum. Org. 192 (1965).
7. Ministry of Economy and Planning of Saudi Arabia, *Seventh Development Plan 1420/21–1424/25 (A.H), 2000– 2004 (A.D)* 52 (Nov. 7, 2015), http://www.mep.gov.sa/themes/GoldenCarpet/index.jsp;jsessionid = F374FDCD0B6758187FA54B943B0D0DF0.alfa?event = SwitchLanguage&Code = EN#1405309588083.

Kingdom's proven reserves of natural gas rose by 2.1% to about 299.74 trillion standard cubic feet at the end of 2014.[8] There is no doubt that these resources have helped the Kingdom to grow its economy rapidly in comparison to other developing countries.

Until a few decades ago, those in the West viewed Saudi Arabia as essentially empty desert with little or no economic value. This lack of interest meant that Saudi Arabia has never been colonized like most other developing countries.[9] So, the Kingdom has achieved political and social stability much more quickly than some other nations – most notably those in Africa, South Asia, and Southeast Asia. Both these factors are indispensable for long-term sustainable development in a nation.

But, Saudi Arabia got a late start in its economic development program. The country showed no real interest in modernization until well into the 1970s. While some may consider this situation to be a liability, it can, in fact, be viewed as a distinct advantage. Saudi Arabia has the benefit of experience of others: the modern Kingdom has the advantage of adopting and using other countries' methods in its development plans and technology utilization, learning from both their triumphs and their setbacks.[10] These primary elements have enabled the government of Saudi Arabia and its agencies to build and develop its economy, starting with its petroleum base and then moving forward.

[A] The Petroleum Platform

In the early 1930s, the economy of Saudi Arabia was characterized by weakness and instability, brought about by King Ibn Saud's serious financial difficulties.[11] John Philby, Ibn Saud's advisor, knew about Ibn Saud's fiscal problems and the threat they represented.[12] Philby told Ibn Saud that there was great mineral wealth beneath the desert and pleaded with the King to conduct appropriate exploration, but Ibn Saud was much more interested in water and neglected oil.[13] When oil was discovered in some places in the 1920s, and in the beginning of the 1930s around the Arabian Gulf, the sudden discoveries created the hope that there may be considerably more underground wealth that could reverse Saudi Arabia's dire financial situation.[14]

Still feeling empowered by their victory in the First World War, and sensing economic opportunity in an unspoiled and nonaligned territory, the Western powers hastily drew up the so-called Red Line Agreement. Much like the "Line of Demarcation" once divided the world between Portugal and Spain, this 1928 agreement among several prominent American, British, and French oil companies divided the oil

8. Saudi Arabian Monetary Agency, *51st Annual Report* 140-141 (2015).
9. Abdullah Alobad, *Egtsad Almmlakh Alarabih Alsaodih* 6 [*The Kingdom of Saudi Arabia Economy*], (Dar Alam Alkotob Press 1994).
10. *Id.* at 7.
11. Yergin, *supra* n. 1, at 286.
12. *Id.* at 287.
13. *Id.* at 288.
14. Federal Research Division, *Country Studies: Saudi Arabia*, Library of Congress (Nov. 8, 2015), http://countrystudies.us/saudi-arabia/.

resources of the former Ottoman Empire within the Middle East.[15] Four of the era's largest oil exploration concerns – the Anglo-Persian, Royal Dutch/Shell, the Compagnie Française des Pétroles, and the Near East Development Corporation – agreed not to make independent deals concerning the Turkish Petroleum Company's ("TPC") territory. Obviously, the Red Line Agreement did not apply to anyone outside these four companies.[16] That loophole opened the door for the Standard Oil Company of California ("SOCAL").[17]

SOCAL negotiated with the Kingdom of Bahrain and soon obtained a concession from a government that was eager not to be left out. SOCAL almost immediately discovered oil in Bahrain, in 1932.[18] Then, having established itself as a major player in the Middle Eastern petroleum exploration industry, SOCAL gained a concession in Saudi Arabia in July 1933.[19]

SOCAL saw King Abdul Aziz's financial problems as an opportunity.[20] The concession between the government of Saudi Arabia and SOCAL provided an annual rental fee of GBP 5,000 in gold or its equivalent until oil was discovered, a direct loan of GBP 50,000 in gold to the government of Saudi Arabia, a royalty payment (in gold) of four shillings per net ton of crude production after the discovery of oil, and free supply to the government of specific quantities of products from the refinery company that was to be built after oil was discovered.[21] The concession gave the company the exclusive rights to explore for, to produce, and to export oil, free of all Saudi taxes and duties, in most of eastern Saudi Arabia for sixty years. The terms in the agreement were liberal, reflecting the King's dire need for additional revenue streams, his low estimate of future oil production, and his weak bargaining position.[22]

Throughout the 1930s and 1940s, the original concession agreement was modified many times. By 1950, a fifty-fifty profit sharing agreement was signed, whereby the government levied a tax. This tax helped the government to augment its revenues,[23] especially because, by that time, production was much higher. Prior to that time, oil had not been produced in significant quantities due to the circumstances that unfolded during and after World War II.[24] However, almost immediately after the war, oil revenues mushroomed to USD 212 million by the end of 1950.[25]

Petroleum quickly became the most important domestic commodity, accounting for the lion's share of the Kingdom's gross domestic product ("GDP"). As the economy

15. U.S. Department of State, Office of Historian, *The 1928 Red Line Agreement* (Nov. 8, 2015), http://history.state.gov/milestones/1921-1936/RedLine; *see* M.S. Vassiliou, *The A to Z of the Petroleum Industry* 448 (Scarecrow Press 2009).
16. *Id.*
17. Vassiliou, *supra* n. 15, at 448.
18. Federal Research Division, *Country Studies*: *Saudi Arabia*, *supra* n. 14.
19. *Id.*
20. *See supra* n. 11, and accompanying text.
21. Federal Research Division, *Country Studies*: *Saudi Arabia*, *supra* n. 14.
22. *Id.*
23. *Id.*
24. Abdulaziz Aldakeel, *Altanmih Alagtsadih Fi Almamlkh Alarabia Alsaodih: Gerah Fi Masirat Altanmih* 89 [*Economic Development in the Kingdom of Saudi Arabia, Reading in the Development Process*], the Article was written in 1986 (Dar Alsaqi Press 2012).
25. *Id.*

and the population grew, oil production increased steadily over the years to keep pace. In 2014, Saudi crude oil production increased by 0.8%, to amount to 3,545.1 million barrels, in comparison to the 3,517.6 million barrels in 2013. The Kingdom's production of refined products in 2014 increased by 19.6% to be 803.8 million barrels compared to 672.2 million barrels in 2013.[26] Moreover, during 2014, Saudi Arabia's crude oil exports decreased by 5.5% to be 2,611.0 million barrels compared to 2,763.3 million barrels in 2013.[27]

Table 1.1 contains oil statistics in the KSA during the last three decades:[28]

Table 1.1 Oil Statistics in Saudi Arabia

Year	*Reserves (Billion Barrels)*	*Production (Million Barrels)*	*Export (Million Barrels)*	*Average OPEC Basket Price (USD)*
1981	164.82	3,579.89	3,291.54	34.2
1982	168.32	2,366.41	2,058.40	31.7
1983	169.02	1,656.88	1,431.08	28.8
1984	171.71	1,492.90	1,167.89	28.1
1985	171.49	1,158.80	760.72	27.5
1986	169.75	1,746.20	1,190.02	13.7
1987	169.59	1,505.40	973.12	17.2
1988	254.99	1,890.10	1,245.49	13.4
1989	260.05	1,848.50	1,217.50	16.2
1990	260.34	2,340.50	1,642.42	20.8
1991	260.93	2,963.00	2,382.11	17.4
1992	261.20	3,049.40	2,408.98	17.9
1993	261.36	2,937.40	2,296.92	15.7
1994	261.38	2,937.90	2,275.27	15.4
1995	261.45	2,928.54	2,296.13	16.9
1996	261.44	2,965.45	2,236.01	20.3
1997	261.54	2,924.28	2,257.33	18.7
1998	261.54	3,022.27	2,332.48	12.3
1999	262.79	2,761.10	2,087.68	17.5
2000	262.76	2,962.60	2,282.38	27.6
2001	262.70	2,879.46	2,203.10	23.1

26. Saudi Arabian Monetary Agency, *51st Annual Report, supra* n. 8, at 141.
27. *Id.* at 143.
28. Ministry of Petroleum and Mineral Resources of Saudi Arabia, *Statistics: Oil* (Nov. 7, 2015), http://www.mopm.gov.sa/Arabic/Statistics/Pages/Oil-Test.aspx; Saudi Arabian Monetary Agency, *Yearly Statistics* (Dec. 31, 2015), http://www.sama.gov.sa/en-us/economicreports/pages/yearlystatistics.aspx; Saudi Arabian Monetary Agency, *51st Annual Report* at 140; Organization of the Petroleum Exporting Countries, *OPEC Basket Price*, (Dec. 31, 2015), http://www.opec.org/opec_web/en/data_graphs/40.htm.

Year	*Reserves (Billion Barrels)*	*Production (Million Barrels)*	*Export (Million Barrels)*	*Average OPEC Basket Price (USD)*
2002	262.79	2,588.98	1,928.89	24.4
2003	262.73	3,069.74	2,380.85	28.1
2004	264.31	3,256.30	2,486.77	36.1
2005	264.21	3,413.94	2,631.24	50.6
2006	264.25	3,360.90	2,565.72	61.1
2007	264.21	3,217.77	2,541.16	69.1
2008	264.06	3,366.34	2,672.42	94.5
2009	264.59	2,987.27	2,287.66	61.1
2010	264.52	2,980.43	2,425.09	77.5
2011	265.41	3,398.52	2,634.59	107.5
2012	265.85	3,573.40	2,783.78	109.4
2013	265.79	3,517.62	2,763.32	105.8
2014	266.58	3,545.14	2,611.01	96.2
2015	N/A	N/A	N/A	49.4

In another energy-related area, Saudi Arabia's proven reserves of natural gas rose by 2.1% to amount to approximately 299.74 trillion standard cubic feet at the end of the year 2014, compared to 293.68 trillion standard cubic feet at the end of 2013.[29]

Table 1.2 contains gas statistics in the KSA during the last two decades:[30]

Table 1.2 Gas Statistics in Saudi Arabia

Year	*Reserves (Trillion SCF)*[31]	*Number of Discovered Fields*	*Natural Gas Production (Billion SCF)*
1990	184,548	N/A	1,741
1991	184,474	N/A	2,283
1992	185,471	N/A	2,334
1993	185,905	N/A	2,377
1994	190,062	N/A	2,479

29. Saudi Arabian Monetary Agency, *51st Annual Report, supra* n. 8, at 141.
30. Ministry of Petroleum and Mineral Resources of Saudi Arabia, *Gas Statistics* (Nov. 7, 2015) http://www.mopm.gov.sa/Arabic/Statistics/Pages/ -الغاز-احصائيات.aspx; U.S. Energy Information Administration, *International Energy Statistics* (Dec. 31, 2015), https://www.eia.gov/cfapps/ipdbproject/iedindex3.cfm?tid = 3&pid = 3&aid = 1&cid = CG9,&syid = 2010&eyid = 2014&unit = BCF; Saudi Arabian Monetary Agency, *Yearly Statistics* (Dec. 31, 2015), http://www.sama.gov.sa/en-us/economicreports/pages/yearlystatistics.aspx.
31. Standard cubic foot.

Year	*Reserves (Trillion SCF)*[31]	*Number of Discovered Fields*	*Natural Gas Production (Billion SCF)*
1995	195,917	N/A	2,612
1996	200,879	N/A	2,742
1997	207,486	N/A	1,680
1998	214,262	3	1,758
1999	217,027	2	1,719
2000	222,493	2	1,888
2001	227,946	1	2,013
2002	234,673	0	2,120
2003	238,492	1	2,399
2004	241,323	1	2,700
2005	243,648	2	2,873
2006	252,607	3	3,002
2007	257,954	1	2,941
2008	267,311	2	3,051
2009	279,670	1	3,165
2010	283,057	1	3,427
2011	287,822	N/A	3,617
2012	290,772	N/A	3,928
2013	293,685	N/A	4,030
2014	299,742	N/A	4,122

For the last eighty years, the KSA has been nearly synonymous with petroleum. There is no reason to believe that this near total dependence will end anytime soon. So, the question is not so much how to change the reliance on petroleum, but rather how to manage this resource and thus diversify the Saudi economy. Management and planning are keys to most any successful economy. While more developed countries can depend on the private sector to perform this function, younger economies need more direction. That is why it is important for the government to have a clear plan of action for the economy, for the management of natural resources, and for the development of valuable financial markets.

[B] The Case for Central Planning and Five-Year Plans

Until the 1950s and 1960s, the KSA achieved consistent growth rates, while maintaining a remarkable degree of stability and security.[32] However, the Middle East crises at

32. Ministry of Economy and Planning of Saudi Arabia, *The First Development Plan 1390-1395 (A.H) 1970-1975 (A.D)* 21 (Nov. 7, 2015) http://www.mep.gov.sa/themes/GoldenCarpet/index.jsp;jsessionid=9081FB102E53B01B5EA4F4C898BD8CE2.beta?event=SwitchLanguage&Code=EN#1370985755188.

that time began to affect Saudi Arabia's economy in areas such as the declines in the rate of growth of GDP, the decreased gold and foreign exchange holdings of the Saudi Arabian Monetary Agency (SAMA), and the relative percentage increase in oil production.[33] Until 1970, Saudi Arabia saw little need for a long-term development plan. It only had one-year development plans based on an annual budget.[34] The problem was that the nation did not use its resources efficiently by looking to the future.[35] Saudi Arabia had many internal social problems as well, such as malnutrition, illiteracy, and sickness.[36] Such problems cannot be addressed in any meaningful way with a one-year plan based solely upon the current budget. Further, the overreliance on petroleum led to an underdeveloped labor force, as well as the neglect of the financial and transportation infrastructures.[37]

In response, the government created the "SAMA" in 1952 to serve as the central bank and, additionally, to provide financial stability.[38] Yet, these same problems persisted. Until the 1970s, due to limited production in previous decades, the government of Saudi Arabia nearly always operated under significant financial constraints, and oil income increased slowly.[39] So, during this same time period, the KSA changed its method of economic planning by creating a Five-Year Plan.[40]

The Five-Year Plan is better and more effective than the one-year development plan based on an annual budget. Essentially, the Five-Year Plan is more about goals and aspirations for that period, using a macroeconomic perspective. The Five-Year Plan concept goes back to the 1950s. After some suggestions by International Monetary Fund (IMF) advisers, the government of Saudi Arabia created a planning agency in 1958.[41] But that agency had limited resources and its work was limited as a result.[42] The agency was given more money and authority when it became the Central Planning Organization in 1965; in 1975, the government reorganized it to become the Ministry of Planning. In 2003, to more accurately reflect its actual role, the name was changed to the Ministry of Economy and Planning.[43]

The general objectives of the five-year development plan policy in the KSA are to maintain its religious and moral values, to raise the living standards and welfare of its people, to maintain national security and economic and social stability, to boost the rate of growth of GDP, to develop human resources through more education, additional

33. *Id.*
34. Alobad, *supra* n. 9, at 17.
35. *Id.*
36. *Id.*
37. Faiz Alhabib, *Mabada Alagtsad Alkoli* 488 [*Principles of Macroeconomics*] (Alfarazdag Press Company 2011).
38. Saudi Arabian Monetary Agency, *SAMA's Functions* (Nov. 7, 2015) http://www.sama.gov.sa/en-US/About/Pages/SAMAFunction.aspx.
39. Federal Research Division, *Country Studies*: *Saudi Arabia*.
40. Alhabib, *Principles of Macroeconomics, supra* n. 37, at 489.
41. Federal Research Division, *Country Studies*: *Saudi Arabia*.
42. *Id.*
43. Ministry of Finance, *Historical Background* (Nov. 7, 2015) http://www.mof.gov.sa/English/MinistryProfile/Pages/AboutUs.aspx.

training, and better health, to diversify sources of national income and limit the dependence on crude oil exports, and to develop the physical infrastructure to support other mentioned goals.[44] These fundamental principles and goals form the basis for long-term economic development in the KSA. They are reflected in every Five-Year Plan, while interim goals adjust according to the circumstances and necessaries of each Five-Year Plan.[45]

Although it laid the groundwork for future plans, the first Five-Year Development Plan left much to be desired. Primarily due to the lack of experience in how to plan long-term resource utilization and an overall lack of money, the Plan had only a bare-bones approach to the period 1970-1974.[46] The total allocations for the Plan were a mere SAR 41.3 billion (approximately USD 11 billion).[47] The Plan focused solely on the core areas of defense, education, transportation, and utilities. Then, in the last two years of the Plan, the government revenues of crude oil production increased significantly, contributing to rapid economic growth.[48] The planners did not anticipate the huge growth in revenues, and the Plan had to be modified. These modifications essentially saved the Plan, because the previous fiscal constraints were largely eliminated.[49] So, the actual budget expenditures were SAR 86.5 billion (USD 23 billion).[50]

As a result, the Saudi economy achieved significant accomplishments in many sectors and the planners were greatly encouraged by these results. Overall, gross domestic production grew by 13.5% annually, well exceeding the original goal of 9.8% annual growth.[51] These results effectively silenced critics of the Five-Year Plan model and convinced the government that it had done the right thing when it replaced the One-Year Plans.

Table 1.3 shows the structure of government expenditure from the First Plan to the Ninth Plan for the period of 1970-2014:[52]

44. Alobad, *supra* n. 9, at 355-356.
45. *Id.* at 356.
46. Alhabib, *Principles of Macroeconomics, supra* n. 37, at 493.
47. Ministry of Economy and Planning of Saudi Arabia, *The First Development Plan 1390-1395 (A.H) 1970-1975 (A.D)* 30 (Nov. 7, 2015), http://www.mep.gov.sa/themes/GoldenCarpet/index.jsp;jsessionid=9081FB102E53B01B5EA4F4C898BD8CE2.beta?event=SwitchLanguage&Code=EN#1370985755188.
48. Alhabib, *Principles of Macroeconomics, supra* n. 37, at 493.
49. Faiz Alhabib, *Altanmih Alagtsadih Bina Alnathorih Oa Oaga Aldola Alnamih* 159 [*Economic Development between the Theory and the Reality of Developing Countries*] (King Saud Library 1985).
50. *Id.*
51. Alobad, *supra* n. 9, at 359.
52. Ministry of Economy and Planning of Saudi Arabia, *The Kingdom of Saudi Arabia Economy in Figures 2013* VIII (Nov. 7, 2015), http://www.mep.gov.sa/themes/GoldenCarpet/index.jsp;jsessionid=30EB1E1954CDF629613F8ACD4693887A.beta?event=SwitchLanguage&Code=EN#1372045463035.

Table 1.3 Structure of Saudi Government Expenditure (1970-2014)

Structure of Government Expenditure (1970-2014) (Percent)					
Development Plans	*Infrastructure* [1]	*Economic Resources* [2]	*Human Resources* [3]	*Social & Health Services* [4]	*Total*
First Plan 1970-1974	41.3	27.9	20.5	10.3	100.0
Second Plan 1975-1979	49.3	28.0	14.7	8.0	100.0
Third Plan 1980-1984	41.1	30.7	18.4	9.8	100.0
Fourth Plan 1985-1989	28.9	20.4	33.0	17.7	100.0
Fifth Plan 1990-1994	21.8	10.0	48.3	19.9	100.0
Sixth Plan 1995-1999	16.2	11.5	51.5	20.8	100.0
Seventh Plan 2000-2004	12.6	11.2	57.1	19.1	100.0
Eighth Plan 2005-2009	14.1	12.2	55.6	18.1	100.0
Ninth Plan* 2010-2014	14.6	15.8	50.6	19.0	100.0

1 Transport, telecommunication services, public works, housing, and municipal affairs.
2 Agriculture, water and electricity, petroleum & mineral resources, and industrial services.
3 General education, higher education, technical & vocational training, science & technology.
4 Health care, social, youth and information services, and cultural activities.
* Planned expenditures.

Policy-makers realized in 1990s that a capital market in Saudi Arabia needed to be developed in the Seventh Development Plan (2000-2004). Market capitalization in 1997 was about 40% of GDP, which was considered low by international standards. Moreover, at that time, there were only seventy-four listed companies in the stock market, and their stocks were traded through commercial banks.[53] In the late 1990s, there were about 105 commercial bank-managed investment funds, which had assets

53. Ministry of Economy and Planning of Saudi Arabia, *Seventh Development Plan 1420/21–1424/25 (A.H), 2000– 2004 (A.D)* 182 (Nov. 7, 2015), http://www.mep.gov.sa/themes/GoldenCarpet/index.jsp;jsessionid = F374FDCD0B6758187FA54B943B0D0DF0.alfa?event = SwitchLanguage& Code = EN#1405309588083.

abroad more than ten times the size of the investments in Saudi Arabia. This capital outflow was due to the limited investment opportunities in the undeveloped Saudi capital market.[54] Therefore, Saudi Arabia concluded "it [was] imperative to take immediate steps to initiate capital market reforms aimed at promoting the development of a strong stock market and encouraging investments in the Kingdom."[55]

A primary objective of the Seventh Development Plan was to develop the Saudi capital market. To enhance market efficiency, a securities market law was enacted. In addition, the capital market infrastructure in the Kingdom was to be developed. This required the preparation and implementation of an adequate framework to regulate the securities issuance operations by nonbank financial institutions, including offshore institutions. A capital market regulatory agency also was established in order to regulate and to oversee the activities of the capital market and to establish procedures for issuing new shares with the objective of encouraging companies to convert to joint-stock companies. Moreover, regulations for converting firms into joint-stock companies would be revised in order to facilitate the process of transformation,[56] to encourage the creation of independent information centers to compile data on joint-stock companies, and to consider the possibility of allowing foreign investors to trade in the Saudi capital market under appropriate regulations.[57]

In effect, during the Seventh Development Plan period, the Saudi capital market was developed through enacting the "CML" in 2003 and establishing the "CMA" in 2004.[58]

Over the years, the Plans have become increasingly better funded and more ambitious. The Ninth Development Plan, which covers the period 2010-2014, has a number of objectives, most notably accelerating economic development and consolidating its sustainability. The planners believe that sustained economic growth should promote a balanced development among the different regions and should continue to improve the standard of living and quality of life for the citizens of Saudi Arabia, especially the needy groups in the community. Secondary and tertiary goals include mitigating the rate of unemployment, developing national human resources and their efficiency, enhancing the private sector to contribute to the development process, supporting the trend away from an industry-based economy and towards a knowledge-based economy, and improving the competitive ability of the Saudi economy in the global economy.[59]

These strategies should support the economy of the KSA, and allow it to continue its growth in order to cope with globalization.[60] As shown in Table 1.3, the planners

54. *Id.* at 183.
55. *Id.* at 184.
56. *Id.*
57. *Id.* at 129.
58. The Capital Market Law, the Council of Ministers, Royal Decree No. M/30, dated 2/6/1424 H (2003). The Capital Market Authority was established under the Capital Market Law. Its website is http://www.cma.org.sa/En/Pages/home.aspx.
59. Ministry of Economy and Planning of Saudi Arabia, *Ninth Development Plan* 25 (Nov. 7, 2015), http://www.mep.gov.sa/themes/GoldenCarpet/index.jsp;jsessionid=E09FE18DA016FEE60A195FCEAE69AA52.beta?event=SwitchLanguage&Code=AR#1372098668716.
60. Alhabib, *Principles of Macroeconomics, supra* n. 37, at 493.

have more than doubled the Plan's budget for human resources since the initial Five-Year Development Plan. The idea is that the government wants to augment the qualifications and the skills of Saudi human resources in order to replace foreign laborers with Saudi citizens' labors.[61]

Central planning has become increasingly more sophisticated in the decades since 1970. The inexperience and timidity of those first few Plans has been replaced by a bold and forward-thinking Plan; this latest Plan also includes an acute understanding of the Kingdom's overall political and economic goals. Central planning may be a hindrance to some economies, but the Kingdom is different in many historical, economic, religious, and political respects. By carefully managing resources according to a Plan, and giving deference to the planner's authority and knowledge, both the private sector and public sector are well on their way towards globalization.

But Plans alone are not enough. Without underlying economic reform, the most well-conceived and well-funded Plan is doomed to failure. The human resources area is a good example. The Kingdom sees the need to move to a more knowledge-based economy; but, without the proper foundation, the Five-Year Plan is an ineffective vehicle to meet this goal. If the Kingdom is to enter the global economy from a position of strength and not of weakness, effective planning is essential to manage limited resources and to build upon the recent reforms in the Saudi economy.

§1.03 THE ROAD TOWARDS GLOBALIZATION AND STABILITY IN SAUDI ARABIA'S ECONOMY

Change is rarely easy, and economic reform is no exception to this rule. It may seem incongruous for an economy that relies on effective central planning to seek privatization, diversification, and other open-market reforms, but that is exactly what needs to happen. Another maxim is that taking calculated risks is one of the best ways to grow, and the Saudi economic authorities need to be willing to try what has been untried before.

The KSA has focused on economic reforms, especially in the past two decades, in order to keep up with the changes and developments in the global economy. Specifically, the Kingdom is looking to achieve sustainable economic growth, continue jobs creation, and enhance the level of welfare of citizens.[62] Acting alone, the state cannot hope to meet this goal. Previously, reform has concentrated in four main areas: privatization, diversification, development of foreign investment, and regulatory modernization. *Vision 2030*, the bold new plan to diversify the economy, modifies these objectives to include "a vibrant society, a thriving economy, and an ambitious nation."[63]

---

61. *Id.*
62. Saudi Arabian Monetary Agency, *Annual Report 42*, 42 (2006).
63. The Saudi Council of Economic Affairs and Development, *Saudi Vision 2030*, p. 2 (Apr. 25, 2016).

[A] The Move Towards Privatization

In the past decade, the government of Saudi Arabia has made a considerable effort to convert enterprises, projects, services, and institutions in the public sector to the ownership and management of the private sector. The Kingdom has used privatization as a useful mechanism to both expand the participation of the private sector in the economic development and amplify competition and efficiency.[64] As far back as 1997, The Council of Ministers placed the country on this path with Resolution No. 60,[65] which defends the objectives of the strategy and policy of privatization in the Kingdom.

The Resolution did not endorse privatization simply for the sake of reform, but rather ascribed eight objectives for the overall strategy. First and foremost, it was expected that privatization would enhance the efficiency and competitiveness of the national economy by making state-run industries more responsive to rapidly changing national and international market conditions. Alongside this goal, the Resolution sought to encourage private investment from both domestic and foreign investors. A sense of ownership almost always increases the willingness to invest. This sense of ownership should extend to the people as well, and not just to corporate leadership. Additionally, citizens should see more and better job opportunities and, consequently, higher incomes.[66]

The Resolution also placed a priority on affordable and timely services for both citizens and investors, which should reduce the public expenditure in these areas and alleviate pressure on the state budget. In fact, the state should see additional funds from privatization as these industries become more efficient and more profitable. Moreover, there is an additional revenue stream from concessions granted to private groups wishing to start or expand a business.[67]

As a follow-up, the Council of Ministers issued Resolution No. 257 in 2001.[68] That resolution allowed the Supreme Economic Council to undertake the responsibility of supervising the privatization program and monitoring its implementation in coordination with the appropriate government agencies.[69] The Supreme Economic Council is responsible for identifying the target activities that would be issued by a Resolution of the Council of Ministers, while the Economic Council would develop the privatization strategy and specify a schedule for its implementation.[70] Essentially, the State sought to retain some control over these privatized industries so that there could still be

64. *Id.*
65. The Council of Ministers, *Privatization Objectives*, Resolution No. 60, dated 1/4/1418 H (1997).
66. Ministry of Economy and Planning of Saudi Arabia, *Achievements of the Plan* 58, Version 29, 2012 (Nov. 9, 2015), http://www.mep.gov.sa/themes/GoldenCarpet/index.jsp#1372627677775.
67. *Id.*
68. The Supreme Economic Council, The Council of Ministers, Resolution No. 257, dated 11/11/1421 H (2001).
69. Water & Electricity L.L.C., *Saudi Privatization Strategy*, (Sept. 27, 2016), http://www.wec.com.sa/PageContentDetails.aspx?menuId=34.
70. Ministry of Economy and Planning of Saudi Arabia, *Achievements of the Plan* 58, Version 29, 2012 (Nov. 9, 2015), http://www.mep.gov.sa/themes/GoldenCarpet/index.jsp;jsessionid=CE72BF929B432B2162EAABA14A68268B.beta?event=SwitchLanguage&Code=EN#1372712260448.

independent oversight of their activities. In other words, the Kingdom took steps to avoid the dark side of privatization: unregulated industries whose only motive is to make money.

It is still fairly early in the program, but the results so far have been encouraging, as they have largely been in line with the goals of Resolution 60. Privatization has progressed nicely in several sectors such as electricity, communications, mineral resources, air transportation, and insurance. The overall participation of the private sector has increased through sale of shares of ownership, operate-manage contracts, leasing assets, and build-operate-transfer contracts.[71] To date, Saudi Telecom Company (STC), Saudi Arabian Airlines, Saudi Ports Services, Saudi Electricity Company, Saudi Railways Organization, and Saudi Postal Corporation either have been privatized or are scheduled for privatization in the near future.[72] The news is not all good. So far, foreign participation has been limited: foreign entities can contribute only as a partner and own shares in a Saudi limited liability company.[73] Otherwise, foreign entities cannot buy shares directly in state-owned enterprises that are subject to privatization.[74]

The privatization movement by the government was an essential first step towards efficient and stable economic reform in the Kingdom. While it is undoubtedly true that the government will have less control over projects, enterprises, services, and institutions, this loss is more than made up for by the economic, social, and fiscal benefits of privatization for both the Saudi government and its citizens. Simply put, competition in the private sector should increase the growth of the Saudi economy. Just as significantly, privatization attracts foreign investors to the Kingdom. The laws may need to be reviewed to help promote the flow of foreign capital that is needed to fuel the other reforms in the Saudi economy. Also, the Supreme Economic Council needs to be vigilant and ensure that the privatization programs are followed as intended, and it needs to monitor its implementation closely with other agencies without being lulled into inactivity by the extra money in the economy. Further, just as the ownership model needs to change, the way the people do business should change as well, if Saudi Arabia is serious about becoming a player in the global economy.

[B] Economic Diversification: Weaning the Kingdom Off a Strict Petroleum Diet

A fundamental rule of business is to never allow one client or customer to dominate the activities because a loss or even a slowdown may have a devastating effect on the bottom line. Countries should operate by the same principle. Any nation that heavily

71. *Id.*
72. Othman Alrouaf, *Engazat Altanoih Fi Almamlkh Alarabih Alsaodih* 396 [*Development Achievements in the Kingdom of Saudi Arabia*], (Alhomathi Press 2010).
73. Ministry of Commerce and Industry, *Tagreer Farig Alamal Hola Inthmam Almamlkh Alarbia Alsaodih Ela Monthmat Altgarh Alalmih* 32, 2005 [*Report on Saudi Arabia's accession to the World Trade Organization 2005*], (Nov. 9, 2015), http://www.mci.gov.sa/Agencies/TechnicalAffairs/ReportsandStatistics/Pages/default.aspx.
74. *Id.*

relies on only one source of income for its economy is at risk of eventual economic collapse.[75] The situation is hardly unique to Saudi Arabia. Because there is little money available to invest in the economy, and because the start-up countries need vast quantities of capital, many developing countries produce and export only one or two commodities. This overreliance may be understandable, at least in the short term, but it makes their economies vulnerable to shocks that inevitably occur in the prices or the productions of these commodities.[76] Moreover, the domestic economies of these developing countries depend on the global effects and variables on these commodities.[77] As such, the economies of these developing countries continually stare economic disaster in the face. They live with the fear that the oil, rubber or tin market will collapse without warning. Because of this fear, they generally have unsustainable and unstable economies.

Fortunately, for all concerned, the KSA has recognized the issue of depending too heavily on oil. Oil is not a renewable resource, and there will come a day when exports will begin to decline and eventually cease altogether. In a planned capacity, assuming an annual output and production level of 12.5 MBPD[78] in Saudi Arabia, the Kingdom may deplete its underground petroleum reserves and cease to export oil by 2075 or 2085, assuming that global consumption continues to grow on a linear path.[79]

The government is not content to count the days until the oil runs out, and it is being proactive in promoting economic diversification. The private sector has been the tip of the spear in terms of the development efforts by the government of Saudi Arabia, in order to diversify the Kingdom's economy and to reduce the dependency on oil revenues.[80] The Ninth Devolvement Plan[81] included several policies intended to promote nonpetroleum economic sectors, such as developing an attractive environment for national and foreign private investments, activating public and private initiatives that are related to small and medium-sized enterprise development, and promoting the incentive packages that are granted to national and foreign private investment to enable them to raise the technical component in non-oil products and exports.[82] Once again, the early returns are encouraging. The non-oil GPD, at 1999 constant prices, has increased at an average annual rate of 5.4% over the period of 1969-2011.[83]

Unfortunately, a look behind the numbers reveals a far different picture. Even though the government of Saudi Arabia has focused on the diversification of its economy through the Five-Year Plans, the reliance on oil revenues and productions is

75. In fact, the International Monetary Fund recently predicted that, due to largely the recent low petroleum prices, the Kingdom might be effectively bankrupt by 2020. *See supra* n. 3.
76. Alhabib, *Principles of Macroeconomics, supra* n. 37, at 486.
77. *Id.*
78. Million barrels per day.
79. Mohamed A. Ramady, *The Saudi Arabian Economy, Policies, Achievements, and Challenges* 15 (2d ed. 2010).
80. Saudi Arabian Monetary Agency, *Annual Report* 42, 42 (2006).
81. The Ninth Development Plane covers the period of 2010-2014.
82. Ministry of Economy and Planning of Saudi Arabia, *Achievements of the Plan* 56, Version 29, 2012 (Nov. 9, 2015).
83. *Id.* at 15.

still a significant issue in the Saudi economy. In fact, actual total revenue for fiscal year 2014 was USD 278.9 billion; 89% of which was petroleum revenue.[84] Despite years of effort to the contrary, diversification is still nowhere near a reality in Saudi Arabia. Nearly the entire GDP is based on petroleum and its derivatives, and *Vision 2030* directly addresses this deficiency.

The government must look for other alternatives in productions in order to create a real diversification in the Kingdom's economy that is not based on petroleum or its derivatives, because prior efforts have clearly been ineffective. Diversification is indispensable, if the Kingdom is to have a stable economy that is not affected by global crises or price changes, and is to avoid the fate of other developing nations that have witnessed economic collapse brought on by forces totally outside their control. Moreover, the underground oil reserves are decreasing every day because of consumption. Though 2075 may seem light years away now, but the time draws closer after every sunset.

More significantly in terms of investment and capital markets, petroleum is not a growth industry in Saudi Arabia. There is really nowhere to go but down, in the long term. Foreign investors are interested in new industries with potential for growth because shares of such companies can be acquired cheaply. Diversification, thus, goes hand-in-hand with increased foreign investment.

[C] Foreign Investment Is Permanently Changing the Saudi Economy

Scarcity plagues all economies, from a household checkbook to a multinational corporation. Oil may be plentiful in Saudi Arabia right now, but capital is not. In order to fuel investment for diversification and growth, the money has to come from somewhere else. That "somewhere else" is foreign investment.

Once again, the government became involved right away. Almost fifteen years ago, the Kingdom launched a concerted effort to attract more foreign investment. In 2000, the government enacted the Foreign Investment Law[85] with high hopes to grow the Saudi economy, to provide the opportunity for the private sector to develop and improve the national economy, and finally, to create a suitable environment for foreign investors to participate in the national economy.[86] The Law was enacted in a bid to align itself with the prevailing international investment trends.[87] In a closely related move, the Kingdom established the Saudi Arabian General Investment Authority

84. For 2013, actual total revenue was USD 301.6 billion, 90% was petroleum revenue; for 2012, actual total revenue was USD 330.5 billion, 92% was petroleum revenue. Ministry of Finance in Saudi Arabia, *Ministry's of Finance Statement About the National Budget for 2015*, (Nov. 9, 2015), https://www.mof.gov.sa/arabic/DownloadsCenter/Pages/Budget.aspx.
85. The Foreign Investment Law, Royal Decree No. M/1 dated 5/1/1421 H (2000).
86. Alrouaf, *Development Achievements in the Kingdom of Saudi Arabia*, *supra* n. 72, at 391.
87. Hussain Agil & Bruno Zeller, *Foreign Investments in Saudi Arabia*, 15 Int'l Trade & Bus. L. Rev., 61 (2012).

("SAGIA") in 2000.[88] SAGIA has the exclusive responsibility for developing, facilitating, and monitoring foreign investments.[89]

The Foreign Investment Law provides a number of key advantages for foreign investors. SAGIA must approve or deny an investment application within thirty days, thus avoiding the long bureaucratic delays that are common in many government agencies, both in Saudi Arabia and elsewhere. To further expedite the process, its application may include more than one license to invest in various activities. Furthermore, an approved private enterprise has all the benefits, incentives, and guarantees that are given to a national enterprise. To enhance transparency and to create a willingness to invest, SAGIA needs to provide all interested investors with required information, clarifications and statistics, as well as all services and procedures needed to facilitate and to complete all investment transactions.[90]

Both the Foreign Investment Law and SAGIA were essential starting points for attracting foreign investors. Clearly, the government of Saudi Arabia is trying to secure another source of revenue whilst encouraging the private sector to grow and to develop, through foreign investment.[91] In just a few years, the Kingdom has already become the eighth largest recipient of foreign direct investment (FDI) in the world.[92] The country's annual inflow of FDI increased exponentially from USD 1.5 billion per year between 1995 and 2005 to USD 25 billion annually between 2005-2009.[93] These achievements came largely as a result of the positive developments in the economy and the improvement of the investment climate in Saudi Arabia. Specifically, the government opened mining, petrochemicals, telecommunications, and other key economic activities to foreign investment. The Kingdom also designated four cities as Special Economic Zones,[94] a model that has worked quite well in China, Korea, and elsewhere. Overall, Saudi Arabia is ranked 22nd out of 185 economies in the World Bank's "Ease of Doing Business"[95] 2013 ranking.[96]

---

88. The Council of Ministers, *The Saudi Arabian General Investment Authority*, Resolution No. 2, dated 5/1/1421 H (2000). The website for the General Investment Authority is http://www.sagia.gov.sa.
89. Alrouaf, *Development Achievements in the Kingdom of Saudi Arabia, supra* n. 72, at 388-89.
90. Foreign Investment Law, Articles 4, 6 &10 (2000).
91. Bob Peake, *Saudi Arabia Plays Safe on Reform*, 11 Int'l Tax Rev., 13 (2000).
92. World Trade Organization, *Trade Policy Review 2012: Saudi Arabia* 8 (Nov. 9, 2015), http://www.wto.org/english/tratop_e/tpr_e/tp356_e.htm.
93. *Id.*
94. *Id.* at 8-9. These four cities are (1) King Abdullah Economic City in Rabigh; (2) Prince Abdulaziz bin Musaid Economic City in Hael; (3) Knowledge Economic City in Madinah; and (4) Jazan Economic City. These cities are under construction. They aim to promote economic diversification, to create 1.3 million jobs, and to be homes for 2.4 million residents by 2020. These cities aim to improve the education and health services and to modernize the infrastructure. Saudi Arabian General Investment Authority, *Saudi Arabia's Economic Cities*, (Nov. 9, 2015), http://www.oecd.org/mena/investment/38906206.pdf; World Trade Organization, *Trade Policy Review 2012: Saudi Arabia* at 14.
95. The World Bank, *Ease of Doing Business* (Sep. 20, 2013), http://www.doingbusiness.org/data/exploreeconomies/saudi-arabia.
96. Saudi Arabia also ranked in other topic rankings in the World Bank as following: starting a business (78); dealing with construction permits (32); getting electricity (12); registering property (12); getting credit (53); protecting investors (19); paying taxes (3); trading across borders (36); enforcing contracts (124); resolving insolvency (107).

However, foreign investment is not without its critics, especially in a traditional society like Saudi Arabia. There is a fear that foreign money would lead to Western influences and the deterioration of the social and religious fabric. So, many activities are excluded from foreign investments such as exploring, excavating and producing petroleum, insurance services, real estate brokerage services, real estate investment in the two holy cities of Mecca and Medina, services of the press and publishing, and services related to the field of fishing.[97] It might be suggested that instead of declaring certain sectors to be "off-limits," the government of Saudi Arabia should consider reviewing its policies and regulations on more of a case-by-case basis regarding the restrictions which foreign investors face in some activities. In particular, and to further encourage economic diversification on a practical level, the services of insurance, the press and publishing, and fishing might be opened to foreign investments in order to create a high level of competition in these services in the national market. Consequently, this would expand the private sector and the Saudi national economy as a whole.

Foreign investment as with privatization has its pros and cons. But, again, the Kingdom should be willing to take a reasonable level of risks in order to grow. If the fears turn out to be legitimate and there are forces introduced in the country that are deemed to be undesirable, assuming that the negative outweighs the positive, these laws can always be reevaluated at a later date.

[D] Restructuring and Modernizing Regulations and Authorities to Keep Pace with Change

Privatization, diversification, and foreign investment are all new ideas to a Saudi mind that is accustomed to government control, a petroleum-based economy and Saudi Riyals.[98] The institutions first designed and built in the 1930s are inadequate to handle the change. Once there has been a decision to change the economy's direction, as has occurred now in the Kingdom, it is essential for the nation to restructure governmental authorities and to develop and to modernize regulations in the nation for the benefits of social and economic growth and development.

Through the past decade, Saudi Arabia has done just that. It has established and reorganized many authorities such as the Supreme Economic Council,[99] the Supreme Council for Petroleum and Minerals,[100] the Saudi Commission for Tourism and

97. Foreign Investment Law, Article 3 (2000).
98. Riyal is the currency of Saudi Arabia.
99. Statute of the Supreme Economic Council, Royal Order No. A/111, dated 17/5/1420 H (1999).
100. The Supreme Council for Petroleum and Minerals, Royal Order No. A 212, dated 27/9/1420 (2000). The Council is composed of members of the royal family, industry leaders, and government ministers. The Council is responsible for petroleum and natural gas policy-making. U.S. Energy Information Administration, *Saudi Arabia* (Nov. 9, 2015), http://www.eia.gov/countries/cab.cfm?fips=SA#note.

Antiquities,[101] the Human Resource Development Fund,[102] the General Investment Authority,[103] the Communications and Technology Commission,[104] the CMA,[105] the Saudi Organization for Industrial Estates and Technology Zones,[106] the Electricity and Co-generation Regulatory Authority,[107] and the Centennial Fund.[108]

The KSA has also enacted several fundamentals laws within the past decade, including the Law of Real Estate Ownership and Investment by Non-Saudis,[109] the Foreign Investment Law,[110] the Telecommunications Act,[111] CML,[112] the Law of Private Health Institutions,[113] the Law of Supervision on Cooperative Insurance Companies,[114] the Law of Gas Supply and Pricing,[115] the Law of Commercial Mortgage,[116] the Law of Benefit Exchange Between the Civil and the Military Pension Laws and the Social Insurance Law,[117] the Income Tax Law,[118] the Labor Law,[119] the Civil Aviation Law,[120] and the E-Business Regulations.[121]

---

101. The Saudi Commission for Tourism and Antiquities, the Council of Ministers, *Resolution*, No. 9, dated 12/1/1421 H (2000). The website for the Saudi Commission for Tourism and Antiquities is http://www.scta.gov.sa/en/Pages/default.aspx.
102. The Human Resource Development Fund, the Council of Ministers, Resolution No. 107, dated 29/4/1421 H (2000). The website for the Human Resource Development Fund is http://www.hrdf.org.sa/?Name = Value.
103. The General Investment Authority, the Council of Ministers, Resolution No. 20, dated 5/1/1421 H (2000).
104. The Communications and Technology Commission, the Council of Ministers, Resolution No. 74, dated 5/3/1422 H (2001). The Commission website is http://www.citc.gov.sa/English/Pages/default.aspx.
105. *See supra* n. 58, and accompanying text.
106. The Saudi Organization for Industrial Estates and Technology Zones, the Council of Ministers, Resolution No. 235, dated 27/8/1422 H (2001). Its website is http://www.modon.gov.sa/English/Pages/default.aspx.
107. The Statute of the Electricity and Co-generation Regulatory Authority, the Council of Ministers, Resolution No. 154, dated 4/5/1428 H (2007). Its website is http://www.ecra.gov.sa/Home.aspx.
108. The Centennial Fund, Royal Decree No. A/190, dated 1425 H (2004). The Centennial Fund is a charity for helping young men and women financially and educationally to start their own businesses and projects. Its website is http://www.tcf.org.sa/dimm/Pages/default.aspx. Ministry of Economy and Planning, *The Saudi Development March 2009*, 37-38 (Nov. 7, 2015), http://www.mep.gov.sa/themes/GoldenCarpet/index.jsp;jsessionid = A81578F940ACA159CC96A6F380C1B98F.alfa?event = SwitchLanguage&Code = EN#1381257481968.
109. The Law of Real Estate Ownership and Investment by Non-Saudis, Royal Decree No. M/15, dated 17/4/1421 H (2000).
110. *See supra* n. 85, and accompanying text.
111. The Telecommunications Law, Royal Decree No. M/12 dated 12/3/1422 H (2001).
112. *See supra* n. 58, and accompanying text.
113. The Law of Private Health Institutions, Royal Decree No. M/40, dated 3/11/1423 H (2003).
114. The Law of Supervision on Cooperative Insurance Companies, Royal Decree No. M/32 dated 2/6/1424 H (2003).
115. The Law of Gas Supply and Pricing, Royal Decree No. M/36, dated 25/6/1424 H (2003).
116. The Law of Commercial Mortgage, Royal Decree No. M/75, dated 21/11/1424 H (2003).
117. The Law of Benefit Exchange between the Civil and the Military Pension Laws and the Social Insurance Law, Royal Decree No. M/53, dated 23/7/1424 H (2003).
118. The Income Tax Law, Royal Decree No. M/1, dated 15/1/1425 H (2003).
119. The Labor Law, Royal Decree No. M/51, dated 23/8/1426 H (2003).
120. The Civil Aviation Law, Royal Decree No. M/44 dated 18/7/1426 H (2005).
121. The E-Business Regulations, Royal Decree No. M/18, dated 27/3/2007 (2007).

On January 29, 2015, a week after King Salman's ascension to the Saudi Arabian throne, he issued royal orders eliminating the following councils and commissions: Higher Committee for Education Policy; Higher Committee for Administrative Organization; Civil Service Council; Higher Commission of King Abdulaziz City for Science and Technology; Council of Higher Education and Universities; Supreme Council for Education; Supreme Council for Petroleum and Minerals; Supreme Economic Council; National Security Council; Supreme Council of; King Abdullah City for Atomic and Renewable Energy; Supreme Council for Islamic Affairs; and Supreme Council for Disabled Affairs. In their place, a Royal Order established two councils that are administratively linked to the Council of Ministers: The Council of Political and Security Affairs[122] and the Council of Economic and Development Affairs.[123] These changes should expedite the decision-making process in the Kingdom.[124]

The establishment of these authorities and enactment of these laws have contributed significantly to the developments in the Kingdom. None of these regulations and authorities existed before 2000, and that innovation indicates the motive of the government to reform and develop the nation.

During the last decade, Saudi Arabia has raised its financial rating in the world. Standard and Poor's Ratings has rated Saudi Arabia at "AA-/A-1 + "[125] on the long- and short-term foreign and local-currency sovereign credit ratings.[126] In addition, in terms

122. The Council of Political and Security Affairs is to be presided over by the Second Deputy Prime Minister and Minister of Interior and composed of the Minister of Foreign Affairs; Minister National Guard; Minister Defense; Minister Islamic Affairs, Endowments, Call and Guidance; Minister of Culture and Information; Chief of General Intelligence; and Ministers of State and Members of the Council of Ministers, namely Dr Musaid bin Muhammad Al-Eiban and Dr Saad bin Khalid Al-Jabri.
123. The Council of Economic and Development Affairs is to be presided over by Prince Mohammed bin Salman bin Abdulaziz, Minister of Defense, and composed of the Minister of Justice; Minister of Petroleum and Mineral Resources; Minister of Finance; Minister of Water and Electricity; Minister of Labor; Minister of Housing; Minister of Hajj; Minister of Economy and Planning; Minister of Commerce and Industry; Minister of Transport; Minister of Communications and Information Technology; Minister of Social Affairs; Minister of Municipal and Rural Affairs; Minister of Health; Minister of Civil Service; Minister of Culture and Information; Minister of Agriculture; Minister of Education; and Ministers of State and Members of the Council of Ministers, namely Dr Musaid bin Muhammad Al-Eiban, Dr Essam bin Saad bin Said, and Mohammed bin Abdulmalik Al-AsShaikh.
124. *Royal Orders Issued*, Riyadh Newpaper, Jan. 31, 2015, http://sites.alriyadh.com/en/article/1017755/Royal-Orders-Issued
125. In Long-Term Issuer Credit Ratings, an obligor rated "AAA" has extremely strong capacity to meet its financial commitments. "AAA" is the highest issuer credit rating assigned by Standard & Poor's. In Short-Term Issuer Credit Ratings, an obligor rated "A-1" has strong capacity to meet its financial commitments, which is the highest category by Standard & Poor's. Within this category, certain obligors are designated with a plus sign (+). This indicates that the obligor's capacity to meet its financial commitments is extremely strong. For more details about Standard and Poor's Ratings definition, *see* http://www.standardandpoors.com/spf/general/RatingsDirect_Commentary_979212_06_22_2012_12_42_54.pdf.
126. Standard and Poor's Rating Services, *Outlook On Saudi Arabia Revised To Positive; Ratings Affirmed At "AA-/A-1 +"* (Sep. 25, 2013), http://www.standardandpoors.com/prot/ratings/articles/en/us/?articleType = HTML&assetID = 1245352279180#ContactInfo.

of transfer and convertibility assessment,[127] Saudi Arabia is "AA + ."[128] Recently, in 2013, Standard and Poor's Rating Services upgraded the outlook on the long-term sovereign credit rating on the Kingdom from stable to positive.[129] However, on October 30, 2015, Standard & Poor's ("S&P's") Ratings Services lowered its long- and short-term foreign and local-currency sovereign credit ratings on Saudi Arabia to "A + /A-1" from "AA-/A-1 + ." The outlook remains negative, as Standard and Poor's Ratings Services expected the KSA's general government fiscal deficit to increase to 16% of the country's GDP in 2015, from 1.5% in 2014, as a result of the sharp drop in oil prices.[130] Moreover, Fitch Rating has also rated the KSA at "AA-" on long-term foreign and local currency Issuer Default Ratings, and upgraded the outlook from stable to positive.[131] It has also rated Saudi Arabia "AA" on Country Ceiling[132] and "F1 + "[133] on its short-term foreign currency.[134] The latest development in this area is designed to alleviate some of these concerns by pushing the economy forward.

[E] *Vision 2030*: The Next Logical Step

[1] Overview

One of the largest oil reserves in the world is under the Saudi Arabian sand, and it may be several decades, if not even longer, before these reserves are fully depleted. However, there will also come a day when petroleum reserves are reduced to the point

127. "AAA" is the highest category assigned by Standard & Poor's. For more details, *see* http://www.standardandpoors.com/prot/ratings/articles/en/us/?articleType = HTML&assetID = 1245360553133.
128. Standard and Poor's Rating, *Outlook On Saudi Arabia Revised To Positive; Ratings Affirmed At "AA-/A-1 + "*, *supra* n. 126.
129. *Id.*
130. *Cf* Standard and Poor's Rating Services, *Ratings On Saudi Arabia Lowered To "A + /A-1"; Outlook Remains Negative,* (Nov. 9, 2015), http://www.standardandpoors.com/en_US/web/guest/article/-/view/type/HTML/id/1473573. This recent rating has become a controversial topic, especially in Saudi Arabia. The Saudi Minister of Finance Ministry described this rating as an unjustified change that ignores the strength of the Saudi economy. The Minister considered "S&P's credit assessment reactionary, driven by fluid market factors rather than changes in the fundamentals of the sovereign." Khalil Hanware, *Kingdom's Growth Trajectory Will Continue Uninterrupted,* Arab News, (Nov. 8, 2015), http://www.arabnews.com/economy/news/832211.
131. Fitch Ratings, *Fitch Affirms Saudi Arabia at "AA-"; Outlook Revised to Positive* (Sep. 25, 2013), http://www.fitchratings.com/creditdesk/press_releases/detail.cfm?pr_id = 786441.
132. "AAA" is the highest rate by Fitch. It indicates the lowest expectation of default risk. "AA" ratings denote expectation of very low default risk. For more details about Fitch rating, *see* https://www.fitchratings.com/web_content/ratings/fitch_ratings_definitions_and_scales.pdf.
133. F1 means highest short-term credit quality. It indicates the strongest intrinsic capacity for timely payment of financial commitments. Fitch Rating, *Definitions of Ratings and Other Forms of Opinion,* (Nov. 9, 2015), http://www.fitchratings.com/web_content/ratings/fitch_ratings_definitions_and_scales.pdf.
134. Fitch Ratings, *Fitch Affirms Saudi Arabia at "AA-"; Outlook Revised to Positive, supra* n. 131.

that these resources cannot be tapped easily, and petroleum exploration and production by itself can no longer be counted on as a pillar in any economy, let alone a nation like Saudi Arabia that is almost entirely dependent on this resource.

Many other countries that are in a similar situation, albeit not to the extent of Saudi dependency, have tried to move away from a petroleum-only economy. For example, Malaysia recently undertook a program to increase foreign investment as a way to diversity its economy. The program worked, although the results were not nearly as eye-popping as planners had hoped. Moreover, when commodity prices started falling, the program lost momentum. The United Arab Emirates is moving in a similar direction by drastically reducing gasoline subsidies; the jury is still out on these reforms.[135] Indeed, a 2014 IMF study concluded that there were "many examples of failure" in this area, and relatively few success stories.[136]

Nevertheless, with a bold new plan conceived by Deputy Crown Prince Mohammed bin Salman, Saudi Arabia hopes to succeed where some other nations have fallen short and fully diversify the economy by 2030.[137]

Although the plan was released in April 2016, the stage was set almost immediately after King Salman ascended to the throne. In January 2015, he replaced a number of economic committees with the twenty-two-member Council of Economic and Development Affairs, which is under the leadership of the aforementioned Prince Mohammed bin Salman.[138] Now, instead of multiple committees who may or may not

135. Katie Paul, et al., *How Saudi Arabia Plans to Shake Up Its Economy*, Reuters, (Apr. 14, 2016), http://www.reuters.com/article/us-saudi-economy-plan-insight-idUSKCN0XB0S8.

136. John Micklethwait, et al., *Saudi Arabia Plans $2 Trillion Megafund for Post-Oil Era: Deputy Crown Prince*, Bloomberg, (Apr. 1, 2016), http://www.bloomberg.com/news/articles/2016-04-01/saudi-arabia-plans-2-trillion-megafund-to-dwarf-all-its-rivals.

137. The Cabinet devoted its session on Monday, Apr. 25, 2016 under the chairmanship of the Custodian of the Two Holy Mosques King Salman bin Abdulaziz Al Saud to consider the draft of the Kingdom of Saudi Arabia's *Vision 2030* on which the Council of Economic Affairs and Development issued the decision No. (3-31/37) dated on 12/7/1437 AH (Apr. 19, 2016), and the contents of the letter of the Deputy Crown Prince, Second Deputy Premier, Minister of Defense and Chairman of the Council of Economic Affairs and Development No. (2719) dated on 18/07/1437 AH (Apr. 25, 2016) on the draft of the vision; and the Cabinet decided the following:

    First: The approval of the Kingdom of Saudi Arabia's Vision 2030 on which the Council of Economic Affairs and Development issued the decision No. (3-31/37) dated on 12/7/1437 AH according to the attaching version of this decision.
    Second: The Council of Economic Affairs and Development shall set the necessary mechanisms and arrangements to implement this vision and follow it up.
    Third: The ministries and other governmental bodies – each in its respective authority – shall take the necessary measures to implement this vision according to the mechanisms and arrangements referred to in item (second) of this decision. Saudi Press Agency, *Cabinet Approves Kingdom of Saudi Arabia s Vision 2030*, (Apr. 25, 2016), http://spa.gov.sa/1493558.

138. The Council of Economic and Development Affairs is to be presided over by Prince Mohammed bin Salman bin Abdulaziz, Minister of Defense, and composed of the Minister of Justice; Minister of Petroleum and Mineral Resources; Minister of Finance; Minister of Water and Electricity; Minister of Labor; Minister of Housing; Minister of Hajj; Minister of Economy and Planning; Minister of Commerce and Industry; Minister of Transport; Minister of Communications and Information Technology; Minister of Social Affairs; Minister of Municipal and Rural Affairs; Minister of Health; Minister of Civil Service; Minister of Culture and Information;

have effectively communicated with each other and worked together, there is one body that makes key decisions for the entire economy.

Vision 2030 itself has three primary visions, according to its architect, which are "[a] vibrant society, a thriving economy and an ambitious nation."[139] There are a number of specific initiatives that are designed to diversify the economy and society.

Approximately 5% of Saudi Aramco, the state-owned oil company, will be placed in an initial public offering ("IPO") and listed in several international stock exchanges.[140] This move should have significant repercussions in the stock market, and these impacts are more fully examined below. Aramco's true value is not known because it is not a publically traded company. But Prince Mohammed bin Salman is confident that a 5% sale will raise about USD 2 trillion. That USD 2 trillion would make the Public Investment Fund[141] larger than the four largest companies in the world - Apple, Microsoft, Alphabet (Google), and Berkshire Hathaway - combined.[142] This money is to be invested in various Saudi and non-Saudi companies, and the return should provide a substantial revenue stream totally unrelated to petroleum production.

In addition to reinvesting its assets, an IPO will make Aramco more transparent because it must publish the same financial reports as other listed companies. Increased transparency is another of *Vision 2030*'s goals. Lack of transparency is a persistent

---

Minister of Agriculture; Minister of Education; and ministers of state and members of the Council of Ministers Dr Musaid bin Muhammad Al-Eiban, Dr Essam bin Saad bin Said, and Mohammed bin Abdulmalik Al-AsShaikh.

139. The Saudi Council of Economic Affairs and Development, *Saudi Vision 2030*, *supra* n. 63, at 2.

140. Hugo Duncan, *World's Biggest Oil Company Set to Join London Stock Exchange in Biggest Share Listing Ever*, This is Money.co.UK, (May 9, 2016), http://www.thisismoney.co.uk/money/markets/article-3581482/World-s-biggest-oil-company-set-join-London-Stock-Exchange-biggest-share-listing-time.html.

141. A Royal Decree established the Public Investment Fund ("PIF") in 1971. The PIF provides financial support for strategically significant economic projects. Specifically, the PIF funds fertilizer, oil refining, electricity, and petrochemical concerns. In July 2014, the Council of Ministers first allowed the PIF to invest in non-Saudi businesses. In March 2015, the Council of Economic and Development Affairs assumed control over the PIF. Since that time, the PIF has acquired a 38% share of the Posco Engineering & Construction Company in South Korea, a 5% stake in Uber, and has made other large foreign investments. The Law of Public Investment Fund, Royal Decree No. M/24, dated 25/6/1391 H (1971); Stefania Bianchi, *The Key Questions Asked About Saudi Arabia's $2 Trillion Fund*, Bloomberg, (May 25, 2016), http://www.bloomberg.com/news/articles/2016-05-25/key-questions-raised-by-the-2-trillion-saudi-wealth-fund-plan; Mohammed Albishi, *Alasaf Le Alsharq Alaosat: Manh Sandug Alestathmarat Salaheit Tasis Alsharikat Siosa Nashatah [Alasif to Alsharq Al-Awsat: Granting the Public Investment Fund the Power to Establish Companies Will Expand Its Activities]*, Alsharq Al-Awsat (Jul. 23, 2014), http://aawsat.com/home/article/143736; *Sandug Alestathmarat Alamah: Maseerah Ala Mada 40 Ama Fi Majal Alanshatah Alegtesadiah Oa Alsenaeih [The Publish Investment Fund: Developmental March Over 40 Years in the Filed of Economic and Industrial Activities]*, Al Eqtisadiah Newspaper (Apr. 4, 2011), http://www.aleqt.com/2011/04/04/article_522656.html; Saudi Press Agency, *Custodian of the Two Holy Mosques Chairs Cabinet Session 3*, (Mar. 23, 2015), http://spa.gov.sa/1341712?lang=ar&newsid=1341715; Stephen Stapczynski, *Saudi Fund Buys $1.1 Billion Stake in Posco Engineering Unit*, Bloomberg, (Jul. 1, 2015), http://www.bloomberg.com/news/articles/2015-07-02/saudi-fund-buys-1-1-billion-stake-in-posco-engineering-unit; Leslie Hook, *Uber Cranks Up Ride-Hailing Battle With $3.5bn Saudi Investment*, Financial Times, (Jun. 2, 2016), https://next.ft.com/content/3ac7c982-2879-11e6-8b18-91555f2f4fde.

142. Micklethwait, *Saudi Arabia Plans $2 Trillion Megafund for Post-Oil Era: Deputy Crown Prince*, *supra* n. 136.

issue in the Saudi government, as well as in the stock market. Moreover, there is considerable anecdotal evidence about bureaucratic delays and other "red tape." Furthermore, *Vision 2030* bluntly states that there will be "zero tolerance for all levels of corruption." Additionally, the Kingdom sets specific goals in terms of the country's efficiency rating in the Government Effectiveness Index and the E-Government Survey Index.[143]

Planners hope that these governmental changes, along with the increased investment, will help propel the economy forward. In addition to the increased transparency, Prince Mohammed bin Salman and his team want to hand over more control to the private sector, specifically in the healthcare and service sectors. The idea is for more Saudi citizens to buy health insurance and not rely on government-provided healthcare, by emphasizing the higher quality, and faster services, that may be available through private healthcare. Furthermore, much of the services sector, including the Interior Ministry, has already been privatized, and the reformers plan to pursue this goal to its logical conclusion.[144]

In a similar vein, *Vision 2030* planners want to localize the defense industry, which is virtually nonexistent in the Kingdom, and develop the mining industry in areas like gold, phosphate, aluminum, and uranium.[145] Currently, the Kingdom uses less than 5% of these mineral resources,[146] and planners believe that it can employ 90,000 workers and generate SAR 97 billion (USD 25.8 billion) in income by 2020.[147]

To support these new sectors, Prince Mohammed bin Salman will rehabilitate the economic cities and take other such actions. The *Vision 2030* plan is somewhat critical of the vaunted King Abdullah Financial District, and planners admit that it was built "without consideration of its economic feasibility." So, the proposal will "repurpose" this area and "change the real estate mix" to keep this project, and other ones like it, moving forward. This structural improvement will work with a more highly developed digital infrastructure and cross-border logistical improvements, such as the mammoth King Salman Bridge across the Red Sea that links Asia and Europe and creates significant development opportunities, to raise the Kingdom's ranking in the Logics Performance Index from 49 to 25.[148]

The lifeblood of any country's economy is its people, so there are plans to invest heavily in educational programs, especially at the early childhood level. When these

143. The Saudi Council of Economic Affairs and Development, *Saudi Vision 2030, supra* n. 63, at 3, 15, 17.
144. Deema Almashabi, et al., *Saudi Arabia's Deputy Crown Prince Outlines Plans: Transcript, Bloomberg,* (Apr. 4, 2016), http://www.bloomberg.com/news/articles/2016-04-04/saudi-arabia-s-deputy-crown-prince-outlines-plans-transcript.
145. The Saudi Council of Economic Affairs and Development, *Saudi Vision 2030, supra* n. 63, at 9, 11.
146. Wael Mahdi, et al., *Aramco IPO Seen by Prince as Tonic for Saudis "Addicted" to Oil, Bloomberg,* (Apr. 25, 2016), http://www.bloomberg.com/news/articles/2016-04-25/saudi-prince-says-aramco-valuation-seen-at-above-2-trillion.
147. The Saudi Council of Economic Affairs and Development, *Saudi Vision 2030, supra* n. 63, at 11.
148. The Saudi Council of Economic Affairs and Development, *Saudi Vision 2030, supra* n. 63, at 12-14; *Highlights of Saudi Deputy Crown Prince's interview with Al Arabiya,* Al Arabiya (Apr. 25, 2016), http://english.alarabiya.net/en/perspective/features/2016/04/25/Highlights-of-Deputy-Crown-Prince-Mohammed-bin-Salman-s-Al-Arabiya-interview.html.

citizens grow up, the government will encourage entrepreneurship and the development of small and medium-sized enterprises ("SMEs") to shift the economy's focus away from huge, energy-driven companies. Women and foreigners will benefit as well. Although the *Vision 2030* plan is a bit short on specifics in this area, other than a stated goal to increase female workforce participation from 22% to 30%,[149] Prince Mohammed bin Salman wants the Kingdom to "develop [women's] talents, invest in their productive capabilities and enable them to strengthen their future."[150] To attract foreign workers, the government will liberalize immigration laws to allow Arabian and Muslim foreigners to remain in the Kingdom for extended periods.[151]

Societal reforms extend to noneconomic areas as well. Prince Mohammed bin Salman wants to attract an additional 22 million *Umrah*[152] visitors each year,[153] partially by constructing the world's largest Islamic heritage museum (Prince Mohammed Bin Salman rhetorically asked an interviewer: "How can the Kingdom be the holiest site for Muslims and have no Islamic museum?").[154] *Vision 2030* also seeks to double the number of the country's UNESCO[155] registered heritage sites.[156]

In order to make Saudi Arabia a more attractive place to live and work, there are a number of other goals in this area, including:

- Moving from 26th to 10th place in the Social Capital index.
- Increasing life expectancy from 74 to 80 years.
- Raising personal savings from 6% to 10% of household income.
- Increasing the nonprofit sector of the GDP from less than 1% to 5%.
- Rallying 1 million volunteers per year (currently, there are about 11,000 per year).
- Increasing entertainment spending from 2.9% to 6% of household income.
- Encouraging at least 40% of citizens to exercise at least once a week (currently, about 13% of the people exercise at least once a week).[157]

There are three overall initiatives that further define these goals: *Daem* (enhancing entertainment and cultural activities in the Kingdom), *Irtiqaa* (helping families

149. The Saudi Council of Economic Affairs and Development, *Saudi Vision 2030, supra* n. 63, at 9.
150. *Id.* at 8.
151. *Highlights of Saudi Deputy Crown Prince's interview with Al Arabiya*, Al Arabiya (Apr. 25, 2016), http://english.alarabiya.net/en/perspective/features/2016/04/25/Highlights-of-Deputy-Crown-Prince-Mohammed-bin-Salman-s-Al-Arabiya-interview.html.
152. Unlike the *Hajj*, a pilgrimage which must occur only in the twelfth month of the Muslim year, an *Umrah* ("to visit a populated place") is a pilgrimage to Mecca, Saudi Arabia that may take place at any time of year. Saudi-National E-Goverment Portal, *Hajj and Umrah*, (Sept. 27, 2016), https://www.saudi.gov.sa/wps/portal/saudi/aboutKingdom/hajjAndUmrah.
153. The Saudi Council of Economic Affairs and Development, *Saudi Vision 2030, supra* n. 63, at 4.
154. *Highlights of Saudi Deputy Crown Prince's interview with Al Arabiya*, Al Arabiya (Apr. 25, 2016), http://english.alarabiya.net/en/perspective/features/2016/04/25/Highlights-of-Deputy-Crown-Prince-Mohammed-bin-Salman-s-Al-Arabiya-interview.html.
155. United Nations Organization for Education, Science, and Culture.
156. The Saudi Council of Economic Affairs and Development, *Saudi Vision 2030, supra* n. 63, at 4.
157. *Id.* at 4, 6, 7, 9, 18.

assume more responsibility for their children's education), and *Qawam* (increasing government spending efficiency).[158]

[2] Specific Programs

The groundwork has already been laid. In fact, there are five executive programs that will serve as a launching pad of sorts for *Vision 2030*'s ambitious goals. One of them – the National Transformation Program 2020 ("NTP") – is already in place.[159] It includes twenty-four government bodies that primarily operate in the development and economic sectors. Many of the plan's goals have a 2020 deadline, and the program will be implemented in phases between 2016 and 2020. The NTP will cost about SAR 270 billion (USD 72 billion) over five years.[160]

In Phase One, which has already been somewhat implemented, the government will examine possible obstacles to fulfillment and set realistic deadlines in light of these challenges. To establish interim targets, the General Authority for Statistics, the National Center for Performance Management, and several other groups all used international and regional benchmarks to assess the current environment and predict what changes may come about in the next few years.[161]

Phase One involves twenty-four different agencies and bodies, primarily the Council of Economic and Development Affairs and various government ministries, that have a total of 178 strategic objectives, 371 indicators, and 346 targets.[162]

In Phase Two, planners will more fully develop the initiatives needed to attain *Vision 2030*'s objectives. After conducting feasibility and best practices studies, and using practical experience to evaluate the results, the government will launch initiatives to improve spending efficiency, obtain new funding methods, and increase the private sector's participation; the outcome should be more collaboration and restructured initiatives that maximize the economic impact.[163]

Phase Three moves *Vision 2030* from the planning to implementation phase, with a detailed breakdown of the different responsibilities of each agency, along with the required financial, legislative, and human resources.[164]

---

158. *Id.* at 5-7, 16-17.
159. One Monday, Jun. 6, 2016, the Saudi Council of Ministers approved the National Transformation Program ("NTP"), a key part of Saudi *Vision 2030.* The NTP emphasizes how the Kingdom will achieve long-term economic change and increase nonoil revenue by 2020. The private sector will invest more than USD 27 billion in the support of 130 initiatives until 2020. Additionally, NTP will generate the creation of more than 450,000 jobs in the private sector by 2020. The Saudi Council of Economic Affairs and Development, *The National Transformation Program 2020,* (Jun. 6, 2016).
160. *Id.* at 7, 16.
161. *Id.* at 13.
162. *Id.* at 15.
163. *Id.* at 13-14.
164. *Id.* at 14.

The critical Phase Four will promote transparency in the publication of targets and outcomes, while at the same time reviewing performance. To carry out this mission, there will be a continually updated dashboard that is publically available.[165]

In the crowning Phase Five, existing initiatives will be thoroughly audited and new ones rolled out on an as-needed basis. This phase will be conducted with the Strategic Management Office and other government bodies, in accordance with the *Vision 2030* model.[166]

Economists predict that the NTP will help the Saudi economy grow by 2.8% in 2017, mostly because of growth in the private sector and higher quality locally produced products. In terms of the public sector, the NTP will have the greatest impact on the Royal Commission for Jubail and Yanbu[167] and the Ministry of Housing. These two growth areas are in line with Vision 2030's overall objectives, which are to remake Saudi society and broaden its economic base.[168] Further down the road, planners predict that the NTP will triple non-oil revenues by 2020, through increased investment, higher "sin taxes" on sugary drinks and tobacco, a value added tax, and higher government fees.[169]

The broad reforms in both the NTP and *Vision 2030* will most likely face both political and logistical challenges. But many observers, such as Moody's Investors Service, believe that the reforms, even if only partially rolled out, are necessary for the Kingdom's long-term societal health and economic viability.[170]

Other implementing programs include the Saudi Aramco Strategic Transformation Program, which aims to remake Aramco into more of an energy company and less of an oil company, the Public Investment Fund Restructuring Program, which should transform the PIF into more of a sovereign wealth fund, and the Human Capital Program, which is designed to nurture and encourage human talent. None of these programs have been implemented and few details are currently available. The same is true for the Strategic Planning Partnership, Privatization Program, and the Program for Strengthening Public Sector Governance.[171]

---

165. *Id.*
166. *Id.*
167. The Royal Commission for Jubail and Yanbu was established as per a Royal Decree issued in Sep. 21, 975. The Royal Decree stated: "A Royal Commission shall be formed to execute the necessary infrastructure plan for the preparation of Jubail and Yanbu Cities as industrial areas. The Commission shall have an independent legal personality." Its mission is to plan, promote, develop, and manage Petrochemicals and Energy intensive industrial cities. The Royal Commission for Jubail and Yanbu, *About Us*, (Jun. 18, 2016), https://www.rcjy.gov.sa/en-US/AboutUs/Pages/Foundation.aspx.
168. *NTP 2020 Promotes Culture of Entrepreneurship in Saudi Arabia*, Arab News, (Jun. 16, 2016), http://www.arabnews.com/node/940476/economy#.
169. *NTP Offers Credible Path to Diversification: Moody's*, Arab News, (Jun. 14, 2016), http://www.arabnews.com/node/939006/economy.
170. *Id.*
171. The Strategic Planning Partnership will "build new strategic partnerships for the twenty-first century;" the Privatization Program will use "international best practices" to reach program goals, and the Program for Strengthening Public Sector Governance will streamline the

[3] Impact on the Saudi Capital Market

The Aramco IPO may start a ripple effect that spreads throughout this sector. This move, and other initiatives designed to increase investment, may roughly double the size of Saudi Stock Exchange ("Tadawul") and transform it from one of the most closed markets in the world to one of the most transparent and investor-friendly markets in the world, and certainly among Gulf Cooperation Council ("GCC") nations.[172] Some of the reforms include:

- Increasing the number of listed companies from 170 to 250.[173]
- Establishing a new equity market, beginning in 2017, that targets SMEs.[174]
- A pending listing on the MSCI Emerging Market Index, to better represent large and mid-capitalization equities.[175]
- Reviewing the Qualified Foreign Investor rules to stimulate demand and increase the number of investors,[176] and
- Lowering the qualified foreign financial institution asset minimum from SAR 18.75 billion (USD 5 billion) to SAR 3.75 billion (USD 1 billion).[177]

These reforms, according to CMA Chairman Mohammed Abdullah Aljadaan, are designed to make the capital market more "efficient" by "enhancing its competitiveness, applying the best practices and international standards, supervise and control it effectively to provide a stable, safe and attractive environment."[178]

---

government to "prevent gaps, duplication or contradiction between agencies' policies and programs." The Saudi Council of Economic Affairs and Development, *Saudi Vision 2030, supra* n. 63, at 19-20.

172. Deema Almashabi & Glen Carey, *Saudis Want to Double Stock Market for a Post-Oil Economy, Bloomberg*, (Apr. 4, 2016), http://www.bloomberg.com/news/articles/2016-04-04/saudis-want-to-double-their-stock-market-for-a-post-oil-economy.
173. *Id.*
174. Saudi Stock Exchange "Tadawul", *The Saudi Stock Exchange (Tadawul) Plans on Establishing an Equity Market Targeting Small and Medium Enterprises (SMEs) Beginning of 2017*, (Apr. 18, 2016), https://www.tadawul.com.sa/wps/portal/tadawul/markets/Press-Release/news-%26-announcements/!ut/p/z1/pY9Rb4IwFIX_yvwBprdQkT12TAHBzg10woup2CCJtAS7Ze7XrzBM9jL3sKYPvSffOfcU5WiLcsnfq5LrSkl-MnOWOzsWxF4ArhVBOgOgy6fF_GWywG4M6LUHLMtz8T2B2A_ZFOgzDTbzTWqDb6P8P34gf_vzHglXPsGhQdzUeQC69mL2yBIME2cAblW8CXQdegB-ORRQZn4x_dGBRTbQGY6ABEsMhKCkyzhwLVairdQBZfZdraQ-dnLDS8EUyvo9WnzoRPC2OJpQM3Mp1VtRC6nTSyNQZu3GuNPPPTNo1_CWy1J8-86Xeq9Ow1sUWrWh2Wq8Tb3eQhWO-f5TXC-lo9EX_uCNyw!!/?1dmy&urile=wcm:path:/Tadawul_en/SA-Tadawul/SA-PricesAndIndeces/SA-News/SA-MarketNews/4708.
175. Alan Larson & Constance Anne Pence, *Saudi Arabia's Vision 2030 – Ambitions to Modernize and Diversify the Economy*, Global Policy Watch, (Jun. 6, 2016), https://www.globalpolicywatch.com/2016/06/saudi-arabias-vision-2030-ambitions-to-modernize-and-diversify-the-economy/.
176. Capital Market Authority, *CMA Chairman: Saudi Vision 2030 Achieves the Diversification of the National Economy with Greater Integration into the Global Economy System*, (Apr. 28, 2016), http://www.cma.org.sa/En/MediaCenter/Events/Pages/Saudivision2030-.aspx.
177. Capital Market Authority, *Aljadaan: Capital Market Authority Renewed the CMA Commitment to Saudi Vision 2030*, (May 25, 2016), http://www.cma.org.sa/En/MediaCenter/Events/Pages/ApsEvent2016.aspx.
178. *Id.*

To support the changes in Tadawul, the government is changing as well. For example, the old "oil ministry" was renamed the Ministry of Energy, Industry, and Mineral Resources and given a new leader, Aramco head Khalid Al-Falih. New real estate laws are designed to increase home ownership and therefore the assets of everyday citizens, and a new proposed 400-article bankruptcy law encourages distressed companies to reconcile and restructure their debts.[179] For both the government and Tadawul, the central aims are increased transparency and the reliance on both key performance indicators and increased investment activity.[180]

While the new proposals hold considerable promise, some international observers are skeptical. Patrick Dennis, an economist at the UK's Oxford Economics, openly doubts that the Kingdom has the resources and resolves to step up its stalled economic diversification program. Jason Tuvey, a Middle East economist at Capital Economics in London, lamented that *Vision 2030* "provided few fresh details on the reform agenda and missed key issues." Nevertheless, most all observers are cautiously optimistic about Tadawul's future and its role in the emerging diversified Saudi economy.[181]

It is a major challenge for a country to anticipate needed reforms and to have the proper institutions in place prior to these reforms actually being passed. So far, Saudi Arabia has been trying to meet the challenge. By creating a new institutional infrastructure, the Kingdom has invited change to come in and to pursue the needed reforms. It is easier to work this way, as opposed to passing reforms and then trying to create new institutions on an ad hoc basis. Saudi Arabia has demonstrated its commitment not only to changing the economy, but also to managing that change for the betterment of the Saudi people.

In the last eighty years, static state-run industries have been privatized to react more quickly to ever-changing conditions, foreign investors are flocking to the Kingdom at a rate that is unmatched at any time in Saudi history, and the government seems willing to make the structural changes that are needed for sustained economic growth and change. The one dark area so far has been diversification. Encouraging investment in nonpetroleum industries should help, along with increased private control in these areas. But, for now, Saudi Arabia's economic reforms remain incomplete, the new *Vision 2030* plan notwithstanding. So far, not all of the Saudi reforms have gone off exactly as hoped, but the movement towards globalization and integration continues, as well it should, and *Vision 2030* is a key component in this movement.[182]

179. Mohieddine Kronfol & Bassel Khatoun, *Vision 2030–Saudi's Bold Move into the Global Financial Market,* Franklin Templeton Investments, (May 18, 2016), http://global.beyondbullsandbears.com/2016/05/18/vision-2030-saudis-bold-move-into-the-global-financial-market/.
180. *Id.*
181. Andrew Torchia, et al., *Analyst View: Saudi Arabia's Vision 2030 Reform Plan*, Reuters (Apr. 25, 2016), http://www.reuters.com/article/us-saudi-plan-reaction-idUSKCN0XM1FX.
182. Ministry of Economy and Planning of Saudi Arabia, *Ninth Development Plan, supra* n. 59, at 25.

But now is not the time for recrimination and second-guessing. Now is the time for moving forward. While domestic prosperity and growth are two important goals in the reform process, the overall goal has always been much bigger. In order to be an advanced-stage developed nation and to have a place at the global table with the Group of 20 major economies, the Kingdom should consider looking outside itself and economically integrate more closely with its neighbors.

This is not to suggest that Saudi Arabia should surrender its sovereignty, but rather to suggest that Saudi Arabia can find its economic future by closer cooperation with economies and parties outside its own borders.

§1.04 SAUDI ARABIA'S MOVEMENT TOWARDS REGIONAL AND GLOBAL ECONOMIC AND FINANCIAL RELEVANCE

The "journey of a thousand miles" begins with a single step.[183] If the ultimate goal for Saudi Arabia is "globalization," in retrospect, the first step could be considered the establishment of a sovereign and independent KSA in 1932. That fledgling Kingdom first looked to petroleum-based, state-run enterprises. The same is largely true today (although Saudi Arabia can hardly be considered "fledgling"): about 90% of the state's revenue is petroleum-based, and the state is largely the lord and master of the economy, certainly from a planning and strategic perspective.

Yet, the journey continues. Economic reform and well-developed planning, as discussed above, have brought Saudi Arabia to the point where globalization is no longer on the distant horizon. Greater integration into the global economic community would be a realistic goal. Saudi Arabia should consider staying on its current path, and begin to explore meaningful "partnerships" with other nations.

Saudi Arabia's first partnerships have been with other Arab-Muslim Gulf states. As experience in international relationships increase, so too can the horizons of the Kingdom's move towards global integration. The KSA has undergone significant changes with respect to its movement towards a "free market" economy within a very short period of time.[184] A society that was largely agrarian just a few decades ago has vastly modernized the infrastructure underpinning the economy, in an important first step towards a meaningful internal modernization.[185] Then, globalization becomes a key component in the Kingdom's Development Plans. In a nutshell, the main strategic objectives of the economic development in Saudi Arabia evolve to enhancing the KSA's position within the global economy, to boost its competitiveness, and to expand regional and international cooperation.[186]

183. A Chinese proverb.
184. Royal Embassy of Saudi Arabia in Washington, DC, *Economy & Global Trade* (Nov. 9, 2015), http://www.saudiembassy.net/about/country-information/economy_global_trade/.
185. *Id.*
186. Ministry of Economy and Planning of Saudi Arabia, *The Kingdom of Saudi Arabia Economy in Figures 2013, supra* n. 52, at VII.

[A] Regional Leadership Opportunities: The Cooperation Council for the Arab States of the Gulf

The Cooperation Council for the Arab States of the Gulf ("GCC")[187] was established on May 25, 1981.[188] The GCC consists of six states: the United Arab Emirates, State of Bahrain, KSA, Sultanate of Oman, State of Qatar, and State of Kuwait.[189] These six states first met in Abu Dhabi, United Arab Emirates, and they "reached a cooperative framework joining the six states to effect coordination, integration and inter-connection among the Member States in all fields."[190]

GCC members share a common language (i.e., Arabic) and, even more importantly, a common cultural (i.e., Muslim) and political history. More recently, these six states have similar economics: together, they account for more than 23% of global natural gas reserves and more than 40% of global oil reserves.[191]

The impetus for the initial "coming-together" was the cumulative effect of a number of incidents over a number of years, most of which are related to international events.[192] The British withdrawal in the 1970s destabilized the region and set a chain of events into motion.[193] At roughly the same time, mushrooming oil prices provided the GCC States with a sudden wealth that was utterly unheard of for any country in the world. Almost immediately thereafter, in 1979, conservative elements took control in Iran, forcing the Shah into exile. The new Iranian regime was openly hostile towards the Gulf States, and towards neighboring Iraq. The Gulf monarchies quickly came to an understanding that the unstable international climate, together with their own economic good fortune, meant that they were tempting targets for aggressive foreign powers. At the very least, there was a general fear that the overall instability might spread to within their borders. It was this need for regional strength and harmony that brought the Gulf States together on that spring day in 1981.[194]

Article 4 of the Cooperation Council Charter ("the Charter") addresses the objectives of the GCC.[195] These objectives revolve around the "coordination, integration and inter-connection between Member States in all fields." It is hoped that such closeness would foster greater unity and the synchronization of some regulations,

---

187. Article one of the Cooperation Council Charter stated that a "Council shall be established hereby to be named The Cooperation Council for the Arab States of the Gulf hereinafter referred to as the Cooperation Council (GCC)". The Cooperation Council for the Arab States of the Gulf, *The Charter*, Article 1 (1981). Available at http://www.gcc-sg.org/eng/indexfc7a.html?action = Sec-Show&ID = 1.
188. The Cooperation Council for the Arab States of the Gulf, *About the GCC- Foundations and Objectives* (Nov. 9, 2015), http://www.gcc-sg.org/en-us/AboutGCC/Pages/StartingPoints AndGoals.aspx.
189. *Id.*
190. *Id.*
191. Mohsin Khan, *The GCC Monetary Union- Choice of Exchange Rate Regime* 5, International Monetary Fund (2008).
192. Joseph Rasquinha, *The Integration of the Gulf Co-Operation Council (GCC): Problems and Prospects*. (September 1991) (Unpublished Ph.D. dissertation, University of St Andrews). A copy of the dissertation is available at http://hdl.handle.net/10023/2754.
193. *Id.*
194. *Id.*
195. The Cooperation Council Charter, Article 4 (1981).

leading to common policies in economic affairs, customs laws, education and culture and international commercial relations. As an example, the GCC States intend to achieve common policies regarding industry, mining, agriculture, water and animal resources. A related goal is the development of scientific and technical research and knowledge, along with the cultivation of foreign investment and the empowerment of the private sector. All these things, along with the establishment of various joint ventures, are designed to work together "for the good of their peoples."[196]

Structurally, the GCC has four main organizations: the Supreme Council, the Commission for Settlement of Disputes, the Ministerial Council, and the Secretariat-General.[197] These organizations are empowered to establish sub-agencies as may be necessary.[198]

A primary motivation for most regional integration efforts is to improve the overall economies of the Member States.[199] The GCC is no exception. Pursuant to this overall goal, the GCC has ratified many documents: one of the most important documents is the 1981 Unified GCC Economic Agreement.[200] In response to the unstable political and economic international situation, the Agreement provided "for the establishment of a Gulf Common Market with free movement of goods, services, capital, and labor among member countries, and of a common external tariff on imports from other countries."[201]

Twenty years later, the region was somewhat more politically stable. Hence, the GCC felt it was time to establish a new Economic Agreement to take the next step towards overall economic integration, with a true common market and a common currency, in accordance with a set timetable. At the same time, the new economic agreement sought to preserve the existing market dynamic of each individual State.[202] Both the 1981 Agreement and 2001 Agreement are essentially snapshots of the region at that particular time: in 1981 the GCC States were concerned about current events while, in 2001, the GCC States were eager to look ahead to their collective economic future.[203]

The establishment of a Monetary Union is not new, having been one of the essential objectives for GCC economic integration since the establishment of GCC in 1981. The 1981 Unified GCC Economic Agreement stated in Article 22 that Member States should "coordinate" their overall fiscal policies, including both monetary and

---

196. *Id.*
197. The Cooperation Council Charter, Article 6 (1981).
198. *Id.*
199. Amr D. Marar, *Cooperation Council for the Arab States of the Gulf*, 10 L. & Bus. Rev. Am. 475 (2004).
200. The GCC Member States signed the GCC Unified Economic Agreement in November 1981, after few months of establishing the GCC. Then, in Dec. 31, 2001, the GCC adopted a new Economic Agreement, which contains a comprehensive revision of the original Economic Agreement. The GCC Unified Economic Agreement 1981 is available at http://sites.gcc-sg.org/DLibrary/index-eng.php?action=ShowOne&BID=170. The new Economic Agreement 2001 is available at http://sites.gcc-sg.org/DLibrary/index-eng.php?action=ShowOne&BID=168.
201. Iqbal Zaidi, *Monetary Coordination among the Gulf Cooperation Council Countries*, 18 World Development, 759 (1990).
202. *See* the Preamble of *the Unified GCC Economic Agreement (2001)*.
203. *Id.*

banking regulations, to enhance the common development of both monetary agencies and central banks. The Agreement was the first call-to-action for a common currency, to promote the region's international economic prestige.[204]

Within the last decade, the Gulf States region has taken many steps towards financial and monetary integration, beginning with the approval of the Monetary Union Agreement in 2008.[205] All GCC States, except for the UAE and Oman, are signatories to this agreement.[206] According to Article 4-1 of the Monetary Union Agreement,[207] Member States are required to establish the Monetary Council as soon as the agreement comes into force.[208] That body had its first meeting in Riyadh in March 2010.[209] Riyadh is also the home of the Council's headquarters.[210]

Article 4 of the Statute of Monetary Council[211] provides the objectives and the goals of the Monetary Council. In general, the Council is empowered to lay the foundation for a Central Bank and Monetary Union. The specific roadmap to this goal includes the enhancement of cooperation among existing National Central Banks ("NCBs"), with an eye towards a total currency integration, the development of common monetary and exchange rate policies, the continued prohibition of NCB loans to a public entity, and the development of the necessary legal framework for a Central Bank to seamlessly replace the NCBs. Additionally, the Council is expected to develop the mechanical structure that achieves the objectives of the Monetary Union, including a statistical system, design of a common currency and plans for its circulation, in the single currency area. Further, the GCC Member States' payment systems would work in conjunction with the new currency; would encourage the fulfillment of the Member States' obligations to the Monetary Union through the introduction of single currency (specifically those items related to the performance of the economic convergence criteria); would specify a timeframe for the rollout of the currency, given all the milestones mentioned in the Statute; and would make recommendations regarding the

204. The Cooperation Council for the Arab States of the Gulf, *Unified GCC Economic Agreement*, Article 22 (1981).
205. The Agreement was signed at Muscat, Sultanate of Oman, on the 2nd day of Muharram 1430 AH, corresponding to Dec. 30, 2008. Then, the parties of the Agreement ratified the Agreement and entered into force on Feb. 27, 2010. The Cooperation Council for the Arab States of the Gulf, *Motatalbat Alathad Alnagdi* (*The Requirements Monetary Union*, (Nov. 9, 2015), http://www.gcc-sg.org/ar-sa/CooperationAndAchievements/Achievements/EconomicCooperation/TheMonetaryUnionandtheSingleCurrency/Pages/Secondthemonetaryunionrequirem.aspx.
206. *Monetary Union Agreement*, the Cooperation Council for the Arab States of the Gulf (2008). The agreement is available at http://en.gmco.int/about/aggrement.
207. *Monetary Union Agreement*, Article 4-1 (2008).
208. The Gulf Monetary Council, *About GMCO* (Nov. 9, 2015), http://en.gmco.int/about.
209. In October 2013, the Gulf Monetary Council opened its headquarter in Riyadh, Saudi Arabia. The efforts by the GCC Members towards economic integration among them are continuing to that goal.
210. *Monetary Union Agreement*, Article 4-4 (2008).
211. The Statute of Monetary Council was approved by the Members States in 2008 and entered into force in March 27, 2010.

enabling legislation that Member States need to pass to make a common currency a reality.[212]

The overall objectives behind establishing Monetary Union in the GCC are to eliminate the risks that are related to the exchange rates of the various current GCC currencies; to promote regional competitiveness in banking and financial services; to increase the ability of GCC corporations to merge or acquire other corporations in the other GCC Member States; to enhance the transparency and financial discipline at the regional level which should positively reflect on the monetary and financial stability in the region; to develop the institutional infrastructure of common economic policies; to stabilize the inflation rate and general level of prices; and to attract more national, regional, and international investments into the GCC Member States.[213] Furthermore, a Monetary Union Regime is less likely to be subject to speculative attacks.[214] A common currency was seen by many as the best way to fulfill all these objectives that are key to the GCC Member States' economic development: rollout was anticipated in 2010 but has now been indefinitely postponed.[215]

As agreed by the GCC Member States, a set of five convergence criteria (on inflation, interest rates, reserves, fiscal balance, and public debt), similar to the European Monetary Union (EMU), has been agreed in principle, while they are not preconditions for entry.[216]

The GCC established a Free Trade Area that entered into force in March 1983. That Free Trade Area exempted the GCC industrial, agricultural, and natural resources products from customs duties and other similar duties.[217] In 2002, the GCC Customs Union[218] replaced the Free Trade Area.[219] The GCC Customs Union goes a bit further, by eliminating all trade barriers between Member States, harmonizing trade procedures among the States, setting common external tariffs on all other imports, and basically treating the area as one political entity for customs and trade purposes.[220] Liberalization of intra-GCC trade is the main objective of the GCC Custom Union.[221] Consequently, the GCC Custom Union allows the flow of goods without tariff or nontariff barriers, so that the private sector in all GCC Member States is influenced directly by such removal of custom barriers.[222]

---

212. Gulf Monetary Council, *The Statute of Monetary Council*, Article 4 (2008). The Statute is available at http://en.gmco.int/about/statute.
213. Information Affair Department, Gulf Cooperation Council, *Almaserah Oa Alanjaz* 100-101 *[The Process and the Achievements]* (7th ed. 2013).
214. Jeffrey A. Frankel, *No Single Currency Regime Is Right For All Countries Or At All Times*, p. 6, Essays In International Finance, No. 215, Princeton University, New Jersey (1999).
215. World Bank, *Economic Integration in the GCC* 13 (World Bank 2010).
216. Khan, *supra* n. 191, at 10.
217. Information Affair Department, Gulf Cooperation Council, *Almaserah oa Alanjaz* 67 *[The Process and the Achievements]* (4th ed. 2009).
218. The GCC Customs Union is available at http://www.gcc-sg.org/eng/indexfef9.html?action=Sec-Show&ID=84.
219. Information Affair Department, Gulf Cooperation Council, *Almaserah oa Alanjaz* 67 *[The Process and the Achievements]* (4th ed. 2009).
220. *Id.*
221. *Id.* at 68.
222. *Id.*

Although the economic integration among GCC Member States is well motivated, the implementation of this goal has yet to be realized. The idea has been in place for over three decades, but the common currency is still bogged down in endless negotiations that have shown little progress. GCC members certainly have the ability to create an integration model, since they have most of the world's oil and gas resources. The GCC needs to be more resolute in its planning, and should make a common currency more of a priority, in order to meet the goals it originally set for itself in 1981.

Part of the problem is that relationships between the GCC States are not always cordial. The KSA's dealings with some of the other GCC Members are tainted by political rivalries such as border disputes and diplomatic punitive measures. Regrettably, it is not unusual for these disputes to erupt into violence.[223] In the past decade, Saudi Arabia withdrew its ambassador in Doha, Qatar from 2002 until 2007, because of that nation's support for the Qatari-based Al Jazeera television network that gave a platform to Osama bin Laden and other prominent Saudi dissidents.[224] More recently, the KSA, United Arab Emirates, and State of Bahrain withdrew their ambassadors in Doha because Qatar has not implemented a signed agreement[225] among GCC States in order to stay out of each other's internal affairs.[226] Qatar is a signatory to the GCC Monetary Union, and this recent event might hinder the Monetary Union and other GCC integration in the near future. If these issues among GCC States are not resolved soon, the GCC integration might be severely hampered. The ultimate result may even be the dissolution of the GCC.

Analysis is mixed as to whether the GCC is ready for a common currency. One study, which focused on generalized purchasing power, cited the Gulf States' overreliance on oil, economic isolation, lack of agreement on fundamental economic policies, and overall absence of economic synchronization as evidence that the GCC countries lacked the foundation necessary for a common currency to be successful.[227] Another study concluded that a common currency would have many benefits, but that the GCC States were not in a position to reap these benefits. Before issuing a common currency, the nations themselves need to set aside their economic and political disputes, which have been outlined above. Only after these nations present a united front can a common currency be implemented with any hope of success.[228] A more recent study

223. Anthony H. Cordesman, *National Security in a Troubled Region* 12 (Center for Strategic and International Studies 2009).
224. *Id.*
225. The six GCC States signed an agreement in Nov. 23, 2013 in Riyadh. Part of the agreement includes a "commitment to the principles that ensure non-interference in the internal affairs of any of the GCC countries, either directly or indirectly, and not to support any activity that would threaten the security and stability of any of the GCC countries from organizations or individuals, including support for hostile media." Paul Iddon, *Why the Gulf States Recalled their Ambassadors from Qatar*, Digital J., Mar. 5, 2014, http://digitaljournal.com/news/politics/why-the-gulf-states-recalled-their-ambassadors-from-qatar/article/374632.
226. Marie-Louise Gumuchian, *Saudi Arabia, UAE, Bahrain Withdraw Envoys from Qatar*, CNN, Mar. 5, 2014, http://www.cnn.com/2014/03/05/world/meast/gulf-qatar-ambassadors/.
227. Belkacem Laabas & Imed Limam, *Are GCC Countries Ready for Currency Union?*, Arab Planning Institute, 32 (2002).
228. *See* Esteban Jadresic, *On a Common Currency for the GCC Countries* (International Monetary Fund 2002).

examined three different economic models, structural VAR, cointegration, and commonality of business cycles, to conclude that the GCC States were not ready for a Monetary Union.[229]

Ever since the establishment of the GCC in 1981, the Member States have expressed a desire for economic unity and free trade, in order to be more competitive in a global sense. The world has changed quite a bit in the ensuing decades, but these same desires remain in place. A common currency is the best way to meet these overall economic goals, but infighting between the GCC Members has been the primary obstacle to this development. Only with a Monetary Union can the Gulf States move to economic relevancy on the world stage, and it is entirely up to them as to when that situation develops. The European Union has seen considerable success with its economic union, and there is no reason to believe that the same thing could not happen in the GCC States.[230]

The GCC is the middle step in the overall Plan; globalization objectives and domestic economic reforms are already largely in place. The current situation in the GCC is far from perfect, and there is much work to be done regarding regional trade and commercial unity, but the Kingdom's experience in the GCC has been reasonably successful, given that the GCC is really the first time that the Kingdom has entered an international agreement with roughly equal partners. So, if the Plan is somewhat on track and if the Plan is to succeed, what should come next?

[B] World Trade Organization: Was It Worth the Wait?

If a regional partnership is an intermediate step towards globalization, the next logical step will be a multilateral and international arrangement. Because of the ongoing conflict with Israel and its own unique cultural identity, meaningful participation in a global organization has been difficult for the Kingdom. Participation in the GCC has helped significantly, even though there have been many problems there also, because the government is learning how to cooperate with others and to work together with other nations towards a common goal.

A unified trade and economic policy is even more important when considering the overall international nature of any one State's, or one region's economy. The

229. Suleiman Abu-Bader & Aamer S. Abu-Qarn, *On the Optimality of a GCC Monetary Union: Structure VRA, Common Trends and Common Cycles Evidence*, 31 The World Economy, 17-18 (2008).

230. Despite its overall success, the European Union has its share of problems. Recently, the European Monetary Union ("EMU") has taken steps to strengthen its economic position by implementing some changes that are designed to "reduc[e] risks and ensur[e] a level playing field in the banking sector [by] limiting the bank-sovereign feedback loop." European Commission, *Completing Europe's Economic and Monetary Union: Commission Takes Concrete Steps to Strengthen EMU*, Oct. 21, 2015, http://europa.eu/rapid/press-release_IP-15-5874_en.htm; the EMU also faces challenges in terms of implementing a common deposit insurance system and is grappling with the fact that five of its Members have recently requested emergency bailouts. Jonathan Stearns, *EU Commission Renews Push for Single Euro-Area Voice at IMF*, Bloomberg Business, Oct. 21, 2015, http://www.bloomberg.com/news/articles/2015-10-21/eu-commission-renews-push-for-single-euro-area-voice-at-imf.

importance of free trade and the exchange among nations have created the necessity of founding a body to design, regulate, and organize international trade. The World Trade Organization ("WTO") was finally established on January 1, 1995 after seemingly endless negotiations in the Uruguay Round from 1986 to 1994 under the General Agreement on Tariffs and Trade ("GATT").[231] The WTO has 162 members, as of November 2015.[232] The organization's underlying objectives are that the international trading system should be without discrimination, more open, more predictable, more competitive, and more beneficial for less-developed countries.[233] The WTO's primary missions are to negotiate the reduction or elimination of obstacles to trade, administer and monitor the application of the agreed rules for trade in goods, trade in services, and trade-related intellectual property rights, monitor and review the trade policies of its Members, ensure transparency of regional and bilateral trade agreements, and settle disputes among its Members regarding the interpretation and application of the applicable agreements.[234]

One of the primary drawbacks to the WTO is the extended delay that often accompanies applications from prospective Members, especially less-developed economies. In the case of Saudi Arabia, the Kingdom became a full Member of the WTO on December 11, 2005, after a decade of negotiations.[235] Saudi Arabia was the final Member of the GCC to join the WTO.[236] This delayed membership is an example of the infighting and disagreements that are widespread in the GCC. Because they pursued their WTO applications separately, the world continues to see the GCC States as separate entities as far as international trade is concerned, which is the exact opposite of the image they wish to project. In short, instead of enhancing the region's economic prestige, the WTO application process has had a damaging effect.[237] Indeed, if it had

231. World Trade Organization, *Understanding the WTO* (Nov. 9, 2015), http://wto.org/english/thewto_e/whatis_e/tif_e/fact1_e.htm.
232. World Trade Organization, *Members and Observers* (Nov. 9, 2015), http://wto.org/english/thewto_e/whatis_e/tif_e/org6_e.htm.
233. World Trade Organization, *Principles of the Trading System* (Nov. 9, 2015), http://wto.org/english/thewto_e/whatis_e/tif_e/fact2_e.htm.
234. World Trade Organization, *What is the WTO* (Nov. 9, 2015), http://wto.org/english/thewto_e/whatis_e/wto_dg_stat_e.htm.
235. Alrouaf, *Development Achievements in the Kingdom of Saudi Arabia*, *supra* n. 72, at 509.
236. The other GCC States entered the WTO as follows:

Bahrain	January 1, 1995
Kuwait	January 1, 1995
Qatar	January 13, 1996
UAE	April 10, 1996
Oman	November 9, 2000
Saudi Arabia	December 11, 2005

237. Rodney Wilson, *Good International Governance: Implications for Saudi Arabia's Political Economy, Good Governance in the Middle East Oil Monarchies*, 85, 97 (Tom Pierre Najem & Martin Hetherington, eds, 2003).

acted in concert with the other GCC States, Saudi Arabia might have been spared the protracted application process it had to endure.

The KSA has taken many steps to achieve globalization: unfortunately, sometimes these steps are taken without its GCC partners. In 1985, GATT approved Saudi Arabia's request to be a preliminary, nonvoting observer member. In response, the government of Saudi Arabia created a Committee headed by the Minister of the Finance and National Economy Ministry. Representatives from the Ministry of Commerce, Ministry of Petroleum and Mineral Resources, Ministry of Industry and Electricity, and Ministry of Planning rounded out the Committee. This body appointed a resident representative in Geneva, Switzerland to represent the Committee.[238] But the KSA did not submit an official accession request to the GATT until June 13, 1993. Almost immediately thereafter, on July 21, the GATT Representatives established a Working Party to examine Saudi Arabia's application to join GATT under Article XXXIII. The process continued to move forward: the GATT Accession Working Party was transformed into a WTO Accession Working Party pursuant to the decision of the General Council of the WTO of January 31, 1995.[239]

Why did it take so long for the world's largest oil producing country to join GATT and the WTO? Before Saudi Arabia joined the WTO, one observer suggested that the "W" in the WTO was a small letter until the KSA has been a full member of the organization, because of its global economic significance.[240] In other words, the WTO was missing a significant player in the world economy. Although there was some opposition to the Saudi Arabian application, that was not the only cause of the delay. One reason for the long process was the attitude of Saudi Arabia itself. The Kingdom was hesitant to join the WTO because of a generalized suspicion and fear of the unknown.[241] Moreover, Saudi Arabia lacked the information and infrastructure needed to make rational choices on fundamental issues and decisions, such as joining GATT and, more recently, the WTO.[242]

Some commentators thought that Saudi Arabia purposefully delayed the process of joining the WTO. They point to the sudden and dramatic rise in world oil prices at the end of 1990s and in the early of 2000s, which strengthened Saudi Arabia's economy and reduced its incentive to join the WTO.[243] There were also moral and religious objections. Some Saudis feared that membership in an international organization such as the WTO would infringe upon the Kingdom's ability to restrict the importation of

238. Alhabib, *Principles of Macroeconomics*, *supra* n. 37, at 548.
239. World Trade Organization, *Report of the Working Party on the Accession of the Kingdom of Saudi Arabia to the World Trade Organization*, 1, WT/ACC/SAU/61(Nov. 1, 2005).
240. Raj Bhala, *Saudi Arabia, the WTO, and American Trade Law and Policy*, 38 Int'l Law. 741, 749 (2004).
241. Abdulaziz Aldakeel, *Altanmih Alagtsadih Fi Almamlkh Alarabia Alsaodih: Almamlakh Alarabiah Alsaodih Oa Monathmat Altgarah Alalmih: Aoagb Altakar Oa Analtathar Fi Itkath Algrar 558* [*Economic Development in the Kingdom of Saudi Arabia: the Kingdom of Saudi Arabia and the World Trade Organization: The Consequences of Hesitation and Waiting in the Decision -Making*], the Article was written in 1999 (Dar Alsaqi Press 2012).
242. *Id.*
243. Amir H. Khoury, *The Development of Modern Trademark Legislation and Protection in Arab Countries of the Middle East*, 16 Transnat'l Law. 249, 311 (2003).

pork, alcohol, pornography, and other items prohibited under Islamic law.[244] Such fears turned out to be unfounded: Saudi Arabia retains, to this day, the power to regulate imports based on concerns of morality, public health, and national security, which are permitted exceptions under the WTO.[245]

When the Kingdom applied to join the GATT/WTO back in 1993, it was a big step for Saudi Arabia's move towards globalization. But, a more intense integration continues to be elusive. Some developed countries, most notably the U.S., demand broader access to Saudi markets. The Kingdom has been hesitant to oblige, partly because of a real or perceived threat to the growing nonpetroleum industries inside Saudi Arabia, and partly due to a fear that a sudden influx of Western goods and culture would undermine traditional Islamic values. At the same time, the U.S. may be suspicious of Saudi motives in terms of trade law, tariff schedules, and import barriers.[246]

It is a fact that the U.S. had a direct hand in delaying Saudi Arabia's accession to the WTO.[247] The U.S. objected to the Kingdom's participation in the Israeli boycott. Moreover, it voiced concerns over Saudi Arabia's human rights record and alleged ties to international terrorism.[248] Indeed, the U.S. threatened to block Saudi membership unless it relented on the secondary boycott against firms doing business with Israel. Such tension has been an impediment to full international cooperation, to say the least.[249]

In the accession process, Saudi Arabia confirmed that "the application of secondary and tertiary boycotts had been terminated[250] in practice and in law."[251] However, the Kingdom did not promise, during the WTO accession process, to terminate the primary boycott against Israel.[252] Shortly after the Kingdom's accession to the WTO, the Saudi Ambassador to the U.S.[253] stated that Saudi Arabia would continue the primary boycott against Israel, and the "primary boycott is an issue of national sovereignty guaranteed within the makeup of the WTO and its rules."[254] A

244. Wynbrandt, *supra* n. 1, at 299.
245. World Trade Organization, *Trade Policy Review: The Kingdom of Saudi Arabia*, WTO Secretariat, xi, WT/TPR/S/256 (Dec. 21, 2011).
246. Raj Bhala, *Challenges of Poverty and Islam Facing American Trade Law*, 17 St. John's J. Legal Comment. 471, 510 (2003).
247. Alhabib, *Principles of Macroeconomics, supra* n. 37, at 552.
248. Bashar H. Malkawi, *Anatomy of the Case of Arab Countries and the WTO*, 20 Arab L.Q. 112, 121 (2006).
249. Wilson, *supra* n. 237, at 97-98. *See* Peter D. Sutberland, *Transforming Nations: How the WTO Boosts Economies and Opens Societies*, 87 Foreign Aff. 125, 132 (2008) (stating that although the Kingdom took some very controversial stances on issues such as religious bans on certain imports, Islamic banking and the Israeli boycott which cast a dark cloud over the early phases of the application process, these positions did not cause significant problems as Saudi Arabia remained focused on opening markets, transparency, fair trading conditions, and nondiscrimination).
250. The Saudi Council of Ministers Decision No. 5 (Jun. 13, 1995).
251. World Trade Organization, *Report of the Working Party on the Accession of the Kingdom of Saudi Arabia to the World Trade Organization*, at 41, WT/ACC/SAU/61 (Nov. 1, 2005).
252. Roger P. Alford, *The Self-Judging WTO Security Exception*, 2011 Utah L. Rev. 697, 724 (2011).
253. Prince Turki Al-Faisal, the former Saudi Ambassador to the U.S. (from 2005 to 2007).
254. Michael Freund, *Saudi Ambassador to US Admits Boycott of Israel Still in Force*, Jerusalem Post (Jun. 22, 2006).

spokesman of the United States Trade Representative's office ("USTR") stated that in the USTR's view, "maintaining the primary boycott of Israel is not consistent with Saudi Arabia's commitment to extend full WTO treatment to all WTO members."[255] In January 2007, the Director General of Saudi Customs[256] reaffirmed "that the Saudi regulations do not permit the import of goods manufactured in Israel."[257] In March 2015, the U.S. Department of Treasury published a current list of nine countries[258] including Saudi Arabia that require or may require participation in, or cooperation with, an international boycott within the meaning of Section 999(b)(3) of the Internal Revenue Code[259] of 1986.[260]

Despite this opposition, and its own misgivings, Saudi Arabia definitely saw the need for WTO membership. During the application process, the Kingdom created nine new regulatory bodies, entered into thirty-eight bilateral trade pacts, and enacted forty-two new trade-related laws.[261] To be compliant with various requests for information, Saudi Arabia provided over 7,000 pages of documents, which included ninety-four basic laws, decrees, and regulations.[262] There were 13 different working party meetings geared exclusively to WTO membership, during which there were 314 rounds of bilateral trade negotiations. Overall, the Saudis promptly responded to 3,400 separate inquiries regarding its trade regime.[263] These efforts had some very practical results. Prior to submitting its application, 75% of import tariffs were 12% or greater; by 2003, 85% of tariffs were 5% or lower, and the Kingdom was poised to make even further reductions as required by the WTO.[264]

---

255. Christopher M. Blanchard, *Saudi Arabia: Background and U.S. Relations* 36, Cong. Research Serv., RL 33533 (2009).
256. Saleh Al-Barak, the Director General of Saudi Customs.
257. *Ban on Israeli Goods in Place: Customs Chief*, Arab News (Jan. 4, 2007), http://www.arabnews.com/node/292917.
258. The current list of countries includes Iraq, Kuwait, Lebanon, Libya, Qatar, Saudi Arabia, Syria, United Arab Emirates, and Yemen.
259. Section 999(b)(3) of the Internal Revenue Code of 1986 states that "a person participates in or cooperates with an international boycott if he agrees (A) as a condition of doing business directly or indirectly within a country or with the government, a company, or a national of a country (i) to refrain from doing business with or in a country which is the object of the boycott or with the government, companies, or nationals of that country; (ii) to refrain from doing business with any United States person engaged in trade in a country which is the object of the boycott or with the government, companies, or nationals of that country; (iii) to refrain from doing business with any company whose ownership or management is made up, all or in part, of individuals of a particular nationality, race, or religion, or to remove (or refrain from selecting) corporate directors who are individuals of a particular nationality, race, or religion; or (iv) to refrain from employing individuals of a particular nationality, race, or religion; or (B) as a condition of the sale of a product to the government, a company, or a national of a country, to refrain from shipping or insuring that product on a carrier owned, leased, or operated by a person who does not participate in or cooperate with an international boycott." Internal Revenue Code of 1986, I.R.C. § 999 (2004).
260. The United States Department of Treasury, Office of the Secretary, *List of Countries Requiring Cooperation with an International Boycott*, Mar. 31, 2015, reprinted in the Federal Register, Vol. 80, No. 31, P.17152 (Nov. 9, 2015).
261. Wynbrandt, *supra* n. 1, at 299.
262. Ramady, *The Saudi Arabian Economy, Policies, Achievements, and Challenges*, *supra* n. 79, at 300.
263. *Id.*
264. Wynbrandt, *supra* n. 1, at 299.

Over the decade-long process, the road was uneven. Although the zeal for open markets "waxed and waned" in Saudi Arabia during this period, the U.S. made very consistent demands for far-reaching free-market reforms. That variance is perhaps the best explanation for the long pre-application process. Indeed, the saga may best be described as "demand-resist-and-concede": the U.S. made a demand, and Saudi Arabia initially resisted but then ultimately conceded, at least in part. These demands covered virtually every area of the economy, from commercial trade to direct foreign investment to intellectual property rights. The end result was not so much a negotiation as a dictation: the U.S., as the ultimate insider, set the conditions for WTO membership and the Kingdom had little choice but to accept the terms that were offered. Even worse, the U.S. has been emboldened to continually increase its demands as the process dragged on.[265]

However, the long wait for membership has been worthwhile for Saudi Arabia. The accession to the WTO has benefited the KSA's economy both during the accession process and after the accession. The accession process enabled the KSA to reform its infrastructure and legal system by enacting many laws and regulations. Specifically, these reforms involved privatization and the attraction of much-needed FDIs.[266] All these changes, along with accession to the WTO, are leading to overall cost-cutting measures and increased efficiency throughout the Saudi economy.[267] The reforms and membership effectively catapulted the Kingdom into the mainstream of international commerce, as Saudi Arabia became more and more cognizant of the unwritten "rules of the game."[268]

WTO membership has some specific perks for the Kingdom. First and foremost, being part of the WTO helps reduce or eliminate the discriminatory trade policies of other nations. Furthermore, Saudi Arabia receives first-hand experience in acceptable trade dispute resolution methods and virtual immunity from many previous anti-dumping practices. Saudi exports automatically attain Most Favored Nation ("MFN") status in other WTO Member States, and internal reforms continue the trend towards privatization, increased FDI and greater internal efficiency.[269]

The bottom line is that membership in the WTO has caused exponential economic growth in Saudi Arabia: growth doubled from 2005 to 2010. That growth has led directly to more foreign investment and a GDP of approximately USD 500 billion. According to the Saudi ambassador to the U.S., this growth has set the stage for long-term job growth and overall economic health and diversity.[270]

In the last twenty years, Saudi Arabia has begun to embrace its role as a global economic player, albeit somewhat reluctantly. But the move towards globalization,

265. Bhala, *Saudi Arabia, the WTO, and American Trade Law and Policy*, *supra* n. 240, at 752-54.
266. M.A. Ramady & Mourad Mansour, *The Impact of Saudi Arabia's WTO Accession on Selected Economic Sectors and Domestic Economic Reforms*, 2 World Rev. Entrep. Mgt. & Sust. Dev. 3, 189-91 (2006).
267. *Id.*
268. Ramady, *The Saudi Arabian Economy, Policies, Achievements, and Challenges*, *supra* n. 79, at 299.
269. *Id.* at 300, 301.
270. Adel Al-Jubeir, *Arab-U.S. Relations: Going Where?* The NCUSAR Annual Conference (Oct. 21, 2010) http://ncusar.org/auspc/2010#20.

although it has been painful at times, is a significant step for the Kingdom, since it has been inward looking for most of its history. That vision is simply not sustainable in the present and future global community. By stretching its horizon, the Saudi economy is expanding in a way that has never been seen before. The WTO is an important part of Saudi Arabia's future, as the Kingdom continues to take further steps towards greater globalization.

The movement towards globalization is not limited to the GCC and WTO. In fact, in the coming years, the Saudi membership in the Group of Twenty ("G-20") may overarch them both.

[C] New Horizons: Participation in the G-20

What began as the G-7 in 1975 (France, UK, U.S., West Germany, Japan, Italy and the European Community) eventually expanded to encompass nations that collectively represent 85% of the world's GDP and two-thirds of the global population.[271] That expansion directly coincides with radical shifts in the global economy. The economic influence wielded by the G-7 began to wane, as economies such as China, India, Brazil, Russia, Mexico, and Saudi Arabia became progressively stronger. As a result, the G-7 (though still in existence and still functioning) can no longer dictate policy in the way in which it was accustomed, given the increased globalization and competition.[272]

These tectonic shifts, along with the global recessions in the 1990s and 2000s, forced the G-7 to become larger and more inclusive, moving from seven members to twenty (nineteen independent states and the European Union.)[273] As gross membership increased, the G-20's ability to influence policy increased commensurately. In fact, in the past few years, the G-20 has moved closer and closer to the forefront of international economics and global trade issues.[274] Especially in the wake of the global financial crisis, the G-20 has been a leading advocate of financial reform, based on a strong regulatory framework, effective supervision, transparent international assessment, peer review, and the balancing of systematic institutions.[275] In fact, in 2009, the G-20 leaders announced that they intended the organization to be "the premier forum

271. The G-7 expanded into the G-8 in the 1990s, until the Russian invasions of Ukraine and Crimea. Subsequently, the global financial crisis further led to the Group of 20. The G-20 currently includes Argentina, Australia, Brazil, Canada, China, the European Union, France, Germany, India, Indonesia, Italy, Japan, South Korea, Mexico, Russia, Saudi Arabia, South Africa, Turkey, the U.K., and the U.S. G-20, *The Group of Twenty: A History*, p. 8 (G-20 2008), www.g20.utoronto.ca/docs/g20history.pdf; *See* Group of Eight, *What Are The G7 And G8?* (Dec. 31, 2015), http://www.g8.utoronto.ca/what_is_g8.html.
272. G-20, *The Group of Twenty: A History*, *supra* n. 271, at 9.
273. *Id.*
274. Arie C. Eernisse, *Banking on Cooperation: The Role of the G-20 in Improving the International Financial Architecture*, 22 Duke J. Comp. & Int'l L. 239, 239 (2012).
275. G-20, *The G-20 Toronto Summit Declaration* 4, 5 (G-20 2010), https://www.g20.org/sites/default/files/g20_resources/library/Toronto_Declaration_eng.pdf.

for our international economic cooperation."[276] One commentator describes the current G-20 as a "qualitatively enhanced international financial architecture."[277]

Even as the G-7 expanded to the G-20 in 1999, which currently includes Argentina, Australia, Brazil, Canada, China, the European Union, France, Germany, India, Indonesia, Italy, Japan, South Korea, Mexico, Russia, Saudi Arabia, South Africa, Turkey, the United Kingdom (U.K.), and the U.S.,[278] the membership process remained somewhat subjective. Beyond the considerations that the group should be regionally balanced and that each Member State should have the capacity to contribute to the global economy in a meaningful way, there are no established membership criteria.[279] Since the 1999 expansion, the G-20 does recognize both established and emerging economies. Saudi Arabia falls squarely into the latter categorization.[280]

Most economists believe that the G-20 saw potential in Saudi Arabia as an emerging economy. They point to the country's vast petroleum reserve, along with its demonstrated record of participation in global and regional economic organizations, i.e., the GCC and WTO. Without both these factors, the G-20's interest in Saudi Arabia would have been minimal, at best.[281] It is noteworthy that Saudi Arabia is the only Organization of the Petroleum Exporting Countries ("OPEC") state in the G-20.[282]

Not all economists agree. The minority view is that Saudi Arabia is in the G-20 solely because of petroleum reserves and the vast financial windfall that the country has inherited as a result of this natural resource. Abdulaziz Aldakeel, a leading voice in this group, maintains that the Western countries that still dominate the G-20 included the KSA into this group primarily because of the Kingdom's ability to influence petroleum supplies and prices.[283]

The reality probably lies somewhere in the middle. While it is certainly true that the industrialized West is almost completely reliant on petroleum, and this reality no doubt carried a considerable amount of weight in the membership decision, it is also true that Saudi Arabia is a much more globally minded economy now than it was ten years ago, as we have already seen. For our purposes, the important thing is that Saudi Arabia is in fact a member but, like its other efforts geared towards globalization, it is fair to say that although it has attained membership among the world's economic elite,

276. G-20, *Leaders' Statement: The Pittsburgh Summit, Sept. 24-25, 2009*, Preamble paragraph 19 (Sep. 24-25, 2009), https://g20.org/wp-content/uploads/2014/12/Pittsburgh_Declaration_0.pdf.
277. Joseph J. Norton, *NIFA-II or "Bretton Woods-II"?: The G-20 (Leaders) Summit Process on Managing Global Financial Markets and the World Economy – Quo Vadis?*, 11 J. Banking Reg. 261, 289 (2010).
278. G-20, *The Group of Twenty: A History*, *supra* n. 271, at 8.
279. *Id.* at 20.
280. The G-20 Research Group, *2011 Cannes G20 Summit Final Compliance Report* 11 (2012), http://www.g20.utoronto.ca/compliance/2011cannes-final/index.html.
281. Fawaz Almoalmi, *Lmath Noshark Fi Majmoat Alashreen [Why Do We Participate in the Group of Twenty]*, Alwatan, Jun. 29, 2010, http://www.alwatan.com.sa/Articles/Detail.aspx?ArticleId=1022.
282. Thijs Van de Graaf & Kirsten Westphal, *The G8 and G20 as Global Steering Committees for Energy: Opportunities and Constraints*, 2 Global Policy 27 (2011).
283. Abdulaziz Aldakeel, *Altanmih Alagtsadih Fi Almamlkh Alarabia Alsaodih: Lmath Noshark Fi Magmoat Alashreen? Shi Men Alwageih* 881[*Why Do We Participate in the Group of Twenty? The Reailty*], the Article was written in 2010 (Dar Alsaqi Press 2012).

there is work still to be done if Saudi Arabia is to assume a leadership position in the G-20 or any other similar organization.

When Saudi Arabia joined the G-20, it, like all other Member States, made a number of commitments to make some substantive changes to its domestic economic policies. Essentially, the G-20 sets a number of goals for its Members, and Member States are expected to act accordingly. Five of these commitments are germane to the issue of financial markets and financial stability, and the Saudi Arabia's performance (or lack thereof) serves as a bellwether to determine its actual commitment to attracting investment, protecting investors and other areas that are relevant to this discussion.

The first, Commitment No. 151, pertains to Systematically Important Financial Institutions ("SIFIs"). In 2011, Member States committed to the full and timely implementation of the financial sector reform agenda agreed upon at the 2011 Cannes G-20 Leader's Summit, including a comprehensive framework to address the risk posed by systemically important financial institutions.[284] The background was the financial crisis of the late 2000s, which saw governments expended considerable sums of money as "bailouts." Determined to prevent future bailouts and crises, the G-20 directed the Financial Stability Board (FSB) to establish a set of procedures that it believed could more effectively regulate SIFIs. The resulting "Key Attributes of Effective Resolution Regimes of Financial Institutions" included such matters as international standards concerning financial solvency and liquidity, a requirement of an additional loss absorption capacity and more purposeful regulation of financial institutions. This third area was perhaps the most important, consisting of stronger government supervision, better risk management structure, and increased resources for appropriate regulatory agencies.[285]

Saudi Arabia has taken some steps in the right direction, by adopting an appropriate legal framework. Specifically, SAMA was empowered to increase its oversight of, and authority over, the Kingdom's SIFIs. SAMA responded to this mandate by publishing its plans that were modeled upon the Basel III implementation process. Moreover, SAMA carefully studied selected banks to make its oversight more effective, in both the short term and the long term.[286] Once put into effect, these measures should serve to bring Saudi Arabia into compliance with the agreed-upon SIFI regulations. But, for whatever reason, these plans were not immediately put into practice. Given its relative inaction, Saudi Arabia received a score of 0.[287]

In fairness, no Saudi bank currently qualifies as a SIFI,[288] a fact that may partially explain the lack of diligence in compliance. Perhaps the Kingdom thinks there is no

284. Group of Twenty, *Cannes Action Plan for Growth and Jobs* (2011), http://www.g20.utoronto.ca/2011/2011-cannes-action-111104-en.html.

285. The G-20 Research Group, *2011 Cannes G20 Summit Final Compliance Report* 144 (2012), http://www.g20.utoronto.ca/compliance/2011cannes-final/index.html.

286. *Id.* at 171.

287. *Id.* The grading scale is as follows: a +1 means that the country has fully complied with the commitment, a 0 means that the country has partially complied, and a -1 indicates that the country has made no progress towards meeting its commitment.

288. *Id.*

need to move forward with these additional SIFI regulations because they are inapplicable to the Saudi economy as it is currently constructed, and that may very well be true. However, the larger question may be a matter of submission to international authority and international standards, and the needs of the world community, as opposed to the present needs of the Kingdom. Saudi Arabia should consider doing more to meet its international obligations, even if doing so does not necessarily advance the Kingdom's own immediate economic interests.

The Basel III/ "Capital Adequacy" Accord involves much more than high-level banking oversight. The 2008 financial crisis exposed weaknesses in both the regulatory structure and capitalization of the world's large banks, and the Basel III initiatives are designed to combat both these problems. At the bank level, Basel III aims to improve the resilience of individual banking institutions during periods of intense financial stress. At the macro prudential level, Basel III reforms attempt to mitigate the procyclical amplification of system-wide risks that build up in the banking sector.[289] These reform objectives are embodied in Commitment 147: "We commit to the full and timely implementation of the financial sector reform agenda agreed up through Seoul, including: implementing Basel II, II.5, and III along the agreed timelines."[290]

In addition to its roots in the Basel Committee and Financial Stability Board, Basel III's structure is related to a G-20 meeting in Korea in 2010, at which time the G-20's finance ministers and central bank governors announced their intention to "propose internationally agreed rules to improve both quantity and quality of bank capital and to discourage excessive leverage and risk taking."[291] The final framework was established about a month later, with implementation to begin in 2013 and conclude by 2019. In 2012, the G-20 added peer review to the already existing plans, hence the name Basel III. The first series of peer reviews took place in December 2012.[292]

Notwithstanding the foregoing, Saudi Arabia might actually have been ahead of the curve, when it comes to embracing Basel III reforms. The Saudi Banking Control Law ("BCL") already had established a clear definition of capital and sets limits regarding capital requirements, liquidity, and leveraging. Furthermore, SAMA has the power to enact additional regulations based on applicable international accords, such as Basel III. Because of its full compliance with Commitment No. 147, Saudi Arabia scored a +1.[293]

Sound banking regulation has been an important policy objective in Saudi Arabia. The Kingdom has the infrastructure in place to help it avoid another financial crisis, and these regulations can be a foundation for effective regulation of capital markets, in accordance with current G-20 standards.

Over-the-counter ("OTC") derivatives are also an issue. In 2009, G-20 leaders set a goal of standardized exchange across international borders by the end of 2012. As a

289. *Id.* at 98.
290. *Cannes Action Plan for Growth and Jobs, supra* n. 284 (2011).
291. Group of Twenty, *Communiqué: Meeting of Finance Ministers and Central Bank Governors*, Republic of Korea (Jun. 5, 2010), http://www.g20.utoronto.ca/2010/g20finance100605.html.
292. The G-20 Research Group, *2011 Cannes G20 Summit Final Compliance Report* 99 (2012), http://www.g20.utoronto.ca/compliance/2011cannes-final/index.html.
293. *Id.* at 117-18. *See supra* n. 290, and accompanying text.

follow-up, in 2010, a G-20 report urged Member States to "improve the functioning, transparency and regulatory oversight of OTC derivatives markets." These observations gave rise to Commitment No. 149: Members committed to the full and timely implementation of the financial sector reform agenda agreed up through Seoul, including: clearing and trading obligations for OTC derivatives.[294] According to that same report, which gave Saudi Arabia a -1 respecting Commitment No. 149, the Kingdom had "failed to take steps towards compliance" on any of these matters.[295]

One can theorize that the same justification behind the lack of full compliance with SIFI regulations may be underlying the lack of effort regarding OTCs. The Kingdom may feel that such measures are largely inapplicable inside its borders. That may very well be true, but if Saudi Arabia is to become a leader in global economic affairs and not just a laggard, it should consider being much more proactive in its economic policies. The essence of international leadership is looking to the interests of other nations and, while not placing such considerations on an equal footing with domestic concerns, at least giving significant weight to these matters. The Kingdom seems unwilling to do that, at least in terms of certain financial regulations.

That is certainly not the case in all such matters. For example, Saudi Arabia has a much better track record regarding the G-20's investment imperative, which requires Member States to "commit to maintaining a supportive business environment for investors."[296] Saudi Arabia has been one of the more proactive Members in the group. As early as 2012, the Kingdom set up Enterprise Zones in six underdeveloped areas of the country – Hai'l, Jazan, Northern Borders, Al Jouf, Najran, and Al Baha – using ten-year tax incentives to attract additional FDI to these areas. The credits include a generous 50% deduction of Saudi employee training expenses, as well as a 50% deduction of some Saudi employee salaries. The following year, SAGIA[297] established a special committee to attract more investment to these areas that would create new jobs. This committee is charged with ending legal red tape and closing loopholes in the law, to attract quality investors to these Enterprise Zones.[298]

The Kingdom has also sought the cooperation of foreign states in this area. In 2012, the Council of Ministers gave SAGIA the authority to conduct bilateral talks with twelve European and Asian nations designed to promote investor protection. The next year, those talks expanded to include India. Saudi Arabia received a +1 as a result of all these efforts.[299]

Why has the Kingdom been enthusiastic about protecting and encouraging foreign investment? The answer may once again be self-interest. Saudi Arabia may see foreign investment as the best way to wean itself from total dependence on petroleum.

294. *Cannes Action Plan for Growth and Jobs, supra* n. 284 (2011).
295. The G-20 Research Group, *2011 Cannes G20 Summit Final Compliance Report* 137 (2012), http://www.g20.utoronto.ca/compliance/2011cannes-final/index.html.
296. Group of Twenty, *G20 Leaders Declaration* 4, Los Cabos (June 2012), http://www.g20.utoronto.ca/summits/2012loscabos.html.
297. Saudi Arabian General Investment Authority.
298. The G-20 Research Group, *2012 Los Cabos G20 Summit Final Compliance Report* 617 (2013), http://www.g8.utoronto.ca/g20/compliance/2012loscabos-final/index.html.
299. *Id.* at 618.

These efforts go in concert with the other initiatives that the Kingdom has put forward to encourage additional foreign investment in the country.

Despite its increasing relevance in international economic organizations, Saudi Arabia is still something of a developing economy. As an Emerging Market and Developing Economy ("EMDE"), the G-20 Cannes Action Plan requires Saudi Arabia to "adopt[] macroeconomic policies to enhance the resilience" of its economy.[300] In 2011, the FSB, the IMF, and the World Bank identified five key issues regarding EMDE stability: promoting cross-border supervisory cooperation, application of international financial standards, management of foreign exchange risks, expanding a supervisory and regulatory perimeter, and developing domestic capital markets.[301]

In 2012, SAMA and CMA signed a memorandum of cooperation that covered many of these points. Broadly speaking, this memorandum provides for coordination between SAMA and CMA in the areas of corporate governance, securities regulation, accounting standards, and other related concerns. The memorandum requires the two agencies to cooperate fully before announcing any new regulations in any affected areas. A joint high-level committee is tasked with handling implementation issues.[302]

For now, these directives are largely theoretical, which is why Saudi Arabia scored a 0.[303] Nonetheless, the extent of these plans clearly indicates Saudi Arabia's commitment to improving its economic stability. Once fully implemented, the SAMA/CMA agreement should form a solid foundation for better governmental monitoring of important economic institutions, a move that should assist the Kingdom in its efforts to attract more foreign investment by making the economy appear to be more stable.

While the GCC attempts to promote regional economic unity, and the WTO is largely committed to free trade, the G-20 exists to strengthen the economies of Member States. That is why it is important for Saudi Arabia to be a major participant in this organization. By adopting the policies that it agreed to embrace, the Kingdom can enhance its international prestige and take an important step towards a global leadership role as a responsible stakeholder.

§1.05 CONCLUSION

It is difficult to believe that the Kingdom has come so far so quickly. Eighty years after its founding, political and economic infighting in the U.S. led to a devastating civil war that nearly destroyed the country. It would be another forty years before an American

300. *Cannes Action Plan for Growth and Jobs, supra* n. 284 (2011).
301. The G-20 Research Group, *2011 Cannes G20 Summit Final Compliance Report* 81 (2012), http://www.g20.utoronto.ca/compliance/2011cannes-final/index.html.
302. Capital Market Authority, *CMA and SAMA Cooperate in Surveillance, Governance, Issuance, and Settlements of Securities of Companies in Financial Sector, 29 Jan. 2012* (Nov. 9, 2015), http://www.cma.org.sa/En/MediaCenter/pr/Pages/CMAandSAMAsignMoC.aspx.
303. The G-20 Research Group, *2011 Cannes G20 Summit Final Compliance Report* 95 (2012), http://www.g20.utoronto.ca/compliance/2011cannes-final/index.html.

President visited a foreign country during his term of office.[304] Saudi Arabia, however, has not only avoided these toxic internal disputes, but also has advanced to the edge of globalization.

Starting with the discovery of oil in the midst of the Great Depression of the 1930s, the Kingdom has moved towards integration with its regional and international neighbors. The journey began in earnest with domestic economic reforms and continued with membership in the GCC, to reach the current point of a place in the WTO and a position among the global economic elite in the G-20. But the adventure is far from over. How do we evaluate the past, and what needs to happen in the future?

The first time that oil gushed out of the ground, Saudi Arabia's identity as a nation was established. Petroleum has been good to the country in an unprecedented way, and that foundation set the Kingdom on the right path. Oil wealth allowed the people to enjoy a standard of living that was undreamed of by their fathers. To their credit, rather than bicker over money, the people chose to move forward.

The next step was to shape the Kingdom into something resembling a post-industrial economy. These reforms are still very much a work in progress, and more changes are needed, specifically in financial transactions and capital markets. These necessary changes will be explored in much more depth in subsequent chapters. For now, it is best to understand that reform is needed, and more reform should come.

All these reforms have had a common purpose: integration into the global community. The GCC was a start, and that organization's potential has yet to be fully tapped. There is no reason to believe that the GCC cannot become this generation's OPEC and have a strong voice in setting global economic policy. For a time beginning in the 1970s, OPEC almost "held the world by the tail." The price collapse of the 1980s effectively ended the group's influence, which underscored the need for a diversified economic base. With a common trade policy and a common currency, the GCC could exert that same type of influence and, as the largest state in the organization, Saudi Arabia has the potential to be the leader of this group.

Membership in the WTO represents a further important step. In roughly ten years of full membership, the Kingdom has seen growth and development that rivals the period 1932-1952: the original oil boom. Even more importantly, the WTO has served as a sort of benchmark for the Saudi economy. MFN status with other WTO Members has given the Kingdom the opportunity to peek inside these economies and find out what makes them tick. The common denominator seems to be controlled and successful capital investment.

Membership in the G-20 is reflective of the efforts the KSA has invested into the GCC and WTO. The G-20 can even be seen as a springboard to further globalization. However, it remains to be seen whether or not the Kingdom can fully take advantage of this opportunity. The future does seem encouraging, as Saudi Arabia has, for the most part, shown considerable diligence in matters of economic regulation and reform. *Vision 2030* picks up where these efforts left off, in a continuing effort to modernize and diversify the economy.

---

304. U.S. Department of State, *Travels of President Theodore Roosevelt* (Nov. 9, 2015), http://history.state.gov/departmenthistory/travels/president/roosevelt-theodore.

If the Kingdom's globalization plan initially involved economic reform and membership in international organizations, the next step is to look inward once again to make a more investment-friendly economy while simultaneously evaluating the strengths, and weaknesses, of the capital market inside Saudi Arabia. Only once that market becomes viable over the long term will Saudi Arabia be able to compete on even terms with other nations.

Bibliography

I. Primary Sources

[A] Saudi Arabia Laws and Regulations

Statute of the Supreme Economic Council, Royal Order No. A/111, dated 17/5/1420 H (1999).

The Capital Market Law, Royal Decree No. M/30, dated 2/6/1424 H (2003).

The Centennial Fund, Royal Decree No. A/190, dated 1425 H (2004).

The Civil Aviation Law, Royal Decree No. M/44 dated 18/7/1426 H (2005).

The Communications and Technology Commission, the Council of Ministers, Resolution No. 74, dated 5/3/1422 H (2001).

The Council of Ministers, *Privatization Objectives*, Resolution No. 60, dated 1/4/1418 H (1997).

The Council of Ministers, *The Saudi Arabian General Investment Authority*, Resolution No. 2, dated 5/01/1421 H (2000).

The E-Business Regulations, Royal Decree No. M/18, dated 27/3/2007 (2007).

The Foreign Investment Law, Royal Decree No. M/1, dated 5/1/1421 H (2000).

The General Investment Authority, the Council of Ministers, Resolution No. 20, dated 5/1/1421 H (2000).

The Human Resource Development Fund, the Council of Ministers, Resolution No. 107, dated 29/4/1421 H (2000).

The Income Tax Law, Royal Decree No. M/1, dated 15/1/1425 H (2003).

The Labor Law, Royal Decree No. M/51, dated 23/8/1426 H (2003).

The Law of Benefit Exchange between the Civil and the Military Pension Laws and the Social Insurance Law, Royal Decree No. M/53, dated 23/7/1424 H (2003).

The Law of Commercial Mortgage, Royal Decree No. M/75, dated 21/11/1424 H (2003).

The Law of Gas Supply and Pricing, Royal Decree No. M/36, dated 25/6/1424 H (2003).

The Law of Private Health Institutions, Royal Decree No. M/40, dated 3/11/1423 H (2003).

The Law of Public Investment Fund, Royal Decree No. M/24, dated 25/6/1391 H (1971).

The Law of Real Estate Ownership and Investment by Non-Saudis, Royal Decree No. M/15, dated 17/4/1421 H (2000).

The Law of Supervision on Cooperative Insurance Companies, Royal Decree No. M/32 dated 2/6/1424 H (2003).
The Saudi Commission for Tourism and Antiquities, the Council of Ministers, Resolution No. 9, dated 12/1/1421 H (2000).
The Saudi Council of Ministers Decision No. 5 (June 13, 1995).
The Saudi Organization for Industrial Estates and Technology Zones, the Council of Ministers, Resolution No. 235, dated 27/8/1422 H (2001).
The Statute of the Electricity and Co-generation Regulatory Authority, the Council of Ministers, Resolution No. 154, dated 4/5/1428 H (2007).
The Supreme Council for Petroleum and Minerals, Royal Order No. A 212, dated 27/9/1420 (2000).
The Supreme Economic Council, The Council of Ministers, Resolution No. 257, dated 11/11/1421 H (2001).
The Telecommunications Law, Royal Decree No. M/12 dated 12/3/1422 H (2001).

[B] GCC Laws and Regulations

Gulf Monetary Council, *The Statute of Monetary Council* (2008).
Monetary Union Agreement, the Cooperation Council for the Arab States of the Gulf (2008).
The Cooperation Council for the Arab States of the Gulf, *The Charter* (1981).
The Cooperation Council for the Arab States of the Gulf, *The Unified GCC Economic Agreement* (2001).
The Cooperation Council for the Arab States of the Gulf, *Unified GCC Economic Agreement* (1981).
The GCC Customs Union (2002).

[C] The U.S. Laws

Internal Revenue Code of 1986, I.R.C. § 999 (2004).

[D] Official/Semi-Official Reports – Government & Nongovernment Bodies

Al-Jubeir, Adel, *Arab-U.S. Relations: Going Where?* The NCUSAR Annual Conference (October 21, 2010) http://ncusar.org/auspc/2010#20.
Blanchard, Christopher M., *Saudi Arabia: Background and U.S. Relations* 36, Cong. Research Serv., RL 33533 (2009).
Capital Market Authority, *Aljadaan: Capital Market Authority Renewed the CMA Commitment to Saudi Vision 2030*, (May 25, 2016), http://www.cma.org.sa/En/MediaCenter/Events/Pages/ApsEvent2016.aspx.
Capital Market Authority, *CMA and SAMA Cooperate in Surveillance, Governance, Issuance, and Settlements of Securities of Companies in Financial Sector, 29 Jan.*

2012 (November 9, 2015), http://www.cma.org.sa/En/MediaCenter/pr/Pages/CMAandSAMAsignMoC.aspx.

Capital Market Authority, *CMA Chairman: Saudi Vision 2030 Achieves the Diversification of the National Economy with Greater Integration into the Global Economy System*, (April 28, 2016), http://www.cma.org.sa/En/MediaCenter/Events/Pages/Saudivision2030-.aspx.

Federal Research Division, *Country Studies, Saudi Arabia*, Library of Congress (November 8, 2015), http://countrystudies.us/saudi-arabia/37.htm.

Fitch Ratings, *Definitions of Ratings and Other Forms of Opinion*, (November 9, 2015), http://www.fitchratings.com/web_content/ratings/fitch_ratings_definitions_and_scales.pdf.

Fitch Ratings, *Fitch Affirms Saudi Arabia at "AA-", Outlook Revised to Positive* (September 25, 2013), http://www.fitchratings.com/creditdesk/press_releases/detail.cfm?pr_id = 78644140.

G-20, *Leaders' Statement: The Pittsburgh Summit, 24-25 Sept. 2009* (September 24-25, 2009), https://g20.org/wp-content/uploads/2014/12/Pittsburgh_Declaration_0.pdf.

G-20, *The G-20 Toronto Summit Declaration* (G-20 2010), http://www.g20.utoronto.ca/2010/to-communique.html .

G-20, *The Group of Twenty: A History* (G-20 2008), www.g20.utoronto.ca/docs/g20history.pdf.

Group of Eight, *What Are The G7 And G8?* (December 31, 2015), http://www.g8.utoronto.ca/what_is_g8.html.

Group of Twenty, *Cannes Action Plan for Growth and Jobs* (2011), http://www.g20.utoronto.ca/2011/2011-cannes-action-111104-en.html.

Group of Twenty, *Communiqué: Meeting of Finance Ministers and Central Bank Governors*, Republic of Korea (June 5, 2010), http://www.g20.utoronto.ca/2010/g20finance100605.html.

Group of Twenty, *G20 Leaders Declaration*, Los Cabos (June 2012), http://www.g20.utoronto.ca/summits/2012loscabos.html.

Information Affair Department, Gulf Cooperation Council, *Almaserah oa Alanjaz [The Process and the Achievements]* (4th ed. 2009).

Information Affair Department, Gulf Cooperation Council, *Almaserah Oa Alanjaz [The Process and the Achievements]* (7th ed. 2013).

International Monetary Fund, *World Economic and Financial Surveys-Regional Economic Outlook: Middle East and Central Asia* (October 15, 2015).

Jadresic, Esteban, *On a Common Currency for the GCC Countries* (International Monetary Fund. 2002).

Khan, Mohsin, *The GCC Monetary Union-Choice of Exchange Rate Regime*, (International Monetary Fund. 2008).

Ministry of Commerce and Industry, *Tagreer Farig Alamal Hola Inthmam Almamlkh Alarbia Alsaodih Ela Monthmat Altgarh Alalmih*, 2005 [*Report on Saudi Arabia's Accession to the World Trade Organization 2005*], (November 9, 2015), http://www.mci.gov.sa/Agencies/TechnicalAffairs/ReportsandStatistics/Pages/default.aspx.

Ministry of Economy and Planning of Saudi Arabia, *Achievements of the Plan*, Version 29, 2012 (November 9, 2015), http://www.mep.gov.sa/themes/GoldenCarpet/index.jsp;jsessionid=CE72BF929B432B2162EAABA14A68268B.beta?event=SwitchLanguage&Code=EN#1372712260448.

Ministry of Economy and Planning of Saudi Arabia, *Ninth Development Plan* (November 7, 2015), http://www.mep.gov.sa/themes/GoldenCarpet/index.jsp;jsessionid=E09FE18DA016FEE60A195FCEAE69AA52.beta?event=SwitchLanguage&Code=AR#1372098668716.

Ministry of Economy and Planning of Saudi Arabia, *Seventh Development Plan 1420/21–1424/25 (A.H), 2000– 2004 (A.D)* (November 7, 2015), http://www.mep.gov.sa/themes/GoldenCarpet/index.jsp;jsessionid=F374FDCD0B6758187FA54B943B0D0DF0.alfa?event=SwitchLanguage&Code=EN#1405309588083.

Ministry of Economy and Planning of Saudi Arabia, *The First Development Plan 1390-1395 (A.H) 1970-1975 (A.D)* (November 7, 2015), http://www.mep.gov.sa/themes/GoldenCarpet/index.jsp;jsessionid=9081FB102E53B01B5EA4F4C898BD8CE2.beta?event=SwitchLanguage&Code=EN#1370985755188.

Ministry of Economy and Planning of Saudi Arabia, *The Kingdom of Saudi Arabia Economy in Figures 2013* (November 7, 2015), http://www.mep.gov.sa/themes/GoldenCarpet/index.jsp;jsessionid=30EB1E1954CDF629613F8ACD4693887A.beta?event=SwitchLanguage&Code=EN#1372045463035.

Ministry of Economy and Planning, *The Saudi Development March 2009* (November 7, 2015), http://www.mep.gov.sa/themes/GoldenCarpet/index.jsp;jsessionid=A81578F940ACA159CC96A6F380C1B98F.alfa?event=SwitchLanguage&Code=EN#1381257481968.

Ministry of Finance in Saudi Arabia, *Ministry's of Finance Statement about the National Budget for 2015,* (November 9, 2015), https://www.mof.gov.sa/arabic/DownloadsCenter/Pages/Budget.aspx.

Ministry of Finance, *Historical Background* (November 7, 2015), http://www.mof.gov.sa/English/MinistryProfile/Pages/AboutUs.aspx.

Ministry of Petroleum and Mineral Resources of Saudi Arabia, *Gas Statistics* (November 7, 2015) http://www.mopm.gov.sa/Arabic/Statistics/Pages/ الغاز-احصائيات-.aspx.

Ministry of Petroleum and Mineral Resources of Saudi Arabia, *Statistics: Oil* (November 7, 2015), http://www.mopm.gov.sa/Arabic/Statistics/Pages/Oil-Test.aspx.

Organization of the Petroleum Exporting Countries, *OPEC Basket Price*, (December 31, 2015), http://www.opec.org/opec_web/en/data_graphs/40.htm.

Royal Embassy of Saudi Arabia in Washington, DC, *Economy & Global Trade* (November 9, 2015), http://www.saudiembassy.net/about/country-information/economy_global_trade/.

Royal Embassy of Saudi Arabia in Washington, DC, *History*, (November 7, 2015), http://www.saudiembassy.net/about/country-information/history/.

Saudi Arabian General Investment Authority, *Saudi Arabia's Economic Cities*, (November 9, 2015), http://www.oecd.org/mena/investment/38906206.pdf.

Saudi Arabian Monetary Agency, *Annual Report 42* (2006).

Saudi Arabian Monetary Agency, *Annual Report 48* (2013).

Saudi Arabian Monetary Agency, *Annual Report 51* (2015).

Saudi Arabian Monetary Agency, *SAMA's Functions* (November 7, 2015), http://www.sama.gov.sa/en-US/About/Pages/SAMAFunction.aspx.

Saudi Arabian Monetary Agency, *Yearly Statistics* (December 31, 2015), http://www.sama.gov.sa/en-us/economicreports/pages/yearlystatistics.aspx.

Saudi Press Agency, *Cabinet Approves Kingdom of Saudi Arabia s Vision 2030*, (April 25, 2016), http://spa.gov.sa/1493558.

Saudi Press Agency, *Custodian of the Two Holy Mosques Chairs Cabinet Session 3*, (March 23, 2015), http://spa.gov.sa/1341712?lang = ar&newsid = 1341715.

Saudi Stock Exchange "Tadawul", *The Saudi Stock Exchange (Tadawul) Plans on Establishing an Equity Market Targeting Small and Medium Enterprises (SMEs) Beginning of 2017*, (April 18, 2016), https://www.tadawul.com.sa/wps/portal/tadawul/markets/Press-Release/news-%26-announcements/!ut/p/z1/pY9Rb4IwFIX_yvwBprdQkT12TAHBzg10woup2CCJtAS7Ze7XrzBM9jL3sKYPvSffOfcU5WiLcsnfq5LrSkl-MnOWOzsWxF4ArhVBOgOgy6fF_GWywG4M6LUHLMtz8T2B2A_ZFOgzDTbzTWqDb6P8P34gf_vzHglXPsGhQdzUeQC69mL2yBIME2cAblW8CXQdegB-ORRQZn4x_dGBRTbQGY6ABEsMhKCkyzhwLVairdQBZfZdraQ-dnLDS8EUyvo9WnzoRPC2OJpQM3Mp1VtRC6nTSyNQZu3GuNPPPTNo1_CWy1J8-86Xeq9Ow1sUWrWh2Wq8Tb3eQhWO-f5TXC-lo9EX_uCNyw!!/?1dmy&urile = wcm:path:/Tadawul_en/SA-Tadawul/SA-PricesAndIndeces/SA-News/SA-MarketNews/4708.

Standard and Poor's Rating Services, *Ratings on Saudi Arabia Lowered To "A + /A-1"; Outlook Remains Negative*, (November 9, 2015), http://www.standardandpoors.com/en_US/web/guest/article/-/view/type/HTML/id/1473573.

Standard and Poor's Rating, *Outlook on Saudi Arabia Revised to Positive; Ratings Affirmed At "AA-/A-1 + "* (September 25, 2013), http://www.standardandpoors.com/prot/ratings/articles/en/us/?articleType = HTML&assetID = 1245352279180#ContactInfo.

The Cooperation Council for the Arab States of the Gulf, *About the GCC- Foundations and Objectives* (November 9, 2015), http://www.gcc-sg.org/en-us/AboutGCC/Pages/StartingPointsAndGoals.aspx.

The Cooperation Council for the Arab States of the Gulf, *Motatalbat Alathad Alnagdi* (*The Requirements Monetary Union*, (November 9, 2015), http://www.gcc-sg.org/ar-sa/CooperationAndAchievements/Achievements/EconomicCooperation/TheMonetaryUnionandtheSingleCurrency/Pages/Secondthemonetaryunionrequirem.aspx.

The G-20 Research Group, *2011 Cannes G20 Summit Final Compliance Report* (2012), http://www.g20.utoronto.ca/compliance/2011cannes-final/index.html.

The G-20 Research Group, *2012 Los Cabos G20 Summit Final Compliance Report* (2013), http://www.g8.utoronto.ca/g20/compliance/2012loscabos-final/index.html.

The Gulf Monetary Council, *About GMCO* (November 9, 2015), http://en.gmco.int/about.

The Royal Commission for Jubail and Yanbu, *About Us*, (June 18, 2016), https://www.rcjy.gov.sa/en-US/AboutUs/Pages/Foundation.aspx.

The Saudi Council of Economic Affairs and Development, *Saudi Vision 2030,* (April 25, 2016).

The Saudi Council of Economic Affairs and Development, *The National Transformation Program 2020,* (June 6, 2016).

The United States Department of Treasury, Office of the Secretary, *List of Countries Requiring Cooperation with an International Boycott*, March 31, 2015, reprinted in the Federal Register, Vol. 80, No. 31, P.17152 (November 9, 2015).

The World Bank, *Ease of Doing Business* (September 20, 2013), http://www.doingbusiness.org/data/exploreeconomies/saudi-arabia.

U.S. Department of State, *Travels of President Theodore Roosevelt* (November 9, 2015), http://history.state.gov/departmenthistory/travels/president/roosevelt-theodore.

U.S. Energy Information Administration, *International Energy Statistics* (December 31, 2015), https://www.eia.gov/cfapps/ipdbproject/iedindex3.cfm?tid = 3&pid = 3&aid = 1&cid = CG9,&syid = 2010&eyid = 2014&unit = BCF.

U.S. Energy Information Administration, *Saudi Arabia* (November 9, 2015), http://www.eia.gov/countries/cab.cfm?fips = SA#note.

U.S. Department of State, Office of Historian, *The 1928 Red Line Agreement* (November 8, 2015), http://history.state.gov/milestones/1921-1936/RedLine.

World Bank, *Economic Integration in the GCC* (World Bank 2010).

World Trade Organization, *Members and Observers* (November 9, 2015), http://wto.org/english/thewto_e/whatis_e/tif_e/org6_e.htm.

World Trade Organization, *Principles of the Trading System* (November 9, 2015), http://wto.org/english/thewto_e/whatis_e/tif_e/fact2_e.htm.

World Trade Organization, *Report of the Working Party on the Accession of the Kingdom of Saudi Arabia to the World Trade Organization*, 1, WT/ACC/SAU/61 (November 1, 2005).

World Trade Organization, *Trade Policy Review 2012: Saudi Arabia* (November 9, 2015), http://www.wto.org/english/tratop_e/tpr_e/tp356_e.htm.

World Trade Organization, *Trade Policy Review: The Kingdom of Saudi Arabia*, WTO Secretariat, WT/TPR/S/256 (December 21, 2011).

World Trade Organization, *Understanding the WTO* (November 9, 2015), http://wto.org/english/thewto_e/whatis_e/tif_e/fact1_e.htm.

World Trade Organization, *What is the WTO* (November 9, 2015), http://wto.org/english/thewto_e/whatis_e/wto_dg_stat_e.htm.

II. Secondary Sources

[A] Books

Aldakeel, Abdulaziz, *Altanmih Alagtsadih Fi Almamlkh Alarabia Alsaodih: Almamlakh Alarabiah Alsaodih Oa Monathmat Altgarah Alalmih: Aoagb Altakar Oa Analtathar Fi Itkath Algrar [Economic Development in the Kingdom of Saudi Arabia: The Kingdom of Saudi Arabia and the World Trade Organization: The*

Consequences of Hesitation and Waiting in the Decision-Making], the Article was written in 1999 (Dar Alsaqi Press 2012).

Aldakeel, Abdulaziz, *Altanmih Alagtsadih Fi Almamlkh Alarabia Alsaodih: Gerah Fi Masirat Altanmih* [*Economic Development in the Kingdom of Saudi Arabia, Reading in the Development Process*], the Article was written in 1986 (Dar Alsaqi Press 2012).

Aldakeel, Abdulaziz, *Altanmih Alagtsadih Fi Almamlkh Alarabia Alsaodih: Lmath Noshark Fi Magmoat Alashreen? Shi Men Alwageih* [*Why Do We Participate in the Group of Twenty? The Reailty*], the Article was written in 2010 (Dar Alsaqi Press 2012).

Alhabib, Faiz, *Altanmih Alagtsadih Bina Alnathorih Oa Oaga Aldola Alnamih* [*Economic Development Between the Theory and the Reality of Developing Countries*], (King Saud Library 1985).

Alhabib, Faiz, *Mabada Alagrsad Alkoli* [*Principles of Macroeconomics*], (Alfarazdag Press Company 2011).

Alobad, Abdullah, *Egtsad Almmlakh Alarabih Alsaodih* [*The Kingdom of Saudi Arabia Economy*], (Dar Alam Alkotob Press 1994).

Alrouaf, Othman, *Engazat Altanoih Fi Almamlkh Alarabih Alsaodih* [*Development Achievements in the Kingdom of Saudi Arabia*], (Alhomathi Press 2010).

Cordesman, Anthony H., *National Security in a Troubled Region* (Center for Strategic and International Studies 2009).

Frankel, Jeffrey A., *No Single Currency Regime Is Right For All Countries or At All Times*, Essays In International Finance, No. 215, (Princeton University 1999).

Ramady, Mohamed A., *The Saudi Arabian Economy, Policies, Achievements, and Challenges* (2nd ed. 2010).

Rasquinha, Joseph, *The Integration of the Gulf Co-Operation Council (GCC): Problems and Prospects*. (September 1991) (unpublished Ph.D. dissertation, University of St Andrews) (A copy of the dissertation is available at http://hdl.handle.net/10023/2754.

Vassiliou, M.S., *The A to Z of the Petroleum Industry* (Scarecrow Press 2009).

Wilson, Rodney, *Good international Governance: Implications for Saudi Arabia's Political Economy, Good Governance in the Middle East Oil Monarchies* (Tom Pierre Najem & Martin Hetherington, eds, 2003).

Wynbrandt, James, *A Brief History of Saudi Arabia* (Facts On File, 2nd ed. 2010).

Yergin, Daniel, *The Prize, the Epic Quest for Oil, Money, and Power* (Simon & Schuster 1992).

[B] Articles

Abu-Bader, Suleiman & Aamer S. Abu-Qarn, *On the Optimality of a GCC Monetary Union: Structure VRA, Common Trends and Common Cycles Evidence*, 31 The World Economy (2008).

Agil, Hussain & Bruno, Zeller, *Foreign Investments in Saudi Arabia*, 15 Int'l Trade & Bus. L. Rev. (2012).

Alford, Roger P., *The Self-Judging WTO Security Exception*, 2011 Utah L. Rev. 697 (2011).
Bhala, Raj, *Challenges of Poverty and Islam Facing American Trade Law*, 17 St. John's J. Legal Comment. 471 (2003).
Bhala, Raj, *Saudi Arabia, the WTO, and American Trade Law and Policy*, 38 Int'l Law. 741 (2004).
Eernisse, Arie C., *Banking on Cooperation: The Role of the G-20 in Improving the International Financial Architecture*, 22 Duke J. Comp. & Int'l L. 239 (2012).
European Commission, *Completing Europe's Economic and Monetary Union: Commission Takes Concrete Steps to Strengthen EMU*, 21 Oct. 2015, http://europa.eu/rapid/press-release_IP-15-5874_en.htm.
Jones, Garth N., *Strategies and Tactics of Planned Organizational Change: Case Examples in the Modernization Process of Traditional Societies*, 24 Hum. Org. 192 (1965).
Khoury, Amir H., *The Development of Modern Trademark Legislation and Protection in Arab Countries of the Middle East*, 16 Transnat'l Law. 249 (2003).
Laabas, Belkacem & Imed Limam, *Are GCC Countries Ready for Currency Union?*, Arab Plan. Inst. (2002).
Malkawi, Bashar H., *Anatomy of the Case of Arab Countries and the WTO*, 20 Arab L.Q. 112 (2006).
Marar, Amr D., *Cooperation Council for the Arab States of the Gulf*, 10 L. & Bus. Rev. Am. 475 (2004).
Norton, Joseph J., *NIFA-II or "Bretton Woods-II"?: The G-20 (Leaders) Summit Process on Managing Global Financial Markets and the World Economy – Quo Vadis?*, 11 J. Banking Reg. 261 (2010).
Peake, Bob, *Saudi Arabia Plays Safe on Reform*, 11 Int'l Tax Rev. (2000).
Ramady, M.A. & Mourad Mansour, *The Impact of Saudi Arabia's WTO Accession on Selected Economic Sectors and Domestic Economic Reforms*, 2 World Rev. Entrep., Mgt. & Sust. Dev. 3 (2006).
Sutberland, Peter D., *Transforming Nations: How the WTO Boosts Economies and Opens Societies*, 87 Foreign Aff. 125 (2008).
Van de Graaf, Thijs & Kirsten Westphal, *The G8 and G20 as Global Steering Committees for Energy: Opportunities and Constraints*, 2 Global Policy 27 (2011).
Zaidi, Iqbal, *Monetary Coordination among the Gulf Cooperation Council Countries*, 18 World Dev. 759 (1990).

[C] News

Albishi, Mohammed, *Alasaf Le Alsharq Alaosat: Manh Sandug Alestathmarat Salaheit Tasis Alsharikat Siosa Nashatah [Alasif to Alsharq Al-Awsat: Granting the Public Investment Fund the Power to Establish Companies Will Expand its Activities]*, Alsharq Al-Awsat (July 23, 2014), http://aawsat.com/home/article/143736.
Almashabi, Deema & Glen Carey, *Saudis Want to Double Stock Market for a Post-Oil Economy, Bloomberg*, (April 4, 2016), http://www.bloomberg.com/news/

articles/2016-04-04/saudis-want-to-double-their-stock-market-for-a-post-oil-economy.

Almashabi, Deema, et al., *Saudi Arabia's Deputy Crown Prince Outlines Plans: Transcript, Bloomberg,* (April 4, 2016), http://www.bloomberg.com/news/articles/2016-04-04/saudi-arabia-s-deputy-crown-prince-outlines-plans-transcript.

Almoalmi, Fawaz, *Lmath Nosharк Fi Majmoat Alashreen [Why Do We Participate in the Group of Twenty]*, Alwatan (June 29, 2010), http://www.alwatan.com.sa/Articles/Detail.aspx?ArticleId = 1022.

Ban on Israeli Goods in Place: Customs Chief, Arab News (January 4, 2007), http://www.arabnews.com/node/292917.

Bianchi, Stefania, *The Key Questions Asked about Saudi Arabia's $2 Trillion Fund*, Bloomberg, (May 25, 2016), http://www.bloomberg.com/news/articles/2016-05-25/key-questions-raised-by-the-2-trillion-saudi-wealth-fund-plan.

Duncan, Hugo, *World's Biggest Oil Company Set to Join London Stock Exchange in Biggest Share Listing Ever*, This is Money.co.UK, (May 9, 2016), http://www.thisismoney.co.uk/money/markets/article-3581482/World-s-biggest-oil-company-set-join-London-Stock-Exchange-biggest-share-listing-time.html.

Freund, Michael, *Saudi Ambassador to US Admits Boycott of Israel Still in Force*, Jerusalem Post (June 22, 2006).

Gumuchian, Marie-Louise, *Saudi Arabia, UAE, Bahrain Withdraw Envoys from Qatar*, CNN, March 5, 2014, http://www.cnn.com/2014/03/05/world/meast/gulf-qatar-ambassadors/.

Hanware, Khalil, *Kingdom's Growth Trajectory Will Continue Uninterrupted*, Arab News, (November 8, 2015), http://www.arabnews.com/economy/news/832211.

Highlights of Saudi Deputy Crown Prince's Interview with Al Arabiya, Al Arabiya (April 25, 2016), http://english.alarabiya.net/en/perspective/features/2016/04/25/Highlights-of-Deputy-Crown-Prince-Mohammed-bin-Salman-s-Al-Arabiya-interview.html.

Hook, Leslie, *Uber Cranks Up Ride-Hailing Battle with $3.5bn Saudi Investment*, Financial Times, (June 2, 2016), https://next.ft.com/content/3ac7c982-2879-11e6-8b18-91555f2f4fde.

Iddon, Paul, *Why the Gulf States Recalled Their Ambassadors from Qatar*, Digital Journal, (March 5, 2014), http://digitaljournal.com/news/politics/why-the-gulf-states-recalled-their-ambassadors-from-qatar/article/374632.

Kronfol, Mohieddine & Bassel Khatoun, *Vision 2030–Saudi's Bold Move into the Global Financial Market,* Franklin Templeton Investments, (May 18, 2016), http://global.beyondbullsandbears.com/2016/05/18/vision-2030-saudis-bold-move-into-the-global-financial-market/.

Larson, Alan & Constance Anne Pence, *Saudi Arabia's Vision 2030 – Ambitions to Modernize and Diversify the Economy*, Global Policy Watch (June 6, 2016), https://www.globalpolicywatch.com/2016/06/saudi-arabias-vision-2030-ambitions-to-modernize-and-diversify-the-economy/.

Mahdi, Wael, et al., *Aramco IPO Seen by Prince as Tonic for Saudis "Addicted" to Oil, Bloomberg*, (April 25, 2016), http://www.bloomberg.com/news/articles/2016-04-25/saudi-prince-says-aramco-valuation-seen-at-above-2-trillion.

Micklethwait, John, et al., *Saudi Arabia Plans $2 Trillion Megafund for Post-Oil Era: Deputy Crown Prince*, Bloomberg, (April 1, 2016), http://www.bloomberg.com/news/articles/2016-04-01/saudi-arabia-plans-2-trillion-megafund-to-dwarf-all-its-rivals.

NTP 2020 Promotes Culture of Entrepreneurship in Saudi Arabia, Arab News, (June 16, 2016), http://www.arabnews.com/node/940476/economy# ....

NTP Offers Credible Path to Diversification: Moody's, Arab News, (June 14, 2016), http://www.arabnews.com/node/939006/economy ....

Paul, Katie, et al., *How Saudi Arabia Plans to Shake Up its Economy*, Reuters, (April 14, 2016), http://www.reuters.com/article/us-saudi-economy-plan-insight-idUSKCN0XB0S8.

Sandug Alestathmarat Alamah: Maseerah Ala Mada 40 Ama Fi Majal Alanshatah Alegtesadiah Oa Alsenaeih [The Publish Investment Fund: Developmental March Over 40 Years in the Filed of Economic and Industrial Activities], Al Eqtisadiah Newspaper (April 4, 2011), http://www.aleqt.com/2011/04/04/article_522656.html.

Stapczynski, Stephen, *Saudi Fund Buys $1.1 Billion Stake in Posco Engineering Unit*, Bloomberg, (July 1, 2015), http://www.bloomberg.com/news/articles/2015-07-02/saudi-fund-buys-1-1-billion-stake-in-posco-engineering-unit.

Stearns, Jonathan, *EU Commission Renews Push for Single Euro-Area Voice at IMF*, Bloomberg Business, October 21, 2015, http://www.bloomberg.com/news/articles/2015-10-21/eu-commission-renews-push-for-single-euro-area-voice-at-imf.

Torchia, Andrew, et al., *Analyst View: Saudi Arabia's Vision 2030 Reform Plan*, Reuters (April 25, 2016), http://www.reuters.com/article/us-saudi-plan-reaction-idUSKCN0XM1FX.

CHAPTER 2

Saudi Capital Market and Its Role in the Saudi Economy

SUMMARY

A thriving capital market, one that not only brings investment funds into a county but also distributes profits in a transparent matter, is essential for any economy, especially a rapidly developing one. Over the past several decades, Saudi Arabia took limited steps in pursuit of this vision, most notably its membership in IOSCO. But the crash of 2006 revealed serious flaws in the capital market, especially with regard to transparency and fairness. The government by itself is not to blame for the crash: media reporting and investor attitudes also played a significant role. However, in the wake of this tragedy, the KSA appears poised to move forward. This chapter examines the level of transparency and fairness among market participants in the Saudi capital market.

§2.01 INTRODUCTION

A growing Saudi capital market first emerged in the 1970s.[1] At that time, the capital market witnessed an increasing number of "listed companies"[2] and also an increase in trading volume. But the roots of the Saudi capital market actually go back much farther, to the Kingdom's beginning in the 1930s. At that time, private brokers who regularly bought and sold securities participated in an unregulated system, but these brokers

1. Mohammed Atta Almadi, Dor Alhaiah Alammh Le Soag Almal Fi Hemait Aglet Almosahemen Fi Alsharekat Almosahemah 17, [The Role of the General Authority of the Capital Market in Protecting the Minority of Shareholders in Joint Stock Companies], (Maktabt Alganon Oa Alagtsad 2012).
2. "Listed companies" are companies whose shares are traded in the Saudi capital market.

lacked experience in a formal capital market.[3] The Saudi Law of Companies in 1965 was the first regulatory law for the primary market.[4]

In 1985, the government enacted Royal Decree No. 8/1230. It restricted trading stocks to local banks.[5] Later, in 1990, the government used a new trading system, the Electronic Securities Information System ("ESIS"), which ushered the Saudi capital market into the digital age.[6] In the ESIS, stock trading went through centralized units in commercial banks that were linked with a central host computer in the "SAMA."[7]

The Saudi government continued to support the private sector, which led to even more growth in the number of listed companies. The figure reached sixty-four large companies by the end of 1996.[8] As of June 2016, there are 175 listed companies in the Saudi capital market,[9] making it one of the largest capital markets in the Arab world in terms of total market capitalization of the listed companies.[10]

One of the most recent developments in the Saudi capital market was the establishment of the "CML" in 2003.[11] The CML aims to regulate the market to operate fairly, to provide equal opportunities to all investors, and to minimize risks involved with trading securities.[12]

Having a regulated capital market with a high level of transparency not only helps ensure a secure and stable market, but also reduces the number of abusive activities and fills possible gaps in procedures.[13] To achieve the desire of having a Saudi modern capital market, the Saudi "CMA," the governmental body responsible for the Saudi capital market, has been a member of the International Organization of Securities

3. At the beginning of the capital market in Saudi Arabia, there were illegal practices that were not regulated as a result of the lack of experience in capital markets by investors and brokers. Ayman Ezzat Albidane, *Asoag Alaorag Almalih Fi Almamlakh Alarabia Alsaodih: Daragt Tatorah Oa Enftaha Alarabi Oa Emkanit Rabtaha Balasoag Almalih Alarabiah, [Stock Markets in Saudi Arabia: Their Openness and the Their Possibility of Liking Them with Arab Stock Markets]*, 12(3), The Arab Magazine for Management 123 (1988).
4. Law of Companies, Royal Decree No. M/6, dated 22/3/1385 H (1965).
5. Royal Decree No. 8/1230, dated 11/7/1403 (1983).
6. Radi Saleh Alhadad, *Daorat Alastathmar Fi Alaorag Almaleah: Grarat Ethafeh [Cycle Investment in Securities: Extra Decisions]* (Riyadh Business 1992).
7. Hisham Aljamal, *Financial Markets and Financial Institutions* 28, (Majmaah University 2013).
8. Almadi, *The Role of the General Authority of the Capital Market in Protecting the Minority of Shareholders in Joint Stock Companies, supra* n. 1, at 18.
9. Saudi Stock Exchange "Tadawul", *Market Watch Today*, (Jun. 30, 2016), https://www.tadawul.com.sa/wps/portal/tadawul/markets/equities/market-watch/market-watch-today.
10. Almadi, *The Role of the General Authority of the Capital Market in Protecting the Minority of Shareholders in Joint Stock Companies, supra* n. 1, at 18.
11. The Capital Market Law, Royal Decree No. M/30, dated 2/6/1424 H (2003).
12. The CML regulates the Capital Market Authority, operates the machinery of the Saudi Stock Exchange, and oversees associated institutions, such as the Depositary Securities Center. The CML also regulates brokerage services and investments funds. To meet these objectives, the CML prohibits individuals from practicing brokerage services without first obtaining a broker's license from the Capital Market Authority. Fahad Alhwimani, *Almal Oa Alastthmar Fi Alasoag Almalih* 475 *[Money and Investment in Capital Markets]*, (Dar Alhilal Offset Printing Press 2006).
13. Alhwimani, *Money and Investment in Capital Markets, supra* n. 12, at 457.

Commissions ("IOSCO") since June 9, 2010.[14] Since then, the CMA has demonstrated its commitment to specific IOSCO objectives and overall principles of securities regulation.[15]

A modern capital market has certainly had beneficial and positive effects on the Saudi economy. However, even though IOSCO membership has been a solid step towards a modern capital market, membership has brought some challenges to Saudi Arabia in general, and the CMA in particular. For Saudi Arabia, the goal remains the same despite any obstacles: i.e., a capital market that fulfills the IOSCO's vision of protection for all investors, fairness, efficiency, and transparency for all capital market transactions, through the implementation and enforcement of clear and precise regulations.

This chapter will focus on the history of Saudi capital market, the need for a modern capital market, the challenges and benefits of IOSCO membership, the role of the Saudi capital market in the economy, and the 2006 crash. The thread that connects all these items is a lack of market transparency.

§2.02 THE NEED FOR, AND IMPACT OF, AN EFFECTIVE CAPITAL MARKET

The economic development of any nation can be measured through studying the development of its financial market, since that market reflects the regulations themselves, as well as their transparency and efficiency.[16] Studies have proved that the economic growth rate increases whenever a capital market develops further, while taking into account the need for a banking sector to serve the needs of the capital market and the overall economy.[17] However, a capital market may also negatively affect an economy if illegal or unprofessional acts are not dealt with effectively.[18] Thus, the role of CMA and other governmental institutions[19] becomes essential to serve and to protect the integrity of the market.[20]

14. The International Organization of Securities Commissions, *IOSCO Expands Its Global Membership to Include Iceland, the Maldives, Saudi Arabia and Syria*, Media Release IOSCO/MR/09/2010, Montreal (Jun. 9, 2010).
15. *Id.*
16. Abdulsabor Abdulkawi Masari, *Altantheem Alganoni Le Haokmat Alsharekat 83, [The Legal Regulation of the Corporate Governance]*, (Maktabt Alganon Oa Alagtsad 2012).
17. Khalid Mohammed Alfaiz, *Dor Soag Alaorag Almaliah Fi Tadaoir Alsoag Almali Fi Almamlakh Alarabiah Alsaodiah, 4-5[the Role of Capital Market in Developing the Financial Market in the Kingdom of Saudi Arabia]*, the 15th Annual Meeting of Saudi Economic Association in Cooperation with Saudi Capital Market Authority (Riyadh, Nov. 13-15, 2005).
18. Masari, *The Legal Regulation of the Corporate Governance*, *supra* n. 16, at 83.
19. These institutions include the Saudi Arabian Monetary Agency.
20. Article 6 of the Capital Market Law states that the Authority shall have the power to "give advice and make recommendations to government authorities in respect of matters that would contribute to the development of the Exchange and the protection of investors in Securities," Capital Market Law, Article 6-4 (2003).

[A] The Beginnings of the Saudi Capital Market

In the mid-1930s, at roughly the same time oil was discovered, Saudi joint-stock companies began their activities. The first joint-stock company, "Arab Automobile,"[21] was established in 1935 with 12 million Saudi Riyals ("SAR") (USD 3,200 million).[22] Then, in 1954, Arabian Cement Company and three electricity companies were founded,[23] along with the National Printing and Publishing Company. Altogether, the total stated capital of these six companies was SAR 78 million (USD 20,800 million). Their capital soon increased to reach SAR 943 million (USD 251,466 million). The number of companies began to increase as well. Between 1955 and 1964, there were eleven new Saudi joint-stock companies such as three electric companies, two cement production companies, and three petroleum service companies.[24]

This period also included two important events in the history and development of Saudi joint-stock companies. In 1956, the first joint-stock company for banking services, "Riyadh Bank," was established by a capital of SAR 50 million (USD 13.3 million) – divided into 50,000 shares.[25] Also, for the first time, mixed joint-stock companies emerged. These companies included foreign investors. Examples include the Arabian Petroleum Supply Company, which was established in 1961 with a capital of SAR 6 million (USD 1.6 million), and with 49% foreign capital. Also, the 100,000-share Arabian Drilling Company was established in 1964 with SAR 10 million (USD 2.6 million), with foreign capital of 49% as well.[26]

In response to this growth and development, and to lay a foundation for future expansion, the government of Saudi Arabia enacted the Law of Companies in 1965. One of its stated goals was the regulation of stock issuance in the primary market.[27] Prior to 1965, there was no law at all regulating the market. The Law of Companies was a turning point for establishing join-stock companies with confidence and clear regulations for investors.[28]

The capital market continued to grow. By 1975, the number of joint-stock companies had increased to fourteen,[29] with total capitalization at about SAR 2 billion

21. Arab Automobile Company was subsequently liquidated. Abdulaziz Mohammed Aldakeel, *Soag Alasahom Alsaodi: Geraah Tarekeeh Oa Estashraf Almostagbl 121 [Saudi Stock Market: Reading the History and an Anticipation the Future]* (Dar Alfarabi 2010).
22. Abdullah Mohammed Alrozain, *Souq Almal* 46 [*the Capital Market*], (Imam Muhammad Ibn Saud Islamic University 2006).
23. Khalid Abdulaziz Bagdadi, *Tadawal Alashom Oa Alquod Aloardah Aliha Fi Alntham Alsaudi* 24 [*Stocks Trading and the Restrictions on them in the Saudi System*], (Maktabt Alganon Oa Alagtsad 2012).
24. Ghazi Mahfoth Falmban, *Alastathmar Balasahom Fi Almamlakh Alharabia Alsaodiah* 79-80 [*Investment in Stocks in the Kingdom of Saudi Arabia*], (Tihama Publications 1986).
25. Alrozain, *supra* n. 22, at 46.
26. Falmban, *supra* n. 24, at 80.
27. Articles 52-65 in Chapter Two of the Law of Companies (1965) regulated the primary market in more detail.
28. Falmban, *supra* n. 24, at 99.
29. Saudi Stock Exchange "Tadawul", *About Us*, (Nov. 12, 2015), http://www.tadawul.com.sa/wps/portal/!ut/p/c1/04_SB8K8xLLM9MSSzPy8xBz9CP0os3g_A-ewIE8TIwODYFMDA08Tn7AQZx93YwN3I_3g1Dz9gmxHRQB7GACB/. "Tadawul" is translated as "trading."

(USD 533 million).[30] Beginning in 1975, more large corporations and joint-stock banks were set up as a result of the rapid economic expansion and the nationalization of some foreign capital.[31] All told, seven foreign joint venture banks were "Saudized,"[32] and the shares made available to the general public.[33] By 1980, the number of joint-stock companies had increased to thirty-three, with total capitalization at about SAR 21 billion (USD 5.6 billion).[34] However, until the early 1980s, the capital market remained largely informal and there was lack of specific regulations, so the government correctly saw the need to set up a regulated market that formalized stock trading.[35]

The secondary market in Saudi Arabia emerged in the late 1970s, when many joint-stock companies were established.[36] The 1965 Law Companies applied only to primary markets. The secondary market remained unregulated until 1984.[37] Before then, a secondary market emerged as an informal market controlled by unauthorized real estate offices. These offices had practiced selling and buying shares without licenses,[38] either for themselves or for their clients, as securities brokers.[39] No license, no minimum capital amount, and no specific competencies were required to practice as a securities broker at that time.[40]

In 1978, there were over eighty securities brokers in Saudi Arabia providing securities brokerage services.[41] Each office worked independently in selling and buying shares as an independent bursa.[42] There were three methods to sell shares at that time: advertising in financial newspapers; trading through banks which served as brokers and dealt with selling and buying shares in exchange of commissions; or going to real

30. Aldakeel, *Saudi Stock Market: Reading the History and Anticipation the Future, supra* n. 21, at 122.
31. Saudi Stock Exchange "Tadawul", *About Us, supra* n. 29.
32. For example, SAMBA, formerly known as Saudi American Bank, has taken over City Bank branches in Jeddah and Riyadh, Saudi Arabia. Also, Saudi British has taken over the British Bank of the Middle East (BBME) branches in the Kingdom of Saudi Arabia. Radi Saleh Alhadad, *Ektbar Alaomel Almoathrah Ala Aoaid Ashom Alsharikat Alsaodiah Almosahemh 49, [Examine the Effecting Factors on Dividends of Saudi Joint-Stock Companies]* (Master Thesis, King Abdulaziz University 1990).
33. Henry T. Azzam, *The Emerging Arab Capital Markets: Investment Opportunities in Relatively Underplayed Markets* 141 (Kegan Paul International 1997).
34. Aldakeel, *Saudi Stock Market: Reading the History and Anticipation the Future, supra* n. 21, at 122.
35. Saudi Stock Exchange "Tadawul", *About Us, supra* n. 29.
36. Ahmed Sulaiman Alsuraiseri, *Saana Alsoag Aldoalih Fi Tadawul Alasahom Almahaleeh 75, [The Maker of International Market in Trading the Local Stocks]* (King Fahad National Library, Riyadh 2008).
37. Masari, *The Legal Regulation of the Corporate Governance, supra* n. 16, at 82.
38. Bagdadi, *Stocks Trading and the Restrictions on Them in the Saudi System, supra* n. 23, at 24.
39. Falmban, *supra* n. 24, at 100.
40. Masari, *The Legal Regulation of the Corporate Governance, supra* n. 16, at 82.
41. There were forty-five securities brokers in Riyadh, thirty in Jeddah, and six in Dammam. Aldakeel, *Saudi Stock Market: Reading the History and Anticipation the Future, supra* n. 21, at 126.
42. Eid Masoud Aljuhane, *Alastathmar Bi Alasaho Fi Alsoug Alsaudi 89 [The Investment in Stocks in the Saudi Market]* (Alsharif Publication 1989).

estate offices which sold and bought shares.[43] The transfer of ownership of shares was through shareholders affairs departments, which were inside the joint-stock companies, after ratifying bills of sale by the Chamber of Commerce.[44]

This situation was unprofessional and unregulated until 1984. It was very difficult for buyers and sellers to meet, and supply and demand of shares was unknown to anyone other than the parties to a transaction. Thus, the shares prices varied greatly from place to place. As a result, many joint-stock companies shares were not traded for long periods of time, simply due to the deficiency in the trading system at that time.[45]

Partly in response to the Al-Manakh crisis,[46] a Ministerial Committee was formed in 1984, consisting of the Ministry of Finance and National Economy, Ministry of Commerce, and SAMA, to regulate and develop the Saudi Arabian Stock Market.[47] Additionally, SAMA was responsible for monitoring and regulating the market's daily business.[48] In June 1984, SAMA issued a regulation covering all banks operating in Saudi Arabia, based upon an agreement with the Ministerial Committee.[49] This regulation included the following: the Ministerial Committee was the responsible body for monitoring stocks market activities, and SAMA was the responsible body for monitoring the market's daily activities; stocks brokerage was limited to commercial banks; banks were responsible for stocks registrations; listed companies were required to publish quarterly financial statements in a local newspaper; and banks were permitted to impose 1% commission for stocks service.[50] "OTC" trading was restricted to twelve banks. Finally, banks were not allowed to be stockholders and brokers[51] in the same transaction.[52] Restricting stocks brokerage exclusively to banks was a good step to avoid using forward contracts based on post-dated checks, as was the case in

43. Researches Department, *Borsat Alaorag Almaleh Oa Ahmitah Fi Kedmat Alsharikat Almosahemh 91-93 [Stock Exchange and Its Importance in Serving Joint-Stock Companies]*, Riyadh Chamber of Commerce and Industry (Alsharif Publication 1980).
44. Saad Hamad Alashre, *Alasahom Oa Asoag Almaal: Doroos Fi Alastathmar 22-23 [Stocks and Capital Markets: Lessons in Investment]* (Arabian Printing and Publishing House 2004).
45. Alsaid Ibrahem Aldsogi, *Almoasherat Alalmih Llasahom Ma Insha Moasher Kas Belasahom Alsaodih 76, [Global Stock Indicators with the Creation of a Special Index for Saudi Stocks]*(King Saud University 1989).
46. In Kuwait, there were an official Kuwaiti stock exchange, which was established in 1978, and an unofficial stock market known as "Souk Al-Manakh" in the late 1970s and early 1980s. Souk Al-Manakh transactions featured contracts based on post-dated checks. The Al-Manakh crisis came to a climax in August 1982, when the official Kuwaiti stock market fell 21% in value and Souk Al-Manakh fell about 60%. For more details, *see* Kirt C. Butler & S. Jamal Malaikah, *Efficiency and Inefficiency in Thinly Traded Stock Markets: Kuwait and Saudi Arabia*, 16 J. Banking & Fin. 197 (1992).
47. Saudi Arabian Monetary Agency, *Historical Preview*, (Nov. 12, 2015), http://www.sama.gov.sa/en-US/About/Pages/SAMAHistory.aspx.
48. Saudi Stock Exchange "Tadawul", *About Us*, *supra* n. 29.
49. Aldakeel, *Saudi Stock Market: Reading the History and Anticipation the Future*, *supra* n. 21, at 126.
50. *Id.*
51. Butler, *supra* n. 46, at 199.
52. Azzam, *supra* n. 33, at 143.

Souk Al-Manakh,[53] because SAMA closely supervised commercial banks' activities, and no others could practice stocks brokerage services except banks.[54]

In 1985, with backing from SAMA, eleven Saudi banks established the Saudi Share Registration Company ("SSRC"),[55] a joint-stock company, to provide automated depository and registration services for all ESIS-traded corporations, and to maintain the Central Share Account as a centralized book-entry depository.[56]

The new regulation, which restricted stock trading to only commercial banks, sharply increased trading volume. The volume in the first year of publishing the regulation reached 2,707,832 shares. In the second year, it reached 7,976,898 shares. Yet, trading volume was still disproportionate to the total volume of about 500 million shares.[57]

In May 1987, the government of Saudi Arabia established a "trading floor," gathered bank brokers into one place, and held trading through an open auction system. SAMA played a supervisory role over the floor's trading activities.[58] However, this new trading system was terminated after less than one month due to technical issues, and stocks trading returned back through phones and telex in the Saudi banks.[59]

A form of central control returned in 1990, when SAMA introduced the ESIS system. All buy and sell orders were funneled through a central computer at SAMA.[60] ESIS was considered one of the most advanced systems in the world at that time. A central host computer in SAMA was connected to remote terminals located in about 500 branches of 12 commercial banks spread throughout the Kingdom.[61] ESIS had been updated nine times until SAMA introduced "Tadawul" in 2001.[62]

In 2001, SAMA implemented a formal structure for the unofficial Saudi stock market, which is known now as "Tadawul."[63] Tadawul, at that time, was an entity owned by banks, but regulated heavily by SAMA.[64] It meets the need of a physical marketplace for trading, clearing, and settling capital market transactions.[65] Moreover,

53. *See supra* n. 46, and accompanying text.
54. Abdulrahman Abdullah Alhamidi & Abdulrahman Abdulmohsen Alkalaf, *Alnagood Oa Albonok Oa Alasoag Almalih 350 [Money, Banks, and Capital Markets]*, (Alfarazdak Press Company, 2009).
55. The Saudi Share Registration Company, Royal Decree No. 1230/8 (1985).
56. Joseph W. Beach, *The Saudi Arabian Capital Market Law: A Practical Study of the Creation of Law in Developing Markets*, 41 Stan. J. Int'l L. 307, 313 (2005).
57. The trading volume was only 2%, which was very low. Aldsogi, *supra* n. 45, at 80.
58. Aldakeel, *Saudi Stock Market: Reading the History and Anticipation the Future, supra* n. 21, at 128.
59. *Id.*
60. Mohammed A. Ramady, *The Saudi Arabian Economy, Policies, Achievements, and Challenges* 155 (2d ed. 2010).
61. Azzam, *supra* n. 33, at 143.
62. Mohammed Ibrahim Alsuhaibani, *Aalaiat Almogasah Oa Altasaoih Fi Alasoag Almalih 50 [Clearing and Settlement Mechanisms in Financial Markets]*, (Dar Kanoze Eshbilia Press 2009).
63. Beach, *supra* n. 56, at 311.
64. *Id.* at 314.
65. Aljazira Capital, *The Financing Role of the Saudi Capital Market 28* (Research Department 2010).

the system enables trading to be easily carried out through the Internet with both security and a short processing time.[66]

There are many benefits for investors. Trading is conducted in a virtual marketplace, and the individual investors can remain in their homes and offices. Real time news and information is available, from sources both inside and outside the Kingdom. Since financial statement and other announcements are published over the Internet, the system has also improved transparency.[67]

In March 2007, the Saudi Council of Ministers updated the system and reformed the Saudi Stock Exchange into a joint-stock company in accordance with Article 20 of the CML.[68] Shortly thereafter, the Council of Ministers converted Tadawul into a state-owned joint-stock company with a capital of SAR 1.2 billion (USD 320 millions) in order to increase the exchange's autonomy and strengthen the capital market regulatory framework.[69]

[B] The Urgent Need to Restructure the Saudi Capital Market

The regulatory structure of the Saudi capital market in the late 1990s was severely underdeveloped. There were two government agencies that shared the responsibilities of supervision: the Ministry of Commerce and SAMA.[70] The primary mission of the Ministry of Commerce was regulating the business entities in Saudi Arabia.[71] However, it used its primary jurisdiction to regulate the primary offering market and took an active role in pricing new shares.[72] At the same time, SAMA's primary mission was the supervision of Saudi banking activities. Because the banks were the only licensed intermediaries in the capital market, SAMA saw itself as having jurisdiction over the entire secondary market. Due to the split between the agencies, there was little or no common direction or central control.[73]

The Law of Companies regulated the primary market in the Kingdom since 1965.[74] The Ministerial Committee issued a regulation in 1984 through SAMA.[75] The regulation governed the secondary market and focused only on banks, excluding all

66. Ramady, *The Saudi Arabian Economy, Policies, Achievements, and Challenges, supra* n. 60, at 155.
67. Saudi Arabian Monetary Agency, *Financial Sector Development for Better Growth: A Future Vision for the Saudi Economy until 2020* (October 2002).
68. Saudi Stock Exchange "Tadawul," *About Us, supra* n. 29.
69. Aljazira Capital, *The Financing Role of the Saudi Capital Market, supra* n. 65, at 4.
70. Beach, *supra* n. 56, at 311.
71. The Ministry of Commerce and Industry, *Historical Overview*, (Nov. 12, 2015), http://www.mci.gov.sa/en/AboutMinistry/Pages/HistoricalOverview.aspx.
72. Beach, *supra* n. 56, at 311.
73. *Id.*
74. Law of Companies, Royal Decree No. M/6, dated 22/3/1385 H (1965). The decision-maker enacted a new Law of Companies in November 2015 and published in the Official Gazette (*Umm Al Qura*) in December 2015. The Law of Companies 2015 entered into force 150 days after its official publication date: enforcement began in May 2016. Law of Companies, Royal Decree No. M/3, dated 28/1/1437 H (2015); Ministry of Commerce and Investment, *The New Corporate Law Comes Into Force Today, Monday 25.07.1437 H, As Confirmed By MCI*, (May 2, 2016), http://mci.gov.sa/en/MediaCenter/News/Pages/02-05-16-01.aspx.
75. *See supra* n. 49, and accompanying text.

other market participants. Moreover, licensing and the activity of market intermediaries were not covered by any specific laws or regulations, so government agencies regulated these actors, primarily the banks, by using laws and rules not specifically geared to the capital market or securities industry.[76]

The Law of Companies did not address some important subjects, such as individual responsibility and liability for misdeeds and deceptive practices.[77] However, while Shari'ah prohibits these items and imposes penalties, Shari'ah courts in Saudi Arabia would disagree on the type of penalties and the degree they should be applied to violators. For example, one judge would impose a USD 3,000 fine and another judge, faced with a similar fact pattern, would impose a USD 20,000 fine and six months' imprisonment. As a result of this discrepancy, foreign investors and issuers were deterred by the lack of specific regulation of the capital market, and they were unwilling to come under the Islamic court's jurisdiction. Moreover, it was impossible to establish a formal stock exchange in Saudi Arabia by using the Regulations for Companies because the regulations were inadequate to that task and outside its scope and authority.[78]

The Law of Companies suffered from other deficiencies. It failed to address some basic concepts, such as mergers and acquisitions, tender offers and proxy solicitations.[79] Additionally, the possible sanctions in the Law of Companies were too weak to combat capital market abuses.[80] Thus, there was a huge demand and need for a more desirable regulation to cover all aspects of the Capital Market in Saudi Arabia, in order to meet the potential growth in the market and the economy.

The regulatory structure in Saudi capital market was insufficient, and both the capital market and the Saudi regulators had been disadvantaged by this deficiency.[81] In an attempt to circumvent the rules, a new class of non-licensed and unregulated financial intermediaries emerged as a result of the rise of the demand for capital. Additionally, both issuers and investors had sought to invest and raise capital in offshore markets due to the restrictions and uncertainties of the Saudi market regulation. This reaction by issuers and investors further undermined the potential capital

76. Beach, *supra* n. 56, at 311.
77. *Id.* at 317.
78. *Id.*
79. *Id.*
80. *See* the Law of Companies, Article 229-231 (1965). For example, Article 229 stated that without prejudice to what is required under Sharia law, a person shall be punishable by imprisonment for a term of not less than three months but not exceeding one year and a fine of not less than SAR 5,000 (USD 1,333) and not exceeding SAR 20,000 (USD 5,333), or either, for any manager, a member of the Board of Directors, an auditor, or a liquidator who intentionally indicates false data in the balance sheet, in the profit and loss account, or in one of the reports of the partners or the General Assembly, or omits from these reports some substantial facts with a view to conceal the financial position of the company from the partners or others. The Law of Companies, Article 229 (1965).

    These sanctions were too weak to deter violators from committing offenses, because the regulation was written back in 1965 and it reflected the financial situation at that time. Yet, the regulation was no longer suitable for the capital market, its activities, and its participants.
81. Beach, *supra* n. 56, at 311.

market growth. The ad hoc system that had been in place since the 1960s was simply no longer up to the task, and additional regulatory oversight was sorely needed.[82]

In the middle 1990s, the Ministry of Finance and National Economy and SAMA asked the World Bank to prepare a study about the reality of the Saudi capital market and its future. The government also asked the World Bank for suggestions to develop the market in order to have a financial market that supported the development process. The World Bank's study recommended that the government of Saudi Arabia enact an integrated regulation for the capital market that included establishing an independent body to monitor the market and promote competition, authorizing brokerage firms other than commercial banks, and establishing a market-owned and managed by a private sector.[83]

In late 1996, Saudi Arabia realized that developing and enacting a comprehensive securities market law and establishing a security market regulator was an important step to develop and enhance the capital market.[84] A vibrant and well-regulated stock market is one of the cornerstones that a national economy relies on for development.[85] Realizing this, the government of Saudi Arabia retained professionals and experts to research and draft the legislation for the capital market.[86] During the period between 1997 and 2003, SAMA worked on preparing an integrated proposed regulation for the capital market, taking into consideration the World Bank recommendations, capital markets experiences in a number of developed and emerging countries, and international trends on the development and modernization of capital markets, particularly those issued by relevant international bodies such as IOSCO.[87]

At the same time, Saudi Arabia was in the midst of a series of Five-Year Economic Plans. The Seventh Development Plan (2000-2004) contained specific provisions about capital market enhancements, including infrastructure development, nonbank securities exchange, the formation of a new regulatory agency and a new CML, and the conversion of existing firms into joint-stock companies.[88] Other Plan objectives included the creation of independent data centers and the encouragement of foreign investment.[89] The Plan highlighted the significance of these capital market reforms, calling them "imperative" to continued economic growth and prosperity in general, and increased foreign investment in particular.[90]

82. *See Id.* at 312.
83. Alhamidi, *Money, Banks, and Capital Markets, supra* n. 54, at 360.
84. Beach, *supra* n. 56, at 309.
85. Abdulaziz Mohammed Aldakeel, *Altanmih Alagtsadih Fi Almamlkh Alarabia Alsaodih: Soag Alashom Alsaudih Bina Aldairh Alhokomih Oa Aldairh Albankeih Oa Ehtkar Algallh 196 [Economic Development in the Kingdom of Saudi Arabia, Saudi Stock Market among government Administration, Banks, and Oligopoly]*(Dar Alsaqi Press 2012).
86. Beach, *supra* n. 56, at 309.
87. Alhamidi, *Money, Banks, and Capital Markets, supra* n. 54, at 361.
88. Ministry of Economy and Planning of Saudi Arabia, *Seventh Development Plan 1420/21–1424/25 (A.H), 2000– 2004 (A.D)* 184 (Nov. 12, 2015), http://www.mep.gov.sa/themes/GoldenCarpet/index.jsp;jsessionid=F374FDCD0B6758187FA54B943B0D0DF0.alfa?event=SwitchLanguage&Code=EN#1405309588083.
89. *Id.* at 129.
90. *Id.* at 184.

The need for a modern capital market in Saudi Arabia was necessary for faster trading, better information availability, more accurate data, and prevention of manipulation and fraud.[91] The undeveloped regulatory structure in the Saudi capital market and the different government regulators made the demand for a new regulation with one regulator a fundamental requirement for the growth of the capital market and the Saudi economy.

[C] The Modern Saudi Capital Market

Currently, thanks in large part to the number of young professionals, the KSA has one of the largest stock markets in the region.[92] This growth is not limited to one economic sector or demographic group. The entire Saudi Arabian economy has been growing rapidly, due to the relative stability of its government and currency, as well as low levels of inflation.[93] The developments in the Saudi Arabian economy have been pronounced in recent decades, and especially in the 2000s.

As briefly referenced above, early in the new millennium, as part of the Seventh Development Plan (2000-2004), the government of Saudi Arabia enacted the CML on July 31, 2003.[94] The law is intended to restructure the capital market in Saudi Arabia by introducing new concepts that help protect investors, enhance the confidence in the market, and attract more potential investors.[95] Furthermore, the CML also contributes to the disclosure process, as well as market fairness and transparency.[96] A well-organized capital market, which has a high level of transparency, should contribute to a safe and stable environment to the market and decrease the number of violations.[97]

With this action, the government of Saudi Arabia hoped that the CML would do more than update the system. The idea was that the CML would unify the regulatory structure, define rules and procedures for all investors and participants in the capital market, and level the playing field in the Saudi financial sector.[98] The extensive CML has sixty-seven articles in ten chapters, covering such diverse topics as the establishment of an independent market regulator, a formal Saudi stock market, and a Securities Depository Center. Moreover, the CML also addresses brokers regulation, investment funds and collective investment schemes, the requirement of public disclosure, the

91. Wadea Kapal, *Hoal Tatoir Soug Alasahom Oa Mostagblah [About the Development of Stock Market and Its Future]*, 230 Alagtasad Magazine 22 (July 1992).
92. John Donboli, *Doing Business in the Middle East: A Primer for U.S. Companies*, 38 Cornell Int'l L.J. 413, 431 (2005).
93. *Id.*
94. Royal Decree No. M/30, dated 2/6/1424 (2003).
95. Saudi Stock Exchange "Tadawul", *Market Rules*, (Nov. 12, 2015) http://www.tadawul.com.sa/wps/portal/!ut/p/c1/04_SB8K8xLLM9MSSzPy8xBz9CP0os3g_A-ewIE8TIwMLf3czA0_vIKegIBN_QwNXQ6B8JJK8e0CYqYGniU-wUXCAl7GBpxEB3X4e-bmp-gW5EeUATNtVlg!!/dl2/d1/L0lDUmlTUSEhL3dHa0FKRnNBL1lCUlp3QSEhL2Vu/.
96. *Id.*
97. Alhwimani, *Money and Investment in Capital Markets*, *supra* n. 12, at 475.
98. *Saudi Stock Exchange Approved*, BBC News, Jun. 17, 2003, http://news.bbc.co.uk/2/hi/business/2998086.stm.

regulation of manipulation and insider-trading behaviors, regulation of proxy solicitations, restricted purchase and restricted offer for shares, and sanctions and penalties for violations.

The CML is a milestone in Saudi CML. Prior to 2003, there was no umbrella law that encompassed multiple aspects of the market, including structures, regulatory, supervisory, and operational entities. Now, the CML clearly defines powers and duties by separating the operational and supervisory roles of the market.[99] The CML established a number of new entities, including the CMA,[100] the Saudi Stock Exchange ("Tadawul"),[101] the Securities Depositary Center,[102] the Committee for the Resolution of Securities Disputes ("CRSD"),[103] and an Appeal Committee for the Resolution Securities Disputes.[104]

With the CML, Saudi Arabia has the foundation for a single and understandable set of rules that govern capital market activities.[105] The Law has been essential for the growth and development of the Saudi Capital Market, and that has positively affected the economic strength in the country.

Shortly after the enactment of the CML, and in accordance with Article 4 of the new law,[106] the CMA was established on July 2, 2004[107] as the primary regulatory and supervisory body over the capital market.[108] Thus, SAMA is no longer responsible for regulating and monitoring capital market activities.[109] As further stated in Article 4, the CMA is a self-contained legal entity with financial and administrative autonomy. It has all the authority as may be necessary to discharge its responsibilities and functions under the CML, and it directly reports to the President of the Council of Ministers.[110] This hierarchical system tends to be inefficient. Instead of reporting to the President of the Council of Ministers (King Salman Bin Abdulaziz), the CMA should report directly to the Minister of Commerce. By tying the CMA to a specialist ministry, it would be easier to make decisions and to implement policies without bureaucratic delay.[111]

To ensure the independence of the CMA and to end any potential conflicts of interests, the CML states that "the Authority shall not have the right to engage in any

99. Alsuraiseri, *supra* n. 36, at 77.
100. Capital Market Law, Article 4 (2003).
101. Article 20-a of the CML states: "a market shall be established in the Kingdom for the trading in Securities, which shall be known as the 'Saudi Stock Exchange', and will have the legal status of a joint-stock company in accordance with the provisions of this Law. This Exchange shall be the sole entity authorized to carry out trading in Securities in the Kingdom." *See supra* n. 63, and accompanying text.
102. Capital Market Law, Article 26 (2003).
103. *Id.* Article 25.
104. *Id.*
105. Beach, *supra* n. 56, at 307.
106. Capital Market Law, Article 4(a) (2003).
107. Alhamidi, *Money, Banks, and Capital Markets, supra* n. 54, at 361.
108. Saudi Stock Exchange "Tadawul", *About Us, supra* n. 29.
109. Saudi Arabian Monetary Agency, *Historical Preview, supra* n. 47.
110. Capital Market Law, Article 4(a) (2003).
111. Almadi, *The Role of the General Authority of the Capital Market in Protecting the Minority of Shareholders in Joint Stock Companies, supra* n. 1, at 19.

commercial activities, to have a special interest in any project intended for profit, to borrow or lend any funds, or to acquire, own, or issue any Securities."[112]

Article 5 of the CML defines the duties and objectives of the CMA. It emphasizes that the CMA is an agency that is responsible for issuing regulations, setting up rules and instructions, and applying the CML in the market.[113] Article 5 also states that the Authority shall regulate and develop the Exchange, monitor securities and dealing in securities, regulate the issuance of securities, regulate and monitor the works and activities of parties subject to the control and supervision of the Authority, protect investors and the public from unfair and unsound practices or practice involving prohibited activities including fraud, deceit, cheating or manipulation, seek to achieve fairness, efficiency and transparency in securities transactions, regulate and monitor the full disclosure of information, and regulate proxy and purchase requests and public offers of shares.[114] As of June 30, 2016, the CMA has authorized eighty-four market intermediaries to carry on securities businesses.[115]

There are also enforcement provisions. The CMA has the power to inspect prior legal violations, as well as investigate a potential violation of the CML or any implementing regulations or rules.[116] Article 5 gives the CMA direction in its basic tasks, while preserving its flexibility to develop and adapt as the Saudi Capital Market grows and develops.[117]

The CMA also has the power to carry out its functions under the CML as well as the regulations, rules and instructions issued pursuant thereto.[118] One of these powers

112. Capital Market Law Article 4(b) (2003).
113. *Id.* Article 5(a).
114. *Id.* The CMA and Saudi Stock Exchange (Tadawul) have continuously endeavored to align the market infrastructure development with the market regulatory environment, under international best practices. In this regard, in May 3, 2016, the CMA has approved Saudi Stock Exchange's (Tadawul) request for amending the transactions settlement cycle of listed shares from (T + 0) to (T + 2). This change is to take effect in the first half of 2017. Settlement cycle is a period between the trade and the moment when securities ownership registered at Securities Depositary Center and corresponding payment is made. Currently, our market is at T + 0 settlement cycle, where settlement of securities happens as soon as trade is executed, and settlement of cash is conducted at the end of the day. In T + 2, compared to the current T + 0 environment, securities and cash will be interchanged between parties two days after the trading day at the same time. For more details, *see* Saudi Stock Exchange "Tadawul", *Frequently Asked Questions on the Amendment of the Settlement Cycle of Listed Securities in the Equity Market*, (May 5, 2016), https://www.tadawul.com.sa/static/pages/en/Publication/PDF/T2E.pdf.

    Additionally, the CMA Board has approved the introduction of securities lending and covered short selling as per the regulations to be issued before the end of the first half of 2017. Capital Market Authority, *CMA Approves Amendments to the Registration Requirements for Qualified Foreign Financial Institutions, Change the Settlement Cycle for Securities Transactions and the introduction of Securities Lending and Covered Short-Selling*, (May 3, 2016), http://www.cma.org.sa/en/News/Pages/CMA_N_2036.aspx.
115. For more details about these authorized persons, *see* Capital Market Authority, *Authorized persons*, (June 30, 2016), http://www.cma.org.sa/en/Pages/AuthorisedPersons.aspx.
116. *Id.* Article 5(c).
117. Beach, *supra* n. 56, at 325.
118. Article Six (a) of the CML states that the CMA "shall have the power to carry out its functions under this Law as well as the regulations, rules and instructions issued pursuant thereto including, but not limited to the power to:

pertains to the issuance and amendment of the implementing regulations as may be necessary. Based on the power that is given by the CML,[119] the CMA has issued many rules and regulations to protect investors, to ensure fairness and to promote efficiency in the capital market. These regulations include Authorized Persons Regulations,[120] Anti-Money Laundering and Counter-Terrorist Financing Rules,[121] Corporate Governance Regulations (CGR),[122] Investment Funds Regulations,[123] Glossary of Defined Terms Used in the Regulations and Rules of the CMA,[124] Listing Rules (LR),[125] Market Conduct Regulations,[126] Merger and Acquisition Regulations,[127] Offers of Securities Regulations (OSR),[128] Real Estate Investment Funds Regulations,[129] Securities Business

---

1. Set forth policies and plans, conduct studies and issue necessary rules to achieve the Authority's objectives.
2. Issue and amend the Implementing Regulations as may be necessary to enforce the provisions of this Law.

...

8. Determine the maximum or the minimum commissions to be charged by brokers to their clients if the Board deems it appropriate, and approve the fees and other commissions to be charged by the Exchange and the Depositary Center."

119. Capital Market Law, Article 6(a) (2003).
120. Authorized Persons Regulations, the Board of the Capital Market Authority Resolution Number 1-83-2005, dated 21/05/1426 H (June 28, 2005). Amended by the Resolution of the Board of the Capital Market Authority Number 1-1-2013, dated 1/3/1434 H (Jan. 13, 2013).
121. Anti-Money Laundering and Counter-Terrorist Financing Rules, the Board of the Capital Market Authority Resolution Number 1-39-2008, dated 3/12/1429 H (Dec. 1, 2008), Amended by the Resolution of the Board of the Capital Market Authority Number 2-54-2013, dated 21/2/1435 H (Dec. 24, 2013).
122. Corporate Governance Regulations, the Board of the Capital Market Authority Resolution Number 1-212-2006, dated 21/10/1427 H (Nov. 12, 2006), Amended by the Resolution of the Board of the Capital Market Authority Number 1-10-2010, dated 30/3/1431 H (Mar. 16, 2010).
123. Investment Funds Regulations, the Board of the Capital Market Authority Resolution Number 1-219-2006, dated 3/12/1427 H (Dec. 24, 2006).
124. Glossary of Defined Terms Used in the Regulations and Rules of the Capital Market Authority, the Board of the Capital Market Authority Resolution Number 4-11-2004, dated 20/8/1425 H (Oct. 4, 2004).
125. Listing Rules, the Board of the Capital Market Authority Resolution Number 3-11-2004, dated 20/8/1425 H (Oct. 4, 2004), Amended by the Resolution of the Board of the Capital Market Authority Number 1-64-2016, dated 19/8/1437 H (May 26, 2016).
126. Market Conduct Regulations, the Board of the Capital Market Authority Resolution Number 1-11-2004, dated 20/8/1425 H (Oct. 4, 2004), Amended by the Resolution of the Board of the Capital Market Authority Number 3-3-2016, dated 27/3/1437 H (Jan. 7, 2016).
127. Merger and Acquisition Regulations, the Board of the Capital Market Authority Resolution Number 1-50-2007, dated 21/9/1428 H (Oct. 3, 2007), Amended by the Resolution of the Board of the Capital Market Authority Number 2-4-2012, dated 28/2/1433 H (Jan. 22, 2012).
128. Offers of Securities Regulations, the Board of the Capital Market Authority Resolution Number 2-11-2004, dated 20/8/1425 H (Oct. 4, 2004), Amended by the Resolution of the Board of the Capital Market Authority Number 1-28-2008, dated 17/8/1429 H (Aug. 18, 2008).
129. Real Estate Investment Funds Regulations, the Board of the Capital Market Authority Resolution Number 1-193-2006, dated 19/6/1427 H (Jul. 15, 2006).

Regulations,[130] the Resolution of Securities Disputes Proceedings Regulations,[131] Prudential Rules,[132] Credit Rating Agencies Regulations,[133] Rules for Qualified Foreign Financial Institutions Investment in Listed Shares,[134] Investment Accounts Instructions,[135] and Procedures and Instructions for Listed Companies on the Market whose Accumulated Losses Amounted to 50% or More of their Capital.[136]

Initially, Tadawul was only open to Saudi nationals.[137] Limited foreign participation began in 1997, when these investors were allowed to participate in banks' mutual funds. Saudi American Bank[138] was the first to introduce a closed-end Saudi mutual fund, the SAIF.[139] Two years later, the Saudi stock market was opened for foreign investment through a wider range of Saudi banks' mutual funds.[140] Later, in December 2007, the Saudi Stock Exchange was opened to Gulf Cooperation Council ("GCC") nationals as a part of the overall move to establish a GCC common market.[141]

---

130. Securities Business Regulations, the Board of the Capital Market Authority Resolution Number 2-83-2005, dated 21/05/1426 H (Jun. 28, 2005).
131. Resolution of Securities Disputes Proceedings Regulations, the Board of the Capital Market Authority Resolution Number 1-4-2011, dated 19/2/1432 H (Jan. 23, 2011).
132. Prudential Rules, the Board of the Capital Market Authority Resolution Number 1-40-2012, dated 17/2/1434 H (Dec. 30, 2012).
133. Credit Rating Agencies Regulations, the Board of the Capital Market Authority Resolution Number 3-58-2014, dated 17/1/1436 H (Nov. 10, 2005).
134. Rules for Qualified Foreign Financial Institutions Investment in Listed Shares, the Board of the Capital Market Authority Resolution Number 1-42-2015, dated 15/7/1436 H (May 4, 2015).
135. Investment Accounts Instructions, the Board of the Capital Market Authority Resolution Number 4-39-2016, dated 25/6/1437 H (Apr. 3, 2016).
136. Procedures and Instructions for Listed Companies on the Market whose Accumulated Losses Amounted to 50% or More of their Capital, the Board of the Capital Market Authority Resolution Number 4-48-2013, dated 15/1/1435 H (Nov. 18, 2013). These implementing regulations are available at http://www.cma.org.sa/en/Pages/Implementing_Regulations.aspx.
137. SAMBA, *The Saudi Stock Market: Structural Issues, Recent Performance and Outlook* 4 (SAMBA Economics Department 2009).
138. Saudi American Bank launched in March 1997 the Saudi Arabian Investment Fund ("SAIF") to server institutional investors. SAIF was the first closed Saudi mutual fund, and was listed in London Stock Exchange. International Monetary Fund- Middle Eastern Department, *Financial Systems and Labor Markets in the Gulf Cooperation Council Countries* 15 (International Monetary Fund 1997).
139. Adli Ali Hammad, *Mosoat Gaoanin Soag Almal Alsaoadi* 28 [*Laws Encyclopedia of the Saudi Capital Market*], (King Fahad National Library 2013); Ramady, *The Saudi Arabian Economy, Policies, Achievements, and Challenges, supra* n. 60, at 156. A "closed-end" mutual fund comes from a publicly traded firm. It is based on a set amount of capital pertaining to an initial public offering. The fund is then listed and traded like a stock on a stock exchange. However, in an "open ended" mutual fund, there are no limits on the number of shares to be issued. Theoretically, if there is sufficient demand, the fund will issue as many shares as there are investors. Most open-end funds also contain a buy back provision for investors wishing to sell. *See* The United States Securities and Exchange Commission, *Closed-End Fund Information*, (Dec. 31, 2015), https://www.sec.gov/answers/mfclose.htm; The United States Securities and Exchange Commission, *Mutual Funds*, (Dec. 31, 2015), https://www.sec.gov/answers/mutfund.htm.
140. Ramady, *The Saudi Arabian Economy, Policies, Achievements, and Challenges, supra* n. 60, at 156.
141. SAMBA, *The Saudi Stock Market: Structural Issues, Recent Performance and Outlook, supra* n. 137, at 4.

In August 2008, the CMA Board made a resolution[142] that allowed nonresident foreign investors, whether individuals or institutions, to participate in share trading through swap agreements with local authorized intermediaries. The agreement is to transfer the economic benefits of the Saudi companies' shares listed on Tadawul while the authorized intermediaries retain the legal ownership of the share under certain conditions and requirements.[143]

More recently, in July 2014, the CMA announced that the Saudi Stock Exchange would be opened to qualified foreign financial institutions beginning in the first half of 2015. In August 2014, the CMA published draft rules for "Qualified Foreign Financial Institutions Investment in Listed Shares." These draft rules allow concerned and interested parties to provide their comments, reviews, observations, and other feedback, for a period of ninety days. Then, the CMA would review the comments and observations, ensure the readiness of the Saudi Stock Exchange, and publish the final regulations.[144] The final rules were published in May 2015,[145] and the Exchange was opened in June 2015 for qualified foreign financial institutions.[146]

---

142. Capital Market Authority, the Board of the Capital Market Authority Resolution Number 2-28-2008, dated 17/08/1429 H (Aug. 18, 2008).
143. Capital Market Authority, *CMA Announces Its Approval for Authorized Persons to Engage in Swap Agreements*, (Nov. 12, 2015), http://www.cma.org.sa/En/News/Pages/CMA_N434.aspx.
144. Capital Market Authority, *CMA Announcement in Regard to the Rules for Qualified Foreign Financial Institutions' Investment in Listed Shares*, (Jul. 22, 2014), http://www.cma.org.sa/En/News/Pages/CMA_N_1506.aspx .
145. Rules for Qualified Foreign Financial Institutions Investment in Listed Shares, the Board of the Capital Market Authority Resolution Number 1-42-2015, dated 15/7/1436 H (May 4, 2015).
146. Capital Market Authority, *CMA Announcement in Regard to the Rules for Qualified Foreign Financial Institutions' Investment in Listed Shares*, (Apr. 16, 2015), http://cma.org.sa/En/News/Pages/CMA_N_1742.aspx. A foreign financial institution may be registered with the CMA as a qualified foreign investor when it meets each of the following conditions: (1) the applicant must be a financial institution that has a legal personality which falls within one of the following types: (a) banks, (b) brokerage and securities firms, (c) fund managers, and (d) insurance companies; (2) the financial institutions must be licensed or otherwise subject to regulatory oversight by a regulatory authority and incorporated in a jurisdiction that applies regulatory and monitoring standards equivalent to those of the CMA or acceptable to it; (3) the applicant must have assets under management of SAR 18.75 billion (USD 5 billion) – or more – the CMA may reduce the minimum for these assets to SAR 11.25 billion (USD 3 billion); (4) and the applicant or any of its affiliates must have been engaged in securities activities and investment therein for a minimum of five years. Rules for Qualified Foreign Financial Institutions Investment in Listed Shares, Articles 4 & 5.

    The Capital Market Authority announced in May 3, 2016 that due to the gradual approach that the CMA has chosen to undertake in the liberalization of the capital market, the CMA board has approved amendments to the criteria and requirements, to register qualified foreign financial institutions, which would include the following:

    1- lowering the minimum value of the assets under management to be SAR 3,750,000,000 (US$1 billion), rather than SAR 18,750,000,000 (US$5 billion). Furthermore, the CMA Board has agreed the inclusion of new foreign financial institutions, including sovereign wealth funds, university endowments and others, as per CMA approval.
    2- The elimination of investment limits as per sub paragraph (A/1), (A/2), (A/4) and (A/5) of article 21 of the qualified foreign investor regulations: (these eliminated limitations in Article 21-A are as following: 1) each QFI, together with its affiliates, or each approved QFI client together with its affiliates may own a maximum of 5% of the shares of any issuer whose shares are listed; 2) where a QFI invests on behalf of an

§2.03 LOOKING OUTSIDE THE BORDERS: IOSCO MEMBERSHIP AND CHALLENGES

Since its founding in 1983, the "IOSCO" has been the international body/association that has brought together many of the world's security regulators into a common forum. Today, the group is recognized as a global standard setter for securities exchanges. The IOSCO has a broader economic role, in addition to its dealings with global stock markets. The group works with both the G20 and the "FSB" on issues of global regulatory and economic reform.[147]

Currently, over 95% of the world's securities markets are members of IOSCO. The membership includes over 200 securities regulators, stock exchanges, financial regions and other similar national and multinational organizations. In fact, IOSCO is the only group of its kind to include both developed and emerging economics in its membership.[148]

IOSCO's governing principles have been endorsed by the FSB and the G20: these principles are internationally recognized as the key standards in the area. The "Objectives and Principles of Securities Regulation" contain comprehensive standards for many phases of a stock market's operation, including regulation, oversight and enforcement. In addition to the agencies mentioned above, both the "IMF" and the

---

approved QFI client, it must not execute a transaction which would result in the relevant client, together with its affiliates, owning more than 5% of the shares of any issuer whose shares are listed; 4) the maximum proportion of the shares of any issuer whose shares are listed that may be owned by QFIs and approved QFI clients is 20%.; 5) and the maximum proportion of the shares of all issuers whose shares are listed that may be owned by QFIs and approved QFI clients in aggregate is 10% by market value, including any interests under swaps.

In addition, the CMA has lower investment limitations on foreign investors in order to allow for higher holding percentage in listed companies as follows:

1- allowing foreign investors to own larger stakes in listed companies not reaching 10% of the shares outstanding of a single issuer for each investor.
2- All foreign investors jointly (whether resident or non-resident) to own no more than 49% of the shares of any listed company on the market, unless company's bylaws or any other regulation provides for foreign ownership to be limited to a lower percentage.

The amended rules will be published and effective before the end of the first half of 2017. Capital Market Authority, *CMA Approves Amendments to the Registration Requirements for Qualified Foreign Financial Institutions, Change the Settlement Cycle for Securities Transactions and the introduction of Securities Lending and Covered Short-Selling*, (May 3, 2016), http://www.cma.org.sa/en/News/Pages/CMA_N_2036.aspx.

147. In 1983, IOSCO was created when eleven securities regulatory bodies from North and South America agreed to build their inter-American regional association into an international cooperative body. In 1984, securities regulators from France, Indonesia, Korea, and the United Kingdom become the first non-American agencies to join the new organization, IOSCO. The International Organization of Securities Commissions, *About IOSCO*, (Nov. 12, 2015), http://www.iosco.org/about/?subsection=about_iosco.
148. *Id.* There are 120 securities regulators and 80 other securities market participants.

World Bank have adopted these standards for use in evaluation of different stock markets.[149]

IOSCO supports its members with education and training programs, technical assistance, and research projects. This support helps the organization build a framework for better global regulation of the various capital markets. In turn, these regulations lead to better efficiency and increased security for all regulated stock transactions.[150]

Collectively, IOSCO members work to develop, to implement, and to promote clear and consistent standards that apply to all markets, regardless of size or location. IOSCO is particularly concerned with oversight and enforcement that exists to protect all investors and promote confidence in the system. These enforcement objectives also include measures to enhance information exchange at regional, national, and global levels. Only then can the market infrastructure be strong enough to support robust economic development for all members.[151]

Simply stated, IOSCO policy is devoted to three different objectives: market transparency and fairness, reduced market risk, and investor protection. These three objectives are grouped into thirty-eight Principles[152] and nine Categories.[153]

---

149. The International Organization of Securities Commissions, *Fact Sheet*, 2 (October 2015), http://www.iosco.org/about/pdf/IOSCO-Fact-Sheet.pdf.
150. *Id.*
151. The International Organization of Securities Commissions, *About IOSCO, supra* n. 147.
152. IOSCO 38 Principles are 1- the responsibilities of the Regulator should be clear and objectively stated; 2- the Regulator should be operationally independent and accountable in the exercise of its functions and powers; 3- the Regulator should have adequate powers, proper resources and the capacity to perform its functions and exercise its powers; 4- the Regulator should adopt clear and consistent regulatory processes; 5- the staff of the Regulator should observe the highest professional standards, including appropriate standards of confidentiality; 6- the Regulator should have or contribute to a process to monitor, mitigate and manage systemic risk, appropriate to its mandate; 7- the Regulator should have or contribute to a process to review the perimeter of regulation regularly; 8- the Regulator should seek to ensure that conflicts of interest and misalignment of incentives are avoided, eliminated, disclosed or otherwise managed; 9- Where the regulatory system makes use of Self-Regulatory Organizations (SROs) that exercise some direct oversight responsibility for their respective areas of competence, such SROs should be subject to the oversight of the Regulator and should observe standards of fairness and confidentiality when exercising powers and delegated responsibilities; 10- the Regulator should have comprehensive inspection, investigation and surveillance powers; 11- the Regulator should have comprehensive enforcement powers; 12- the regulatory system should ensure an effective and credible use of inspection, investigation, surveillance and enforcement powers and implementation of an effective compliance program; 13- the Regulator should have authority to share both public and non-public information with domestic and foreign counterparts; 14- Regulators should establish information sharing mechanisms that set out when and how they will share both public and non-public information with their domestic and foreign counterparts; 15- the regulatory system should allow for assistance to be provided to foreign Regulators who need to make inquiries in the discharge of their functions and exercise of their powers; 16- there should be full, accurate and timely disclosure of financial results, risk and other information which is material to investors' decisions; 17- holders of securities in a company should be treated in a fair and equitable manner; 18- accounting standards used by issuers to prepare financial statements should be of a high and internationally acceptable quality; 19- auditors should be subject to adequate levels of oversight; 20- auditors should be independent of the issuing entity that they audit; 21- audit standards should be of a high and internationally acceptable quality; 22- credit rating agencies should be subject to adequate levels of oversight; 23- other entities that offer

On June 9, 2010, the KSA joined IOSCO and has demonstrated its commitment to IOSCO's Objectives and Principles of Securities Regulation.[154] Additionally, the CMA is a signatory to IOSCO's Multilateral Memorandum of Understanding ("MMOU") Concerning Consultation and Cooperation and the Exchange of Information.[155] More specifically, to date, Saudi Arabia has taken action to incorporate all thirty-eight Principles into its capital market. Some areas have been fully implemented, while others remain a work in progress. In a recent survey,[156] based on the old thirty IOSCO Principles,[157] the IMF stated that the Kingdom had "fully implemented" the following

---

investors analytical or evaluative services should be subject to oversight and regulation appropriate to the impact their activities have on the market or the degree to which the regulatory system relies on them; 24- the regulatory system should set standards for the eligibility, governance, organization and operational conduct of those who wish to market or operate a collective investment scheme; 25- the regulatory system should provide for rules governing the legal form and structure of collective investment schemes and the segregation and protection of client assets; 26- Regulation should require disclosure, as set forth under the principles for issuers, which is necessary to evaluate the suitability of a collective investment scheme for a particular investor and the value of the investor's interest in the scheme; 27- Regulation should ensure that there is a proper and disclosed basis for asset valuation and the pricing and the redemption of units in a collective investment scheme; 28- Regulation should ensure that hedge funds and/or hedge funds managers/advisers are subject to appropriate oversight; 29- Regulation should provide for minimum entry standards for market intermediaries; 30- there should be initial and ongoing capital and other prudential requirements for market intermediaries that reflect the risks that the intermediaries undertake; 31- market intermediaries should be required to establish an internal function that delivers compliance with standards for internal organization and operational conduct, with the aim of protecting the interests of clients and their assets and ensuring proper management of risk; 32- there should be procedures for dealing with the failure of a market intermediary in order to minimize damage and loss to investors and to contain systemic risk; 33- the establishment of trading systems including securities exchanges should be subject to regulatory authorization and oversight; 34- there should be ongoing regulatory supervision of exchanges and trading systems which should aim to ensure that the integrity of trading is maintained through fair and equitable rules that strike an appropriate balance between the demands of different market participants; 35- Regulation should promote transparency of trading; 36- Regulation should be designed to detect and deter manipulation and other unfair trading practices; 37- Regulation should aim to ensure the proper management of large exposures, default risk and market disruption; and 38- Securities settlement systems and central counterparties should be subject to regulatory and supervisory requirements. The International Organization of Securities Commissions, *Objectives and Principles of Securities Regulation*, 3 (June 2010).

153. These nine categories include Principles Relating to the Regulator, Principles for Self-Regulation, Principles for the Enforcement of Securities Regulation, Principles for Cooperation in Regulation, Principles for Issuers, Principles for Auditors, Credit Rating Agencies, and other information providers, Principles for Collective Investment Schemes, Principles for Market Intermediaries, and Principles for Secondary Markets.

154. The International Organization of Securities Commissions, *IOSCO Expands Its Global Membership to Include Iceland, the Maldives, Saudi Arabia and Syria*, Media Release IOSCO/MR/09/2010, Montreal (Jun. 9, 2010).

155. The International Organization of Securities Commissions, *Current Signatories and Members Listed on Appendix B*, (Nov. 12, 2015), http://www.iosco.org/about/?subSection=mmou&subSection1=signatories.

156. International Monetary Fund, *Saudi Arabia: Financial Sector Assessment Program- Detailed Assessment of Observance of the IOSCO Objectives and Principles of Securities Regulation*, IMF Country Report No. 13/212 (July 2013).

157. The IOSCO 30 Principles of 1998 was revised in 2010 to become 38 Principles. The International Organization of Securities Commissions, *IOSCO Annual Report*, 7 (2010).

areas: Principle 3, 5, 8, 9, 11, 13, 14, 17, 19, 21, 22, 23, 26, 27, 28, and 29.[158] In other words, these Principles have been almost completely fulfilled.[159]

Saudi Arabia has created an independent body - the CMA - that meets ISOCO standards. The CMA has the authority to establish regulations and set procedures that are geared towards market improvement. Moreover, the CMA also has broad enforcement powers.[160] The CML addresses standards of conduct designed to insure the integrity and professionalism of the CMA core staff. Therefore, the CMA adopted a Code of Conduct that imposed a duty to take necessary precautions to prevent the disclosure of any confidential or inside information obtained while working for the CMA, and all CMA personnel are subject to this code.[161] Additionally, the CML gives the CMA the authority to investigate potential violations and to bring legal actions before the CRSD seeking civil[162] and criminal penalties.[163] There are also other powers. The CML[164] authorizes the CMA to share information with other domestic and foreign regulators, and to share information that it receives from issuers.[165]

In 2013, Tadawul signed a Memorandum of Understanding ("MOU") with Abu Dhabi Securities Exchange[166] pledging cooperation in strengthening the bilateral relations between the two markets. According to this MOU, the two markets agreed to exchange information and experiences in order to enhance communication and cooperation, explore opportunities to work together, exchange financial market information, and cooperate to develop the markets.[167] Similarly, Tadawul signed another MOU in 2013 with Bahrain Bourse[168] in order to enhance the bilateral relations and joint cooperation between those two markets. The memorandum also included a statement that the two markets can benefit from the capabilities, competences, and

---

158. These old principles are roughly equal to the new 38 principles and their new numbers are 3, 5, 10, 11, 13, 15, 16, 24, 26, 29, 30, 31, 34, 35, 36, and 37. *See supra* n. 152.
159. The results of the survey are as following: fully implemented (16 Principles); broadly implemented (5 Principles); partly implemented (6 Principles); not implemented (0 Principle); not applicable (2 Principles). *See* International Monetary Fund, *Saudi Arabia: Financial Sector Assessment Program- Detailed Assessment of Observance of the IOSCO Objectives and Principles of Securities Regulation, supra* n. 156, at 21.
160. International Monetary Fund, *Saudi Arabia: Financial Sector Assessment Program- Detailed Assessment of Observance of the IOSCO Objectives and Principles of Securities Regulation, supra* n. 156, at 13.
161. *Id.* at 14.
162. *Id.*
163. *See* Capital Market Law, Article 59 (2003).
164. *See Id.* Articles 17 & 46.
165. International Monetary Fund, *Saudi Arabia: Financial Sector Assessment Program- Detailed Assessment of Observance of the IOSCO Objectives and Principles of Securities Regulation, supra* n. 156, at 15.
166. Abu Dhabi Securities Exchange is in the United Arab Emirates, and it was established on Nov. 15, 2000. For further details, *see* https://www.adx.ae/English/Pages/default.aspx.
167. Saudi Stock Exchange "Tadawul", *2013 Annual Report* 25 (Dec. 31, 2013).
168. Bahrain Bourse was established as a shareholding company in 2010 and replaced the Bahrain Stock Exchange, which was established in 1987. For further details, *see* http://www.bahrainbourse.net/bhb/default.asp?language=en.

experiences of leadership in the two markets. Moreover, the memorandum emphasized that the two markets will work together to develop administrative abilities in both markets and to develop the capital markets.[169]

Because of Tadawul's achievements, Capital Finance International ("CFI") recognized Tadawul as the best stock exchange in Middle East and North Africa region ("MENA") for 2013. The CFI praised Tadawul for its "exemplary" work in "executing a well-prepared and skillfully thought out plan that will increase market ability" in both Saudi Arabia and the entire MENA region. The judges specifically noted the "solid foundations and outstanding expertise of the Exchange."[170]

Some work does remain, such as providing immunity from lawsuits to help ensure independence, formalizing an individual's right to a hearing before any adverse action is taken, augmenting the information available in published reports, and improving professional conduct and anti-conflict of interest statutes.[171] The CMA might also consider increasing the maximum fines, better controlling the flow of international information, adding additional auditing requirements, and producing a contingency plan for insolvency of a market intermediary.[172] The CMA should also consider being more transparent when exercising its enforcement powers in all cases by publishing all outcomes to demonstrate regulatory action and to obtain the maximum deterrent effect.[173]

One of the more significant challenges that the Saudi capital market faces is enhancing transparency and disclosure. Even though the CML addresses transparency and disclosure in considerable detail in Chapter 7,[174] the law is useless if there is no implementation. To promote transparency and disclosure, the CMA should consider publishing daily, weekly, and monthly reports that contain information about the market, decisions of boards of directors, trading volume, and price indices. The CMA should consider also contracting with a reputable company to publish all trading

---

169. Saudi Stock Exchange "Tadawul", *2013 Annual Report, supra* n. 167, at 25.
170. CFI.co, *the Saudi Stock Exchange Wins the CFI.co MENA Award for 2013,* (Oct. 29, 2014), http://cfi.co/awards/africa/2013/the-saudi-stock-exchange-wins-the-cfi-co-mena-award-for-2013/. More recently, the Saudi Stock Exchange was voted the best Exchange for the 2015 year in Middle East and North Africa at the Global Investor/ISF MENA Awards 2015. During the 2014 year, the Exchange had developed including the transition of operations to the world-leading Nasdaq X-Stream INET trading platform and a number of significant reforms most notably the successful launch of the Qualified Foreign Investors framework that allowed direct foreign investment in the Saudi stock market for the first time. The Global Investor/ISF, *Middle East Awards 2015: Winners announced,* (Nov. 2, 2015), http://www.globalinvestormagazine.com/Article/3502629/Middle-East-Awards-2015-Winners-announced.html; The Saudi Stock Exchange "Tadawul", *The Saudi Stock Exchange Voted MENA Exchange of the Year at Global Investor/ISF MENA Awards 2015,* (Oct. 31, 2015), http://www.tadawul.com.sa/wps/portal/!ut/p/c1/04_SB8K8xLLM9MSSzPy8xBz9CP0os3g_A-ewIE8TIwN_D38LA09vV7NQP8cQQ3dnA6B8JJK8e0CYqYGniU-wUXCAl7GBpxEB3X4e-bmp-sGJRfoFuRHlAP-C3us!/dl2/d1/L0lHSkovd0RNQUZrQUVnQSEhL1lCWncvZW4!/?PRESS_REL_NO=4472.
171. International Monetary Fund, *Saudi Arabia: Financial Sector Assessment Program- Detailed Assessment of Observance of the IOSCO Objectives and Principles of Securities Regulation, supra* n. 156, at 22.
172. *Id.* at 23-24.
173. *Id.* at 23.
174. Capital Market Law, Articles 40-48 (2003).

information in one place.[175] Increasing the availability of information is generally one of the best ways to improve transparency, and this situation is no exception.[176]

The CMA might provide more intensive investment and legal education to all investors, especially small investors. The CMA also might raise the level of awareness among investors and encourage them to make long-term investments. These efforts would require investment in a media campaign inside Saudi Arabia.[177] The CMA has already commenced many educational programs since 2006.[178] One of these programs established a website in Arabic specifically for investor awareness.[179] However, these programs are not known to many investors, with the exception of those investors who have visited the CMA's website. The CMA should consider publishing these investor awareness reports in many newspapers and magazines in Arabic and English in order to spread the awareness programs nationwide and promote investor awareness. Furthermore, representatives from the CMA might hold television programs monthly to talk about the development of the capital market, legal and investment information, and any strategies for the future.

§2.04 WHAT DOES THE CAPITAL MARKET MEAN TO THE SAUDI ECONOMY?

Capital markets have fundamental roles in supporting economic growth by encouraging additional investment.[180] Interest in the connection between financial development and economic growth has increased globally in the past few decades.[181] Through various "channels," including a securities market, financial development can contribute to and therefore foster economic growth. The fundamental role of capital markets is seen as distributing capital efficiently by allocating funds to investment projects with the highest marginal product of capital.[182] Moreover, recent studies attempt to show

175. Moftah Saleh & Maarfi Fareedah, *Motatalabat Kafaat Soug Alaorag Almalieh: Derasah Leoaka Asoag Alaorag Almalieh Alarabiah Oa Sobal Rafa Kafataha [the Requirements for the Securities Market Efficiency: A Study of the Reality of Arabian Capital Markets and How to Promote Their Efficiency]*, 7 El-Bahith Review 192 (2010).
176. The disclosure regime in the Saudi Arabia's capital market will be examined, analyzed, and evaluated in terms of its compliance with international standards in Chapter 4, *infra*.
177. *Id.* at 193.
178. In the CMA website, the CMA has published many reports for investor awareness in both English and Arabic, including Investor Awareness Guidebooks, Investor Awareness Brochures, Reports, Smart Investor Project, and Smart Investor Magazine. The Capital Market Authority, *Investor Awareness Center*, (Nov. 12, 2015) http://www.cma.org.sa/en/IA/Pages/default.aspx .
179. Capital Market Authority, *Maoga Taoeat Almostathmar, [Investor Awareness Website]*, (Oct. 10, 2014) http://www.cma.org.sa/IA/index.html.
180. Mostafa Yousef Kafi, *Borsat Alaorag Almalih 25, [Securities Exchange]*, (Dar Moasasat Raslan for Printing, Publishing, and Distributing 2009).
181. Geert Bekaert & Campbell R. Harvey, *Capital Markets: An Engine for Economic Growth*, 5 Brown J. World Aff. 33, 34 (1998).
182. *Id.*

that economic growth and stock market growth are intertwined on a long-term basis. These studies point out that a future economy can be improved through securities market liquidity.[183] Moreover, a related study postulates that stock market liquidity[184] is positively and significantly correlated with current and future rates of economic growth, capital accumulation, and productivity growth.[185] As such, developing the Saudi capital market should benefit Saudi Arabia's economic growth in several specific ways.

Capital markets can provide an alternative funding or capital flow sources for emerging economies. In effect, capital markets can provide a "funding bridge" that connects economic needs with foreign and domestic capital resources. In this respect, a capital market may offer a funding alternative that is as good as, or maybe even better than, private loans.[186] There are a variety of funding mechanisms, such as bonds, sukuk, and securities.[187] Moreover, capital markets offer a broad range of funding short, medium, and long term, for investors and companies.[188] Thus, capital markets are intended to support the delivery of funds to the right place at the right time,[189] and that dynamic should potentially lead to economic growth.

The financial impact of capital market development is not limited to full-time investors. The Saudi capital market produces investment opportunities to the general public to invest their savings, regardless of the amount, in the market within the borders of Saudi Arabia. The investment of the general public inside the Kingdom can benefit the Saudi economy in general.[190] Capital markets provide "alternative vehicles" for national savings through several means, such as collective investment schemes, mutual funds, and pension funds.[191] Additionally, these investments provide funds for establishing new companies in different businesses.[192] These new corporations probably will lead to the growth of the Saudi economy in the long term.

Establishing new corporations and increasing the number of listed companies in the Saudi capital market in different sectors[193] leads to the development of the private

183. Ake Boubakari & Dehuan Jin, *the Role of Stock Market Development in Economic Growth: Evidence From Some Euronext Countries*, 1 Int'l J. Fin. Res. 14, 17 (2010).
184. Stock market liquidity was measured in this study by both the value of stock trading relative to the size of the market and by the value of trading relative to the size of the economy.
185. Ross Levine & Sara Zervos, *Stock Markets, Banks, and Economic Growth*, 88 Am. Econ. Rev. 537, 538 (1998).
186. Joseph Jude Norton, *Financial Sector Law Reform in Emerging Economies* 126 (The British Institute of International and Comparative Law and the London Institute of International Banking, Finance and Development Law 2000).
187. Mohammed Alsirefi, *Alborasat 84 (Exchanges*] (Dar Alfakar Aljamae 2007).
188. *Id.* at 63.
189. Mohammed Tanweer Alrafii, *Segar Almostathmareen Oa Daor Haiat Soag Almal Fi Hemaitahm* 354-55, *[The Small Investors and the Role of the Capital Market Authority to Protect Them]*, (Dar Alnahathah Alarabia 2007).
190. Falmban, *supra* n. 24, at 119.
191. Norton, *Financial Sector Law Reform in Emerging Economies*, *supra* n. 186, at 127.
192. Falmban, *supra* n. 24, at 119.
193. As of Jun. 30, 2016, the number of listed companies in the Saudi Stock Exchange is 175 companies in 15 sectors, compared to 68 listed companies in 2002. These sectors with the

sector in the Kingdom. The expanded number of new and better-funded business enterprises has the potential of increasing the growth rate in the private sector and the GDP of Saudi Arabia respecting critical nonpetroleum sectors.[194] Through the promotion of nonpetroleum sectors, investment diversifies the economy. Furthermore, increasing the number of corporations in the Kingdom should promote production efficiency in the private sector, decrease production prices as a result of economic competition, and generate new jobs.[195] These results will have a significant, and positive, impact on both the Saudi people and on the Saudi economy as a whole.

Currently, the Saudi capital market is large and active. The number of shares traded in the Saudi market during 2013 was 52,502 million, and the total value of shares traded was SAR 1,369,665.79 million (USD 365,244.211 million). Moreover, the number of transactions in the market was 28,967,694 million during 2013. The market value of shares was SAR 1752.86 billion (USD 467.43 billion) at the end of 2013.[196] These figures show substantial growth since 2002, when the number of shares traded was 1736.0 million and the total value of shares traded was SAR 133.8 billion (USD 35.68 billion). The number of transactions executed in the market during 2002 was 1033.7 thousand transactions. The market capitalization of issued shares was SAR 280.7 billion (USD 74.9 billion) at the end of 2002.[197] These numbers reflect the developments in the Saudi capital market and how the market can have positive impacts in the economic growth and development of the country.

Traded securities prices in capital markets are thought to be a mirror for future national economies. Securities prices can be an early warning to those who are in charge of economic affairs in a country to take corrective actions when necessary. When securities prices decrease – which is often an indicator of potential economic downturn in a nation – economic officials can then take necessary measures to prevent the depression in the country. Likewise, economic analysts provide their views about the status of the economy and propose necessary measures to confront the possible downturn.[198]

Capital markets place an unofficial and external oversight on certain economic policies, especially regarding efficiency of investment, financing, and operation for listed companies. Capital markets also reveal the true financial positions of listed

number of companies in 2016 are as following: Banks & Financial Services 12; Petrochemical Industries 14; Cement 14; Retail 17; Energy & Utilities 2; Agriculture & Food Industries 16; Telecommunication & Information Technology 4; Insurance 35; Multi-Investment 7; Industrial Investment 15; Building & Construction 18; Real Estate Development 9; Transport 5; Media and Publishing 3; Hotel & Tourism 4. Saudi Stock Exchange "Tadawul", *Market Watch Today*, (Jun. 30, 2016), https://www.tadawul.com.sa/wps/portal/tadawul/markets/equities/market-watch/market-watch-today; Saudi Arabian Monetary Agency, *39th Annual Report* 155 (2003).

194. Falmban, *supra* n. 24, at 119.
195. *Id.*
196. Saudi Stock Exchange "Tadawul", *Annual Report*, (Oct. 30, 2014), http://www.tadawul.com.sa/Resources/Reports/Yearly_en.html.
197. Saudi Arabian Monetary Agency, *39th Annual Report, supra* n. 193, at 146.
198. Munir Ibrahim Hindi, *Alaorag Almaleih Oa Asoag Almal* 670, *[Securities and Capital Markets]*, (Monshat Almaraf Press 2007).

companies and provide an evaluation of listed companies' projects and investments.[199] Markets can contribute to increase investors' awareness about companies' positions and whether listed companies have successful projects, investments, and managements.[200] A decreasing value of shares of a listed company often leads the affected company to change some of its policies and its management in order to improve its position.[201] As such, Saudi stock market evaluations of listed companies should improve companies' performances, investments, managements, and productions to positively impact the growth of Saudi economy.

A modern capital market can attract a steady flow of foreign capital to finance important domestic projects.[202] A related study proved that there is a causal link between "FDI" and economic growth. The study indicates that FDI promotes economic growth in a nation through a financial market.[203] Having a suitable securities and stock exchange regulation structure would provide a highly desirable opportunity to attract even more FDI.[204] From one perspective, the CMA has made progress by gradually opening up the Saudi capital market since 1997. However, at a practical level, the progress has been slow.[205]

The Saudi Chamber of Commerce in Riyadh gave five motivated causes for creation of the Saudi stock market. All of them are directly related to the growth of the Saudi economy.[206] First, the Saudi stock market should increase the rate of economic growth. The Saudi stock market aims to mobilize financial resources, to develop savings, and then to direct these funds to finance investment projects. These efforts will improve income levels, will decrease unemployment rates, and will raise the level of Saudi economic growth.[207]

Second, the market should increase the role of the private sector in the economic growth of the Kingdom to crease new investment opportunities and new jobs. The private sector is seen as having a fundamental role in supporting the economic growth.[208]

Third, the stock market should support the privatization project, which has been in place since 1997.[209] This process should expand stock markets. Mobilizing savings

199. Zakaria Salamah Shatnawi, *Alathar Alagtsadih Lasoag Alaorag Almalih Men Manthor Alagtsad Alaslami* 63 *[the Economic Effects of the Securities Markets From the Perspective of Islamic Economy]*, (Dar Alnafaes for Publishing and Distributing 2009).
200. Alsirefi, *Exchanges, supra* n. 187, at 85.
201. *Id.*
202. Shatnawi, *supra* n. 199, at 67.
203. Laura Alfaro, et al, *FDI and Economic Growth: the Role of Local Financial Markets*, 64 J. Int'l Econ. 89, 108 (2004).
204. Norton, *Financial Sector Law Reform in Emerging Economies, supra* n. 186, at 127-28.
205. *See supra* nn. 137-146, and accompanying text.
206. Saudi Chamber of Commerce in Riyadh, *Istakshaf Mada Kafat Soag Alasahom Almahalih Oa Dorah Fi Daam Alagtsad Aloatani* 5-6 [*Explore to What Extend the Efficiency of the Local Stock Market and Its Role in Supporting the National Economy*], the 15th Annual Meeting of Saudi Economic Association (Riyadh, Nov. 13-15, 2005).
207. *Id.* at 5.
208. *Id.*
209. The Council of Ministers, *Privatization Objectives*, Resolution No. 60, dated 1/4/1418 H (1997). This Resolution defends the objectives of the strategy and policy of privatization in Saudi Arabia.

and operating them in investment projects can only exist in the presence of an organized and regulated capital market.[210]

Fourth, the banking sector in Saudi Arabia has a low capability to attract domestic savings. Despite the importance of Saudi banks in attracting and mobilizing domestic savings, there are many restrictions and constraints that inhibit the ability of banks to attract a significant proportion of these savings. These restrictions are associated with Shari'ah law or with financial returns. As a result of these constraints, the Kingdom was losing a significant proportion of these funds because these funds had outflow outside Saudi Arabia, or the funds were directed to other investment channels that might not benefit the national economy. Thus, Saudi Arabia was in urgent need of finding a new channel that is able to attract savings and funds and to be free from concerns among investors.[211]

Fifth, the Saudi stock market should attract foreign investments and return outflow capital to the Kingdom. An organized and regulated market is considered one of the most important factors that attract foreign capital. Moreover, in order to draw outflow capital back into the Kingdom, a stock market is needed to attract domestic investors and to direct them to good investment opportunities in the Kingdom.[212]

A most recent study conducted by Alshammary further defined the relationship between the Saudi capital market development and Saudi economic growth.[213] The results of the study proved a long-run relationship between the capital market development and economic growth in Saudi Arabia.[214]

Part of the reason for the slow progress in this area, and the dire need for additional action, may be because one of the most traumatic events in the Kingdom's economic history occurred just a few short years ago.

§2.05 THE CRASH OF 2006

The Saudi capital market had not experienced a major crash until 2006. Beginning in 2003, the capital market expanded significantly, and the Tadawul All Share Index ("TASI") closed at 4437.6 points at the end of the year, compared with a 2518.1 close at the end of 2002. As a SAMA annual report indicated, the growth and expansion in the capital market was caused by the growth of the domestic economy, enhanced confidence in the market, high earnings of many companies, the declining rate of return on deposits, and a large number of new market investors.[215] At the end of 2004,

210. Saudi Chamber of Commerce in Riyadh, *Explore to What Extend the Efficiency of the Local Stock Market and Its Role in Supporting the National Economy*, *supra* n. 206, at 6.
211. *Id.*
212. *Id.*
213. "This study investigated the relationship between stock market development and the real GDP growth rate per capita of the Saudi economy from January 1993 to December 2009. The secondary data was collected from the IMF, SAMA and TadawuL. The VAR model was used to estimate the effects of stock market development on economic growth." Meshaal J. Alshammary, *Stock Market Development and Economic Growth in Developing Countries: Evidence from Saudi Arabia*, 11 Corp. Ownership & Control 193, 208 (2014).
214. *Id.*
215. Saudi Arabian Monetary Agency, *40th Annual Report* 140, 141(2004).

the TASI increased 84% to 8,206.23 points.[216] At the end of 2005, the TASI closed at 16,712.64 points, rising by 103.7%.[217]

Behind the numbers, the market capitalization of issued shares increased rapidly from USD 75 billion in 2002[218] to USD 157 billion in 2003,[219] and again from USD 306 billion in 2004[220] to USD 650 billion by the end of 2005.[221] Eventually, the TASI registered the highest point in its history, 20,634.86, on February 25, 2006.[222]

The main reason for the dramatic and sustained rise was the large increase in demand due to a large number of additional investors in the stock market, either directly or through banks with various types of portfolios.[223] At one point, more than half of Saudi adults had invested money in the capital market. Unfortunately, many of these people borrowed money or liquidated their assets to finance stock purchases.[224]

According to SAMA annual reports, the gross loan balance among individuals in 2002 was SAR 50.5 billion (USD 13.4 billion);[225] and, only three years later, the outstanding balance increased sharply to over SAR 180 billion (USD 48 billion).[226] Consumer lending patterns changed dramatically as well. In 2002, most of these loans were granted for real estate, durable goods and equipment, and lines of credit. Also, there is a classification for "Other Purposes," which amounted to a mere SAR 29.5 billion (USD 7.8 billion) in 2002.[227] However, in 2005, "Other Purposes" loans exceeded SAR 137 billion (USD 36 billion out of a total USD 180 billion). In other words, more than three-quarters of consumer loans in 2005 were for something other than real estate, durable goods or lines of credit.[228] It seems apparent that many people saw an opportunity to invest in the capital market at a time when the market showed evidence of high growth. To many, it apparently was worth the additional risk of investing money that they did not have.

According to a Saudi expert, other factors were at work as well. After "9/11," a large amount of capital returned to the Kingdom from abroad, due to investor fears of overseas instability. Since there were no effective investment alternatives at the time, much of that money went directly into the stock market. Trading shares was largely unsupervised, banks provided both easy credit and physical facilities for investors, and there was a considerable amount of legal and illegal speculation in the shares of some companies. Ultimately, after a series of decisions by the CMA, most notably one that

216. Saudi Arabian Monetary Agency, *41st Annual Report* 137 (2005).
217. Saudi Arabian Monetary Agency, *42nd Annual Report* 105 (2006).
218. Saudi Arabian Monetary Agency, *39th Annual Report, supra* n. 193, at 146.
219. Saudi Arabian Monetary Agency, *40th Annual Report, supra* n. 215, at 141.
220. Saudi Arabian Monetary Agency, *41st Annual Report, supra* n. 216, at 138.
221. Saudi Arabian Monetary Agency, *42nd Annual Report, supra* n. 217, at 106.
222. Saudi Stock Exchange "Tadawul", *2006 Annual Report* 3 (Dec. 31, 2006).
223. Abdulrahman A. Al-Twaijry, *Saudi Stock Market Historical View and Crisis Effect: Graphical and Statistical Analysis*, 34 J. Human Sciences 1, 8 (2007).
224. Tim Niblock & Monica Malik, *the Political Economy of Saudi Arabia* 218 (Routledge 2007).
225. Saudi Arabian Monetary Agency, *39th Annual Report, supra* n. 193, at 108.
226. Saudi Arabian Monetary Agency, *42nd Annual Report, supra* n. 217, at 69.
227. Saudi Arabian Monetary Agency, *39th Annual Report, supra* n. 193, at 111.
228. Saudi Arabian Monetary Agency, *42nd Annual Report, supra* n. 217, at 69.

the daily stock price fluctuation limit of listed companies decreased to 5%,[229] the bubble burst in February 2006.[230]

The TASI started to fall dramatically at the end of February 2006 and quickly lost about 13,000 points. Within the first three weeks after November 25, 2006, TASI fell from 20,634.86 to 15,000 points, decreasing 25%. The TASI then appeared to stabilize, hovering above 15,000 for several weeks. But the TASI then fell for the second time to reach almost 10,000 points within less than a month. The total loss of the TASI during these two and a half months was 50%.[231] By the end of 2006, TASI had bottomed out at 7,933.29 points, decreasing 52.53% from the previous year.[232] Ultimately, TASI lost about 65% of its value during 2006 from its highest level, 20,634.86 points.[233] Moreover, the market capitalization dropped to USD 326.9 billion by the end of 2006, falling 49.72% from 2005.[234]

During this period, over 4 million Saudis had invested money in the stock market.[235] Many of these investors were rather unsophisticated and inexperienced. Moreover, a number were widows, retired persons and other lower-income people who liquidated their savings and other assets, unrealistically expecting big returns. These persons could ill afford to lose significant sums of money in the stock market, and their losses had repercussions throughout the economy.[236] To make matters worse, instead of making investment decisions based on a company's performance, the overall economic outlook, and other related factors, these people based decisions on advice from family and friends, public announcements, and prior pricing patterns.[237]

The crash hit working families the hardest. Many people lost their jobs and/or sought psychiatric help, while others resorted to begging or were incarcerated because of a failure to pay debts, largely because they had essentially lost their entire life savings.[238] Since the crash was unprecedented, many investors had a difficult time coping with this new economic reality. Many became physically ill, even to the point of death in some cases.[239] All told, the country lost a significant portion - SAR 2 trillion (USD 533 billion) - of its overall wealth.[240]

229. Capital Market Authority, the Board of the Capital Market Authority Resolution Number 1-141-2006, dated 24/01/1427 H (Feb. 23, 2006). On Mar. 37, 2006, the Capital Market Authority issued a decision to return the daily stock price fluctuation limit of listed companies back to 10% starting Apr. 1, 2006, because the risks associated with market prices correction have decreased. Capital Market Authority, the Board of the Capital Market Authority Resolution Number 3-154-2006, dated 27/02/1427 H (Mar. 27, 2006).
230. Abdulsalam S. Al-Ghamidi, *Thababiat Enhiar Soag Almal Alsaodiah Aam 2006 Oathar Alada Almali Llsharikah Almosahemah [the Fogginess of Saudi Stock Market Crash 2006 and the Effect of Firm's Financial Performance]*, 13 the Arab J. Acct. 86, 89 (2010).
231. Al-Twaijry, *supra* n. 223, at 9.
232. Saudi Stock Exchange "Tadawul", *2006 Annual Report, supra* n. 222, at 15.
233. Al-Twaijry, *supra* n. 223, at 26.
234. Saudi Stock Exchange "Tadawul", *2006 Annual Report, supra* n. 222, at 3.
235. Sami Al-Nwaisir, *Saudi Stock Market Needs to Be Reformed*, Arab News, Jan. 11, 2012, http://www.eurasiareview.com/11012012-saudi-stock-market-needs-to-be-reformed-oped/.
236. *Id.*
237. Al-Twaijry, *supra* n. 223, at 18.
238. *Id.*
239. *Id.* at 2.
240. Al-Nwaisir, *supra* n. 235.

Unrealistic expectations may have fueled investment, but certain aspects of the market itself also contributed to the stock market bubble of 2004 and 2005. Prices rose artificially, because certain wealthy investors essentially bought and sold stock among themselves, thus creating the illusion of high margins and fervent trading activity. There were noneconomic factors as well which contributed to spiraling prices. Inside information was certainly an issue in some cases, and in other cases, the rumored profits simply did not exist. Smaller investors took note of these trends and, after assuming that the spiral would continue, purchased shares at already inflated prices. Too many times, instead of providing sound financial advice, banks acted as enablers by granting credit to overextended borrowers.[241]

The crash was not bad news for everyone. The economic elite took full advantage of the artificially high prices by selling their shares just before the fall. Most of these people were from very wealthy Saudi families.[242] There were also a significant number of speculators in the market as the bubble grew. Since these investors cared little about the market's long-run share performance, they helped prop up prices and reaped high profits when they suddenly withdrew their money.[243]

The Saudi stock market might be seen differently from most other markets in the world during and after the 2006 crash. Because of the speculation and artificial spiral, a company's performance had little, if anything, to do with share prices. In fact, some of the worst performing companies in 2005 and 2006 had some of the highest values on the capital market.[244] At the same time, many large speculators bought and sold these shares as both individuals and groups, so the price went up even further based on trading volume. Because of the lack of oversight and penalties, some of these acts continued even after the 2006 crash.[245] The CMA finally intervened in 2007, by suspending trading in companies whose losses exceeded 75% of their capital.[246]

There were other factors at work that artificially increased prices. First, domestic liquidity was still growing, so prices increased to an unreasonable level regardless of the listed companies' financial statements. In effect, some companies were able to use their capital reserve to disguise their operating losses. Second, abusive practices occurred continually because the CMA feared possible negative consequences from any tough action that might be taken against manipulators in the market. The CMA's hesitation encouraged violators to persist in their untoward behavior and their illegal acts.[247] Many of these behaviors were evident as far back as 2000, but the speculation and counter-speculation continued almost unabated. At the same time, these speculators purchased as many inflated shares as possible, to maximize their financial return.

241. Niblock, *supra* n. 224, at 218.
242. *Id.* at 219.
243. Al-Twaijry, *supra* n. 223, at 21.
244. Abdulrahman Mohammed Alsultan, *Fogah Jadidah Tatakon Fi Soag Alashom Alsaodiah [New Bubble is Forming in the Saudi Stock Market]*, Al Eqtisadiah Newspaper, Jul. 3, 2006, http://www.aleqt.com/2006/07/03/article_5702.html.
245. *Id.*
246. Masari, *The Legal Regulation of the Corporate Governance, supra* n. 16, at 150.
247. *Id.*

Along with inexperienced investors who may have made questionable decisions, for whatever reason, the speculators essentially created the bubble.[248]

Some other factors also contributed in the 2006 crash. One of them was the lack of transparency and disclosure by listed companies, banks, and some governmental agencies that are related to the stock market. Many listed companies failed to disclose their financial statements. These, and other, violations occurred continually with little, or no, response from the government. These violations included insider trading, price manipulation, and false statements. Rumors steadily increased during 2005 and 2006, and there was no effective method to detect and to punish violators, partially because some investors had power and relationships that allowed them access to material inside information. These investors used the inside information as individuals or groups to speculate in the market illegally. Furthermore, the large size of liquidity in the Saudi economy with few listed companies led to inflation in the market. Also, the selfishness, greed and the lack of accountability in some Saudi banks led these banks to expand their lending policy, instead of restricting it, which flooded the capital market with liquidity.

The CMA's lack of experience in dealing with the emerging market led the CMA to issue decisions, procedures, and statements without fully examining them. These actions by the CMA made the capital market unstable, and many investors lost confidence in the market. The CMA could not identify the real issue at the time of the crash so that the CMA followed unsound procedures that worsened an already deteriorating situation. Finally, some government officials and analysts continued to issue statements until the end of 2005 encouraging citizens to invest in the market. These statements brought new investors to a market that was on the verge of collapse.[249]

The unprecedented nature of the crash may have caught some officials off-guard. The Kingdom had never experienced an economic crisis of this magnitude. But, crashes are not unknown in the capital markets. So, the real question is not so much what happened, but rather what should the government do to prevent, or at least contain, the next economic catastrophe?

[A] The Government's Response

Based on Article IV of the IMF's Articles of Agreement,[250] the Fund concluded at the end of 2005 that "IMF observed that the authorities needed to be cautious in light of the

248. Mohammad Al-Aqeel & Nasser Spear, *Private Information Trading in Emerging Markets: Evidence from GCC Security Markets*, p. 3, paper presented at Nadoat Sobal Tatuair Almohasab [Ways to Develop Accounting Conference], 11th Meeting, Riyadh (Dec. 5-6, 2006).
249. Hamdi Hamzah Aljuhani, *Azamat Soag Alasahom 2006 Enthar Fiah Daoah Llaslah 178-181[The Stock Market Crisis in 2006 Is a Warning and a Call for Reforming]* (Obekan Printing and Packaging 2006).
250. Under Article IV of the IMF's Articles of Agreement, the IMF holds bilateral discussions with members. A staff team visits the country, collects economic and financial information, and discusses the country's economic developments and policies with the proper officials. On return to headquarters, the staff prepares a report, which forms the basis for discussion by the Executive Board.

continuing strong increase in stock prices. IMF commended the authorities for the steps already implemented, and encouraged them to further strengthen prudential oversight on stock market-related lending and on consumer lending."[251] Based on the IMF's conclusions, SAMA, Ministry of Commerce, CMA, and CRSD were encouraged to take some measures to prevent the stock market crash.

Official action began almost immediately. On January 1, 2006, SAMA started to enforce the Regulation for Consumer Finance, which is applicable to financing contracts and all related guarantee agreements executed by banks and authorized institutions by SAMA.[252] The next day, the CMA published a CRSD decision regarding three defendants who violated Article 49 of the CMA and Article 3 of the Market Conduct Regulations. The three defendants conducted manipulative and deceptive acts in eight listed companies in the Saudi stock market. CRSD-imposed penalties on these three defendants totaling SAR 169 million (USD 45 million). This money went directly to the CMA. Additionally, CRSD barred these three defendants from working in the listed companies in the stock market or membership in a Board of Directors for three years.[253]

Next, on January 22, 2006, the CMA changed Articles 25 and 30 of the LR.[254] These changes aimed to impose greater transparency and disclosure about transactions made by big investors, members of boards of directors, and senior executives. The new Articles also monitored any changes in their investments.[255]

On January 23, 2006, the CMA Board issued a resolution[256] that prohibited listed companies from buying or selling shares of other joint-stock companies, unless their articles of incorporation allow them to do so and the transaction was not inconsistent with relevant regulations. Also, the resolution required joint-stock companies whose investment did not comply with the resolution to correct their statuses within a period of three months from the date of the resolution and to provide the CMA with their plans to correct their conditions within one month from the resolution.[257]

251. International Monetary Fund, *IMF Executive Board Concludes 2005 Article IV Consultation with Saudi Arabia*, Public Information Notice No. 05/161 (Dec. 5, 2005).
252. Saudi Arabian Monetary Agency, *Thaoabd Altamoial Alastahlaqi [the Regulation for Consumer Finance]*, (Nov. 25, 2014), http://www.sama.gov.sa/News/Pages/News14270214.aspx.
253. Capital Market Authority, *Elan Beshan Tagraeem Thlathah Mokalefeen Lentam Alsoag Almaleih Bemablag Maah Oa Tesah Oa Setoon Malion Riyal Oa Manahom Men Alamal Fi Alsharikat Almosahemah [Announcement Regarding Imposing Penalties on Three Violators Who Violated the Capital Market Law Amount of Hundred and Sixty Nine Million Riyals and Ban Them from Working in Joint Stock Companies]*, (Nov. 12, 2015), http://www.cma.org.sa/Ar/News/Pages/CMA_N151.aspx.
254. The Board of the Capital Market Authority Resolution Number 2-128-2006, dated 22/12/1426 H (Jan. 22, 2006).
255. Capital Market Authority, *Garar Majals Haiat Alsoag Almaleih Ragom 2-128-2006 Oa Taraik 22/12/1426 H Almoafag 22/1/2006 [The Decision of the Capital Market Authority Board No. 2-128-2006, Dated 12/22/1426 H Corresponding to 01/22/2006 AD]*, (Nov. 12, 2015), http://www.cma.org.sa/Ar/News/Pages/CMA_N156.aspx.
256. The Board of the Capital Market Authority Resolution Number 5-126-2006, dated 23/12/1426 H (Jan. 23, 2006).
257. Capital Market Authority, *Garar Men Majals Haiat Alsoag Almaleih Beshan Istathmar Alsharikat Almosahimah Fi Asahom SHarikat Okrah [A Decision from the Capital Market Authority Board Regarding the Investment of Joint Stock Companies In the Share of Other Joint Stock Companies]*, (Nov. 12, 2015), http://www.cma.org.sa/Ar/News/Pages/CMA_N157.

Many Saudi experts welcomed the CMA's decision, even though it was late. The CMA found that many listed companies invested primarily in the stock market when their business types were in something else, which caused them to neglect their main course of investments. But, while it was intended to refocus investors, this decision would cause many of these listed companies to liquidate their stock portfolios, thereby decreasing the market prices. Moreover, the CMA failed to coordinate with the Minister of Commerce, which is responsible for business registrations and licensing, among other things. Some experts criticized the CMA's decision because it did not contain any sanctions for any companies that violated the decision.[258]

Tadawul announced on January 29, 2006 that after the CMA approval, the "tick size"[259] would be changed from SAR 0.25 to SAR 1.00 starting in February 4, 2006. As Tadawul mentioned, this change was due to the huge increase in many stock prices in the market.[260]

On February 14, 2006, the CMA Board requested a department in the CMA to accelerate the investigative procedures in the activities of a number of traders in the capital market. This request came when the trading data showed abnormal increase in the speculations by a number of traders over a period of a few weeks. As the CMA's Board stated, these activities improperly influenced the prices of some listed companies because these companies did not disclose any information to justify these high price levels. These activities would threaten the integrity of the capital market and harm investors, especially small investors. Thus, the Board ordered the specialized department to speed up the inquiry and investigation procedures to detect any manipulation or misleading transactions, and then take the necessary actions in accordance with the CML.[261]

On the same day it requested an accelerated investigation, the CMA's Board ordered Tadawul to immediately stop executing any buying orders in the Saudi capital market for a certain trader who engaged in abusive practices. The CMA had evidence that this trader intentionally sold and bought stocks with huge amounts of money to create a false impression of the prices of some companies stocks. The decision also

aspx. On Jun. 24, 2006, the CMA Board extended the correction period for joint-stock companies for three more months, until Oct. 23, 2006. Capital Market Authority, *Garar Majalos Alhaiah Betamadid Almohalh Almamnoha Llsharikat Letasahih Aotaoa Estathmaratah [CMA Board's Decision to Extend the Period of Correction for Joint Stock Companies to Correct Its Investments]* (Nov. 12, 2015), http://www.cma.org.sa/Ar/News/Pages/CMA_N235.aspx.

258. Ali Albashari, *Kobara: Tantheem Estathmar Alsharikat Alsaodih Fi Soag Alasahom Ohaviz Nashatah Alraiasiah [Experts: Regulating the Investment of Saudi Companies in the Stock Market Stimulates their Main Businesses Activities]*, Alsharq Al-Awsat News, Jan. 28, 2006, http://awsat-a.com/details.asp?section = 6&article = 345409&issueno = 9923#.VIDeR74kNUQ.

259. The tick size is the minimum price movement of a stock.

260. Saudi Stock Exchange "Tadawul", *Ealan Bekasos Tadail Oahadat Altagaior Fi Asaar Alashom [Announcement Regarding Changing the* Tick Size, (Nov. 12, 2015), http://www.tadawul.com.sa/wps/portal/!ut/p/c0/04_SB8K8xLLM9MSSzPy8xBz9CP0os3g_A-ewIE8TIwN_D38LA09vV7NQP8cQQ3dnA_3gxCL9gmxHRQCtDLXm/?x = 1&PRESS_REL_NO = 601.

261. Capital Market Authority, *Ealan Men Hiait Alsoag Almalih Beshan Tasarea Egraaalt Altahari Oa Altahaqiq Fi Shan Nashatat Adad Men Almotadaolaien [Announcement from the Capital Market Authority Regarding the Acceleration of the Investigative Procedures in the Activities of a Number of Traders in the Capital Market]*, (Nov. 12, 2015), http://www.cma.org.sa/Ar/News/Pages/CMA_N170.aspx.

included a lawsuit to be filed against this trader before the CRSD in accordance with the CML.[262] Similarly, on February 21, 2006, the CMA made a similar request to Tadawul to stop a trader from buying stocks. Allegedly, the trader was engaging in abusive practices and circulating untrue statements of material facts and statements of opinions on the Internet for the purpose of influencing the price of a security. These acts are prohibited under Article 49 of the CML and Article 8 of the Market Conduct Regulations.[263] It is worth noting that the CMA prevented these two traders from only buying stocks, not selling. Thus, these two big investors would likely increase the market supply that caused the market prices to decrease.

On February 23, 2006, the Board of CMA made a decision[264] to change the daily stock price fluctuation limit of listed companies in the Saudi capital market to 5% instead of 10%. This new policy started on February 25, 2006,[265] which was one day before the crash. Also, on February 23, the CMA requested Tadawul not to execute any buying orders for one trader due to abusive practices.[266] Again, the CMA prevented this large investor only from buying stock, which would likely increase supply and reduce stocks prices. These actions were a surprise to many investors and served as a warning for the beginning of the market crash.[267]

On February 26, 2006, the Saudi capital market started to fall from its highest point of 20,634.86.[268] The market continued to fall until it reached 7,933.29 points at the end of 2006, losing 52.53% comparing to the previous year.[269] In the first two days, the market lost over 1,500 points and most of the listed companies reached the maximum decline, which was 5%.[270] After the second day of the crash, the stock market sent a clear message to investors that the trip for prices declining had already started.[271]

262. Capital Market Authority, *Elan Men Haiat Alsoag Almaleih Beshan Egaf Altadaol Ma Alhesabat Alestathmareih Leahad Almotadaolain [Announcement from the Capital Market Authority Regarding Stopping Dealing with Investment Accounts for One Trader]* (Nov. 12, 2015), http://www.cma.org.sa/Ar/News/Pages/CMA_N171.aspx.
263. Capital Market Authority, *Elan Men Haiat Alsoag Almaleih Beshan Egaf Altadaol Ma Alhesabat Alestathmareih Leahad Almotadaolain [Announcement from the Capital Market Authority Regarding Stopping Dealing with Investment Accounts for One Trader]* (Nov. 12, 2015), http://www.cma.org.sa/Ar/News/Pages/CMA_N178.aspx.
264. The Board of the Capital Market Authority Resolution Number 1-141-2006, dated 24/1/1427 H (Feb. 23, 2006).
265. Capital Market Authority, *Elan Men Haiat Alsoag Almaleih Beshan Tadaeel Nesabat Altathabthb Aliomi Men Asharah Bealmeih Ela Kamsah Bealmeih [Capital Market Authority Announcement in Regarding to a Change in the Daily Stock Price Fluctuation Limit of Listed Companies from 10% to 5%]* (Nov. 12, 2015), http://www.cma.org.sa/Ar/News/Pages/CMA_N179.aspx.
266. Capital Market Authority, *Elan Men Haiat Alsoag Almaleih Beshan Egaf Altadaol Ma Alhesabat Alestathmareih Leahad Almotadaolain [Announcement from the Capital Market Authority Regarding Stopping Dealing with Investment Accounts for One Trader]* (Nov. 12, 2015), http://www.cma.org.sa/Ar/News/Pages/CMA_N180.aspx.
267. Aljuhani, *supra* n. 249, at 119.
268. *See* Saudi Stock Exchange "Tadawul", *2006 Annual Report, supra* n. 222, at 13.
269. *Id.*
270. Aljuhani, *supra* n. 249, at 119.
271. *Id.* at 120.

On March 1, 2006, the CMA published a statement saying that Alhayat Newspaper had published untrue statements on its front page stating that the CMA forgave speculators and detainees. The Board of the CMA also confirmed its intention to apply all the CML articles and its regulations on all violators. Moreover, the CMA declared its intention to take legal action against anyone who published or promoted untrue statements.[272]

On March 11, 2006, the Board of the CMA made a decision[273] to impose fines on two listed companies because these two companies failed to disclose their financial statements during the required period. The Board's decision was enforced immediately.[274] It is worth noting that the CMA has started to impose fines against companies who fail to meet the deadlines for financial statements disclosures only on July 20, 2005.[275]

The Supreme Economic Council held a meeting headed by King Abdullah on March 14, 2006 to discuss recent events in the Saudi stock market, specifically the sharply declining prices. The Council expressed its confidence in the strength of the Saudi economy and its ability to grow and to flourish in various types of economic sectors, which, according to the Council, meant a suitable investment future. Furthermore, the Council also expressed its confidence in national companies, likening the investments in these companies to investments in the nation and for the future of its citizens. The Council encouraged the citizens not to follow rumors and misleading information but to make their investment decisions on a sound basis.[276]

On March 15, 2006, according to King Abdullah's instructions, the Minister of Finance held a meeting with a group of Saudi private sector representatives to discuss the Saudi stock market situation. The Minister confirmed that what was currently happening in the capital market was not supported by national economic indicators. The Minister also confirmed what the Supreme Economic Council expressed regarding the investments in the national economy and its companies are an investment in the

272. Capital Market Authority, *Elan Ma Nasharatah Sahefat Alhayat Hatha Aliom Alarba [Announcement Regarding What Alhayat Newspaper Has Published Today, Wednesday]* (Nov. 12, 2015), http://www.cma.org.sa/Ar/News/Pages/CMA_N184.aspx.

273. The Board of the Capital Market Authority Resolution Number 1-148-2006, dated 11/2/1427 H (Mar. 11, 2006).

274. The decision contained (1) a fine of SAR 50,000 (USD 13,333) – on the Saudi Fisheries Company because it failed to disclose its financial statement for the fourth quarter of 2005; (2) a fine of SAR 100,000 (USD 26,000) – on the Saudi Fisheries Company because it failed to disclose its annual financial statement for the year of 2005; and (3) a fine of SAR 100,000 (USD 26,000) – on the Saudi Industrial Development Company because it failed to disclose its annual financial statement for the year of 2005. Capital Market Authority, *Elan Beshan Farad Garamat Malieh Ala Sharikateen Leadam Alefsah An Gaoaemah Almaleih Kelal Almodah Alnedamiah [Announcement Regarding Imposing Fines Against Two Companies for Not Disclosing Financial Statements During the Required Period]* (Nov. 12, 2015), http://www.cma.org.sa/Ar/News/Pages/CMA_N187.aspx.

275. The Board of the Capital Market Authority Resolution Number 11-57-2005, dated 28/2/1426 H (Apr. 7, 2005).

276. Capital Market Authority, *Baian Sahafe An Ejtma Almjlas Alagtsadi Alala Almonagd Iaom Altholatha Almoafag 14/2/1427H [Press Release about the Supreme Economic Council Meeting Which Held on Tuesday 3/14/2006]* (Nov. 12, 2015), http://www.cma.org.sa/Ar/News/Pages/CMA_N191.aspx.

nation and for the future of its citizens. Far from discouraging additional investment, the Minister stressed that the government expected businesses to accelerate their investments for the good of the economy. Furthermore, the Minister revealed some of the Supreme Economic Council's recommendations from its meeting the previous day regarding supporting the stock market and allowing investors to take advantage of the available opportunities in the Saudi capital market. Some of these recommendations were to allow non-Saudi residents to invest directly in the stock market and not limited to investment funds, and to reduce the par value of stock that would allow splitting the stocks.[277]

Less than a week after King Abdullah's instructions, the CMA announced on March 20, 2006 that non-Saudi residents could invest in the Saudi capital market, and that they were no longer limited to investment funds. Non-Saudi residents could start investing directly in the market beginning on March 25, 2006.[278] A day later, the CMA also announced that the Minster of Commerce and the Head of the CMA had agreed to submit a proposal to the King to change the par value of the stocks in the listed companies in the market to SAR 10.[279] On March 23, 2006, the CMA published the terms and requirements for opening investment portfolios for non-Saudi residents, allowing them to trade in the Saudi capital market.[280] However, even with these actions that were designed to prop up prices, the market index continued to decline, and many investors began to question the level of market transparency. The market at that time was characterized by unstable prices that seemed to rise and fall randomly without any interpretation or clue.[281]

On March 27, 2006, the CMA's Board issued a decision[282] to change the daily stock price fluctuation limit of listed companies in the capital market back to 10% instead of 5%. Moreover, the decision also changed the tick size back to SAR 0.25.[283]

277. Capital Market Authority, *Baian An Ejtma Oazeer Almaleeh Ma Momthli Algta Alkas [Press Release About the Minister of Finance's Meeting with Private Sector Representatives]* (Nov. 12, 2015), http://www.cma.org.sa/Ar/News/Pages/CMA_N192.aspx.

278. Capital Market Authority, *Baian Beshan Alsamah Llmogimin Belsatathmar Almobashar Fi Alasahom Alsaodiah [Announcement Regarding Allowing Non-Saudis Residents to Invest Directly in the Saudi Stocks]* (Nov. 12, 2015), http://www.cma.org.sa/Ar/News/Pages/CMA_N193.aspx.

279. Capital Market Authority, *Baian Beshan Takfeed Algaimah Alasmaih Llsahom Bima Easmah Betajasat Asahom Alsharikat Almosaheimal Almodrajah [Announcement Regarding Reducing the Par Value of Stock Which Would Allow Splitting Listed Companies' Stocks]* (Nov. 12, 2015), http://www.cma.org.sa/Ar/News/Pages/CMA_N195.aspx.

280. Capital Market Authority, *Thaoabt Fatah Mahavith Estathmariah Llmogimin Ltadaoal [The Terms for Opening Investment Portfolios for Non-Saudi Residents for Trading]* (Nov. 12, 2015), http://www.cma.org.sa/Ar/News/Pages/CMA_N196.aspx.

281. Aljuhani, *supra* n. 249, at 120.

282. The Board of the Capital Market Authority Resolution Number 3-154-2006, dated 27/2/1427 H (Mar. 27, 2006).

283. The tick size was changed for the third time on Sep. 13, 2008 to a new formula. The tick size is based on the share price, at three new bands. In band one, which is shares SAR 25.00 or below, the tick size would be SAR 0.05. In band two, which is shares SAR 25.10-SAR 50.00, the tick size would be SAR 0.10. In the last band, which is shares SAR 50.25 and above, the tick size would be SAR 0.25. Tadawul aimed the new implementation to pace with the increasing growth in the Saudi Stock Market trading. Moreover, the new implementation aimed to improve the quality and efficiency of share pricing, as well as to boost liquidity and the volume

The reason for these changes, as the CMA alleged, was because the risks that were associated with the market had been reduced.[284] Moreover, the CMA made another decision[285] regarding the reduction of the par value of stock, which would allow splitting the stocks. The par value of a stock was reduced from SAR 50 to SAR 10 and the stocks of listed companies in the market were splitting to five shares in a gradual manner, based on the number of shareholders in these listed companies. Splitting the stocks started on April 1, 2006 and ended on the 22nd of the same month.[286]

On April 9, 2006, the CMA's Board made a decision[287] that contained sanctions against two traders who violated Article 49 of the CML and Article 3 of the Market Conduct Regulations. The decision ordered Tadawul immediately to stop executing any buying orders in the Saudi capital market for these two traders due to abusive practices. The CMA had evidence that these two traders intentionally sold and bought stocks with large amounts of money in order to create a false impression of the prices of some companies stocks. This decision also included the intention to file a lawsuit against these two traders before CRSD in accordance with the CML.[288] Once again, the CMA prevented these two big investors only from buying stocks, which (again) was likely to increase market supply.

On May 12, 2006, King Abdullah issued a Royal Decree[289] to relieve the Chairman of the CMA, Jammaz Al-Suhaimi, from his duties and to appoint a new Chairman for the CMA, Abdulrahman Altuwaijri.[290] Many experts and investors were pleased with the decision as they were looking for positive reform in the capital market.[291]

---

of share trading. For more details, *see* Saudi Stock Exchange "Tadawul", *Tick Size,* (Nov. 12, 2015), http://www.tadawul.com.sa/static/pages/en/TickSize/TickSize.html; *Tatbeeg Oahadat Altagaior Aljadidh Leasar Alasahom Bada Esboa Ofaga 3 Netagat Tatoafag Ma Alasoag Alalamih [Applying a New Tick Size for Stock Prices After a Week According to 3 Bands Which Are Congruence with Global Markets]*, Alriyadh Newspaper, Sep. 4, 2008, http://www.alriyadh.com/371886.

284. Capital Market Authority, *Ealan Men Haiat Alsoag Almalieh Beshan Zisat Niesbat Altathbthb Aliomi Leasaar Alasahom [Capital Market Authority Announcement in Regarding Increasing the Daily Stock Price Fluctuation Limit of Listed Companies from 5% to 10%]* (Nov. 12, 2015), http://www.cma.org.sa/Ar/News/Pages/CMA_N202.aspx.
285. The Board of the Capital Market Authority Resolution Number 4-154-2006, dated 27/2/1427 H (Mar. 27, 2006).
286. Capital Market Authority, *Ealan Men Hiaat Alsoag Almalih Beshan Tajaziat Ashom Alsharikat Almodaragah Fi Alsoag [Announcement for CMA Regarding Splitting the Stocks of Listed Companies in the Market]* (Nov. 12, 2015), http://www.cma.org.sa/Ar/News/Pages/CMA_N203.aspx.
287. The Board of the Capital Market Authority Resolution Number 1-160-2006, dated 11/3/1427 H (Apr. 9, 2006).
288. Capital Market Authority, *Elan Men Haiat Alsoag Almaleih Beshan Egaf Altadaol Ma Alhesabat Alestathmareih Leathnain Men Almotadaolain [Announcement from the Capital Market Authority Regarding Stopping Dealing with Investment Accounts for Two Traders]* (Nov. 12, 2015), http://www.cma.org.sa/Ar/News/Pages/CMA_N208.aspx.
289. Royal Decree No. A/41, dated 14/4/1427 H (Dec. 5, 2006).
290. Abdulrahman Altuwaijri was also relieved from his duties in Feb. 5, 2013. Mohammed Alsheikh appointed by a Royal decree as the new chairman of the CMA. Royal Decree No. A/92, dated 24/3/1434 H (May 3, 2013). In January 2015, Mohammed Aljadaan was appointed as the new chairman of the CMA by a Royal Decree number A/90, dated 9/4/1436 H (Jan. 29, 2015). Mr Aljadann has served until now as the chairman of the CMA.
291. Abdulaziz Alaqrara, *Soag Alasaho Toang Altuwaijri Belaon Alakdar Oalmostathmoron entathron Gararat Alraees Aljadid [the Saudi Stock Market is Hugging Altuwaijri by the Green Color,*

On the whole, the government, the media, and the traders themselves share responsibility for the crash. Some decisions came late, or not at all. At the same time, the investing public was largely unaware of investing protocol and strategy. In fact, many leapt at the opportunity to make money without really knowing how to invest at all. Instead of sound financial advice, many Saudis made decisions based on informal recommendations and media reports. This same media indirectly encouraged continued speculation, even though prices were unreasonably high, because there was no real warning about an imminent collapse and many writers lacked financial and capital market expertise.[292]

The 2006 crash brought about a major change in many peoples' attitudes about the government's ability to manage the economy. Some investors openly questioned the integrity of the system, and called for more intensive government supervision and intervention to better control market dynamics. Specifically, many were concerned that the market favored large investors at the expense of smaller ones, by giving these large investors access to information that resulted in an unfair advantage.[293]

Properly grounded investor confidence and equal access to information are two major keys to a successful capital market. The government may have performed a disservice by pumping up prices and confidence at a time when the market was clearly at a breaking point; and, the media was unwilling, or unable, to question these government policies. So, instead of prompt and effective intervention that could have possibly contained the damage, problems festered and, in many cases, actually became worse.

We now move to the common question that many investors asked in the wake of the crash: is the Saudi capital market, as it is presently constituted, consistent with the Kingdom's overall economic goals?

[B] Is the Saudi Capital Market Efficient?

Over the past several decades, a number of studies have been conducted to try and answer this question, and the majority of this research has concluded that the Saudi stock market is inefficient. The study authors cite various reasons for this deficiency, including high transaction costs, lack of information, inadequate infrastructure, lack of transparency, and several other factors.

A study by Butler and Malaikah tested the efficiency of Saudi Arabia and Kuwaiti stock markets over the period of 1985-1989. Along with volatile prices and a rather weak rate of return, the authors concluded that high transaction costs contributed

and Investors Are Waiting the New President's Decisions] Alriyadh Newspaper, May 14, 2006, http://www.alriyadh.com/154289; Hazem Sharkawy & Munira Almoshkas, *Amar Malake: Eafa Al-Suhaimi Oatakaleef Altuwaijri Beraasat Haiat Soag Almal [Royal Decree: Relieve Al-Suhaimi from his Duties and Appointed Altuwaijri to Be the Head of the Capital Market Authority]*, Aljazirah Newspaper, May 13, 2006, http://www.al-jazirah.com/2006/20060513/ec1t.htm.

292. Al-Twaijry, *supra* n. 223, at 28.
293. Al-Aqeel, *supra* n. 248, at 3.

significantly to overall inefficiency. The two researchers also cited illiquidity, trading delays and market fragmentation, and the absence of official market makers.[294]

A pair of studies examined the capital market's performance in the late 1980s to the mid-1990s. One study, conducted by Al-Razeen, examined the efficiency of the Saudi stock market by applying the "weak-form test"[295] for the period of 1992-1995. The study result was that the Saudi stock market had a low level of efficiency.[296] Another study, from Khababa in 1998, examined the efficiency of the Saudi stock market for the period of 1985-1997.[297] The results strongly suggested inefficiency for the Saudi stock market in both informational and operational aspects.[298] Later, Alkholifey examined the informational efficiency of the Saudi stock market in 2000. This study concluded that the Saudi stock market was weak and informationally inefficient.[299]

The Saudi Chamber of Commerce in Riyadh conducted a survey in 2005 in order to examine both the Saudi capital market's efficiency and its role in supporting the Saudi economy.[300] The finding of the survey was that the market did not have the fundamental factors needed to be efficient. One of the major drawbacks was the difficulty to access information about the listed companies and shares. Many traders in the market had the ability to influence stock prices, and due to high costs for trading in the market, stock prices in the market moved in random paths and away from available information about listed companies, and many traders in the market did not have the same opportunities to gain profits. Moreover, a large class of traders and market makers could make higher profits than other traders in the market. Also, the number of listed companies, seventy-seven at that time,[301] was inadequate.[302] Specifically, the result of the analysis was that the Saudi stock market had, at best, a medium level of efficiency, yet the level of efficiency was closer to the weak level than a strong level.

294. Butler, *supra* n. 46, at 209, 210.
295. The weak-form test considers only historical prices. Weak efficiency means the price of a stock reflects all the historical prices of such a stock. Abdullah Mohamed Al-Razeen, *the Weak-Form Efficiency of the Saudi Stock Market* 129 (PhD Thesis, University of Leicester, United Kingdom 1997).
296. Al-Razeen, *supra* n. 295, at 233.
297. Nourredine Khababa, *Behavior of Stock Prices in the Saudi Arabian Financial Market: Empirical Research Findings*, 11 J. Fin. Mgmt. & Analysis 48, 50 (1998). This study applied two tests to find evidence for weak-form efficiency, namely Autocorrelation and Runs test.
298. The study found several reasons behind the informational and operational inefficiency that were associated with the natural and structure of the Saudi stock market. First, the absence of official traders market and brokers in the market caused significant delays in operation and the associated high transaction costs. Second, the government and/or a few investors dominated shareholding, leading to a thinness of trading that affected the behavior of price movement and price level in the market. The third reason was related to illiquidity in the market, because banks were not allowed to trade stocks for their own accounts. *Id.* at 54.
299. Ahmed Alkholifey, *the Saudi Arabian Stock Market: Efficient Market Hypothesis and Investors Behavior* 105 (PhD Thesis, Colorado State University, 2000).
300. Saudi Chamber of Commerce in Riyadh, *Explore to What Extend the Efficiency of the Local Stock Market and Its Role in Supporting the National Economy, supra* n. 206, at 24.
301. Saudi Arabian Monetary Agency, *42nd Annual Report, supra* n. 217, at 115.
302. Saudi Chamber of Commerce in Riyadh, *Explore to What Extend the Efficiency of the Local Stock Market and Its Role in Supporting the National Economy, supra* n. 206, at 24.

Moreover, the survey pointed out that the Saudi stock market had, to that point, not played a fundamental role in the economy.[303]

In 2008, Elango and Hussein examined the efficiency of the capital markets across the GCC countries[304] during the period of 2001-2006.[305] The results of this study was that the hypothesis pertaining to random walk and weak-form efficiency of the seven capital markets in GCC countries was rejected for all these markets during the target period of this study.[306]

Onour's study[307] used a number of tests in 2009 to examine the weak-form efficiency of the Saudi capital market.[308] The findings of the tests in the study rejected the hypothesis of random walk behavior of Saudi stock price returns at all three levels including individual, sectoral, and aggregate levels.[309] The study indicated that the major causes of the inefficiency of the Saudi capital market are inadequate information and lack of market transparency.[310]

Al-Ashikh examined also the efficiency of the Saudi stock market in 2012. The result was that the Saudi stock market was inefficient and the day-of-the-week effect existed. The study indicated that the returns of the Saudi market are high on the first trading day of the week, and the lowest volatility in Saudi market occurs on the last two trading days of the week. Moreover, the main factors of the existence of seasonal patterns in returns and volatility are measurement errors, trading delay and settlement differences, and non-trading periods, timing of corporate news releases, and time zone differences.[311]

Asiri and Alzeera conducted a test for the weak-form market efficiency of the Saudi stock market from 2006 to the end of 2012. The study concluded that the Saudi stock market was weak-form efficient,[312] because there are no investors who could

303. *Id.*
304. The six GCC countries have seven capital markets including: Saudi Stock Market-Tadawul (Saudi Arabia); Kuwait Stock Exchange (Kuwait); Doha Securities Market (Qatar); Dubai Financial Market (United Arab Emirates); Abu Dhabi Securities Market (United Arab Emirates); Bahrain Stock Exchange (Bahrain); and Muscat Securities Market (Oman).
305. Rengasamy Elango & Mohammed Ibrahim Hussein, *An Empirical Analysis on the Weak-Form Efficiency of the GCC Markets Applying Selected Statistical Tests,* 4 Int'l Rev. Bus. Res. Papers 140, 146 (2008).
306. Elango and Hussein's study analyzed the market efficiency of the GCC stock markets over the period between October 2001 and October 2006 based on the data available of these exchanges at the time of conducting this study. The study used the "Kolmogorov Smirnov test" and Runs test to examine the normality and randomness respectively. *Id.* at 152.
307. Ibrahim A. Onour, *Testing Efficiency Performance of Saudi Stock Market,* 23 JKAU:Econ. & Admin. 15, 16 (2009).
308. Onour's study employed unit root test, stationarity test, and variance ratio test to examine whether the Saudi capital market is efficient. *Id.* at 23-24.
309. *Id.* at 25.
310. *Id.*
311. Abdullah I. Al Ashikh, *Testing the Weak-Form of Efficient Market Hypothesis and the Day-Of-The-Week Effect in Saudi Stock Exchange: Linear Approach,* 8 Int'l Rev. Bus. Res. Papers 27, 48 (2012).
312. Batool Kasim Asiri & Hamad Alzeera, *Is the Saudi Stock Market Efficient? A Case of Weak-Form Efficiency,* 4 Res. J. Fin. & Acct. 35, 41 (2013). In this study, four tests are applied: Dicky-Fuller unit root, Pearson correlation coefficient, Durbin-Watson (autocorrelation), and Wald-Wolfowitz runs-tests.

generate significant returns with an investment formula based on information gleaned from prior data and technical analysis, at least on an ongoing basis.[313]

In 2012, Al-Ajmi and Kim evaluated the GCC stock markets to determine whether these markets are efficient in the weak form. The study used three new multiple variance tests, including wild bootstrap test of Kim, joint sign test of Kim and Shamsuddin, and the Chen and Deo's test.[314] The study concluded that all GCC markets are inefficient in the weak form. The findings hold for both observed returns and the returns corrected for thin trading in all markets. The result against market efficiency is stronger when the daily data is used.[315] The study indicated the factors behind inefficiency in the weak form in the GCC markets. These included relatively low institutional ownership, significant government ownership of listed companies, prohibition of short sales in all markets, and the limited number of brokerage firms publishing analysts' recommendations. None of these published analyses forecast nonavailability of derivatives for trading in all markets, with the exception of Kuwait, and the failure in matching international standards, although all markets had taken a number of measures to improve disclosure level, transparency, and corporate governance requirements.[316]

However, a recent study was more hopeful. In 2014, Jamaani and Roca tested the GCC stock markets to find out whether GCC stock markets are weak-form efficient both as single markets and as a regional stock market.[317] This study employed daily index prices denominated in local currencies for the period from the end of December 2003 to the end of January 2013 by applying a number of tests.[318] Findings and results of the study purported to prove that all GCC stock markets are not weak-form efficient, in the sense that current stock price movement can be predicted from past price movements. As the efficiency of GCC as a regional stock market, the result is that GCC stock market prices is cointegrated in the long run, so that the past movements of other GCC market prices can predict the movement of individual GCC stock market prices.[319]

The inefficiency that contributed to the 2006 crash can be traced back several decades. The bottom line is that the market's infrastructure was insufficient to support a growing economy. Although the existing capital market served a vital function until the economic expansion in the 1970s and 1980s, it was inadequate for a modern economy and a modern people. For whatever reason, the government chose not to take remedial action until after the crisis was already in motion. Progress has been made, but some substantial structural deficiencies still need to be addressed, particularly in terms of transparency and the flow of information.

313. *Id.*
314. These tests are well known to have desirable small sample properties. Jasim Al-Ajmi & J.H. Kim, *Are Gulf Stock Markets Efficient? Evidence from New Multiple Variance Ratio Tests*, 44 Applied Econ. 1737, 1746 (2012).
315. *Id.*
316. *Id.* at 1746, 1747.
317. Fouad Jamaani & Eduardo Roca, *Are the Regional Gulf Stock Markets Weak-Form Efficient as Single Stock Markets and as a Regional Stock Market?*, 33 Res. Int'l Bus. & Fin. 221, 244 (2014).
318. Jamaani and Roca applied in the study different tests including a battery of parametric, nonparametric, unit root, and Johansen cointegration tests. *Id.*
319. *Id.*

§2.06 CONCLUSION

Developing economies experience growing pains, and it is up to the countries' respective governments to respond to these issues and to minimize the effects that its citizens feel. From its inception, the capital market has been an important part of Saudi Arabia's economy, and appropriate steps should be taken to help ensure that it retains that position. The Kingdom needs a strong capital market, and a vigorous capital market requires the proper level of oversight.

IOSCO membership was an important step in the Saudi capital market's development. Moreover, some of the necessary infrastructure simply is not available by looking inside the Kingdom. By expanding its horizons, Saudi Arabia can look to the other GCC States, and even beyond the Arabian Gulf nations, to find a suitable model for a thriving, and fair capital market.

Among the more significant challenges is to foster enhanced transparency in market transactions. The lack of transparency came to light in the crash of 2006. It was, in many ways, the perfect storm: as indicated above, the government, the media, and the investors themselves all bear some measure of responsibility for the crash.

The fact that the crash was an unprecedented event helps explain some of the actions, and inactions, that took place around that time, and in the years leading up to the crash. Government policies at the time are a very good example. Due to their inexperience, the decision-makers often took actions without considering the long-term consequences. In many cases, these shortsighted moves simply made a difficult situation almost unbearable. Now, with the benefit of experience, the State should be prepared to help ensure fairness and transparency in the market. Such a development is particularly welcome now that the Saudi capital market is open to foreign investors.

The crash of 2006 has taught both investors and the government a painful lesson. While investors have hopefully learned more about the overall process, the State should enact measures that both minimize the possibility of future collapses and that limit the damage that they cause. This author suggests that the best way to achieve these goals is to create a trading environment based on fairness, transparency, and accountability. Only then can the Saudi capital market be a key element in a sustainable economic future for the Saudi people.

Bibliography

I. Primary Sources

[A] Saudi Arabia Laws and Regulations

Anti-Money Laundering and Counter-Terrorist Financing Rules, the Board of the Capital Market Authority Resolution Number 1-39-2008, dated 3/12/1429 H (December 1, 2008), Amended by the Resolution of the Board of the Capital Market Authority Number 2-54-2013, dated 21/2/1435 H (December 24, 2013).

Authorized Persons Regulations, the Board of the Capital Market Authority Resolution Number 1-83-2005, dated 21/05/1426 H (June 28, 2005). Amended by the Resolution of the Board of the Capital Market Authority Number 1-1-2013, dated 1/3/1434 H (January 13, 2013).

Capital Market Authority, the Board of the Capital Market Authority Resolution Number 1-141-2006, dated 24/01/1427 H (February 23, 2006).

Capital Market Authority, the Board of the Capital Market Authority Resolution Number 2-28-2008, dated 17/08/1429 H (August 18, 2008).

Capital Market Authority, the Board of the Capital Market Authority Resolution Number 3-154-2006, dated 27/02/1427 H (March 27, 2006).

Corporate Governance Regulations, the Board of the Capital Market Authority Resolution Number 1-212-2006, dated 21/10/1427 H (November 12, 2006), Amended by the Resolution of the Board of the Capital Market Authority Number 1-10-2010, dated 30/3/1431 H (March 16, 2010).

Credit Rating Agencies Regulations, the Board of the Capital Market Authority Resolution Number 3-58-2014, dated 17/1/1436 H (November 10, 2005).

Glossary of Defined Terms Used in the Regulations and Rules of the Capital Market Authority, the Board of the Capital Market Authority Resolution Number 4-11-2004, dated 20/8/1425 H (October 4, 2004).

Investment Accounts Instructions, the Board of the Capital Market Authority Resolution Number 4-39-2016, dated 25/6/1437 H (April 3, 2016).

Investment Funds Regulations, the Board of the Capital Market Authority Resolution Number 1-219-2006, dated 3/12/1427 H (December 24, 2006).

Law of Companies, Royal Decree No. M/6, dated 22/3/1385 H (1965).

Law of Companies, Royal Decree No. M/3, dated 28/1/1437 H (2015).

Listing Rules, the Board of the Capital Market Authority Resolution Number 3-11-2004, dated 20/8/1425 H (October 4, 2004), Amended by the Resolution of the Board of the Capital Market Authority Number 1-64-2016, dated 19/8/1437 H (May 26, 2016).

Market Conduct Regulations, the Board of the Capital Market Authority Resolution Number 1-11-2004, dated 20/8/1425 H (October 4, 2004), Amended by the Resolution of the Board of the Capital Market Authority Number 3-3-2016, dated 27/3/1437 H (January 7, 2016).

Merger and Acquisition Regulations, the Board of the Capital Market Authority Resolution Number 1-50-2007, dated 21/9/1428 H (October 3, 2007), Amended by the Resolution of the Board of the Capital Market Authority Number 2-4-2012, dated 28/2/1433 H (January 22, 2012).

Offers of Securities Regulations, the Board of the Capital Market Authority Resolution Number 2-11-2004, dated 20/8/1425 H (October 4, 2004), Amended by the Resolution of the Board of the Capital Market Authority Number 1-28-2008, dated 17/8/1429 H (August 18, 2008).

Procedures and Instructions for Listed Companies on the Market whose Accumulated Losses Amounted to 50% or More of their Capital, the Board of the Capital Market Authority Resolution Number 4-48-2013, dated 15/1/1435 H (18 Nov. 2013).

Prudential Rules, the Board of the Capital Market Authority Resolution Number 1-40-2012, dated 17/2/1434 H (December 30, 2012).

Real Estate Investment Funds Regulations, the Board of the Capital Market Authority Resolution Number 1-193-2006, dated 19/6/1427 H (July 15, 2006).

Resolution of Securities Disputes Proceedings Regulations, the Board of the Capital Market Authority Resolution Number 1-4-2011, dated 19/2/1432 H (January 23, 2011).

Royal Decree No. 8/1230, dated 11/7/1403 (1983).

Royal Decree No. A/41, dated 14/4/1427H (5/12/2006).

Royal Decree No. A/92, dated 24/3/1434 H (3/5/2013).

Rules for Qualified Foreign Financial Institutions Investment in Listed Shares, the Board of the Capital Market Authority Resolution Number 1-42-2015, dated 15/7/1436 H (May 4, 2015).

Securities Business Regulations, the Board of the Capital Market Authority Resolution Number 2-83-2005, dated 21/05/1426 H (June 28, 2005).

The Board of the Capital Market Authority Resolution Number 1-141-2006, dated 24/1/1427 H (February 23, 2006).

The Board of the Capital Market Authority Resolution Number 1-148-2006, dated 11/2/1427 H (March 11, 2006).

The Board of the Capital Market Authority Resolution Number 1-160-2006, dated 11/3/1427 H (April 9, 2006).

The Board of the Capital Market Authority Resolution Number 11-57-2005, dated 28/2/1426 H (April 7, 2005).

The Board of the Capital Market Authority Resolution Number 2-128-2006, dated 22/12/1426 H (January 22, 2006).

The Board of the Capital Market Authority Resolution Number 3-154-2006, dated 27/2/1427 H (March 27, 2006).

The Board of the Capital Market Authority Resolution Number 4-154-2006, dated 27/2/1427 H (March 27, 2006).

The Board of the Capital Market Authority Resolution Number 5-126-2006, dated 23/12/1426 H (January 23, 2006).

The Capital Market Law, Royal Decree No. M/30, dated 2/6/1424 H (2003).

The Council of Ministers, *Privatization Objectives*, Resolution No. 60, dated 1/4/1418 H (1997).

The Saudi Share Registration Company, Royal Decree No. 1230/8 (1985).

[B] Official/Semi-Official Reports-Government & Nongovernment Bodies

Capital Market Authority, *Authorized Persons*, (June 30, 2015), http://www.cma.org.sa/en/Pages/AuthorisedPersons.aspx.

Capital Market Authority, *Baian An Ejtma Oazeer Almaleeh Ma Momthli Algta Alkas [Press Release About the Minister of Finance's Meeting with Private Sector Representatives]* (November 12, 2015), http://www.cma.org.sa/Ar/News/Pages/CMA_N192.aspx.

Capital Market Authority, *Baian Beshan Alsamah Llmogimin Belsatathmar Almobashar Fi Alasahom Alsaodiah [Announcement Regarding Allowing Non-Saudis Residents to Invest Directly in the Saudi Stocks]* (November 12, 2015), http://www.cma.org.sa/Ar/News/Pages/CMA_N193.aspx.

Capital Market Authority, *Baian Beshan Takfeed Algaimah Alasmaih Llsahom Bima Easmah Betajasat Asahom Alsharikat Almosaheimal Almodrajah [Announcement Regarding Reducing the par value of Stock Which Would Allow Splitting Listed Companies' Stocks]* (November 12, 2015), http://www.cma.org.sa/Ar/News/Pages/CMA_N195.aspx.

Capital Market Authority, *Baian Sahafe An Ejtma Almjlas Alagtsadi Alala Almonagd Iaom Altholatha Almoafag 14/2/1427H [Press Release about the Supreme Economic Council Meeting Which Held on Tuesday 3/14/2006]* (November 12, 2015), http://www.cma.org.sa/Ar/News/Pages/CMA_N191.aspx.

Capital Market Authority, *CMA Announcement in Regard to the Rules for Qualified Foreign Financial Institutions' Investment in Listed Shares*, (April 16, 2015), http://cma.org.sa/En/News/Pages/CMA_N_1742.aspx.

Capital Market Authority, *CMA Announcement in Regard to the Rules for Qualified Foreign Financial Institutions' Investment in Listed Shares*, (July 22, 2014), http://www.cma.org.sa/En/News/Pages/CMA_N_1506.aspx.

Capital Market Authority, *CMA Announces Its Approval for Authorized Persons to Engage in Swap Agreements*, (November 12, 2015), http://www.cma.org.sa/En/News/Pages/CMA_N434.aspx.

Capital Market Authority, *CMA Approves Amendments to the Registration Requirements for Qualified Foreign Financial Institutions, Change the Settlement Cycle for Securities Transactions and the Introduction of Securities Lending and Covered Short-Selling*, (May 3, 2016), http://www.cma.org.sa/en/News/Pages/CMA_N_2036.aspx.

Capital Market Authority, *Ealan Men Haiat Alsoag Almalieh Beshan Zisat Niesbat Altathbthb Aliomi Leasaar Alasahom [Capital Market Authority Announcement in Regarding Increasing the Daily Stock Price Fluctuation Limit of Listed Companies from 5% to 10%]* (November 12, 2015), http://www.cma.org.sa/Ar/News/Pages/CMA_N202.aspx.

Capital Market Authority, *Ealan Men Hiaat Alsoag Almalih Beshan Tajaziat Ashom Alsharikat Almodaragah Fi Alsoag [Announcement for CMA Regarding Splitting the Stocks of Listed Companies in the Market]* (November 12, 2015), http://www.cma.org.sa/Ar/News/Pages/CMA_N203.aspx.

Capital Market Authority, *Ealan Men Hiait Alsoag Almalih Beshan Tasarea Egraaalt Altahari Oa Altahaqiq Fi Shan Nashatat Adad Men Almotadaolaien [Announcement from the Capital Market Authority Regarding the Acceleration of the Investigative Procedures in the Activities of a Number of Traders in the Capital Market]*, (November 12, 2015), http://www.cma.org.sa/Ar/News/Pages/CMA_N170.aspx.

Capital Market Authority, *Elan Beshan Farad Garamat Malieh Ala Sharikateen Leadam Alefsah An Gaoaemah Almaleih Kelal Almodah Alnedamiah [Announcement Regarding Imposing Fines Against Two Companies for Not Disclosing Financial*

Statements During the Required Period] (November 12, 2015), http://www.cma.org.sa/Ar/News/Pages/CMA_N187.aspx.

Capital Market Authority, *Elan Beshan Tagraeem Thlathah Mokalefeen Lentam Alsoag Almaleih Bemablag Maah Oa Tesah Oa Setoon Malion Riyal Oa Manahom Men Alamal Fi Alsharikat Almosahemah [Announcement Regarding Imposing Penalties on Three Violators Who Violated the Capital Market Law Amount of Hundred and Sixty Nine Million Riyals and Ban Them from Working in Joint Stock Companies*], (November 12, 2015), http://www.cma.org.sa/Ar/News/Pages/CMA_N151.aspx.

Capital Market Authority, *Elan Ma Nasharatah Sahefat Alhayat Hatha Aliom Alarba [Announcement Regarding What Alhayat Newspaper Has Published Today, Wednesday]* (November 12, 2015), http://www.cma.org.sa/Ar/News/Pages/CMA_N184.aspx.

Capital Market Authority, *Elan Men Haiat Alsoag Almaleih Beshan Egaf Altadaol Ma Alhesabat Alestathmareih Leahad Almotadaolain [Announcement from the Capital Market Authority Regarding Stopping Dealing with Investment Accounts for One Trader]* (November 12, 2015), http://www.cma.org.sa/Ar/News/Pages/CMA_N171.aspx.

Capital Market Authority, *Elan Men Haiat Alsoag Almaleih Beshan Egaf Altadaol Ma Alhesabat Alestathmareih Leahad Almotadaolain [Announcement from the Capital Market Authority Regarding Stopping Dealing with Investment Accounts for One Trader]* (November 12, 2015), http://www.cma.org.sa/Ar/News/Pages/CMA_N178.aspx.

Capital Market Authority, *Elan Men Haiat Alsoag Almaleih Beshan Egaf Altadaol Ma Alhesabat Alestathmareih Leahad Almotadaolain [Announcement from the Capital Market Authority Regarding Stopping Dealing with Investment Accounts for One Trader]* (November 12, 2015), http://www.cma.org.sa/Ar/News/Pages/CMA_N180.aspx.

Capital Market Authority, *Elan Men Haiat Alsoag Almaleih Beshan Egaf Altadaol Ma Alhesabat Alestathmareih Leathnain Men Almotadaolain [Announcement from the Capital Market Authority Regarding Stopping Dealing with Investment Accounts for Two Traders]* (November 12, 2015), http://www.cma.org.sa/Ar/News/Pages/CMA_N208.aspx.

Capital Market Authority, *Elan Men Haiat Alsoag Almaleih Beshan Tadaeel Nesabat Altathabthb Aliomi Men Asharah Bealmeih Ela Kamsah Bealmeih [Capital Market Authority Announcement in Regarding to a Change in the Daily Stock Price Fluctuation Limit of Listed Companies from 10% to 5%]* (November 12, 2015), http://www.cma.org.sa/Ar/News/Pages/CMA_N179.aspx.

Capital Market Authority, *Garar Majalos Alhaiah Betamadid Almohalh Almamnoha Llsharikat Letasahih Aotaoa Estathmaratah [CMA Board's Decision to Extend the Period of Correction for Joint Stock Companies to Correct its Investments]* (November 12, 2015), http://www.cma.org.sa/Ar/News/Pages/CMA_N235.aspx.

Capital Market Authority, *Garar Majals Haiat Alsoag Almaleih Ragom 2-128-2006 Oa Taraik 22/12/1426 H Almoafag 22/1/2006 [The Decision of the Capital Market Authority Board No. 2-128-2006, Dated 12/22/1426 H Corresponding to*

01/22/2006 AD], (November 12, 2015), http://www.cma.org.sa/Ar/News/Pages/CMA_N156.aspx.

Capital Market Authority, *Garar Men Majals Haiat Alsoag Almaleih Beshan Istathmar Alsharikat Almosahimah Fi Asahom SHarikat Okrah [A Decision from the Capital Market Authority Board Regarding the Investment of Joint Stock Companies In the Share of Other Joint Stock Companies]*, (November 12, 2015), http://www.cma.org.sa/Ar/News/Pages/CMA_N157.aspx.

Capital Market Authority, *Maoga Taoeat Almostathmar, [Investor Awareness Website]*, (October 10, 2014) http://www.cma.org.sa/IA/index.html.

Capital Market Authority, *Thaoabt Fatah Mahavith Estathmariah Llmogimin Ltadaoal [The Terms for Opening Investment Portfolios for Non-Saudi Residents for Trading]* (November 12, 2015), http://www.cma.org.sa/Ar/News/Pages/CMA_N196.aspx.

CFI.co, *the Saudi Stock Exchange Wins the CFI.co MENA Award for 2013*, (October 29, 2014), http://cfi.co/awards/africa/2013/the-saudi-stock-exchange-wins-the-cfi-co-mena-award-for-2013/.

International Monetary Fund – Middle Eastern Department, *Financial Systems and Labor Markets in the Gulf Cooperation Council Countries* (International Monetary Fund 1997).

International Monetary Fund, *IMF Executive Board Concludes 2005 Article IV Consultation with Saudi Arabia*, Public Information Notice No. 05/161 (December 5, 2005).

International Monetary Fund, *Saudi Arabia: Financial Sector Assessment Program-Detailed Assessment of Observance of the IOSCO Objectives and Principles of Securities Regulation*, IMF Country Report No. 13/212 (July 2013).

Ministry of Commerce and Investment, *The New Corporate Law Comes Into Force Today, Monday 25.07.1437 H, As Confirmed By MCI*, (May 2, 2016), http://mci.gov.sa/en/MediaCenter/News/Pages/02-05-16-01.aspx.

Ministry of Economy and Planning of Saudi Arabia, *Seventh Development Plan 1420/21–1424/25 (A.H), 2000– 2004 (A.D)* (November 12, 2015), http://www.mep.gov.sa/themes/GoldenCarpet/index.jsp;jsessionid=F374FDCD0B6758187FA54B943B0D0DF0.alfa?event=SwitchLanguage&Code=EN#1405309588083.

Researches Department, *Borsat Alaorag Almaleh Oa Ahmitah Fi Kedmat Alsharikat Almosahemh [Stock Exchange and its Importance in Serving Joint-Stock Companies]*, Riyadh Chamber of Commerce and Industry (Alsharif Publication 1980).

Saudi Arabian Monetary Agency, *39th Annual Report* (2003).

Saudi Arabian Monetary Agency, *40th Annual Report* (2004).

Saudi Arabian Monetary Agency, *41st Annual Report* (2005).

Saudi Arabian Monetary Agency, *42nd Annual Report* (2006).

Saudi Arabian Monetary Agency, *Financial Sector Development for Better Growth: A Future Vision for the Saudi Economy until 2020* (October 2002).

Saudi Arabian Monetary Agency, *Historical Preview*, (November 12, 2015), http://www.sama.gov.sa/en-US/About/Pages/SAMAHistory.aspx.

Saudi Arabian Monetary Agency, *Thaoabd Altamoial Alastahlaqi [the Regulation for Consumer Finance]*, (November 25, 2014), http://www.sama.gov.sa/News/Pages/News14270214.aspx.

Saudi Chamber of Commerce in Riyadh, *Istakshaf Mada Kafat Soag Alasahom Almahalih Oa Dorah Fi Daam Alagtsad Aloatani* [*Explore to What Extend the Efficiency of the Local Stock Market and its Role in Supporting the National Economy*], the 15th Annual Meeting of Saudi Economic Association (Riyadh, November 13-15, 2005).

Saudi Stock Exchange “Tadawul”, *Ealan Bekasos Tadail Oahadat Altagaior Fi Asaar Alashom [Announcement Regarding Changing the* Tick Size, (November 12, 2015), http://www.tadawul.com.sa/wps/portal/!ut/p/c0/04_SB8K8xLLM9MSSzPy8xBz9CP0os3g_A-ewIE8TIwN_D38LA09vV7NQP8cQQ3dnA_3gxCL9gmxHRQCtDLXm/?x = 1&PRESS_REL_NO = 601.

Saudi Stock Exchange “Tadawul”, *Frequently Asked Questions on the Amendment of the Settlement Cycle of Listed Securities in the Equity Market*, (May 5, 2016), https://www.tadawul.com.sa/static/pages/en/Publication/PDF/T2E.pdf.

Saudi Stock Exchange “Tadawul”, *Market Watch Today*, (June 30, 2016), https://www.tadawul.com.sa/wps/portal/tadawul/markets/equities/market-watch/market-watch-today.

Saudi Stock Exchange “Tadawul”, *2006 Annual Report* (December 31, 2006).

Saudi Stock Exchange “Tadawul”, *2013 Annual Report* (December 31, 2013).

Saudi Stock Exchange “Tadawul”, *Annual Report*, (October 30, 2014), http://www.tadawul.com.sa/Resources/Reports/Yearly_en.html.

Saudi Stock Exchange “Tadawul”, *About Us*, (November 12, 2015), http://www.tadawul.com.sa/wps/portal/!ut/p/c1/04_SB8K8xLLM9MSSzPy8xBz9CP0os3g_A-ewIE8TIwODYFMDA08Tn7AQZx93YwN3I_3g1Dz9gmxHRQB7GACB/.

Saudi Stock Exchange “Tadawul”, *Market Rules*, (November 12, 2015) http://www.tadawul.com.sa/wps/portal/!ut/p/c1/04_SB8K8xLLM9MSSzPy8xBz9CP0os3g_A-ewIE8TIwMLf3czA0_vIKegIBN_QwNXQ6B8JJK8e0CYqYGniU-wUXCAl7GBpxEB3X4e-bmp-gW5EeUATNtVlg!!/dl2/d1/L0lDUmlTUSEhL3dHa0FKRnNBL1lCUlp3QSEhL2Vu/.

Saudi Stock Exchange “Tadawul”, *Tick Size*, (November 12, 2015), http://www.tadawul.com.sa/static/pages/en/TickSize/TickSize.html.

The Capital Market Authority, *Investor Awareness Center*, (November 12, 2015) http://www.cma.org.sa/en/IA/Pages/default.aspx.

The Global Investor/ISF, *Middle East Awards 2015: Winners Announced*, (November 2, 2015), http://www.globalinvestormagazine.com/Article/3502629/Middle-East-Awards-2015-Winners-announced.html.

The International Organization of Securities Commissions, *About IOSCO*, (November 12, 2015) http://www.iosco.org/about/.

The International Organization of Securities Commissions, *Current Signatories and Members Listed on Appendix B*, (November 12, 2015) http://www.iosco.org/library/index.cfm?section = mou_siglist#AnnexB.

The International Organization of Securities Commissions, *Fact Sheet* (October 2015), http://www.iosco.org/about/pdf/IOSCO-Fact-Sheet.pdf.

The International Organization of Securities Commissions, *IOSCO Annual Report* (2010).

The International Organization of Securities Commissions, *IOSCO Expands its Global Membership to Include Iceland, the Maldives, Saudi Arabia and Syria*, Media Release IOSCO/MR/09/2010, Montreal (June 9, 2010).

The International Organization of Securities Commissions, *Objectives and Principles of Securities Regulation* (June 2010).

The Ministry of Commerce and Industry, *Historical Overview*, (November 12, 2015), http://www.mci.gov.sa/en/AboutMinistry/Pages/HistoricalOverview.aspx.

The Saudi Stock Exchange "Tadawul", *The Saudi Stock Exchange Voted MENA Exchange of the Year at Global Investor/ISF MENA Awards 2015*, (October 31, 2015), http://www.tadawul.com.sa/wps/portal/!ut/p/c1/04_SB8K8xLLM9MSSzPy8xBz9CP0os3g_A-ewIE8TIwN_D38LA09vV7NQP8cQQ3dnA6B8JJK8e0CYqYGniU-wUXCAl7GBpxEB3X4e-bmp-sGJRfoFuRHlAP-C3us!/dl2/d1/L0lHSkovd0RNQUZrQUVnQSEhL1lCWncvZW4!/?PRESS_REL_NO = 4472.

The United States Securities and Exchange Commission, *Closed-End Fund Information*, (December 31, 2015), https://www.sec.gov/answers/mfclose.htm.

The United States Securities and Exchange Commission, *Mutual Funds*, (December 31, 2015), https://www.sec.gov/answers/mutfund.htm.

II. Secondary Sources

[A] Books

Alashre, Saad Hamad, *Alasahom Oa Asoag Almaal: Doroos Fi Alastathmar [Stocks and Capital Markets: Lessons in Investment]* (Arabian Printing and Publishing House 2004).

Aldakeel, Abdulaziz Mohammed, *Altanmih Alagtsadih Fi Almamlkh Alarabia Alsaodih: Soag Alashom Alsaudih Bina Aldairh Alhokomih Oa Aldairh Albankeih Oa Ehtkar Algallh [Economic Development in the Kingdom of Saudi Arabia, Saudi Stock Market among Government Administration, Banks, and Oligopoly]*, (Dar Alsaqi Press 2012).

Aldakeel, Abdulaziz Mohammed, *Soag Alasahom Alsaodi: Geraah Tarekeeh Oa Estashraf Almostagbl [Saudi Stock Market: Reading the History and an Anticipation the Future]* (Dar Alfarabi 2010).

Aldsogi, Alsaid Ibrahem, *Almoasherat Alalmih Llasahom Ma Insha Moasher Kas Belasahom Alsaodih, [Global Stock Indicators with the Creation of a Special Index for Saudi Stocks]*(King Saud University 1989).

Alhadad, Radi Saleh, *Daorat Alastathmar Fi Alaorag Almaleah: Grarat Ethafeh [Cycle Investment in Securities: Extra Decisions]* (Riyadh Business 1992).

Alhamidi, Abdulrahman Abdullah & Abdulrahman Abdulmohsen Alkalaf, *Alnagood Oa Albonok Oa Alasoag Almalih [Money, Banks, and Capital Markets]*, (Alfarazdak Press Company 2009).

Alhwimani, Fahad, *Almal Oa Alastthmar Fi Alasoag Almalih [Money and Investment in Capital Markets]*, (Dar Alhilal Offset Printing Press 2006).

Aljamal, Hisham, *Financial Markets and Financial Institutions*, (Majmaah University 2013).

Aljazira Capital, *The Financing Role of the Saudi Capital Market* (Research Department 2010).

Aljuhane, Eid Masoud, *Alastathmar Bi Alasaho Fi Alsoug Alsaudi [The Investment in Stocks in the Saudi Market]* (Alsharif Publication 1989).

Aljuhani, Hamdi Hamzah, *Azamat Soag Alasahom 2006 Enthar Fiah Daoah Llaslah [The Stock Market Crisis in 2006 is a Warning and a Call for Reforming]* (Obekan Printing and Packaging 2006).

Alkholifey, Ahmed, *The Saudi Arabian Stock Market: Efficient Market Hypothesis and Investors Behavior* (PhD Thesis, Colorado State University 2000).

Almadi, Mohammed Atta, *Dor Alhaiah Alammh Le Soag Almal Fi Hemait Aglet Almosahemen Fi Alsharekat Almosahemah, [The Role of the General Authority of the Capital Market in Protecting the Minority of Shareholders in Joint Stock Companies*], (Maktabt Alganon Oa Alagtsad 2012).

Alrafii, Mohammed Tanweer, *Segar Almostathmareen Oa Daor Haiat Soag Almal Fi Hemaitahm, [The Small Investors and the Role of the Capital Market Authority to Protect Them]*, (Dar Alnahathah Alarabia 2007).

Al-Razeen, Abdullah Mohamed, *the Weak-Form Efficiency of the Saudi Stock Market* (PhD Thesis, University of Leicester 1997).

Alrozain, Abdullah Mohammed, *Souq Almal* [*The Capital Market*], (Imam Muhammad Ibn Saud Islamic University 2006).

Alsirefi, Mohammed, *Alborasat (Exchanges*] (Dar Alfakar Aljamae 2007).

Alsuhaibani, Mohammed Ibrahim, *Aalaiat Almogasah Oa Altasaoih Fi Alasoag Almalih [Clearing and Settlement Mechanisms in Financial Markets]*, (Dar Kanoze Eshbilia Press 2009).

Alsuraiseri, Ahmed Sulaiman, *Saana Alsoag Aldoalih Fi Tadawul Alasahom Almahaleeh, [The Maker of International Market in Trading the Local Stocks]* (King Fahad National Library, 2008).

Azzam, Henry T, *The Emerging Arab Capital Markets: Investment Opportunities in Relatively Underplayed Markets* (Kegan Paul International 1997).

Bagdadi, Khalid Abdulaziz, *Tadawal Alashom Oa Alquod Aloardah Aliha Fi Alntham Alsaudi* [*Stocks Trading and the Restrictions on Them in the Saudi System*], (Maktabt Alganon Oa Alagtsad 2012).

Falmban, Ghazi Mahfoth, *Alastathmar Balasahom Fi Almamlakh Alharabia Alsaodiah* [*Investment in Stocks in the Kingdom of Saudi Arabia*], (Tihama Publications 1986).

Hammad, Adli Ali, *Mosoat Gaoanin Soag Almal Alsaoadi* [*Laws Encyclopedia of the Saudi Capital Market*], (King Fahad National Library 2013).

Hindi, Munir Ibrahim, *Alaorag Almaleih Oa Asoag Almal, [Securities and Capital Markets]*, (Monshat Almaraf Press 2007).

Kafi, Mostafa Yousef, *Borsat Alaorag Almalih, [Securities Exchange]*, (Dar Moasasat Raslan for Printing, Publishing, and Distributing 2009) 31.

Masari, Abdulsabor Abdulkawi, *Altantheem Alganoni Le Haokmat Alsharekat, [The Legal Regulation of the Corporate Governance]*, (Maktabt Alganon Oa Alagtsad 2012).

Niblock, Tim, & Monica Malik, *The Political Economy of Saudi Arabia* (Routledge 2007).

Norton, Joseph Jude, *Financial Sector Law Reform in Emerging Economies* (The British Institute of International and Comparative Law and the London Institute of International Banking, Finance and Development Law 2000).

Ramady, Mohammed A, *The Saudi Arabian Economy, Policies, Achievements, and Challenges* (2nd ed. 2010).

SAMBA, *The Saudi Stock Market: Structural Issues, Recent Performance and Outlook* (SAMBA Economics Department 2009).

Shatnawi, Zakaria Salamah, *Alathar Alagtsadih Lasoag Alaorag Almalih Men Manthor Alagtsad Alaslami [the Economic Effects of the Securities Markets from the Perspective of Islamic Economy]*, (Dar Alnafaes for Publishing and Distributing 2009).

[B] Articles

Al Ashikh, Abdullah I., *Testing the Weak-Form of Efficient Market Hypothesis and the Day-Of-The-Week Effect in Saudi Stock Exchange: Linear Approach*, 8 Int'l Rev. Bus. Res. Papers 27 (2012).

Al-Ajmi, Jasim & J.H. Kim, *Are Gulf Stock Markets Efficient? Evidence from New Multiple Variance Ratio Tests*, 44 Applied Econ. 1737 (2012).

Al-Aqeel, Mohammad & Nasser Spear, *Private Information Trading in Emerging Markets: Evidence from GCC Security Markets*, paper presented at Nadoat Sobal Tatuair Almohasab [Ways to Develop Accounting Conference], 11th Meeting, Riyadh (December 5-6, 2006).

Albidane, Ayman Ezzat, *Asoag Alaorag Almalih Fi Almamlakh Alarabia Alsaodih: Daragt Tatorah Oa Enftaha Alarabi Oa Emkanit Rabtaha Balasoag Almalih Alarabiah, [Stock Markets in Saudi Arabia: Their Openness and the Their Possibility of Liking them with Arab Stock Markets]*, 12(3) The Arab Magazine for Management (1988).

Alfaiz, Khalid Mohammed, *Dor Soag Alaorag Almaliah Fi Tadaoir Alsoag Almali Fi Almamlakh Alarabiah Alsaodiah,[the Role of Capital Market in Developing the Financial Market in the Kingdom of Saudi Arabia]*, the 15th Annual Meeting of Saudi Economic Association in Cooperation with Saudi Capital Market Authority (November 13-15, 2005).

Alfaro, Laura, et al., *FDI and Economic Growth: The Role of Local Financial Markets*, 64 J. Int'l Econ. 89 (2004).

Al-Ghamidi, Abdulsalam S., Thababiat Enhiar Soag Almal Alsaodiah Aam 2006 Oathar Alada Almali Llsharikah Almosahemah *[the Fogginess of Saudi Stock Market Crash 2006 and the Effect of Firm's Financial Performance]*, 13 the Arab J. Acct. 86 (2010).

Alhadad, Radi Saleh, *Ektbar Alaomel Almoathrah Ala Aoaid Ashom Alsharikat Alsaodiah Almosahemh, [Examine the Effecting factors on Dividends of Saudi Joint-Stock Companies]* (Master Thesis, King Abdulaziz University 1990).

Alshammary, Meshaal J., *Stock Market Development and Economic Growth in Developing Countries: Evidence from Saudi Arabia*, 11 Corp. Ownership & Control 193 (2014).

Al-Twaijry, Abdulrahman A., *Saudi Stock Market Historical View and Crisis Effect: Graphical and Statistical Analysis*, 34 J. Human Sciences 1 (2007).

Asiri, Batool Kasim & Hamad Alzeera, *Is the Saudi Stock Market Efficient? A Case of Weak-Form Efficiency*, 4 Res. J. Fin. & Acct. 35 (2013).

Beach, Joseph W., *The Saudi Arabian Capital Market Law: A Practical Study of the Creation of Law in Developing Markets*, 41 Stan. J. Int'l L. 307 (2005).

Bekaert, Geert & Campbell R. Harvey, *Capital Markets: An Engine for Economic Growth*, 5 Brown J. World Aff. 33 (1998).

Boubakari, Ake & Dehuan Jin, *The Role of Stock Market Development in Economic Growth: Evidence from Some Euronext Countries*, 1 Int'l J. Fin. Res. 14 (2010).

Butler, Kirt C & S Jamal Malaikah, *Efficiency and Inefficiency in Thinly Traded Stock Markets: Kuwait and Saudi Arabia*, 16 J. Banking & Fin. 197 (1992).

Donboli, John, *Doing Business in the Middle East: A Primer for U.S. Companies*, 38 Cornell Int'l L.J. 413 (2005).

Elango, Rengasamy & Mohammed Ibrahim Hussein, *An Empirical Analysis on the Weak-Form Efficiency of the GCC Markets Applying Selected Statistical Tests*, 4 Int'l Rev. Bus. Res. Papers 140 (2008).

Jamaani, Fouad & Eduardo Roca, *Are the Regional Gulf Stock Markets Weak-Form Efficient as Single Stock Markets and as a Regional Stock Market?*, 33 Res. Int'l Bus. & Fin. 221 (2014).

Kapal, Wadea, *Hoal Tatoir Soug Alasahom Oa Mostagblah [About the Development of Stock Market and Its Future]*, 230 Alagtasad Magazine 22 (July 1992).

Khababa, Nourredine, *Behavior of Stock Prices in the Saudi Arabian Financial Market: Empirical Research Findings*, 11 J. Fin. Mgmt. & Analysis 48 (1998).

Levine, Ross & Sara Zervos, *Stock Markets, Banks, and Economic Growth*, 88 Am. Econ. Rev. 537 (1998).

Onour, Ibrahim A., *Testing Efficiency Performance of Saudi Stock Market*, 23 JKAU:Econ. & Admin. 15 (2009).

Saleh, Moftah & Maarfi Fareedah, *Motatalabat Kafaat Soug Alaorag Almalieh: Derasah Leoaka Asoag Alaorag Almalieh Alarabiah Oa Sobal Rafa Kafataha [the Requirements for the Securities Market Efficiency: A Study of the Reality of Arabian Capital Markets and How to Promote Their Efficiency]*, 7 El-Bahith Rev. 192 (2010).

[C] News

Alaqrara, Abdulaziz, *Soag Alasaho Toang Altuwaijri Belaon Alakdar Oalmostathmoron entathron Gararat Alraees Aljadid [the Saudi Stock Market is Hugging*

Altuwaijri by the Green Color, and Investors Are Waiting the New President's Decisions] Alriyadh Newspaper, May 14, 2006, http://www.alriyadh.com/154289.

Albashari, Ali, *Kobara: Tantheem Estathmar Alsharikat Alsaodih Fi Soag Alasahom Ohaviz Nashatah Alraiasiah [Experts: Regulating the Investment of Saudi Companies in the Stock Market Stimulates their Main Businesses Activities]*, Alsharq Al-Awsat News, January 28, 2006, http://awsat-a.com/details.asp?section = 6& article = 345409&issueno = 9923#.VIDeR74kNUQ.

Al-Nwaisir, Sami, *Saudi Stock Market Needs to Be Reformed*, Arab News, January 11, 2012, http://www.eurasiareview.com/11012012-saudi-stock-market-needs-to-be-reformed-oped/.

Alsultan, Abdulrahman Mohammed, *Fogah Jadidah Tatakon Fi Soag Alashom Alsaodiah [New Bubble Is Forming in the Saudi Stock Market]*, Al Eqtisadiah Newspaper, July 3, 2006, http://www.aleqt.com/2006/07/03/article_5702.html.

Saudi Stock Exchange Approved, BBC News, June 17, 2003, http://news.bbc.co.uk/2/hi/business/2998086.stm.

Sharkawy, Hazem, & Munira Almoshkas, *Amar Malake: Eafa Al-Suhaimi Oatakaleef Altuwaijri Beraasat Haiat Soag Almal [Royal Decree: Relieve Al-Suhaimi from His Duties and Appointed Altuwaijri to Be the Head of the Capital Market Authority]*, Aljazirah Newspaper, 13 May, 2006, http://www.al-jazirah.com/2006/20060513/ec1t.htm.

Tatbeeg Oahadat Altagaior Aljadidh Leasar Alasahom Bada Esboa Ofaga 3 Netagat Tatoafag Ma Alasoag Alalamih [Applying a New Tick Size for Stock Prices After a Week According to 3 Bands Which Are Congruence with Global Markets], Alriyadh Newspaper, September 4, 2008, http://www.alriyadh.com/371886.

CHAPTER 3

Developing an Effective Securities Dispute Resolution Mechanism

SUMMARY

Shari'ah courts have a general jurisdiction to hear almost all disputes in Saudi Arabia and resolve them by referring to principles embedded in *Shari'ah* and enacted laws. There are certain disagreements, however, that cannot be resolved in this manner. Securities law matters are an example. The Kingdom has tasked the Committee for the Resolution of Securities Disputes ("CRSD") with jurisdiction over securities-related matters. But there are serious questions about the CRSD's independence, given its financial and administrative ties to the "CMA." The new Judiciary Law of 2007 partially put these questions to rest, but that Law has not yet been fully implemented. Therefore, an arguably nonindependent CRSD continues to function. This chapter examines securities disputes resolution methods, as well as the CRSD's constitutionality given the apparent conflict between the CML and the Basic Law of Governance.

§3.01 INTRODUCTION

Saudi Arabian law, as is the case with the laws of many other predominately Muslim countries, has deep religious roots. The *Qur'an* and the *Sunnah* are much more than a moral compass: they are at the heart of the judicial system. While this structure is effective in many respects, the *Shari'ah* courts struggle to deal with commercial and financial issues that are not fully addressed in these holy works or are not compliant with *Shari'ah* Law.

Historically, the Kingdom has dealt with this issue by creating quasi-judicial committees to hear disputes that arise in specific contexts. For example, the Committee of Security Disputes Resolution ("CRSD") was tasked with matters that involve the capital market. A glaring weakness of the CRSD was that it was effectively part of the

"CMA." This issue is not unique, as many quasi-judicial committees share a similar structure: government ministries and agencies either directly or indirectly control them.

While the CMA does not control any aspect of the CRSD's day-to-day operations or have direct influence over its decisions, there are very close financial and administrative ties between the two. There are even some who question the CRSD's constitutionality, since its establishment in Article 25 of the "CML" appears to violate Article 46 of the Basic Law of Governance. Regardless, the seeming lack of judicial independence, especially in a specialized area such as securities law, affects public confidence in the system and may not provide an effective forum for dispute resolution. Meeting these challenges is crucial to further capital market development in the Kingdom. Although a new Judiciary Law was enacted in 2007 that is designed to address some of these problems, this Law has not yet been fully implemented.

This chapter examines the history of the Saudi judicial system, particularly as it applies to the capital market; discusses the quasi-judicial committees and their structure, with a focus on the CRSD; and, evaluates the constitutionality of this Committee.

§3.02 ROOTS OF ISLAMIC LAW IN THE SAUDI JUDICIAL SYSTEM

Saudi Arabia is the "heartland" of Islam,[1] and the majority of Saudis are Muslim.[2] In the KSA, *Shari'ah*, or Islamic Law, is the paramount body of law.[3] *Shari'ah* Law is a collection of fundamental principles derived from a number of different sources.[4] These sources of *Shari'ah* comprise two primary and three secondary sources. The *Qur'an* and *Sunnah* are the two primary sources of *Shari'ah*.[5] The three secondary sources are *Consensus* of the legal scholars, deduction from analogy, and *Ijtihad*, the use of individual reasoning by those scholars.[6]

The *Qur'an* is the Muslim Holy Book, and it is considered as the verbatim word of God. This source is continuous and unchangeable. Most of the *Qur'an* principles and rules are general sayings and guidelines without specific details.[7] For example, one verse in the *Qur'an* says: "O you who have believed, fulfill all contracts."[8] Another

1. The Kingdom is the heartland of Islam because it is the birthplace of Islam history, the site of the two Holy Mosques, and the focus of Islamic devotion and prayer. The Royal Embassy of Saudi Arabia in Washington, DC, *Saudi Arabia: Islam's Heartland,* (Nov. 12, 2015), http://www.saudiembassy.net/about/country-information/Islam/saudi_arabia_Islam_heartland.aspx.
2. Janet K. Mullin Marta, et al., *Some Important Factors Underlying Ethical Decisions of Middle-Eastern Marketers*, 21 Int'l Marketing Rev. 53, 55 (2004); Central Intelligence Agency, *The World Factbook, Middle East: Saudi Arabia,* (Nov. 12, 2015), https://www.cia.gov/library/publications/the-world-factbook/geos/sa.html.
3. Latham & Watkins, *Doing Business in Saudi Arabia 2* (Latham & Watkins 2010).
4. *Id.*
5. Frederick V. Perry, *Shari'ah, Islamic Law and Arab Business Ethics*, 22 Conn. J. Int'l L. 357, 365 (2007).
6. *Id.*
7. Abdulallah Mohammed Almullh & Essat Shahatah Karrar, *Alnezam Almale Oalaqtasadi Fi Alaslam 28[Financial and Economic System in Islam 28],* (Husseini Modern Press, 3rd ed. 2006).
8. The *Qur'an, Surat Almaidah*, verse 1.

example is that "O you, who have believed, when you contract a debt for a specified term, write it down."[9] These verses, and more, discuss principles and rules in the life of the economy without explaining these principles and its procedures, or how they should be implemented on a day-to-day basis. The *Qur'an* left the explanation to the *Sunnah*.

The *Sunnah*, which is the written record of the way the Prophet Mohammed led his life and practiced his faith, is the second primary source of *Shari'ah*.[10] The *Sunnah* is comprised of the sayings and deeds of the Prophet Mohammed. It generally emphasizes the principles in the *Qur'an*, explains them, specifies them, or adds new principles and rules that are not in the *Qur'an*.[11]

An example of the *Sunnah* is this saying from the Prophet Muhammad: "The seller and the buyer have the right to keep or return goods as long as they have not parted. If both parties speak the truth and point out the defects and qualities [of the goods], then they will be blessed in their transaction. But if they tell lies or hide something, then the blessings of their transaction will be destroyed."[12]

Consensus is the first of the secondary sources in the *Shari'ah* Law. It can be defined as an agreement among scholars in the same era after the death of Prophet Muhammad, regarding a particular problem in *Shari'ah*.[13] There was a need to create a new source of *Shari'ah* Law after the death of Prophet Muhammad to cover new topics that come up in life.[14] The *consensus* cannot be contrary to the primary sources, the *Qur'an* and the *Sunnah*, and it depends on them. The idea of *consensus* is to have an answer to a problem and to share the responsibility among scholars, instead of one scholar who may get the answer wrong.[15]

The fourth source of *Shari'ah* Law is *Qiyas*, which means to transform something undecided into something that is decided, because these two things are similar in their reasoning. For example, the *Qur'an* prohibits drinking wine. However, there is nothing in the *Qur'an* that prohibits other alcoholic drinks. Yet, the reasoning to prohibit drinking wine is intoxication. Both wines and other alcoholic drinks have similar intoxicating properties. Since there is similarity in the reasoning, alcoholic drinks generally are prohibited by *Qiyas*.

Finally, *Ijtihad* is the fifth source of *Shari'ah* Law. *Ijtihad* is an Arabic term, which literally means to "exert oneself."[16] It is the concept of exerting one's judgment within the scope of free thought and individual opinion, so long as that opinion does not

9. The *Qur'an, Surat Al-Baqarah*, verse 282.
10. Perry, *supra* n. 5, at 365.
11. Almullh, *supra* n. 7, at 29.
12. Mohammed Zohair Alnasser, *Sahih Al-Bukari 58 [the Authenticity of Al-Bukari 58]*, (Dar Toag Alnajat 2001). Sahih Al-Bukari is a collection of *Sunnah* conducted by Mohammed Al-Bukari in the 800 century, and the majority of Muslims recognizes this collection as the most authentic collection of *Sunnah*.
13. Abbas Shoman, *Massader Al-Tashri'e Al-Eslamy 63 [the Sources of Islamic Legislation 63]*, (Aldar Althgafih Press 2000).
14. Wahba Alzuhaily, *Asuol Alfaqh Alaslami 486 [Principles of Islamic Jurisprudence* 486], (Dar Alfiker 1986).
15. *Id.*
16. Hisham M. Ramadan, *Understanding Islamic Law From Classical to Contemporary* 5 (Rowman and Littlefield Publisher 2006).

contravene the plain meaning and spirit of *Shari'ah*.[17] Islamic scholars are expected to reason within the scope of the spirit and principles of *Shari'ah* in all circumstances.

In addition to the *Shari'ah*, enacted legislation is also part of the Saudi Arabian legal system.[18] However, these laws cannot conflict with the *Shari'ah*.[19] Thus, all Saudi laws, including laws that are related to the capital market, are subject to the compliance with the *Shari'ah*, and *Shari'ah* courts must apply the *Qur'an*, the *Sunnah*, and enacted laws by the government that do not conflict with *Shari'ah* Law.[20]

§3.03 THE JUDICIAL SYSTEM IN THE KINGDOM

The judicial system in Saudi Arabia has been reformed and developed over the years since the foundation of the Kingdom.[21] After its establishment in 1970,[22] the Ministry of Justice has worked to further develop the judicial system through the proposal of a new judiciary law.[23] The Law of Judiciary[24] was enacted in 1975: this Act reformed the legal system in the Kingdom by adding new courts levels,[25] defining the jurisdictions of each court, and ensuring explicitly for the first time the independence of the judiciary and its guarantees in Chapter One of the Law.[26] *Shari'ah* courts have a general jurisdiction over all disputes and crimes except claims that their jurisdictions have been granted to other judicial bodies, such as the Board of Grievances.[27]

17. *Id.*
18. Latham & Watkins, *Doing Business in Saudi Arabia, supra* n. 3, at 2.
19. *Id.*
20. The Law of Procedure Before *Shari'ah* Courts, Article 1, Royal Decree No. M/1, dated 22/1/1435 (Nov. 25, 2013). Moreover, Article 48 of the Basic Law of Governance states "the Courts shall apply rules of the Islamic *Shari'ah* in cases that are brought before them, according to the Holy Qur'an and the Sunna, and according to laws which are decreed by the ruler in agreement with the Holy Qur'an and the Sunna." The Basic Law of Governance, Royal Decree No. A/90, dated 27/8/1412 H (Mar. 2, 1992).
21. For more details about the development of the judicial system in Saudi Arabia, *See* Suliman Alsalim, *Altantheem Algadai Fi Almamlakah Alarabiah Alsaodiah 3[the Judicial Regulation in the Kingdom of Saudi Arabia 3]*, (Institute of Public Administration 1971); Abdurahman Abdulaziz Algasam, *Alnedam Algadai Aleslami Mogaranan Bealndam Algadai Alodai Oatatbegah Fi Almamlakh Alarabiah Alsaodiah 582 [the Islamic Judicial System Comparing by the Enacted Laws and Applying them in the Kingdom of Saudi Arabia 582]*, (Alsaadah Press 1973); Mohammed Barak Alfozan, *Altantheem Algadai Aljadid Fi Almamlakah Alarabiah Alsaodiah 53 [The New Judicial Regulation in the Kingdom of Saudi Arabia 53]*, (Maktabt Alganon Oa Alagtsad 2010).
22. Royal Decree No. A/105, dated 21/7/1390 (Sep. 9, 1970).
23. Ali Ramadan Ali Barakat, *Aloaseed Fi Sharah Nedam Algada Alsaoadi Aljadid 20 [The Mediator in Explaining the New Saudi Judicial Law 20]*, (Maktabt Alganon Oa Alagtsad 2014).
24. The Law of Judiciary, Royal Decree No. M/64, dated 14/7/1395 H (Jul. 23, 1970).
25. According to Article 5 of the Law of Judiciary 1970, *Shari'ah* courts shall consist of: (a) the Supreme Judicial Council, (b) the Appellate Court, (c) General Courts, and (d) Summary Courts. The Law of Judiciary, Article 5 (1970).
26. Barakat, *supra* n. 23, at 20; Alfozan, *supra* n. 21, 76; Fadi Mohammed Ahmed Shaysha, *Altandaim Algadaei Aljadid Fi Almamlakah Alarabiah Alsaoudiah 240 [the New Judicial Regulation in the Kingdom of Saudi Arabia 240]* (Alrushd for Publishing and Distribution 2014).
27. The Law of Judiciary, Article 26 (1970).

In May 1982, the Law of the Board of Grievances[28] was enacted: it recognized the Board of Grievances to be an independent administrative judicial commission responsible directly to the King of Saudi Arabia. The Board of Grievances functions as an administrative court.[29] In addition to jurisdiction over administrative cases, Article 8 of the Law gave the Board jurisdiction over penal cases for forgery crimes and crimes mentioned in the Law of Combating Bribery and the Law of Handling Public Funds.[30] In 1987, the Council of Ministers issued a resolution to transfer the jurisdiction of the Settlement of Commercial Disputes Committees that set forth in laws and resolutions, including disputes related to the Law of Companies, to the Board of Grievances.[31] Later, in January 2003, the Council of Ministers issued a resolution to provide the Board of Grievances broader jurisdiction to rule in business cases until the establishment of commercial courts.[32]

The *Shari'ah* courts and the Board of Grievances are not the only judicial bodies in Saudi Arabia. Quasi-judicial committees first emerged in 1926, when the government established the Commercial Council in Jeddah to rule in issues arising among traders, as well as matters involving commercial and maritime affairs.[33] Since then, the number of quasi-judicial committees has increased dramatically to reach almost one hundred committees in Saudi Arabia.[34] These committees[35] are separate from the two branches, *Shari'ah* courts and the Board of Grievances.[36] Thus, the judicial system in the KSA is divided into three legal bodies: general judiciary, administrative judiciary, and quasi-judicial committees.[37]

In a theocratic society, the courts often struggle to deal with secular matters involving criminal laws and civil disputes. Saudi Arabia is no exception. In fact, the courts in the Kingdom have been criticized, by some, due to what these detractors see as overly rigid interpretation of the *Shari'ah* Laws by appointed judges, inadequate legal procedures, and red tape. In addition to these quantitative matters, the Kingdom's judicial system may have some qualitative issues as well. An acute shortage of qualified judges has created overburdened courts that are, in many ways, overwhelmed by the volume of cases. For example, ruling on a simple divorce or family law

28. The Law of the Board of Grievances, Royal Decree No. M/51, dated 17/7/1402 H (May 10, 1982).
29. Ayoub M. Al-Jarbou, *The Role of Traditionalists and Modernists on the Development of the Saudi Legal System*, 21 Arab L.Q. 191, 193(2007).
30. The Law of the Board of Grievances 1982, Article 8.
31. Council of Ministers' Resolution No. 241, dated 26/10/1407 (Jun. 23, 1987).
32. Council of Ministers' Resolution No. 261, dated 17/11/1423 (Jan. 20, 2003).
33. Alfozan, *supra* n. 21, at 76.
34. *See* Omer Alkoli, *Gada Altheel Oa Almahakm Alkafiah [The Shadow of Judiciary or the Hidden Courts]* (King Fahad National Library 2010).
35. Examples of these committees include Committee for the Resolution of Securities Disputes, the Committee for the Settlement of Banking Disputes, Committees for the Settlement of Labor Disputes, Commercial Paper Committee, investment disputes settlement committee, Committee for Combating Commercial Fraud, Insurance Committee, and the Committee for Reviewing Patent Disputes. For more details about quasi-judicial committees, *see* Legal Department in Riyadh Chamber of Commerce, *the Guide for Judicial Authorities in Saudi Arabia*, Chamber of Commerce (Institute of Public Administration 2006); Alkoli, *supra* n. 34.
36. Latham & Watkins, *Doing Business in Saudi Arabia, supra* n. 3, at 2.
37. Alkoli, *supra* n. 34, at 8.

matter may take years, and most all litigants experience significant delays because of red tape and a bloated bureaucracy.[38]

On October 1, 2007, the late King Abdullah issued a Royal Decree with two new laws, the Law of Judiciary (2007) and the Law of the Board of Grievances (2007).[39] These two new laws replace the 1975 Law of Judiciary and the 1982 Law of the Board of Grievances.[40] In addition to providing a new structure, other provisions in these laws address court specialization and judicial training, in an effort to decide cases more efficiently.[41] However, the Ministry of Justice is still in the process of implementing these two laws, and their application is being enforced gradually.[42] In order to implement these two laws perfectly, the King also allocated SAR 7 billon (USD 1.8 billion) – to improve and develop the entire judiciary in the Kingdom.[43]

Under the new Law of Judiciary, each court has a particular jurisdiction, which depends on the type of dispute. These specialized courts will have jurisdiction in only one or more kinds of disputes. According to Article 9 of the law, there will be general, criminal, personal status, commercial, and labor courts.[44] Moreover, the law allows litigation to be in two levels, a trial court and an appeal court,[45] to provide a more complete dispute resolution process.[46] Furthermore, the new Law of Judiciary establishes a Supreme Court for the first time.[47] Prior to enacting the new law, the Supreme Judicial Council had a judicial function, as an addition to its administrative and supervisory responsibilities.[48] The new law renamed the Supreme Judicial Council to be the Supreme Council for Judiciary and specified its responsibilities to be only the administration and supervision of the judiciary.[49]

The 2007 Law of the Board of Grievances restructured the Board by establishing the Administrative Judicial Council, which is similar to the Supreme Council for Judiciary.[50] The Board of Grievances will have jurisdiction only over administrative cases[51] and will function as an independent administrative judicial authority. Also, courts in the Board of Grievances will be in three levels, the Administrative Supreme

38. Joseph A. Kechichian, *Legal and Political Reforms in Saudi Arabia* 7-8 (Routledge, 2013).
39. The Law of Judiciary, Royal Decree No. M/78, dated 19/9/1427 H (Oct. 1, 2007); The Law of the Board of Grievances, Royal Decree No. M/78, dated 19/9/1427 H (Oct. 1, 2007).
40. The Law of Judiciary 2007, Article 85 (2007); The Law of the Board of Grievances 2007, Article 26 (2007).
41. Kechichian, *supra* n. 38, at 8.
42. Alfozan, *supra* n. 21, at 53.
43. *Alsaodiah: Garar Malakei Belmoafagah Ala Nethamain Algadah Oa Dewan Almadaleem, [Saudi Arabia: A Royal Decree Approving the Law of Judiciary and the Law of the Board of Grievance]*, Alsharq Al-Awsat News, Oct. 2, 2007, http://classic.aawsat.com/details.asp?article=439632&issueno=10535#.VIzA8r4kNUR.
44. The Law of Judiciary 2007, Article 9 (2007).
45. Under the old 1975 Law of Judiciary, appeal courts did not listen to litigants, and losing parties were not allowed to argue in person in appeals courts. Litigants could only file their briefs to an appeal court for review. Alfozan, *supra* n. 21, at 107.
46. Barakat, *supra* n. 23, at 24.
47. The Law of Judiciary 2007, Article 10 (2007).
48. The Law of Judiciary 1975, Article 8 (2007).
49. The Law of Judiciary 2007, Article 6 (2007).
50. The Law of the Board of Grievances 2007, Articles 4, 5 (2007).
51. *See Id.* at Articles 1, 13.

Court, administrative appeal courts, and the lower administrative courts.[52] The Board of Grievances no longer will have jurisdiction over business and crimes cases after the establishment of the specialized courts in the general judiciary.[53] However, commercial courts have not been established yet, and implementation by the Ministry of Justice has been slow since 2007 when the Law of Judiciary (2007) and the Law of the Board of Grievances (2007) were enacted.

§3.04 THE QUASI-JUDICIAL COMMITTEES

In the Saudi system, independent committees supplement the *Shari'ah* courts, Board of Grievances, and other judicial bodies. These quasi-judicial committees have increased over the years without any clear comprehensive regulation that defines these committees in one place.[54] Typically, enacted laws include an order to form a quasi-judicial committee in general, without specific details. The details regarding jurisdiction, litigation procedures, and committee members' appointments are left up to the related authorities or ministries.[55] Furthermore, these committees are not related to the Ministry of Justice, and have commercial, criminal, or administrative judicial jurisdictions.[56] How did these quasi-judicial committees come into being?

Some commentaries state that these committees were a result of the rapid developments in the Saudi economy, laws, and society. These effects made it necessary to find a quick solution that was easily implemented. Moreover, it was thought that these quasi-judicial committees would temporarily ease the burden on the *Shari'ah* courts and their judges, and the *Shari'ah* courts would resume jurisdiction when they were able to assume a larger caseload.[57]

However, others have a different view. They believe that the passive attitude of *Shari'ah* courts, coupled with their outright refusal to consider certain banking, insurance and other issues, led to the creation of these committees.[58] For example, even though interest on borrowed funds is prohibited by *Shari'ah* Law and the courts will not always enforce it in banking disputes, the Committee for the Settlement of Banking Disputes ("CSBD") typically looks only at the terms of the contract, and is willing to enforce them, regardless of whether or not the provision is consistent with

52. *Id.* at Article 8.
53. Alfozan, *supra* n. 21, at 112.
54. Alkoli, *supra* n. 34, at 8.
55. Fahad Hamoud, *Lejan Fad Almonazat Altaminih Oaallegan Shabah Algadaiah: Kaifa Takon Almogaranah [Committees for Insurance Disputes Resolution and Quasi-Judicial Committees: How to Compare?]*, Al Eqtisadiah Newspaper, Aug. 25, 2008, http://www.aleqt.com/2008/08/25/article_152200.html.
56. Naseer Zaid Aldaoud, *Aldaoud: Otalb Beahmal Oahadat Algada Oathag Fi Emkaniat Roat Almohkamah Aldostodiah Gariban [Aldaoud: I Call for the Realization of the Unity of Judicial Principle and I am Confident of the Possibility of Having the Constitutional Court Soon]*, Al Madina Newspaper, Oct. 28, 2011, http://www.al-madina.com/node/335460?risala.
57. *See* Abdullah Hammad Alrashed, *Alegan That Alektsas Algadai* 9-10 [*Quasi-Judicial Committees* 9-10] (Institute of Public Administration 1985); Abdurahman Aiad, *Osoal Elam Algada: Gaoaid Almorafahat* 235-39 [*Judicial Principles: Procedures Rules* 235-39] (Institute of Public Administration 1985); Aldaoud, *supra* n. 56.
58. Al-Jarbou, *supra* n. 29, at 223.

Shari'ah Law. In practical terms, then, the CSBD may put the agreement of the parties on a higher plane than *Shari'ah* Law, at least as far as the contract is concerned.[59] Because of this conflict, there was the necessity of finding an alternative judiciary. In the Saudi system, the quasi-judicial committees are this alternative judiciary.

The fact that these committees exist outside the general judicial jurisdictions has some negative impacts in the judicial system in the KSA. The sheer number of these committees leads to overlap in cases, which, in turn, leads to the possible conflict of jurisdictions among these committees and the general judiciary.[60] Moreover, these committees lack both judicial immunity and judicial independence, which are key components in a country's judicial system.[61] Most of these committees are unstable, because their members usually work in these committees as part-time jobs.[62] Furthermore, many parties are unaware of the procedures to litigate before these committees, because almost every committee has unique procedures. These unknown procedures lead to error and delay, thus wasting the time of both litigants and committee members.[63] Also, most of these committees have only one location, which creates a significant hardship for people to come to these committees from all over the Kingdom.[64] Most importantly, the Ministry of Justice and the Supreme Council for Judiciary do not monitor or have authority over these committees, weakening the judicial system and its authority in the Kingdom.[65] Instead, these committees are regulated and overseen by an executive body such as the CMA, SAMA, and the Ministry of Commerce.

To overcome the drawbacks of the quasi-judicial committees, it was necessary to join them to specialized courts under the general judiciary, thus allowing the Ministry of Justice and the Supreme Council for Judiciary to have proper supervisory oversight. In fact, this necessity has been evident for over three decades, even inside the government itself. As far back as 1981, the Council of Ministers issued a resolution to establish specialized courts for commercial, labor, and traffic disputes.[66] But these specialized courts have not been established, while the number of committees increased. The 2007 Law of Judiciary reaffirmed the commitment to the establishment of

59. Michael J.T. McMillen, *Islamic Shari'ah-Compliant Project Finance: Collateral Security and Financing Structure Case Studies*, 24 Fordham Int'l Law J. 1184, 1197 (2001).
60. Abdulmoniem Abdulazeem Jeirah, *Dorose Fi Altantheem Algadai Oalagtesaas* 35-36 [*Lessons in Judicial and Jurisdiction Regulation* 35-36], (Institute of Public Administration 1986).
61. Abdulaziz Abdullah Hassan Al-Shaikh, *Lamahat Hoala Algada Fi Almamlakah Alarabia Alsaodiah* 143 [*Overview About the Judiciary in the Kingdom of Saudi Arabia* 143], (Dar Alshabal for Publishing, Printing, and Distribution 1991); Mahmoud Mohammed Hashim, *Algada Onedam Alethbat Fi Alfagah Aleslame Oalanzemmah Aloadaiah 48 [the Judiciary and the Prove System in Islamic Jurisprudence and Enacted Laws 48]*, (King Saud University Press 1988); Jeirah, *supra* n. 60, at 35; Nasser Mohammed Alghamdi, *Alegtsas Algadai Fi Alfagah Aleslame 144 [The Jurisdiction in Islamic Jurisprudence 144]*, (Alrushd for Publishing and Distribution 2000).
62. Mohammed Mustafa Alzoheily, *Altandeem Algadai Fi Alfagah Aleslami 118-119 [Judicial Regulation in the Islamic Jurisprudence 118-119]* (Dar Alfakar 1982); Mahmoud Mohammed Hashim at 48; Alghamdi, *supra* n. 61, at 144.
63. Alghamdi, *supra* n. 61, at 144.
64. *Id.* at 144-45.
65. Alzoheily, *supra* n. 62, at 118-19; Alghamdi, *supra* n. 61, at 144.
66. Council of Ministers' Resolution No. 167, dated 14/9/1401 (Jul. 16, 1981).

specialized courts.[67] In 2014, the Ministry of Justice set up personal status courts in various cities in the Kingdom, and the Ministry is in the process of establishing the other new specialized courts.[68]

Under the Mechanism for Enforcing the 2007 New Law of Judiciary and the 2007 Law of the Board of Grievances,[69] the jurisdictions for all quasi-judicial committees for criminal cases, commercial and civil disputes will be transferred to the specialized courts in the general judiciary.[70] However, committees that are related to the capital market, banks, and customs are exempted from the transfer. For example, the CRSD and the Appeal Committee for the Resolution Securities Disputes are specifically exempted. Instead, the Supreme Council for Judiciary is legally required to conduct a comprehensive study about status of these exempted committees, and report its findings within one year, in order to complete the regulation procedures.[71] At this point, it is not clear whether the Supreme Council for Judiciary has conducted the study or not, and whether these exempted committees will continue to have an exempt status.[72]

It is important to accelerate the implementation of the 2007 Law of Judiciary and to establish commercial courts that have jurisdiction over all commercial cases, including capital market and banking disputes, because these bodies should have the power to make independent decisions. To better understand where the quasi-judicial committees need to be, we should first examine these bodies as they are presently constituted. The CRSD is a fairly typical example, and an excellent vehicle for further analysis.

§3.05 THE COMMITTEE FOR THE RESOLUTION OF SECURITIES DISPUTES ("CRSD")

Securities disputes require qualified professionals and specialists to deal with securities cases, because these disputes are complicated and require an extensive background in securities to deal with and resolve securities cases. Therefore, Article 25 of the CML requires the CMA to establish the Committee for the Resolution of Securities Disputes.[73]

67. The Law of Judiciary 2007, Article 9.
68. Hamad Alfaraj, *Wazeer Aladal Uodashen Manazomat Almahakem Almotakasesah Fi Almamlaka [Minister of Justice will Establish the Specialized Courts in the Kingdom: Tuesday]*, Sabq Newspaper, Aug. 17, 2014, http://sabq.org/EFigde.
69. The Mechanism for Enforcing the New Law of Judiciary and The Law of the Board of Grievances, Royal Decree No. M/78, dated 19/9/1427 H (Oct. 1, 2007).
70. *Id.* section 1, Article 9-1.
71. *Id.* section 3, Article 2.
72. Majed Mohammed Garoub, *Alejan Shebah Algadaiah [Quasi-Judicial Committees]*, Okaz Newspaper, Jul. 31, 2013, http://www.okaz.com.sa/new/mobile/20130731/Con20130731624581.htm.
73. A part of Article 25(a) of the CML states that the Authority shall establish a committee known as the "Committee for the Resolution of Securities Disputes". Capital Market Law, Article 25(a) (2003).

[A] Formation

As distinguished from *Shari'ah* courts, the CRSD consist of legal advisors who specialize in the doctrine of transactions and capital markets, along with experts in commercial and financial affairs and securities.[74] The Law gives the Board of the CMA power to appoint the members of the Committee for a renewable three-year term.[75] The capital market cases operate on a two-tier system, with initial cases before the Committee and appeals before the Appeal Panel.

According to Article 25(g) of the CML, the Appeal Panel is formed by a Council of Ministers' decision, and the Appeal Panel has three members representing the Ministry of Finance, the Ministry of Commerce and Industry and the Bureau of Experts at the Council of Ministers for a renewable three-year term.[76] The same Article stipulates that the members of the Committee must not have any direct or indirect financial or commercial interest in the suit brought before the Committee, or have a family relationship up to the fourth degree with the parties to the complaint.[77]

[B] Jurisdiction and Procedure

The CRSD has sole and exclusive jurisdiction over any dispute, with respect to public and private actions, that arises under the CML, implementing regulations, and the regulations, rules and instructions issued by the CMA and Tadawul.[78] Article 25 of the Law gives the CRSD all necessary powers to investigate and settle complaints and suits, including the power to issue subpoenas, issue decisions, impose sanctions, and order the production of evidence and documents.[79]

Moreover, this Committee has jurisdiction over claims against decisions and actions taken by the CMA, Tadawul, or any other agency, and also has the right to issue a decision awarding damages, order a return to a prior state of affairs, or issue another decision as appropriate that would guarantee the rights of the aggrieved party.[80]

A complaint must be filed first with the CMA and lodged there for ninety days before it is brought to the CRSD, unless the CMA agrees and approves an expedited proceeding.[81] The idea behind this waiting period is to give the parties an opportunity to amicably resolve their disputes before they ask the CRSD to intervene, thus reducing the litigation volume.[82] Furthermore, once a complaint is presented to the CRSD, the

74. Capital Market Law, Article 25(b) (2003).
75. *Id.* Article 25(b).
76. *Id.* Article 25(g).
77. *Id.* Article 25(b).
78. Tadawul is the name of the Saudi Stock Exchange.
79. Capital Market Law, Article 25(a) (2003).
80. *Id.* Article 25(c).
81. *Id.* Article 25(e).
82. Mohammed Alkhaldi, *Lagnata Alfasal Mostaglatan Ola Takthan Letatherat Hiat Alsoag Almaleih [The CRSD Committee and the Appeal Panel are Independent, and the Capital Market Authority Has No Influence Upon them]*, Aljazira Newspaper, Jun. 8, 2011, http://www.al-jazirah.com.sa/20110608/ec5d.htm.

Committee must begin considering the complaint or suit within fourteen days from the day of filling.[83]

Decisions from the Committee may be appealed before the Appeal Panel within thirty days from the notification date.[84] The Appeal Panel can refuse to review the matter, affirm the CRSD's decision, or conduct a *de novo* review and issue an appropriate decision concerning the complaint.[85] More importantly, the Appeal Panel decisions are final and cannot be the subject of any further judicial review.[86]

On January 23, 2011, the CMA issued the Resolution of Securities Disputes Proceedings Regulations.[87] It aims to regulate and to facilitate the litigation procedures in securities before the CRSD Committee and the Appeal Panel.[88] This step is intended to protect the interests and rights of investors and all market participants; and, thus, to promote justice and transparency in the securities litigations.

Another recent change took place effective on December 31, 2014 when a High Order transferred authority for the investigation and prosecution of criminal offenses to the Bureau of Investigation and Public Prosecution ("BIPP").[89] Specifically, the BIPP now handles all matters related to Articles 31, 49, and 50 of the CML, which are serving as a broker without a license, market manipulation and insider trading.[90] The CMA no longer has any jurisdiction in this area; the BIPP is the exclusive agency to bring these matters before the CRSD.

§3.06 THE RELATIONSHIPS BETWEEN THE CMA AND THE CRSD AND THE CONSTITUTIONALITY OF ARTICLE 25 OF THE CML

The "rule of law" and the independence of the judiciary are fundamental to any society for the growth and development of its economy and the equal distribution of justice among its people.[91] Thus, Article 46 of the Basic Law of Governance of Saudi Arabia emphasizes that the Judiciary is an independent authority; the decisions of judges shall not be subject to any authority other than the authority of the Islamic *Shari'ah*.[92] But, the CMA and the CRSD have both administrative and financial relationships.

83. Capital Market Law, Article 25(b) (2003).
84. *Id.* Article 25(f).
85. *Id.* Article 25(g).
86. *Id.*
87. Resolution of Securities Disputes Proceedings Regulations, the Board of the Capital Market Authority Resolution Number 1-4-2011, dated 19/2/1432 H (Jan. 23, 2011).
88. Al Eqtisadiah Newspaper, *Alsoug Almaliah: Laihat Alfasal Fi Almonazaat Tahadaf Ela Tanzeem Ejraat Altarafa Oa Altagadi [Capital Market: The Regulations for Dispute Regulations Aims to Regulate the Procedures for Litigation]*, Al Eqtisadiah Newspaper, Jan. 31, 2011, http://www.aleqt.com/2011/01/31/article_498177.html.
89. This is in pursuant to the High Order No. (4690) and dated 6/2/1435. Capital Market Authority, *CMA Announces the Start of the Referral of Criminal Offences to the Bureau of Investigation and Public Prosecution*, Dec. 31, 2014, http://www.cma.org.sa/en/News/Pages/CMA_N_1589.aspx.
90. Capital Market Law, Articles 31, 49, 50 (2003).
91. Amr Daoud Marar, *Saudi Arabia: The Duality of the Legal System and the Challenge of Adapting Law to Market Economies*, 19 Arab L.Q. 91, 100 (2004).
92. The Basic Law of Governance, Article 46 (1992).

The Administrative relationship was created with the enactment of the CML. The CML gave the CMA the jurisdiction to establish the CRSD in accordance with Article 25.[93] The same Article gave the Board of the CMA the jurisdiction to appoint the members of the CRSD for a renewable three-year term.[94] Employment is an administrative function. The CMA is the executive branch that is responsible for applying the CML and bringing lawsuits before the CRSD against any violation of the Law and its regulations.

Leaving the appointment of the CRSD members to the hand of an executive branch when the CRSD may have an occasion to rule against the CMA is against the judicial independence principle, and it directly violates Article 46 of the Basic Law of Governance. The CMA has the discretion to renew the term of the CRSD's members. Thus, the members of the CRSD may hesitate to refuse or disappoint the CMA in its requests. Although the Law does not limit how many times the terms can be renewed, the Law gives the Board the discretion summarily to remove any member at the end of the member's term, without even having to give a cause.

However, the Appeal Panel's members are appointed by a Council of Ministers' decision. The panel has three members representing the Ministry of Finance, the Ministry of Commerce and Industry, and the Bureau of Experts at the Council of Ministers.[95] The members of the Appeal Panel represent executive branches, which directly contradicts the principle of judicial independence.

In contrast, judges in the general judiciary are not subject to removal from offices except in the cases set forth in the law.[96] Also, judges in the general judiciary are appointed by a royal decree based on a proposal of the Supreme Council for Judiciary.[97] These rules help ensure the independence of the judicial system and its neutrality.

The second strong relationship between the CMA and the CRSD is financial. The CMA is a separate legal, financial, and administrative entity,[98] with its own annual budget.[99] The financial relationship is evident in two areas: (a) salaries and bonuses, and (b) sanctions and fines.

All employees in the CRSD - including members, legal advisors, and other employees - receive their salaries and bonuses directly from the CMA.[100] Furthermore, Article 7(g) of the CML states that the Board of the CMA is responsible for determining the salaries and remunerations of all employees.[101] The ties go beyond words on paper. The CRSD's offices are actually located inside the CMA facility.[102] The CRSD's financial dependence on the CMA contributes to the lack of judicial independence.

93. Capital Market Law, Article 25(a) (2003).
94. *Id.* Article 25(b).
95. *Id.* Article 25(g).
96. The Law of Judiciary 1975, Article 2 (1975); The Law of Judiciary 2007, Article 2 (2007).
97. The Basic Law of Governance, Article 52 (1992).
98. Capital Market Law, Article 4(a) (2003).
99. *Id.* Article 14.
100. Mohammad Abdullah Alsahali, *Nezam Alsoag Almaleh Oa Mokalafat Aldastor [The Capital Market Law and the Violation of the Constitution]*, Alriyadh Newspaper, Jun. 24, 2011, http://www.alriyadh.com/2011/06/24/article644668.html.
101. Capital Market Law, Article 7(g) (2003).
102. Alsahali, *supra* n. 100.

Article 13 of the CML states that the financial resources of the CMA include fees for services and commissions charged by the CMA, charges against using its facilities, fines and financial penalties imposed on violators of the provisions of this Law, funds provided by the government to the Authority, and any other resources determined by the Board.[103] CMA has the right to bring a legal action against any person who violates the CML or its regulations before the CRSD.[104] Indemnification is one of the sanctions that the CRSD may impose after any violation of the CML and its regulations.[105] The CMA may seek an order to indemnify the investors who have suffered damages as a consequence of a violation or to oblige the violator to pay to the Authority's account the gains realized as a consequence of such violation.[106] Thus, the CMA has direct interests in bringing lawsuits before the CRSD, because it gains the financial penalties.

It is possible to locate and to identify investors who have suffered losses as a consequence of a violation, and then determine each investor's loss. But, when the Agency files an action, it always simply requests that violators forfeit their profits.[107] Based on the cases that are published by the CMA, the CMA has never asked the CRSD to directly indemnify investors who have suffered damages as a result of legal violations. This dynamic indicates that the CMA may have more of an interest in the financial windfall than in restoring an investor's losses.[108]

In fact, prior to 2012, the CRSD had never ordered the Authority to indemnify investor losses. Then, the CRSD made a decision that surprised many commentators and investors alike. It ruled against the CMA and ordered it to distribute some of the money it had obtained from a violator to the persons who have suffered damages as a consequence of that violation.[109] In this particular case, the CMA brought a lawsuit against an investor who has violated the CML and gained SAR 16 million (USD 4.26 million) – in unlawful profits. The CRSD ordered the violator to forfeit profits to the CMA. After the violator paid the money to the CMA's account, other aggrieved investors filed their own lawsuits, demanding indemnification of around SAR 4 million (USD 1 million). The CRSD ruled in favor of these investors. Faced with the possibility of having to pay twice, the violator filed a lawsuit asking the CMA to distribute SAR 4 million to the investors who had suffered damages. The CRSD held against the CMA, for the first time ordering the Authority to indemnify the investors from the money that it had gained from the violator.[110]

However, even though the door for indemnification claims has started to open, domestic and foreign investors need to know immediately about all lawsuits that have been filed and the judgments of the CRSD and the Appeal Panel in order for investors and all market participants who have suffered losses as a result of unlawful activities

103. Capital Market Law, Article 13(a) (2003).
104. *Id.* Article 59(a).
105. *Id.* Article 59(a-4).
106. *Id.*
107. Alsahali, *supra* n. 100.
108. *Id.*
109. Shalah Althofari, *Hokom Lajanat Alfasal Eafatah Albab Mashroan Amam Matalab Altaoiad [The Committee's Ruling Will Open the Door for Indemnification Claims]*, Aljazira Newspaper, Jan. 30, 2012, http://www.al-jazirah.com/2012/20120130/ec23.htm.
110. *Id.*

to have the opportunity to claim indemnification. Moreover, all market participants need to be educated about their rights. It is the responsibility of the CMA to educate all investors on their rights and how they can claim them before the CRSD.

Article 25 of the CML should be changed because it violates Article 46 of the Basic Law of Governance of Saudi Arabia that ensures judicial independence. An executive branch, CMA, appoints the members of the CRSD, which creates the fusion of powers. To ensure the legitimacy of the Committee and be consistent with the Basic Law of Government, Article 25 of the CML should be changed to make the CRSD and the Appeal Panel's members appointed by a royal decree based on a proposal of the Supreme Council for Judiciary, similar to the appointment of judges in the general judiciary.[111] This system should help ensure the separation of powers and prove the independence of the CRSD and the Appeal Panel, thus giving more legitimacy to their judgments. The independence of the Committee will lead to more confident market participants, as well as overall fairness and justice in the market judicial system.

The Ministry of Justice and the Supreme Council for Judiciary should consider accelerating the establishment of the commercial courts and joining the CRSD to the general judiciary. For example, Egypt has a successful system that features economic courts with jurisdiction over capital market cases.[112] By joining the CRSD to the general judiciary, disputes that are arising under the CML and its regulations will be under the umbrella and supervision of the Ministry of Justice and the Supreme Council for Judiciary, not under the executive branches supervision.

In an interview with the CRSD's Secretary-General, he maintained that the committee is independent, regardless of what the laws may stipulate.[113] But, while CSRD may be free from day-to-day interference from the CMA or any other entity, the financial and administrative links should not be overlooked. As long as there is a significant potential for interference, the committee cannot be considered "independent," at least as far as the "rule of law" is concerned.

The Saudi judicial system is a combination of religious and civil law that has served the Kingdom well, but it may not be ideal for the resolution of certain commercial and financial disputes. Some basic changes can make the system more efficient and resolve litigation issues quickly and fairly.

§3.07 CONCLUSION

Since Saudis are a people of deep religious faith, *Shari'ah* courts are empowered to hear most civil and criminal matters. However, this general rule may not apply to specific situations, especially matters such as commercial and financial disputes in general and securities law disputes in particular.

111. The Basic Law of Governance, Article 52 (1992).
112. The Law of Establishing Economic Courts In Egypt, No. 120 (May 22, 2008). Article 6 of the Law states that the Economic Courts have jurisdiction over, among others, disputes and cases arising under the CML. *See* Ahmed Hindi, *Ganon Almorafaht Almadani Oa Altagari 88,89 [Civil and Commercial Procedures Law 88-89]* (Dar Aljammiah Aljadidh 2010).
113. Interview with Adel Gabani, Secretary-General of the Committees for the Resolution of Securities Disputes, in Riyadh, Saudi Arabia (Aug. 14, 2014).

Therefore, to deal with this dilemma, Saudi law has turned to a number of quasi-judicial committees. Many of these bodies share close ties with the government ministries that created them, so the line between executive and judicial functions is at least somewhat blurred. The same can be said of the CRSD. While it is effective in most respects, the administrative and financial ties between the Committee and the CMA create at least the appearance of nonindependence.

There has been progress in this area. Passed in the wake of the stock market crash, the 2007 Law of Judiciary is a significant ray of light. Its objectives to reshape the Saudi judicial system, especially in terms of commercial disputes, are significant indeed. But, for whatever reason, the law has been largely unimplemented. Changes to the CRSD and to the whole of the commercial court system should be pursued, if the capital market is to continue to thrive. The best way to facilitate change may be to join the CRSD with the rest of the general judiciary system, giving the Supreme Council for the Judiciary and Ministry of Justice supervisory power in these matters.

Independence is perhaps the most important pillar of the Saudi dispute resolution system. When the inevitable disagreements between parties occur, an independent judiciary, and not a quasi-judicial committee whose very existence probably violates Article 46 of the Basic Law of Governance, should be fully empowered to resolve these matters, consistent with the "rule of law."

Saudi Arabia is at a critical point in its economic development. If the country is to continue its desired development plan and to join the world's economic elite in a meaningful way, the judicial system should be further reformed and equipped to deal with commercial and financial decisions, including insider-trading issues. Justice should be both swift and fair, and only an independent judiciary most likely will carry out these functions.

Bibliography

I. Primary Sources

[A] Saudi Arabia Laws and Regulations

Council of Ministers' Resolution No. 167, dated 14/9/1401 (July 16, 1981).

Council of Ministers' Resolution No. 241, dated 26/10/1407 (June 23, 1987).

Council of Ministers' Resolution No. 261, dated 17/11/1423 (January 20, 2003).

Resolution of Securities Disputes Proceedings Regulations, the Board of the Capital Market Authority Resolution Number 1-4-2011, dated 19/2/1432 H (January 23, 2011).

Royal Decree No. A/105, dated 21/7/1390 (September 9, 1970).

The Basic Law of Governance, Royal Decree No. A/90, dated 27/8/1412 H (March 2, 1992).

The Capital Market Law, Royal Decree No. M/30, dated 2/6/1424 H (2003).

The High Order No. (4690) and dated 6/2/1435 (December 9, 2013).

The Law of Judiciary, Royal Decree No. M/64, dated 14/7/1395 H (July 23, 1970).

The Law of Judiciary, Royal Decree No. M/78, dated 19/9/1427 H (October 1, 2007).
The Law of Procedure Before Shari'ah Courts, Royal Decree No. M/1, dated 22/1/1435 (November 25, 2013).
The Law of the Board of Grievances, Royal Decree No. M/51, dated 17/7/1402 H (May 10, 1982).
The Law of the Board of Grievances, Royal Decree No. M/78, dated 19/9/1427 H (October 1, 2007).
The Mechanism for Enforcing the New Law of Judiciary and The Law of the Board of Grievances, Royal Decree No. M/78, dated 19/9/1427 H (October 1, 2007).
The Holy Qur'an

[B] Other Counties' Laws

The Law of Establishing Economic Courts, No. 120 (May 22, 2008) (Egypt).

[C] Official/Semi-Official Reports – Government & Nongovernment Bodies

Capital Market Authority, *CMA Announces the Start of the Referral of Criminal Offences to the Bureau of Investigation and Public Prosecution*, December 31, 2014, http://www.cma.org.sa/en/News/Pages/CMA_N_1589.aspx.
Central Intelligence Agency, *The World Factbook, Middle East: Saudi Arabia,* (November 12, 2015), https://www.cia.gov/library/publications/the-world-factbook/geos/sa.html.
Interview with Adel Gabani, Secretary-General of the Committees for the Resolution of Securities Disputes, in Riyadh, Saudi Arabia (August 14, 2014).
Legal Department in Riyadh Chamber of Commerce, *the Guide for Judicial Authorities in Saudi Arabia*, Chamber of Commerce (Institute of Public Administration 2006).
The Royal Embassy of Saudi Arabia in Washington, DC, *Saudi Arabia: Islam's Heartland,* (November 12, 2015), http://www.saudiembassy.net/about/country-information/Islam/saudi_arabia_Islam_heartland.aspx.

II. Secondary Sources

[A] Books

Aiad, Abdurahman, *Osoal Elam Algada: Gaoaid Almorafahat [Judicial Principles: Procedures Rules]* (Institute of Public Administration 1985).
Alfozan, Mohammed Barak, *Altantheem Algadai Aljadid Fi Almamlakah Alarabiah Alsaodiah [The New Judicial Regulation in the Kingdom of Saudi Arabia]*, (Maktabt Alganon Oa Alagtsad 2010).
Algasam, Abdurahman Abdulaziz, *Alnedam Algadai Aleslami Mogaranan Bealndam Algadai Alodai Oatatbegah Fi Almamlakh Alarabiah Alsaodiah [the Islamic*

Judicial System Comparing by the Enacted Laws and Applying them in the Kingdom of Saudi Arabia], (Alsaadah Press 1973).

Alghamdi, Nasser Mohammed, *Alegtsas Algadai Fi Alfagah Aleslame [the Jurisdiction in Islamic Jurisprudence]*, (Alrushd for Publishing and Distribution 2000).

Alkoli, Omer, *Gada Altheel Oa Almahakm Alkafiah [the Shadow of Judiciary or the Hidden Courts*] (King Fahad National Library 2010).

Almullh, Abdulallah Mohammed & Essat Shahatah Karrar, *Alnezam Almale Oalaqtasadi Fi Alaslam [Financial and Economic System in Islam]*, (Husseini Modern Press, 3rd ed. 2006).

Alnasser, Mohammed Zohair, *Sahih Al-Bukari [the Authenticity of Al-Bukari]*, (Dar Toag Alnajat 2001).

Alrashed, Abdullah Hammad, *Alegan That Alektsas Algadai* [*Quasi-Judicial Committees*] (Institute of Public Administration 1985).

Alsalim, Suliman, *Altantheem Algadai Fi Almamlakah Alarabiah Alsaodiah [the Judicial Regulation in the Kingdom of Saudi Arabia]*, (Institute of Public Administration 1971).

Al-Shaikh, Abdulaziz Abdullah Hassan, *Lamahat Hoala Algada Fi Almamlakah Alarabia Alsaodiah [Overview About the Judiciary in the Kingdom of Saudi Arabia]*, (Dar Alshabal for Publishing, Printing, and Distribution 1991).

Alzoheily, Mohammed Mustafa, *Altandeem Algadai Fi Alfagah Aleslami [Judicial Regulation in the Islamic Jurisprudence]* (Dar Alfakar 1982).

Alzuhaily, Wahba, *Asuol Alfaqh Alaslami [Principles of Islamic Jurisprudence*], (Dar Alfiker 1986).

Barakat, Ali Ramadan Ali, *Aloaseed Fi Sharah Nedam Algada Alsaoadi Aljadid [the Mediator in Explaining the New Saudi Judicial Law]*, (Maktabt Alganon Oa Alagtsad 2014).

Hashim, Mahmoud Mohammed, *Algada Onedam Alethbat Fi Alfagah Aleslame Oalanzemmah Aloadaiah [the Judiciary and the Prove System in Islamic Jurisprudence and Enacted Laws]*, (King Saud University Press 1988).

Hindi, Ahmed, *Ganon Almorafaht Almadani Oa Altagari [Civil and Commercial Procedures Law]* (Dar Aljammiah Aljadidh 2010).

Jeirah, Abdulmoniem Abdulazeem, *Dorose Fi Altantheem Algadai Oalagtesaas* [*Lessons in Judicial and Jurisdiction Regulation*], (Institute of Public Administration 1986).

Kechichian, Joseph A., *Legal and Political Reforms in Saudi Arabia* (Routledge, 2013).

Latham & Watkins, *Doing Business in Saudi Arabia* (Latham & Watkins 2010).

Ramadan, Hisham M., *Understanding Islamic Law From Classical to Contemporary* (Rowman and Littlefield Publisher 2006).

Shaysha, Fadi Mohammed Ahmed, *Altandaim Algadaei Aljadid Fi Almamlakah Alarabiah Alsaoudiah [the New Judicial Regulation in the Kingdom of Saudi Arabia*] (Alrushd for Publishing and Distribution 2014).

Shoman, Abbas, *Massader Al-Tashri'e Al-Eslamy [the Sources of Islamic Legislation]*, (Aldar Althgafih Press 2000).

[B] Articles

Al-Jarbou, Ayoub M., *the Role of Traditionalists and Modernists on the Development of the Saudi Legal System*, 21 Arab L.Q. 191 (2007).

Marar, Amr Daoud, *Saudi Arabia: The Duality of the Legal System and the Challenge of Adapting Law to Market Economies*, 19 Arab L.Q. 91 (2004).

Marta, Janet K. Mullin, et al., *Some Important Factors Underlying Ethical Decisions of Middle-Eastern Marketers*, 21 Int'l. Marketing Rev. 53 (2004).

McMillen, Michael J.T., *Islamic Shari'ah-Compliant Project Finance: Collateral Security and Financing Structure Case Studies*, 24 Fordham Int'l Law J. 1184 (2001).

Perry, Frederick V., *Shari'ah, Islamic Law and Arab Business Ethics*, 22 Conn. J. Int'l L. 357 (2007).

[C] News

Al Eqtisadiah Newspaper, *Alsoug Almaliah: Laihat Alfasal Fi Almonazaat Tahadaf Ela Tanzeem Ejraat Altarafa Oa Altagadi [Capital Market: The Regulations for Dispute Regulations Aims to Regulate the Procedures for Litigation]*, Al Eqtisadiah Newspaper, January 31, 2011, http://www.aleqt.com/2011/01/31/article_498177.html.

Aldaoud, Naseer Zaid, *Aldaoud: Otalb Beahmal Oahadat Algada Oathag Fi Emkaniat Roat Almohkamah Aldostodiah Gariban [Aldaoud: I Call for the Realization of the Unity of Judicial Principle and I am Confident of the Possibility of Having the Constitutional Court Soon]*, Al Madina Newspaper, October 28, 2011, http://www.al-madina.com/node/335460?risala.

Alfaraj, Hamad, *Wazeer Aladal Uodashen Manazomat Almahakem Almotakasesah Fi Almamlaka [Minister of Justice Will Establish the Specialized courts in the Kingdom: Tuesday]*, Sabq Newspaper, August 17, 2014, http://sabq.org/EFigde.

Alkhaldi, Mohammed, *Lagnata Alfasal Mostaglatan Ola Takthan Letatherat Hiat Alsoag Almaleih [The CRSD Committee and the Appeal Panel are Independent, and the Capital Market Authority Has No Influence Upon them]*, Aljazira Newspaper, June 8, 2011, http://www.al-jazirah.com.sa/20110608/ec5d.htm.

Alsahali, Mohammad Abdullah, *Nezam Alsoag Almaleh Oa Mokalafat Aldastor [The Capital Market Law and the Violation of the Constitution]*, Alriyadh Newspaper, June 24, 2011, http://www.alriyadh.com/2011/06/24/article644668.html.

Alsaodiah: Garar Malakei Belmoafagah Ala Nethamain Algadah Oa Dewan Almadaleem, [Saudi Arabia: A Royal Decree Approving the Law of Judiciary and the Law of the Board of Grievance], Alsharq Al-Awsat News, October 2, 2007, http://classic.aawsat.com/details.asp?article=439632&issueno=10535#.VIzA8r4kNUR.

Althofari, Shalah, *Hokom Lajanat Alfasal Eafatah Albab Mashroan Amam Matalab Altaoiad [The Committee's Ruling Will Open the Door for Indemnification Claims]*, Aljazira Newspaper, January 30, 2012, http://www.al-jazirah.com/2012/20120130/ec23.htm.

Garoub, Majed Mohammed, *Alejan Shebah Algadaiah [Quasi-Judicial Committees]*, Okaz Newspaper, July 31, 2013, http://www.okaz.com.sa/new/mobile/20130731/Con20130731624581.htm.

Hamoud, Fahad, *Lejan Fad Almonazat Altaminih Oaallegan Shabah Algadaiah: Kaifa Takon Almogaranah [Committees for Insurance Disputes Resolution and Quasi-Judicial Committees: How to Compare?]*, Al Eqtisadiah Newspaper, August 25, 2008, http://www.aleqt.com/2008/08/25/article_152200.html.

CHAPTER 4

Disclosure Regulations and Their Enforcement in the Saudi Capital Market

SUMMARY

The history of the disclosure regime in the Saudi stock market begins in earnest in 2003, with the passage of the "CML" and subsequent creation of the "CMA." Today, there is a fully developed disclosure structure that is in compliance with international standards.

Although the CML gives the CMA sweeping powers to enforce these disclosure requirements, the CMA is hesitant to wield its sword in this area. Specifically, both the potential and actual fines for disclosure violations are rather low, the CMA is not particularly insistent as to the timeliness and contents of reports, and the agency itself is lacking in this area.

This chapter examines the historical contributions of the disclosure laws to promote the level of disclosure and transparency in the Saudi capital market, as well as ongoing efforts to protect investors and uphold the integrity of the capital market. These rules must be vigorously and fairly enforced, to both deter current and future illegal activity as well as promote investor and public confidence in the system. In other words, well-developed disclosure rules and a strong enforcement regime work together to produce high level of disclosure, transparency, and fairness in the market.

In short, the theme of this chapter is that to make the regulatory structure and enforcement mechanisms work in concert, Saudi Arabia should strengthen its enforcement when dealing with disclosure violations to better enforce existing laws.

Therefore, Part II of this chapter will focus on mandatory disclosure of listed companies before the enactment of the CML in 2003. Then, Part III will discuss the new Saudi disclosure regime and whether the rules are in compliance with international standards. Part IV will address the CMA's role towards a high level of disclosure in the market. This section will focus on the CMA efforts to promote disclosure and transparency in the market, and the enforcement tools that are available to the CMA.

To gain a better understanding of how these tools are used in practice, this section will also examine some of the CMA's published actions against disclosure violations. Moreover, this chapter will evaluate whether or not the CMA has promoted a high disclosure level in the Market.

§4.01 INTRODUCTION

The rules and principles related to mandatory disclosure and transparency exist in many laws that regulate companies, banks and capital markets in the Arab region and in the world.[1] However, these rules exist in more detailed, and perhaps more necessary, in the world's most developed countries, such as the U.S.[2] where principles of mandatory disclosure and transparency are adopted and enforced based on the concepts of the principles of corporate governance.[3] These regulations are issued either as mandatory laws or as guiding principles and standards, as they are in Saudi Arabia.

In 2006, Saudi Arabia enacted[4] "CGR," partially to regulate the management of joint-stock companies listed in the capital market, and also "to ensure the protection of shareholder's rights as well as the rights of stakeholders."[5] Moreover, the CGR aimed to increase transparency and disclosure in the capital market in order to avoid conflict of interests between directors of companies and their shareholders.[6] However, the rules in the CGR are only guiding principles and standards for listed companies in the capital market, unless other laws or resolutions of the Board of the CMA provide for binding effect of some of the provisions of the CGR.[7]

With the Saudi "CML" enactment in 2003,[8] the establishment of the "CMA" in 2004,[9] and CMA issuance of many regulations during the past decade, the Saudi government hopes to increase transparency and disclosure in the capital market, and to protect investors from abusive conducts such as insider trading through the use of appropriate enforcement tools. In fact, Chapter Eight of the CML is titled "Manipulation and Insider Trading,"[10] which indicates that the Saudi government is concerned about the integrity of the capital market and its transparency. Moreover, the CMA issued

1. Ahmed Ali Khdar, *Alefsah Oa Alshafafiah Kaahad Mabada Alhokmah Fi Ganon Alsharekat 47 [Disclosure and Transparency Are One of Corporate Governance Principles in the Companies Law 47]*, (Dar Alfakar Aljamae 2012).
2. Sarbanes-Oxley Act of 2002, Pub. L. No. 107-204, 116 Stat. 745 (2002).
3. Khdar, *supra* n. 1, at 47.
4. Corporate Governance Regulations, the Board of the Capital Market Authority Resolution Number 1-212-2006, dated 21/10/1427H (Nov. 12, 2006), Amended by the Resolution of the Board of the Capital Market Authority Number 1-10-2010, dated 30/3/1431H (Mar. 16, 2010).
5. *Id.* Article 1(a).
6. Adli Ali Hammad, *Mosoat Gaoanin Soag Almal Alsaoadi* 293 [*Laws Encyclopedia of the Saudi Capital Market* 293], (King Fahad National Library 2013).
7. Corporate Governance Regulations, Article 1 (b) (2006).
8. The Capital Market Law, Royal Decree No. M/30, dated 2/6/1424 H (2003).
9. The Capital Market Authority was established in Jul. 2, 2004 in accordance with Article Four of the Capital Market Law in order to regulate and supervise the capital market. Abdulrahman Abdullah Alhamidi & Abdulrahman Abdulmohsen Alkalaf, *Alnagood Oa Albonok Oa Alasoag Almalih 361 [Money, Banks, and Capital Markets 361]*, (Alfarazdak Press Company, 2009).
10. The Capital Market Law, Chapter Eight.

Market Conducts Regulations ("MCR") in 2004 to provide further details about illegal conduct in the capital market, including insider trading.[11]

This chapter will examine the historical contributions of the disclosure laws to promote the level of disclosure and transparency in the Saudi capital market, as well as ongoing efforts to protect investors and to uphold the integrity of the capital market. These laws are an important component of the Kingdom's movement towards a modern market that embraces the "rule of law," increases investor awareness, and contributes to the market's overall strength. The government has developed a mandatory disclosure regime, which is one of the fundamental mechanisms to promote transparency and fairness in the market and to deter violations conducts. In any successful economy, these rules need to be vigorously and fairly enforced so as to deter current and future illegal activity and to promote investor and public confidence in the system. In other words, well-developed disclosure rules and a strong enforcement regime should work together to produce a high level of disclosure, transparency, and fairness in the market.

In particular, Part II of this chapter will focus on mandatory disclosure of listed companies before the enactment of the CML in 2003. Then, Part III will discuss the new Saudi disclosure regime and whether the rules are in compliance with international standards. Current law requires listed companies to disclose certain data, in order to help ensure transparency and fairness in the market. Part IV will address the CMA's role as to moving towards a high level of disclosure in the market. This section will focus on the CMA's efforts to promote disclosure and transparency in the market, and on the enforcement tools that are available to the CMA. To gain a better understanding of how these tools are used in practice, this section will also examine some of the CMA's published actions against disclosure violations. Moreover, this chapter will evaluate whether the CMA has promoted a high disclosure level in the capital market.

§4.02 DISCLOSURE OBLIGATIONS OF LISTED COMPANIES PRIOR TO 2003

Corporate transparency is a core element both in financial market development and in overall economic growth. Mandatory disclosure regimes are a key subpart because, simply stated, these transparency laws force companies to disclose critical information that they would have otherwise kept private, to the clear detriment of investors.[12] To be effective, the disclosure rules must require these companies to provide accurate, timely, and complete information, so that investors have the opportunity to make well-grounded purchase and sales decisions based on reliable and current information about the issuer's activities and overall market conditions. In this respect, disclosure rules have a direct impact on market efficiency, because these rules are designed to

11. Market Conduct Regulations, the Board of the Capital Market Authority Resolution Number 1-11-2004, dated 20/8/1425 H (Oct. 4, 2004), Amended by the Resolution of the Board of the Capital Market Authority Number 3-3-2016, dated 27/3/1437 H (Jan. 7, 2016).
12. Merritt B. Fox, *Civil Liability and Mandatory Disclosure*, 109 Colum. L. Rev. 237, 239 (2009).

help ensure effective distribution of data that is central to investing decisions, thus facilitating a positive capital flow in a timely and cost-effective manner.[13]

A market with a greater disclosure has three possible benefits, including a more level playing field in the capital market, more manageable risk levels for investors, and a more efficient allocation of resources.[14]

Beginning in 1965, the Law of Companies (1965) required listed companies[15] to disclose certain information relevant to capital market activity.[16] Initially, a company had to file a public report with the Ministry of Commerce in order to register as an issuer;[17] these requirements were "administrative." Later, in 1997, the Ministry of Commerce issued guidelines for the conversion of companies to joint-stock companies in considerably more detail than set forth in the Law of Companies.[18]

Initially, when companies became publicly traded, the 1965 Law of Companies required them to disclose merely annual reports.[19] Approximately twenty years later, more detailed disclosure requirements developed, beginning in 1984. That was the year the Saudi Arabia Monetary Agency ("SAMA") issued Executive Rules to regulate the stock market and protect investors.[20] The Executive Rules required listed companies to publish reports quarterly in two daily newspapers.[21] Nevertheless, it was not until 1997 that listed companies were required to disclose vital information on an ongoing basis, as nothing in the Law of Companies required such disclosure.

The Ministerial Committee[22] issued in March 1997 the Disclosure Rules[23] to increase the level of transparency and disclosure in the market.[24] The Disclosure Rules imposed a broad duty upon chairmen or managing directors of listed companies to disclose any major event or material information that may affect share prices, either directly or indirectly.[25] Listed companies must disclose major events and material

13. Janis Sarra, *Disclosure as a Public Policy Instrument in Global Capital Markets*, 42 Tex. Int'l L. J. 875, 876 (2007).
14. Merritt B. Fox, *Securities Disclosure in a Globalizing Market: Who Should Regulate Whom*, 95 Mich. L. Rev. 2498, 2533(1997).
15. "Listed companies" are companies whose shares are publicly traded in the Saudi capital market.
16. Law of Companies, Royal Decree No. M/6, dated 22/3/1385 H (1965).
17. *Id.* Articles 52 & 64.
18. *See* the Guidelines for the Conversion of Companies to Joint Stock Companies, The Ministry of Commerce, Circular 495, dated 25/3/1418, 7/29/1997 (1997).
19. Law of Companies, Article 123 (1965).
20. The Executive Rules to Regulate Share Dealing in Company Shares Through Commercial Banks, The Saudi Arabia Monetary Agency, December 1984 (1984).
21. *Id.* Article 19 (d).
22. The Ministerial Committee was formed in 1984 by Royal Decree Number 1230/8 to regulate and develop the Saudi Arabian Stock Market. The committee consisted of the Ministry of Finance and National Economy, Ministry of Commerce, and SAMA. For more details, *See* Kirt C. Butler & S. Jamal Malaikah, *Efficiency and Inefficiency in Thinly Traded Stock Markets: Kuwait and Saudi Arabia*, 16 J. Banking & Fin. 197 (1992); Alhamidi, *supra* n. 9, at *348*; Saudi Arabian Monetary Agency, *Historical Preview*, (Dec. 31, 2015), http://www.sama.gov.sa/en-US/About/Pages/SAMAHistory.aspx.
23. Disclosure Rules, Ministerial Committee, Minister of Commerce Circular Reference Number 2222/221/9/3340, Dated 8/11/1417, Mar. 17, 1997 (1997).
24. Alhamidi, *supra* n. 9, at 354.
25. Disclosure Rules 1997, Article 2 (a) (1997).

information "immediately"[26] to the Share Control Department of SAMA for dissemination through the "ESIS"[27] and to the mass media.

Another major development in market transparency was that the Disclosure Rules addressed directly, for the first time, the prohibition of insider trading by any person.[28] Before 1997, directors of listed companies could trade freely and legally on the companies they were managing without violating the law because there was no law at all prohibiting them to trade based on inside information.[29]

However, violations of the requirements of publishing quarterly information on the financial position, as required by the Executive Rules of 1984, were punishable in accordance with the sanctions mentioned in the Law of Companies, which were weak and ineffective in those days.[30] Sadly, the weak enforcement pattern is a continuing theme with regard to the Saudi capital market, as will be seen below. The 1997 Disclosure Rules contained no additional sanctions for any other violations, but it mentioned that violations of these rules would be punishable according to the existing regulations in Saudi Arabia.[31]

Even with the progress towards increasing transparency and improving disclosure regime in the Saudi capital market, these developments were too weak as to effectively promoting an efficient, fair, and sustainable capital market. The government realized this weakness in the capital market by the early 2000s, and therefore launched a major development towards a modern capital market that has a fully developed disclosure regime. But, as enforcement remains somewhat suspect, the full potential behind these new laws and regulatory entities has not fully been realized.

§4.03 2003 AND A NEW PUSH TOWARDS TRANSPARENCY

Beginning in 2003, the KSA significantly restructured the capital market in order to address its deficiencies with regard to the lack of information and transparency. The CML was enacted in 2003: an independent body, the CMA, was created in 2004, and the CMA has enacted several key regulations over the past decade. These developments aimed to improve transparency in the market, to protect investors, and to move the

26. The Disclosure Rules did not mention how long a company had to disclose the material information. The Rules stated the disclosure need to be "immediately." It was not clear whether the information should be released within hours or within weeks, and a violation occurred.
27. In 1990, the government of Saudi Arabia introduced a new trading system, the Electronic Securities Information System "ESIS," which ushered the Saudi capital market into the digital age. In ESIS, stock trading went through centralized units in commercial banks that were linked with a central host computer in SAMA. For more details, *see* Radi Saleh Alhadad, *Daorat Alastathmar Fi Alaorag Almaleah: Grarat Ethafeh [Cycle Investment in Securities: Extra Decisions]* (Riyadh Business 1992); Mohammed Ibrahim Alsuhaibani, *Aalaiat Almogasah Oa Altasaoih Fi Alasoag Almalih [Clearing and Settlement Mechanisms in Financial Markets]*, (Dar Kanoze Eshbilia Press 2009); Hisham Aljamal, *Financial Markets and Financial Institutions* 28, Majmaah University (2013).
28. Disclosure Rules 1997, Article 4 (a) (1997).
29. More details and analyses on the matter of insider trading are in the next chapter.
30. The Executive Rules to Regulate Share Dealing in Company Shares Through Commercial Banks, Article 19 (d) (1984).
31. Disclosure Rules 1997, Article 5 (1997).

market towards modernization.[32] One of the most important matters that the CML addresses is transparency and disclosure in the capital market.[33] The CML considers public disclosure and transparency as one of its fundamental principles in order to be used as "a shield against fraud, deception, and manipulation, and as the building block of an efficient market."[34]

The CML addresses the disclosure principle in Chapter Seven and indicates two types of disclosures that the CMA monitors and regulates: initial disclosure and ongoing disclosure.[35] Additionally, the CMA issued "LR" in 2004 to serve as protection for investors and increase the levels of disclosure and transparency.[36] The LR discusses in more detail the information that must be disclosed, and the initial procedures that must be followed, before their shares can be traded in the market. This law also sets forth the information that must be disclosed continuously and periodically while these shares are listed in the market.

[A] Initial Disclosure

Before going public and offering shares to the public in the market, the CML, LR, and "OSR"[37] require companies to disclose information to the CMA and to the public through a prospectus.[38] Similar to the U.S. laws,[39] an issuer, its affiliate, or its underwriter must provide the CMA with a prospectus[40] before offering securities.[41] Unless the issuer or the offering is exempted, the CMA must receive and approve the prospectus, and the issuer must publish the prospectus before offering[42] and selling

32. Ahmed Sulaiman Alsuraiseri, *Saana Alsoag Aldoalih Fi Tadawul Alasahom Almahaleeh 77, [The Maker of International Market in Trading the Local Stocks 77]* (King Fahad National Library, Riyadh 2008).
33. Alhamidi, *supra* n. 9, at 370.
34. Joseph W. Beach, *The Saudi Arabian Capital Market Law: A Practical Study of the Creation of Law in Developing Markets*, 41 Stan. J. Int'l L. 307, 338 (2005).
35. The Capital Market Law, Chapter Eight. This Chapter of the CML consistes of Articles Fourty to Fourty Eight.
36. Listing Rules, the Board of the Capital Market Authority Resolution Number 3-11-2004, dated 20/8/1425 H (Oct. 4, 2004), Amended by the Resolution of the Board of the Capital Market Authority Number 1-64-2016, dated 19/8/1437 H (May 26, 2016).
37. Offers of Securities Regulations, the Board of the Capital Market Authority Resolution Number 3-11-2004, dated 20/8/1425 H (Oct. 4, 2004), Amended by the Resolution of the Board of the Capital Market Authority Number 1-28-2008, dated 17/8/1429 H (Aug. 18, 2008).
38. Prospectus is defined as a required document in order to offer securities in accordance with the Capital Market Law and Listing Rule. Glossary of Defined Terms Used in the Regulations and Rules of the Capital Market Authority, the Board of the Capital Market Authority Resolution Number 4-11-2004, dated 20/8/1425 H (Oct. 4, 2004), Amended by the Resolution of the Board of the Capital Market Authority Number 3-58-2014, dated 17/1/1436 H (Nov. 10, 2014).
39. *See* U.S. Securities Act 1933, § 5 (codified as amended at 15 U.S.C. § 77f (2012)).
40. It is worth mentioning that the CML does not distinct between a prospectus and a registration statement. On the contrary, U.S. laws make differences between these two statements. *See* U.S. Securities Act 1933, §§ 5, 7 (codified as amended at 15 U.S.C. § 77e, 77g (2012)).
41. The Capital Market Law, Article 40 (b) (2003).
42. Placement or offering of securities is defined in Article One of the CML as "issuing securities, inviting the public to subscribe therefor or the direct or indirect marketing thereof; or any statement, announcement or communication that has the effect of selling, issuing or offering securities, but does not include preliminary negotiations or contracts entered into with or among

any securities.[43] The issuer cannot publish the prospectus to the public without first obtaining written approval from the CMA.[44]

The CML gives the CMA power to exempt the issuer from some of these requirements. According to the CML, such an exemption may be based on "the manner of the offering, the amount of the offering, the number of investors and their characteristics, or the characteristic of the issuer of the Security or the Security itself."[45]

In terms of content, the CML provides only general requirements of necessary information that must be included in a prospectus. These categories include an "adequate" description of the issuer, the securities, financial position of the issuer, and any other information that is deemed to be necessary in assisting investors to make investing decisions.[46] Ultimately, the CMA has the final authority to regulate and specify the exact requirements of a prospectus.[47]

---

underwriters." *Id.* Article 1. The Capital Market Law uses an extremely broad effects-based definition, which covers all possible scenarios in which the communication has the effect of offering to sell the security and results in an objective standard. In contrast, the Securities Act uses a more specific "intent-based formula" to identify offering of securities, which is a more subjective approach. *See* Beach, *supra* n. 34, at 340. The U.S. Securities Act of 1933 states that "offer to sell," "offer for sale," or "offer" shall include every attempt or offer to dispose of, or solicitation of an offer to buy, a security or interest in a security, for value." U.S. Securities Act 1933, § 2(a)(3) (codified as amended at 15 U.S.C. § 77b (2012)).

43. *See* The Capital Market Law, Articles 40 (a)-(b), 41 (2003). Article 41 states that "an issuer, an affiliate of the issuer or an underwriter may not sell any Security owned by that issuer before the prospectus is approved by the Authority and becomes effective, provided that the approved prospectus shall be sent to the buyer prior to the sale date in accordance with such rules as the Authority may issue." Similarly, in Egypt, "no offer of securities by any company, including Public Business Sector Companies, and Public Sector Companies, shall be made for public subscription without a prospectus to be filed with and certified by the Authority, and published in two widely circulated daily morning newspapers, one of which at least should be an Arabic newspaper. The prospectus should be prepared according to the forms provided by the Authority." Egyptian Capital Market Law, Article 4, Law No. 95 of 1992 (1992).
44. Listing Rules, Article 22 (a) (2004).
45. Capital Market Law, Article 40 (b) (2003).
46. Article 42 of the CML states that the prospectus must contain the following:

    a. Information required by the Authority's rules which give an adequate description of the issuer, the nature of its business, the individuals in charge of its management such as members of the board of directors, executive officers, senior staff, and its major shareholders.
    b. Information required by the Authority's rules which give an adequate description of the Securities to be issued, their number, price, and related rights, preferences or privileges of the issuer's other Securities, if any. The description will set forth how the issue proceeds will be disbursed, and the commissions levied by persons connected with the issue.
    c. A clear statement of the financial position of the issuer and any significant financial data including the audited financial balance sheet, profit and loss account and cash flow statement as the rules of the Authority may require.
    d. Any other information required or authorized by the Authority in accordance with rules issued by the Authority, which it deems necessary to assist investors and their advisers in making decisions about investing in the Securities to be issued. Capital Market Law, Art. 42 (2003).

47. *See* Capital Market Law, Articles 41-44 (2003). In Egypt, the Capital Market Law provides the general elements that need to be in a prospectus. "The prospectus of a company at incorporation should disclose the following information: purpose and duration of the company, issued and paid up capital of the company; characteristics of the shares being offered, advantages and the

The LR goes further into the specific requirements of a prospectus. Article 21(a) states that "the prospectus must contain all information which is necessary to enable an investor to make an assessment of the activities, assets and liabilities, financial position, management and prospects of the issuer and of its profits and losses and must include information in relation to the number and price of the securities and any obligations, rights, powers and privileges attaching to them."[48]

Unlike U.S. regulations in terms of the schedules or annexes that contain the instructions for disclosure within the laws,[49] the CML gives the power to the CMA to issue detailed requirements and instructions for disclosure based on the principles and standards of the CML.[50] The LR sets out in Annex 4[51] and Annex 5[52] the minimum information that must be included in a prospectus.[53] This required information is more detailed and includes information such as the corporate directory, an offer summary, the business nature and structure, legal information, and financial information. Annex 4 and Annex 5 are both fourteen pages long.

The CMA must approve the prospectus before it becomes valid. However, the CML restricts the CMA's authorization to reject a prospectus to only four situations.[54] The CMA has the power to require the issuer to disclose further information where it deems such behavior to be appropriate.[55]

---

terms of offer; names of founders, capital subscribed by each and payment in kind, if any; the company's plan for the use of proceeds of shares sale and expected results; places where the Authority's certified prospectus could be obtained; any other information as defined by the Executive Regulations." Egyptian Capital Market Law, Article 5. Also, the Executive Regulations of Egyptian Capital Market Law provides sixteen elements that need to be added in a prospectus in addition to the elements that are stated in the Egyptian Capital Market Law. *See* the Executive Regulations of Egyptian Capital Market Law, Article 42, Law No. 95 of 1992 (1992).

48. Listing Rules, Article 21 (a) (2004).
49. *See* U.S. Securities Act 1933, § 10 & sched, A (1933).
50. *See* Capital Market Law, Articles 41-44 (2003). Article 6 of the CML gives the CMA the power to Issue and amend the Implementing Regulations as may be necessary to enforce the provisions of this Law. Capital Market Law, Article 6 (a)-6 (2003). Moreover, Article 48 of the CML states that the CMA "shall specify the disclosure forms and instructions, including the information which must be included in the prospectuses and periodical reports which must be provided to the Authority by the parties that are subject to its control and supervision or which must be announced to the public, as the case may be." Capital Market Law, Article 6 (a) (2003). The rules that are issued by the CMA are much easier to be changed than laws. These rules should continue to grow and develop new topic as the Saudi capital market demands. Beach, *The supra* n. 34, at 342.
51. Annex 4 of the Listing Rules sets out the minimum information that the issuer must include them in a prospectus for shares. Annex 4 has twenty-seven major items with sub-items to be included in a prospectus.
52. Annex 5 of the Listing Rules sets out the minimum information, twenty-five major items, that an issuer must include them in a prospectus for debt instruments and convertible debt instruments.
53. Listing Rules, Article 21 (b)-(c) (2004).
54. Article 44 states that the CMA may reject a prospectus if: (1) the prospectus does not contain the information required by Article 42 of CML; (2) "the prospectus contains incorrect information pertaining to material matters, false or misleading statements or omits to state material information or statements that would under the circumstances render the prospectus misleading or incorrect"; (3) "the prospectus issuance fees have not been paid in full to the Authority"; or (4) "the issuer has failed to provide any of the reports stipulated in Article 45 of" the Capital Market Law, which are quarterly and annual reports for whose securities are already traded in the market. Capital Market Law, Articles 44-45 (2003).
55. Listing Rules, Article 26 (a) (2004).

An issuer must notify the CMA immediately in writing of any "material change" in the prospectus, as soon as the issuer becomes aware of such change.[56] The CML defines material changes as "any information that may affect the price or value of the security."[57] Thus, the standard used in the CML is an objective standard. Moreover, the CML also requires the issuer to disclose any material change to the public in a press release.[58] The LR sets forth the information to be disclosed and when an issuer is required to submit and to publish a "supplementary prospectus" before starting the offering.[59] In the U.S., "material" is defined for the purposes of a 1933 Act registration statement as "matters to which there is a substantial likelihood that a reasonable investor would attach importance in determining whether to purchase the security registered."[60]

A prospectus must be published and be available to the public at least fourteen days before an issuer begins the offering.[61] The LR requires the issuer to publish the initial prospectus, and any supplementary prospectus, in both printed and electronic forms.[62] However, to keep pace with constantly changing market conditions, disclosure other than a one-time prospective is required.

[B] Periodic and Continuous Disclosure

[1] Periodic Disclosure

Periodic and continuous disclosure is the second type of disclosure in both the CML and the LR. In terms of periodical disclosure, the law requires listed companies to submit reports to the CMA both quarterly[63] and annually.[64] These reports need to

56. Capital Market Law, Article 43 (b) (2003).
57. *Id.*
58. *Id.*
59. Listing Rules, Article 24 (2004).
60. Thomas Lee Hazen, Federal Securities Law 35 (2nd. 2003).
61. Listing Rules, Article 25 (a) (2004). As an exception from paragraph (a) of Article 25, "an issuer must publish the prospectus and must ensure that it is made available to the public at least 14 days prior to the general assembly meeting where an offering of a rights issue is to be made." *Id.* Article 25 (b).
62. *Id.* Article 25 (c). The prospectus and the supplementary prospectus must be available to the public (1) "in printed form, free of charge, at the offices of the Exchange, the issuer's registered office, the head office of the financial advisor, the offices of the financial advisor and the offices of any authorized persons whom are placing or selling the securities to which the prospectus relates; and (2) in electronic form, on the websites of the issuer, the Exchange, the Authority and the financial advisor."
63. Within a period of thirty days after the end of the financial period, listed companies are required to submit their quarterly reports to the CMA and announce to their shareholders of such financial statements. Listing Rules, Article 42 (d) (2004).
64. Similarly, annual reports must be provided to the CMA and announced by listed companies as soon as they have been approved and within a period of three months after the end of the annual financial period of such financial statements. *Id.* Article 42 (e). Capital Market Law, Article 45(a) (2003). Part of the Article states that "every issuer offering Securities to the public or whose Securities are traded on the Exchange must submit to the Authority quarterly and annual reports." Capital Market Law, Article 45(a) (2003).

contain a balance sheet, a profit and loss account, a cash flow statement, and any other information as required by the rules of the CMA.[65]

Further in terms of annual reports, the full requirements extend well beyond these basic elements. These reports must be audited as required by the CMA's rules.[66] The LR requires the auditing of these annual reports to be prepared and reviewed in accordance with the accounting standards approved by Saudi Organization for Certified Public Accountants ("SOCPA").[67] Additionally, annual reports must include: (a) an adequate description of the issuer and its business; (b) information regarding the board of directors, officers, and major investors; (c) an evaluation of the issuing company management of current and future developments and any future possibilities that may have significant effect on financial position of the company;[68] and (d) any other information as may be required by the CMA.[69]

Interim and annual reports of listed companies must be approved by directors and signed by an authorized director and by a chief executive officer prior to their publication and circulation to shareholders and third parties.[70] Also, interim and annual reports must be submitted immediately upon directors' approval.[71] In a similar vein, listed companies must announce their interim and annual financial statements immediately upon approval by directors and such statements must not be published to the shareholders or third parties prior to their announcement in the Exchange.[72]

Along with annual reports, the LR requires listed companies to provide the CMA and announce to the shareholders within a period of three months after the end of the annual financial period a report issued by the board of directors. A directors' report includes a review of the operations of the company during the last financial year and of all relevant factors affecting the issuer's business that an investor requires to assess the assets, liabilities, and financial position of the company.[73] Moreover, the CGR also

65. Capital Market Law, Article 45 (a) (2003).
66. *Id.* Article 45.
67. Listing Rules, Article 42 (e) (2004).
68. Part (c) of these requirements is similar to U.S. Regulation S-K § 229.303 Management's Discussion and Analysis of Financial Condition and Results of Operations ("MD&A"). MD&A presents "the company's operations and financial results, including information about the company's liquidity and capital resources and any known trends or uncertainties that could materially affect the company's results. This section may also discuss management's views of key business risks and what it is doing to address them." Regulation S-K, 17 C.F.R. §229.303 (2011); U.S. Securities & Exchange Commission, *How to Read a 10-K*, Dec. 31, 2015, http://www.sec.gov/answers/reada10k.htm.

    MD&A disclosure required in the Securities Act registration statements and the Exchange Act Forms: annual reports and quarter reports. Henry TC Hu, *Disclosure Universes and Modes of Information: Banks, Innovation, and Divergent Regulatory Quests*, 31 Yale J. On Reg 565, 593 (2014).
69. Capital Market Law, Article 45 (b) (2003).
70. Listing Rules, Article 42 (a) (2004).
71. *Id.* Article 42 (b).
72. *Id.* Article 42 (c).
73. *Id.* Article 43. Corporate Governance Regulation ("CGR") also requires additional information to be included in board of directors' reports. These additional contents includes information such as any punishment or penalty imposed on the listed company by the CMA, the implemented and unimplemented provisions of the CGR, and the justification for any inaction. This Article 9 is a mandatory provision, as of 2008. *See* Corporate Governance Regulations, Article 9 (2006). It is

requires listed companies to have, in writing, the policies, procedures and supervisory rules related to disclosure in accordance to the law.[74]

As a way to protect both investors and the market from abusive conduct, such as insider trading, financial reports[75] and current and future management evaluations of listed companies[76] are confidential until they are released to the public.[77] The CML prohibits listed companies from disclosing such information to "parties not bound by a confidentiality obligation and an obligation to protect such information."[78] Undisclosed information obtained by the CMA is deemed to be confidential; however, the CMA may reveal this undisclosed information whenever the Board of the CMA believes such action to be necessary for the protection of investors.[79]

Similar to the U.S. laws,[80] issuers must disclose all required information to the public and to the CMA in a way that is "complete, clear, accurate, and not misleading."[81] As a general rule, the LR emphasizes that all issuers must provide to the CMA, without delay, all information and explanations that the CMA may require, which "must be complete, clear, accurate and not misleading."[82] Moreover, effective in March 31, 2016 and as per Article 40 of the LR, disclosures to the public of any information or material developments, including periodic and current disclosures, must be made "at least half an hour before the start of the trading period."[83]

---

worth noting that most other CGR provisions are only guiding principles and standards for listed companies. *See* Corporate Governance Regulations, Article 1 (b) (2006).

74. Corporate Governance Regulations, Article 8 (2006).
75. Financial reports include a balance sheet, a profit and loss account, and a cash flow statement. These financial reports are stated in Article 45 (a) of the CML. Capital Market Law, Article 45 (a) (2003).
76. These current and future management forecasts are stated in Article 45 (b) (3) of the Capital Market Law.
77. Capital Market Law, Article 45 (c) (2003).
78. *Id.*
79. *Id.* Article 17.
80. *For example* Sarbanes-Oxley Act of 2002, § 401; 17 C.F.R. §§ 230.421 (b), (d), 240.13a-20. Section § 240.13a-20 – Plain English presentation of specified information – requires that any information that must be disclosed under Section 13 of the Securities Exchange Act of 1934 "must be presented in a clear, concise and understandable manner."
81. Listing Rules, Article 40 (a) (2004). Prior to April 2016, the Article required all disclosures to be "clear, fair, and not misleading."
82. Listing Rules, Article 34 (a) (2004). Amendments on Mar. 31, 2016 added the word "complete" to this Article.
83. Article 40 of the Listing Rules was Article 25. In 2006, Article 25 obligated listed companies to inform the CMA and the public "without delay" of any material information which could lead to movements in the price of the listed securities or other securities or significantly affect a listed company's ability to meet its obligations regarding debts. In 2006, the Board of the CMA amended Article 25 of the Listing Rules to require listed companies to disclose such information "at least two hours" before the start of the trading period. Very recently, on Mar. 31, 2016, the Board of the CMA amended Article 40 to require the public disclosure of any information or material developments to be made "at least half an hour before the start of the trading period." *See* the Board of the Capital Market Authority Resolution Number 2-128-2006, dated 22/12/1426 H (Jan. 22, 2006), http://www.cma.org.sa/Ar/News/Pages/CMA_N156.aspx; Capital Market Authority, *An Announcement of the Issuance of the Board of the CMA Resolution Number (1-38-2016) Dated 22/6/1437H Corresponding to 31/3/2016G to Adopt the Amended Listing Rules*, (Mar. 31, 2016), http://cma.org.sa/en/News/Pages/CMA_N_1990.aspx; Listing Rules, Article 40 (b) (2004).

In 2006, the CMA issued the Instructions for Regulating Announcements of Listed Companies in the Saudi Capital Market and updated them in 2008.[84] These instructions aim to assist listed companies in complying with the LR and other rules related to disclosure. Moreover, these instructions intend to enhance transparency and disclosure level in the capital market, thereby helping investors to make their financial decisions based on accurate and adequate information.[85] However, these instructions are only available in Arabic.[86]

In a similar manner, U.S. laws and regulators focus heavy amounts of attention on the disclosure requirements. The two main objectives of disclosure regulations in the U.S. are: (a) to provide investors with financial and other significant information about securities; and (b) to reduce the frequency of deceit, misrepresentations and fraud in the purchase and sale of securities.[87]

The Securities Exchange Act 1934 ("1934 Act") requires companies[88] to disclose and to provide the Securities and Exchange Commission ("SEC") with current and periodic reports under §13 of the 1934 Act.[89] These companies are required to file annual reports (Form 10-K), quarterly reports (Form 10-Q), and current reports (Form 8-K).[90] Similar to Saudi laws, §13(a) of the U.S. 1934 Act grants the SEC broad power to set such additional disclosure rules and regulations as the SEC "may prescribe as necessary or appropriate for the proper protection of investors and to ensure fair dealing in the security."[91]

[2] Continuous Disclosure

In addition to periodic disclosure, Saudi-listed companies are required to inform the CMA about material developments on an ongoing basis. The CML obligates issuers to inform the CMA in writing upon awareness of any material development that may affect the prices of the securities that are issued by such party. In a case that such issuer has a security traded on the Exchange "Tadawul," the issuer must inform Tadawul of the material development in writing as well.[92] The CML uses an objective standard

84. Instructions for Regulating Announcements of Listed Companies in the Saudi capital Market, the Board of the Capital Market Authority Resolution Number 1-199-2006, dated 18/07/1427 H (Aug. 12, 2006), Amended by the Resolution of the Board of the Capital Market Authority Number 4-38-2008, dated 26/11/1429 H (Nov. 11, 2008).
85. *Id.*
86. Capital Market Authority, *Disclosure*, Dec. 31, 2015, http://www.cma.org.sa/en/FormsSite/Pages/Disclosure.aspx.
87. Debra Van Alstyne & Stephanie Tsacoumis, *Periodic Reporting Under the Federal Securities Laws*, Corporate Practice Portfolio Series 89-2nd, 1 (BNA 2015). These objectives can be seen, for example, in §§5, 6 and 7 of the U.S. Securities Exchange Act of 1933.
88. A company generally becomes subject to the reporting requirements of the 1934 Act in three categories: (1) Exchange-listed issuers, (2) issuers with USD 10 million in assets and a specified number of equity holders, and (3) issuers with effective registration statements. Alstyne, *supra* n. 87, at 2.
89. U.S. Securities Exchange Act of 1934, § 13(a) (codified as amended at 15 U.S.C. § 78m (2012).
90. Alstyne, *supra* n. 87, at 4.
91. U.S. Securities Exchange Act of 1934, § 13(a) (codified as amended at 15 U.S.C. § 78m (2012).
92. Capital Market Law, Article 46 (a) (2003).

rather than a subjective standard in determining the materiality of an event.[93] The CMA and the Exchange have the power to request any information and data pertaining to any issuer, and the issuer must provide such information within a specific time.[94] The Board of the CMA, along with the Exchange, also has the power to require the issuing party to disclose such information to the public.[95] Besides that, the CML grants the Board of the CMA and the Exchange the right to publish such information and data at the expense of such issuer.[96]

The obligation to disclose material developments aims to protect investors in the market from the adverse effects of these developments, whether they act positively or negatively on the price of securities, and to prevent the abuse of nonpublic information related to such developments, especially insider trading.[97]

The LR requires issuers to disclose material information and developments at least half an hour before the start of the trading period.[98] However, the LR makes an exception to this rule so that an issuer is not required to disclose such information within the period specified.[99] An issuer may request "a temporary trading halt"[100] when an unexpected event occurs during trading hours. Two conditions must be met: (a) the event requires immediate disclosure under the LR; and (b) the issuer cannot maintain the confidentiality of the information until the end of the trading period.[101] Such issuer must submit a request to the CMA to enable the agency to assess the need for a trading halt. The request must include specific reasons for the request, the duration of the requested trading halt, and a copy of the announcement.[102]

At the CMA's discretion, the CMA may grant or refuse any such temporary halt request.[103] In the event that the CMA accepts a temporary trading halt request, the issuer must announce as soon as possible the reasons for the trading halt, the anticipated period of such halt, and the event affecting the issuer's activities.[104] The LR grants the CMA the power to impose a trading halt without a request where the CMA becomes aware of a material development related to an issuer, if the CMA considers it

93. *Id.* The language of Article 46 (a) is that "a party who issues Securities must inform the Authority in writing upon becoming aware of any material developments which may affect the prices of the Securities issued by such party."
94. Article 46 (b) of the CML states that "the Authority or the Exchange may request the party issuing Securities to provide any information or data pertaining to such party and the issuing party shall provide the same within the period of time specified in the request." Capital Market Law, Article 46 (b) (2003).
95. *Id.* Article 46 (c).
96. *Id.*
97. Hammad, *Laws Encyclopedia of the Saudi Capital Market, supra* n. 6, at 142.
98. *See supra* n. 83, and accompanying text.
99. Listing Rules, Article 40 (b) (2004).
100. "Trading halt" is defined as the temporary suspension of trading in the securities during the trading period. *See* Glossary of Defined Terms Used in the Regulations and Rules of the Capital Market Authority (2004).
101. Listing Rules, Article 37 (a) (2004).
102. *Id.* Article 37 (b).
103. *Id.* Article 37 (d).
104. *Id.* Article 37 (c).

is likely that such an event will interrupt the market or will place investors at an unfair disadvantage.[105]

The LR provides further details about material developments disclosure. Issuers must inform the CMA and the public without delay of any private developments in their sphere of activity that affects the issuer's assets, liabilities, financial position, or course of business, if that development may create movement in the security's price or affect the issuer's abilities in terms of debt servicing.[106] Similar to the CML, the LR emphasizes an objective standard to determine the materiality of information.[107] To make the determination even more objective, the LR provides twelve events[108] where a material development occurs.[109]

---

105. *Id.* Article 37 (e). An example of that is the announcement of the CMA on Aug. 13, 2015. "The Capital Market Authority announces the suspension of trading the shares of Al-Ahsa Development Co. starting from today Thursday 28/10/1436H corresponding to 13/8/2015 until 2 p.m. upon its request as it will announce a material development related to the letter received by the company from Department of Zakat and Income Tax." Capital Market Authority, *CMA Announcement in Regard to the Suspension of Trading the Shares of Al-Ahsa Development Co.* (Aug. 14, 2015), http://www.cma.org.sa/En/News/Pages/CMA_N_1846.aspx.
106. Listing Rules, Article 41 (a) (2004). The language of this provision is as follows:

> An issuer must notify the Authority and the public without delay of any material developments in its sphere of activity which are not public knowledge and which may effect the assets and liabilities or financial position or on the general course of business of the issuer or its subsidiaries and which may: 1) lead to movements in the price of the listed securities; or 2) significantly affect an issuer's ability to meet its commitments in respect of debt instruments.

107. In determining whether a development is a material, "an issuer must assess whether any investor would be likely to consider information about the development in making his investment decisions." Listing Rules, Article 41 (a) (2004).
108. In the U.S., Form 8-K is created for current disclosure. Form 8-K includes a list of events where disclosure is required. These events include entry into a material definitive agreement, termination of a material definitive agreement, bankruptcy or receivership, completion of acquisition or disposition of assets, results of operations and financial condition, creation of a direct financial obligation or an obligation under an off-balance sheet arrangement of a registrant, triggering events that accelerate or increase a direct financial obligation or an obligation under an off-balance sheet arrangement, costs associated with exit or disposal activities, material impairments, notice of delisting or failure to satisfy a continued listing rule or standard; transfer of listing, unregistered sales of equity securities, material modification to rights of security holders, changes in registrant's certifying accountant, nonreliance on previously issued financial statements or a related audit report or completed interim review, changes in control of registrant, departure of directors or certain officers, election of directors, appointment of certain officers, compensatory arrangements of certain officers, amendments to articles of incorporation or bylaws, change in fiscal year, amendments to the registrant's code of ethics, or waiver of a provision of the code of ethics, and submission of matters to a vote of security holders. *See* The U.S. Securities and Exchange Commission, Form 8-K.
109. Material developments include, but not limit to: (1) any transaction to purchase, sell, lease or mortgage an asset at a price equal to or greater than 10% of the net asset of the issuer according to the latest reviewed interim financial statements or audited annual financial statements, whichever is later; (2) any debt outside the issuer's ordinary course of business, of a value equal to or greater than 10% of the issuer's net assets; according to the latest reviewed interim financial statements or audited annual financial statements, whichever is later; (3) any losses equal to or greater than 10% of the issuer's net assets; according to the

These rules do not exist in isolation. To judge properly their effectiveness, they should be evaluated in terms of applicable international standards.

[C] Is the Saudi Periodic and Continuous Disclosure Regime in Compliance with International Standards?

All stock market rules have a common purpose: to protect investors and level the playing field. In pursuit of this overall goal, the "IOSCO" set forth clear standards that these types of rules should follow, and it appears that Saudi rules conform to these standards.[110]

[1] International Standards for Periodic Disclosure

Specifically, the periodical disclosure laws of Saudi Arabia are compliant with the IOSCO's nine principles for periodic disclosure by listed companies that were published in 2010.[111] First, periodic reports of listed companies should contain relevant information.[112] In terms of annual reports, these reports should contain audited financial statements,[113] Management's Discussion and Analysis of Financial Condition and

---

latest reviewed interim financial statements or audited annual financial statements, whichever is later; (4) any significant change in the issuer's production environment or activity including but not limited to the availability of resources and the possibility of obtaining them; (5) any changes in the composition of the directors or to CEO's position of the issuer; (6) any dispute including any litigation, arbitration, or mediation where the value involved is equal to or greater than 5% of the net assets of the issuer according to the latest reviewed interim financial statements or audited annual financial statements, whichever is later; (7) any judicial decision issued against the board or any of the directors where the subject of the decision involved relates to the business of the board or any of the directors in the issuer; (8) the increase or decrease in the net assets of the issuer equal to or greater than 10% according to the latest reviewed interim financial statements or audited annual financial statements, whichever is later; (9) the increase or decrease in the gross profit of the issuer equal to or greater than 10% according to the latest audited annual financial statements; (10) the entering into, or the unexpected termination of, any contract with revenues equal to or greater than 5% of the gross revenues of the issuer according to the latest audited annual financial statements; (11) any transaction between the issuer and a related party or any arrangement through which the issuer and a related party invest in any project or asset or provide financing therefor if this transaction or arrangement is equal to or greater than 1% of the gross revenues of the issuer according to the latest audited annual financial statements; and (12) any interruption in the principal activities of the issuer or its subsidiaries equal to or greater than 5% of the gross revenues according to the latest audited annual financial statements. Listing Rules, Article 41 (b) (2004).

110. In July 2013, the Financial Sector Assessment Program of the International Monetary Fund evaluated the Saudi capital market with regard to the IOSCO Principles. This report has been discussed early in Chapter 2, §2.03, *supra*.

111. The International Organization of Securities Commissions, *Principles for Periodic Disclosure By Listed Entities* (February 2010).

112. *Id.* at 7.

113. *See* Capital Market Law, Article 45 (a) (2003).

Results of Operations ("MD&A"),[114] material-related party transactions,[115] compensation disclosure,[116] corporate governance disclosure,[117] disclosure related to market risk sensitive instruments,[118] and security ownership in the issuer.[119]

In contrast, interim periodic reports must contain information related to the performance of a company,[120] sufficient financial information,[121] MD&A, and other similar information,[122] such as data related to party transactions disclosures.[123] However, no Saudi laws require listed companies to include MD&A in their quarter reports. Thus, the CMA should consider adding the MD&A to requirements of quarterly reports. Overall, Saudi capital market regulations substantially meet the first principle of the IOSCO for periodic disclosure by listed companies.

The second principle[124] of the IOSCO regarding periodic disclosure is that periodic reports, which include financial statements, should identify the persons responsible for the financial statements[125] and clearly affirm that the financial information provided in the report is fairly presented.[126]

The third principle[127] is that the issuer's internal control over reporting should be assessed or reviewed by a comprehensive internal audit.[128] Article 10(b) of the Saudi

114. *See Id.* Article 45 (b) (3).
115. *See Id.*; Listing Rules, Article 43 (18) (2004).
116. *See* Listing Rules, Article 43 (20) (2004); Corporate Governance Regulations, Article 9 (e) (2006).
117. *See* Listing Rules, Article 43 (25) (2004); *see* Corporate Governance Regulations (2006).
118. *See* Listing Rules, Article 43 (2, 3) (2004).
119. *See Id.* Article 43 (7-11).
120. *See* Capital Market Law, Article 45 (a) (4) (2003); *See* Instructions for Regulating Announcements of Listed Companies in the Saudi capital Market (2006).
121. *See* Listing Rules, Article 42 (d) (2004).
122. *See* Capital Market Law, Article 45 (a) (4) (2003); *See* Instructions for Regulating Announcements of Listed Companies in the Saudi capital Market (2006).
123. The International Organization of Securities Commissions, *Principles for Periodic Disclosure By Listed Entities* (2010).
124. The International Organization of Securities Commissions, *Principles for Periodic Disclosure By Listed Entities* at 20 (2010).
125. *See* Listing Rules, Article 42 (a) (2004); Listing Rules, Annex 7 (2004).
126. *See* Listing Rules, Article 40 (a) (2004); Listing Rules, Annex 6 (1) (e) (2004).
127. The International Organization of Securities Commissions, *Principles for Periodic Disclosure By Listed Entities* at 22 (2010).
128. *See* Listing Rules, Article 43 (2004) (stating that the "issuer must provide the Authority and announce to the shareholders within a period not exceeding 75 calendar days after the end of the annual financial period a report issued by the directors including a review of the operations of the issuer during the last financial year and of all relevant factors affecting the issuer's business which an investor requires to assess the assets, liabilities and financial position of the issuer." In Article 43 (24), board of directors' reports must include a declaration that: (1) proper books of account have been maintained, (2) the system of internal control is sound in design and has been effectively implemented, and (3) there are no significant doubts concerning the issuer's ability to continue as a going concern). Listing Rules, Article 43 (24) (2004).

CGR, which is a mandatory article,[129] charges the board of directors with establishing and supervising the rules for internal control systems.[130]

The fourth principle of the IOSCO is that information of the listed companies should be made available to the public on a timely basis.[131] The LR sets out the timing for filing and announcing the periodic reports of listed companies. Specifically, listed companies must provide information to the CMA and announce it to shareholders within thirty days after the end of the financial period for their interim financial statements, and within three months after the end of the annual financial period for their annual financial statements.[132] Also, annual financial statements must be provided to the CMA, and announced to shareholders, in not less than fifteen calendar days before the date of convening the issuer's annual general assembly.[133] Moreover, listed companies must announce their interim and annual financial statements immediately upon approval by the directors.[134] These statements must not be published to the shareholders or third parties prior to their announcement in the Saudi Stock Exchange "Tadawul."[135]

The Technical Committee of the IOSCO[136] suggested that the size of the listed companies might be taken into consideration when establishing the due dates for

---

129. Capital Market Authority, the Board of the Capital Market Authority Resolution Number 1-33-2011, dated 03/12/1432 H (Oct. 30, 2011), (making paragraph (b) of Article 10 of the Corporate Governance Regulations mandatory on all companies listed on the Exchange effective from Jan. 1, 2012).
130. Corporate Governance Regulations, Article 10 (b) (2006). It states that the board of directors shall lay down, and supervise, rules for internal control systems, including:

    1. Developing a written policy that regulates conflict of interest and remedies any possible cases of conflict by members of the Board of Directors, executive management and shareholders. This includes misuse of the company's assets and facilities and the arbitrary disposition resulting from dealings with the related parties.
    2. Ensuring the integrity of financial and accounting procedures, including procedures related to the preparation of the financial reports.
    3. Ensuring the implementation of control procedures appropriate for risk management by forecasting the risks that the company could encounter, and disclosing them with transparency.
    4. Reviewing annually the effectiveness of the internal control systems.

131. The International Organization of Securities Commissions, *Principles for Periodic Disclosure By Listed Entities* at 23 (2010).
132. Listing Rules, Article 42 (d)-(e) (2004).
133. *Id.* Article 42 (e).
134. *Id.* Article 42 (c).
135. *Id.*
136. The Technical Committee does not exist anymore. In 2012, "IOSCO constituted a new Board that absorbed the functions of the Executive Committee, the Technical Committee and the Emerging Markets Committee Advisory Board. The Emerging Market Committee continued as a separate body renamed the Growth and Emerging Markets Committee." The IOSCO Board is composed of thirty-three members, and it is IOSCO's governing and standard-setting body. Saudi Arabia is a member of both the IOSCO Board and the Growth and Emerging Markets Committee. The International Organization of Securities Commissions, *Annual Report 2014*, p. 64 (2014); The International Organization of Securities Commissions, *Growth and Emerging Markets Committee*, (Dec. 31, 2015), https://www.iosco.org/about/?subsection=display_committee&cmtid=8; The International Organization of Securities Commissions, *IOSCO Board*, (Dec. 31, 2015), https://www.iosco.org/about/?subsection=display_committee&cmtid=11.

periodic reports.[137] However, the CML, CMA, LR, and other regulations do not distinguish between listed companies in terms of size. This might be due to the relative size of the market and lack of experience on the part of authorities. The CMA should consider altering the due dates for small and medium-sized listed companies, due to their lack of experience and limited resources.

The fifth principle is that periodic reports should be filed with the relevant regulator.[138] The CML requires listed companies to submit their periodic reports to the CMA.[139] Prior to providing periodic reports to the CMA, issuers shall not disclose such information to parties not bound by a confidentiality agreement or any similar obligation to protect such information.[140]

Next, the information of periodic reports should be stored to facilitate public access to such information.[141] The CML allows the public to review and copy the prospectus and periodic reports, as well as any other information and data that has been filed with the CMA and made public.[142] The CML also authorizes the CMA to determine the fees for providing access to such information;[143] such charges are acceptable under the IOSCO principles.[144]

Disclosure criteria are the subject of the seventh principle. The information disclosed in periodic reports should be fairly presented, not be misleading or deceptive, and should not contain any material omission of information. Also, the information disclosed in periodic reports should be presented in a clear and concise manner.[145] The LR requires that all disclosure made by listed companies to the CMA, and to the public, must be "complete, clear, accurate, and not misleading."[146] All disclosures must be in Arabic: listed companies have the option to translate them to English.[147] However, Arabic is the official language in order to explain and to interpret any disclosures that are made by listed companies.[148]

IOSCO's eighth principle is the equal access to disclosure.[149] In order to ensure equal access, the LR prohibits listed companies from releasing interim and annual financial statement to shareholders or others, prior to their disclosure in Tadawul.[150]

137. The International Organization of Securities Commissions, *Principles for Periodic Disclosure By Listed Entities* at 23 (2010) (pointing out that small and medium-sized listed companies may need more time to prepare their reports because of their more limited resources).
138. The International Organization of Securities Commissions, *Principles for Periodic Disclosure By Listed Entities* at 24 (2010).
139. Capital Market Law, Article 45 (a) (2003); Listing Rules, Article 42 (b) (2004).
140. Capital Market Law, Article 45 (c) (2003).
141. The International Organization of Securities Commissions, *Principles for Periodic Disclosure By Listed Entities* at 25 (2010).
142. Capital Market Law, Article 47 (2003).
143. *Id.*
144. The International Organization of Securities Commissions, *Principles for Periodic Disclosure By Listed Entities* at 25 (2010).
145. *Id.* at 26.
146. Listing Rules, Article 40 (a) (2004).
147. *Id.* Article 48 (a).
148. *Id.* Article 48 (b).
149. The International Organization of Securities Commissions, *Principles for Periodic Disclosure By Listed Entities* at 27 (2010).
150. Listing Rules, Article 42 (c) (2004).

However, the LR provides some exceptions that allow disclosure to some persons before the information is filed with the CMA or otherwise made public. These persons are the issuer's advisors to the extent necessary for those advisors to provide advice in relation to the LR; the issuer's agent employed to release the information; and, persons with whom the issuer is negotiating with a view to effecting a transaction or raising funds, including prospective underwriters of an issue of securities or lenders.[151] To avoid insider trading, listed companies are to advise excepted persons in writing that the information is confidential and that they must not deal in the issuer's securities or any other related securities before the information has been made available to the public.[152]

The ninth principle is the equivalence of disclosure in which an entity is listed or admitted to trading in more than one jurisdiction. In that case, periodic reports made available to one market should be made available promptly to all other markets in which the entity is listed.[153] In this regard, Saudi laws do not spell out this principle directly. However, as a condition for listing foreign issuers in the Saudi Stock Exchange, the LR applicable in the foreign issuer's jurisdiction of listing must be at least equivalent to the LR.[154] Thus, the LR requires listed companies to disclose periodic reports in a timely manner, and any foreign issuer's jurisdiction is to be the same. Moreover, Article 14 of the LR states that foreign issuers are subject to the provisions of the LR.[155] However, the CMA should address clearly the equivalence of disclosure in the LR so that periodic reports made available to one market should be made available promptly to all markets in which the entity is listed, even if there is no obligation to disclose such information in the other jurisdiction.

Overall, the Saudi periodic disclosure regime is generally compliant with the IOSCO's principles: in fact, some relevant Saudi laws track the IOSCO's standards almost word for word.

[2] International Standards for Continuous Disclosure

In 2002, the Technical Committee of the IOSCO developed International Ongoing Disclosure Standards ("IODS").[156] The intent of the IODS is to "facilitate the agreement on minimum standards for ongoing disclosure and material development reporting for listed entities and provide guidance to jurisdictions reviewing and/or developing an

151. *Id.* Article 26 (c).
152. *Id.*
153. The International Organization of Securities Commissions, *Principles for Periodic Disclosure By Listed Entities* at 28 (2010).
154. Listing Rules, Article 14 (a) (2004).
155. *Id.* Article 14 (b).
156. The International Organization of Securities Commissions, *Principles for Ongoing Disclosure and Material Development Reporting by Listed Entities* (October 2002). The term "ongoing disclosure" in the Principles for Ongoing Disclosure and Material Development Reporting by Listed Entities is meant by the Technical Committee of the IOSCO to include current and periodic disclosure. *See* The International Organization of Securities Commissions, *Principles for Ongoing Disclosure and Material Development Reporting by Listed Entities* at 4 (2002).

ongoing disclosure and material development reporting regime for listed entities."[157] The Technical Committee recognizes the principle that timely, reliable, and readily accessible information is fundamental for investors. Therefore, such information should be disclosed on a consistent and timely basis, whether it is in connection with an IPO or other listing.[158]

The first principle of the IODS is that listed companies have an obligation for ongoing disclosure that applies to all material information that is important for investors' investment decisions.[159] Both the CML and the LR require issuers to disclose material developments that any investor would be likely to consider information about the development in making his investment decisions.[160] Moreover, the LR provides a list of events that are typically material developments, and issuers must disclose these events to both the CMA and the general public.[161]

The second IODS principle is that listed companies must disclose ongoing information on a timely basis, and material developments on an immediate basis.[162] The CML and the LR both require listed companies to disclose, without delay, any material developments to the CMA and the public. The CMA requires listed companies to disclose and report material developments at least half an hour prior to the start of the trading period immediately after the material development occurs.[163] If any such material development occurs less than half an hour prior to the start of the trading period, or during trading, the issuer must wait until the end of the trading period, and then announce the information publically.[164] During such a waiting period, the issuer must take all necessary precautions to ensure that the material information does not leak before the disclosure.[165] However, in case that the issuer cannot maintain the confidentiality of the information until the end of the trading period, the issuer may request a temporary trading halt and immediately inform the CMA about the event.[166]

In the U.S., the general rule is that Form 8-K[167] must be filed within four business days after a triggering event,[168] unless a different deadline is specified in the

157. The International Organization of Securities Commissions, *Principles for Ongoing Disclosure and Material Development Reporting by Listed Entities* at 3 (2002).
158. *Id.* at 2.
159. *Id.* at 4.
160. Capital Market Law, Article 46 (2003); Listing Rules, Article 41 (2004).
161. Listing Rules, Article 41 (b) (2004). These events are listed in *supra* n. 109.
162. The International Organization of Securities Commissions, *Principles for Ongoing Disclosure and Material Development Reporting by Listed Entities* at 4 (2002). The Technical Committee of the IOSCO suggested a definition for the team "an immediate basis" to be "as soon as possible" or prescribed as a maximum of specified days. *See* the International Organization of Securities Commissions, *Principles for Ongoing Disclosure and Material Development Reporting by Listed Entities* at 4 (2002).
163. Capital Market Authority, *CMA: Listed Companies are Obligated to Inform the Public about Any Significant Developments Which Are Not Available to the Public,* (May 27, 2015), http://cma.org.sa/Ar/MediaCenter/PK/Pages/Disclosure-Awareness-Report.aspx; Listing Rules, Article 40 (b) (2004).
164. Instructions for Regulating Announcements of Listed Companies in the Saudi capital Market at 3 (2006).
165. *Id.*
166. Listing Rules, Article 37 (2004).
167. *See supra* n. 108, and accompanying text.
168. These events are listed in *supra* n. 108.

Form.[169] Particularly, these exceptions are as follows: first, Regulation FD filings must be made simultaneously with the release of the relevant material if it is intentionally released, or the next trading day, if such release was unintentional;[170] second, voluntary disclosures, other than those made to satisfy a Regulation FD obligation, have no deadline;[171] third, firms that invoke the forty-eight-hour rule[172] for conference calls or earnings presentations must file the related earnings release on Form 8-K[173] prior to the related event; fourth, information on Form 8-K relating to a new officer appointment may be released after these appointments are publically announced;[174] fifth, a Form 8-K filing related to suspension of trading under employee benefit plans must be done on the same day that the company notifies any affected directors or officers.[175]

The third principle of the IODS applies to entities listed in multiple jurisdictions: these companies must release the same information in all jurisdictions, at the same time.[176] According to Saudi laws,[177] the CMA may admit the securities of a foreign issuer to listing, provided that "the listing rules applicable in the foreign issuer's jurisdiction of listing are at least equivalent to these Rules."[178] A foreign issuer is subject to the provisions of the LR[179] that require foreign issuers to promptly disclose any material developments to both the CMA and the public.[180]

The fourth principle of the IODS is that "listed entities should ensure that full information is promptly made available to the market by using efficient, effective, and timely means of dissemination."[181] In a similar fashion, the fifth principle states that "ongoing disclosure of information should be fairly presented, not be misleading or deceptive and contain no material omission of information."[182] Saudi capital market rules meet these two principles. The Instructions for Regulating Announcements of Listed Companies ("IRALC") in the Saudi capital market covers many aspects of

169. Alstyne, *supra* n. 87, at 67; Form 8-K, General Instructions, B.
170. Regulation FD, Rule 100(a), 17 C.F.R. § 243.100; Form 8-K, General Instructions, B.
171. Form 8-K, Item 8.01.
172. "Item 2.02(b) provides that a Form 8-K is not required to report the disclosure of material nonpublic information that is disclosed orally, telephonically, by webcast, broadcast or similar means if, among other things, that presentation is complementary to and initially occurs within 48 hours following a related written announcement or release that has been furnished on an Item 2.02 Form 8-K. This 48-hour safe harbor is construed literally and is not the equivalent of two business or calendar days." The U.S. Securities and Exchange Commission, *Exchange Act Form 8-K*, (Jun. 1, 2015), https://www.sec.gov/divisions/corpfin/guidance/8-kinterp.htm.
173. Form 8-K, Item 2.02 (b).
174. *Id.* Item 5.02 (b).
175. *Id.* Item 5.04; Alstyne, *supra* n. 87, at 67.
176. "This will mean disclosing information in a jurisdiction where: (a) the obligation may not technically require disclosure but disclosure is required in another jurisdiction in which the entity is listed; or (b) such information is exempted from ongoing disclosure obligation but it is not exempted in another jurisdiction in which the entity is listed." The International Organization of Securities Commissions, *Principles for Ongoing Disclosure and Material Development Reporting by Listed Entities* at 5 (2002).
177. *See supra* nn. 154 & 155, and accompanying text.
178. Listing Rules, Article 14 (2004).
179. *Id.* Article 14.
180. *Id.* Article 41.
181. The International Organization of Securities Commissions, *Principles for Ongoing Disclosure and Material Development Reporting by Listed Entities* at 5 (2002).
182. *Id.* at 6.

material developments disclosures, in addition to the release of financial reports, interim reports, and annual reports, while giving many specific rules regarding their structure.[183] Also, listed companies have the duty of due diligence to make sure that all information and data related to the material development are accurate and not misleading. Moreover, listed companies must not exclude, omit, or hide any information that can affect the content or the results of the material development. Also, if the material developments created financial obligations on behalf of the listed company, the announcement must contain the terms, duration, value of the financial obligation, related parties, and impact on the financial statements.[184]

Furthermore, the LR states "all disclosures made by an issuer to the public and to the Authority must be complete, clear, accurate and not misleading."[185] Additionally, the LR requires issuers to inform the CMA and the public "without delay" of any material developments.[186] All material information must be published on the Saudi Stock Exchange's website, according to the CMA's directions regarding the content and timing of any listed companies' announcements.[187]

The sixth IODS principle is that "the information to be disclosed in compliance with the ongoing disclosure obligation should not be disclosed to selected investors or other interested parties before it is released to the public."[188] The LR states "information that is required to be disseminated pursuant to these Rules must not be given to a third party before the information has been filed with the Authority and has been published."[189] However, issuers may disclose information to certain persons[190] before others, with the condition that the issuer must advise these persons in writing that the information is confidential, and that they must not deal in the issuer's securities before the information is made public.[191]

The seventh principle of the IODS is that "the listed entity is responsible for compliance with the ongoing disclosure obligation."[192] Article 34 of the LR states that "the issuer must comply with these Rules and must provide to the Authority without

183. With regard to sudden material developments, any announcement must include: (1) a clear title that reflects the material development, (2) a detailed description of the material development, (3) factors and reasons that have led to the material development, (4) and the effects on the financial statement, or the reasons the development has no effect on the financial statement. *See* Instructions for Regulating Announcements of Listed Companies in the Saudi Capital Market, 3. (2006).
184. Instructions for Regulating Announcements of Listed Companies in the Saudi Capital Market at 3 (2006).
185. Listing Rules, Article 40 (a) (2004).
186. *Id.* Article 41 (a); *See supra* nn 163-166, and accompanying text.
187. Capital Market Authority, *Annual Report 2014*, 74 (2014).
188. The International Organization of Securities Commissions, *Principles for Ongoing Disclosure and Material Development Reporting by Listed Entities* at 6 (2002).
189. Listing Rules, Article 26 (b) (2004).
190. These persons are: (1) the issuer's advisors to the extent necessary for those advisors to provide advice in relation to these Rules; (2) the issuer's agent employed to release the information; and (3) persons with whom the issuer is negotiating with a view to effecting a transaction or raising finance, including prospective underwriters of an issue of securities or lenders. Listing Rules, Article 26 (c).
191. Listing Rules, Article 26 (c) (2004).
192. The International Organization of Securities Commissions, *Principles for Ongoing Disclosure and Material Development Reporting by Listed Entities* at 6 (2002).

delay all information, explanations, books and records that the Authority may require, which must be complete, clear, accurate and not misleading."[193]

Assuming they are fully implemented and diligently enforced, these seven principles, when working together, should help create a capital market that is both transparent and equitable. These two principles are intended to be synchronistic: one cannot exist without the other. After reviewing the principles of the IODS, and their application in Saudi laws, it appears that the Saudi disclosure laws, regulations, and regime are in substantial compliance with international standards, and that the Saudi capital market is moving towards transparency and fairness.[194]

These guiding principles exist on top of the periodic and continuous disclosure requirements discussed above, which intensify the effect. In a similar fashion, the Kingdom has expressed a genuine interest in promoting capital investment in a common marketplace, although the extent of this commitment may be limited, as will be evaluated more fully below.

§4.04 THE CMA'S ROLE TOWARDS HIGH LEVEL OF DISCLOSURE IN THE MARKET

[A] Overall Goals

The primary force behind the capital market's movement towards fairness is the CMA. In fact, Article 5 of the CML gives the CMA broad powers to measure and observe all data that is associated with either the securities themselves or the entities that issue them, in addition to additional matters, including the behavior of informed persons (insiders), major shareholders and investors. The CMA then processes this information and makes it available to company shareholders, actual or potential investors, and the public at large. Furthermore, Article 6 of the CML grants the CMA the power to oversee the entire process, by issuing any required resolutions, instructions, or procedures for monitoring and regulating the disclosure process. As mentioned previously, the CMA relies on two primary types of disclosures to accomplish this mission: continuous disclosure and initial disclosure.[195]

After gathering this information, the CMA reviews and condenses it into annual and quarterly financial statements of listed companies, which are then published on the Saudi Stock Exchange Co.'s website. This scrutiny helps ensure that the reports meet all disclosure requirements according to the CML and any relevant Implementing

193. Listing Rules, Article 34 (a) (2004).

194. In July 2013, the IMF's Financial Sector Assessment Program published the *Detailed Assessment of Observance of the IOSCO Objectives and Principles of Securities Regulation* regarding Saudi capital market. This report concluded that the existing capital market regulatory framework in Saudi Arabia had no major gaps, while it encouraged ongoing revisions with regard to compliance and transparency issues. International Monetary Fund, *Saudi Arabia: Financial Sector Assessment Program- Detailed Assessment of Observance of the IOSCO Objectives and Principles of Securities Regulation*, p. 4, IMF Country Report No. 13/212 (July 2013). *See also* Chapter 2, §2.03, *supra*.

195. Capital Market Authority, *Annual Report 2015*, 64 (2015).

Regulations. In 2015, the CMA reviewed 841 condensed financial statements and 833 detailed financial statements.[196]

[B] Specific Activities

In collecting and distributing this information, the CMA's overall goal is to ensure that listed companies fully comply with the disclosure of any material information that has any possible significance for market participants. The most visible sign of this goal, and the most effective way to track the CMA's progress in this area, is to review listed companies' announcements on "Tadawul," especially with regard to content and timing. Overall, in 2015, there were 4,105 corporate announcements, which was a 9.1% increase from 2014. Furthermore, the number of general assembly announcements and invitations increased by 3.0%, as compared with the previous year. Finally, from 2014 to 2015, the volume of announcements related to financial results decreased by 0.6%.[197]

In addition to purely financial data, the CMA requires companies to establish regulations and rules for both internal controls and conflict of interest policies, in order to apply the best standards and rules for corporate governance.[198]

Within the CMA, the Continuous Disclosure Department has the primary responsibility for monitoring company compliance with the disclosure requirements of both the CML and LRs. The department has fifty staff persons and is divided into three thematic units: Daily Monitoring Unit, Review of Financial Statements Unit, and Qualified/Unqualified Opinion Unit. In addition to these three, there is an Enforcement Department that conducts on-site inspections, upon the recommendation of investigators' reports. Although this division currently has fewer than twenty employees, the staffing level has increased recently.[199]

The Enforcement Department was rather active in 2014, having conducted several supervisory inspections to raise awareness of the rules and support communication with the boards of those companies in order to achieve the highest possible compliance level with the CML in general, and its Implementing Regulations and other related regulations in particular. When it conducts an inspection, this division evaluates the company's current status, encourages it to apply the best practices, and ensures that the boards have adequate policies and procedures in place.[200]

Another CMA function is to monitor the financial health of listed companies. To fulfill this part of its mission, the CMA board passed Resolution No. (4-48-2013) dated November 18, 2013. It mandates that the CMA should scrutinize instructions and procedures concerning certain listed companies, namely those whose accumulated losses amount to 50% or more of their capital endowment. There were nine targeted

196. *Id.* at 65.
197. *Id.* at 67.
198. Saudi Arabian Monetary Agency, *51st Annual Report* 93 (2015).
199. The World Bank, *Report on the Observance of Standards and Code: Corporate Governance Country Assessment: Kingdom of Saudi Arabia 28* (20 Aug. 2015), http://www.worldbank.org/ifa/rosc_cg_saudia_arabia.pdf.
200. Capital Market Authority, *Annual Report 2014*, 75 (2014).

companies in 2015; four of these firms had registered losses exceeding 75% of their capitalized value by the end of 2014.[201]

The CMA also uses methods that are not as adversarial as the full inspections. It organizes conferences and seminars that promote awareness of the disclosure requirements in a much less intimidating fashion that rely on interactive dialogue. In 2014, the CMA conducted six sessions of the workshop entitled "Requirements of Continuous Disclosure for Listed Companies" in Jeddah, Riyadh, and Al-Khobar.[202]

In keeping with the theme of transparency, the CMA releases capital market news and Board resolutions on its website, as a way to communicate this information to all investors at the same time. To supplement these releases, the CMA issued 200 press releases and other materials in 2014, in addition to 5 awareness reports that were distributed to the media. These awareness reports appeared in 132 print and online newspapers. In addition to these traditional outlets, the CMA transmitted 510 messages over social media and other channels to communicate its message, distributed over 32,000 publications in public places and industry conferences, and published close to 10,000 copies of the eighth edition of *Smart Investor Magazine*.[203]

The CMA also relies on personal interaction. Some 3.7 million visitors attended at least one mobile exhibition during a five-city tour of the Kingdom. To connect with future investors, the agency connected with over 7,000 students during 251 school visits in nine cities and conducted various training courses throughout the country. All this activity occurred in 2014.[204]

[C] CMA Enforcement Tools with Respect to Disclosure Requirements

The Saudi CML provides the CMA with the tools necessary to protect the market and its investors, and to enforce fully the provisions of the CML and its regulations.[205] These tools can be used individually or together, in order to enforce the disclosure requirements.

As an initial matter, the CMA has the power to subpoena witnesses, to collect evidence, and to compel the production of documents and other tangible items, if the agency deems them relevant to a current or potential investigation.[206] In a similar vein, the Authority can conduct inspections of records and other materials to determine whether a person has violated, or is about to violate, any provision of a CML.[207]

201. In 2015, five companies listed accumulated losses between 50% and 74%. One company recorded accumulated losses between 75% and 99%; three companies accumulated losses of at least 100%. Capital Market Authority, *Annual Report 2015*, 70 (2015).
202. Capital Market Authority, *Annual Report 2014*, 77 (2014).
203. Saudi Arabian Monetary Agency, *51st Annual Report* 97-99 (2015).
204. *Id.*
205. *See* Capital Market Law, Articles 5 & 6 (2003).
206. *Id.* Article 5 (c).
207. *Id.*

If further action is necessary, the CMA can suspend the Exchange's activities up to one trading day; if the Authority or the Minister of Finance believes that a longer suspension is necessary, the Minister of Finance needs to approve that action.[208]

Furthermore, the CMA has the power to "approve the listing, cancel or suspend the listing, of any Saudi Security traded on the Exchange of any Saudi issuer, on any stock exchange outside the Kingdom"[209] or "prohibit any Security or suspend the issuance or trading of any Securities on the Exchange, as the Authority may deem necessary."[210]

In support of this activity, the CMA may issue instructions and decisions for the implementation of the provisions of the CML and any accompanying Implementing Regulations: it may also conduct investigations and inquiries regarding actual or potential violations.[211]

Additionally, the CMA has the right to bring a legal action before the Committee for the Resolution of Securities Disputes (CRSD) to impose an appropriate sanction, if it appears to the Authority that any person has engaged, is engaging, or is about to engage in acts or practices constituting a violation of any the CML or regulatory provisions.[212]

These sanctions include the following: warning the person concerned; obliging the person concerned to cease or refrain from carrying out the act which is the subject of the suit; obliging the person concerned to take the necessary steps to avert the potential violation, or address the results of a prior violation; indemnifying the persons who have suffered damages as a consequence of a prior violation; obliging the violator to remit any illegal gains to the CMA; suspending trading in the affected security; prohibiting the offending person from acting as a broker, portfolio manager or investment adviser for such period of time as is necessary for the safety of the market and the protection of investors; seizing and executing on property; imposing a travel ban; and barring persons from working with companies whose Securities are traded on the Exchange.[213] The CMA may request CRSD to impose additional financial fines on defendants who "intentionally" violate the CML, its regulations, or CMA rules.[214]

As an alternative to a demand for additional financial penalties, the Board may impose a financial fine upon any person responsible for the violation of the CML, its Implementing Regulations, the rules of the CMA, and the regulations of the Exchange. The fine that the CRSD or the Board of the CMA can impose shall not be less than SAR 10,000 and shall not exceed SAR 100,000 (USD 2,666-USD 26,666) per violation.[215]

The primary distinction between CRSD-imposed fines and those levied by the CMA is that the CRSD may only impose financial fines upon those who intentionally violate the CML or its regulations, while the Board of the CMA can impose monetary

208. Capital Market Law, Article 6 (a) (5) (2003).
209. *Id.* Article 6 (a) (6).
210. *Id.* Article 6 (a) (7).
211. *Id.* Article 6 (a) (12).
212. *Id.* Article 59 (a).
213. Capital Market Law, Article 59 (a) (2003).
214. *Id.* Article 59 (b).
215. *Id.* Article 59 (b).

fines upon those who are "responsible" for the violations, "apparently even if they did not do or have conscious knowledge of the act in question."[216] In other words, the Board can impose a monetary fine upon unintentional violations.

[D] Recently Published CMA Actions Against Disclosure Violations

To better evaluate the CMA's policies and enforcement tools, below is a summary of some of the more recent activity in this sector:

- On August 10, 2015 the CMA Board imposed a fine of SAR 20,000 (USD 5,333) on the Alinma Tokio Marine Company due to its violation of clause (B) of Article (40) of the LR, or failure to timely disclose interim financial results for the period ending on June 30, 2014 (Six Months). The information was eventually disclosed at (10:51:20),[217] which was less than two hours before the market opened on July 16, 2014.[218]
- On August 10, 2015 the CMA Board imposed a fine of SAR 20,000 (USD 5,333) on the Ash-Sharqiyah Development Company due to its violation of clause (B) of Article (40) of the LR. In this incident, the company was late to announce its receipt of the cadastral for the company's reclaimed land and report it to the Ministry of Agriculture, to complete the procedures to issue the resolution of ownership. It was later announced on June 3, 2014 at (09:28:54) less than two hours before the market opens on June 3, 2014.[219]
- The CMA announced in August 10, 2015 the issuance of a CMA Board resolution to impose a fine of SAR 10,000 (USD 2,666) on the Jarir Marketing Co. due to its violation of clause (A) of Article (40) of the LR and clause (8) of

216. Beach, *supra* n. 34, at n.223.
217. At that time, trading started at 11:00 AM and ended at 3:30 PM. Effective Apr. 3, 2016, the trading hours changed to be from 10:00 AM until 3:00 PM. Saudi Stock Exchange "Tadawul", *The Saudi Stock Exchange (Tadawul) Announces Changes to its Equities and ETF Markets Trading Hours*, (Jun. 9, 2016), https://www.tadawul.com.sa/wps/portal/tadawul/markets/Press-Release/news-details/!ut/p/z1/rVNNc9owEP0tPeTo0cqSPzi6QDCYmDQYEvvCCHshbrDsGKUp-fWVPzLNJTCZVqPDPs3b1du3EknIA0mk-JXvhcpLKQ4ax4m9Cf350AfXDMA3R-DZ4yAYDS0TmE3uW4JpDl064DCfTEMHvB-ev75eRwwmjCT_kg_8Uv6aJCRJparUI4mVyMTry2GD8gqOwuhhG1d1nuJRyCyXGeqoPZT42gWFqJ9QdZBbFm-KVmmekZiD5TiCgWHt0DU4c7gxoGxnDEyHI4XtbgtZ38T0dsLpVKt0I_s7eKvhPByFSwqWfdmEpKWcq9ASzvl8lgC8J8AnywMS6y6cDxrCgIE3pgFw_4YC52TZ1MiEwlus81KbY9DWKLHHsCQxhQYp_K2WKOpUz6PBQsryJS1QquhUIYnNTZd1bDn92XvhWsg9dnnHU7EtD32MqSrraXdjJ_Ovm9FYq79ZzK7vrBldLKCT-YXpzS6NR3-C_Ofzc-Lpl1bKpkHy8P-eWlWsVoXLTsbTnf8W4fbtfbvArMP-2x-8PVON/dz/d5/L0lDUmlTUSEhL3dHa0FKRnNBLzROV3FpQSEhL2Vu/.
218. At that time, the CMA required listed companies to disclose and report material developments at least two hours prior to the start of the trading period immediately after the material development occurs. Now, the CMA only requires listed companies to disclose material developments at least half an hour prior to the start of the trading period immediately after the material development occurs. *See supra* n. 83, and accompanying text.
    Capital Market Authority, *Imposition of a Fine on Alinma Tokio Marine Co.* (Aug. 11, 2015), http://www.cma.org.sa/En/News/Pages/CMA_N_1841.aspx.
219. Capital Market Authority, *Imposition of a Fine on Ash-Sharqiyah Development Co.* (Aug. 11, 2015), http://www.cma.org.sa/En/News/Pages/CMA_N_1842.aspx.

the Instructions for companies' Announcements regarding their financial results. The company failed to mention in its announcement on its interim financial results for the period ending on December 31, 2013 (twelve months), which was published on the Saudi Stock Exchange (Tadawul)'s website on January 19, 2014, all the reasons for the net profit decrease in the fourth quarter of 2013 compared to the same quarter of the previous year.[220]

- On February 26, 2015, the CMA assigned a special team to examine the Etihad Etisalat Co. (Mobily)'s financial statements, conduct site visits, obtain documents, and hear concerned parties' statements. The assigned specialized team submitted a preliminary report containing the results of its examination. Later, on June 8, 2015, the team presented a report summary to Etihad Etisalat Co. (Mobily); based on this report, the CMA's Board of Commissioners directed the company to study and ascertain the extent of the financial impact on the company's financial statements. On that same date, based on the CML and its implementing regulations, the Board suspended the trading of Etihad Etisalat Co. (Mobily) shares in the Saudi Stock Exchange ("Tadawul") effective June 9, 2015, until the company disclosed the financial impact on its financial statements, in light of the observations that had been submitted to the company.[221]
- On July 7, 2015, the CMA imposed a fine of SAR 20,000 (USD 5,333) on the Al-Baha Investment and Development Co. due to its violation of clause (A) of Article (34) of the LR;[222] specifically, the company presented misleading information to CMA.[223]
- On July 6, 2015, the CMA imposed a fine of SAR 10,000 (USD 2,666) on the Saudi Marketing Co. due to its violation of clause (A) of Article (46) of the CML and clause (A) of Article (41) of the LR.[224] The company signed an amendment on the Murabaha financing contract with Gulf International Bank signed on

220. Capital Market Authority, *Imposition of a Fine on Jarir Marketing Co.* (Aug. 11, 2015), http://www.cma.org.sa/En/News/Pages/CMA_N_1752.aspx.
221. Capital Market Authority, *CMA Announcement in Regards to the Suspension of Trading the Shares of Etihad Etisalat Co. (Mobily)*, (11 Aug. 2015), http://www.cma.org.sa/En/News/Pages/CMA_N_1801.aspx. The company announced on Jul. 30, 2015 its restated consolidated financial statements for the year 2014 and the restated consolidated financial statements for the first quarter of 2015. Also, the company published the restated financial statements on The Saudi Stock Exchange (Tadawul) website. As a result, the CMA announced the lift of the suspension of trading the shares of the company beginning Aug. 3, 2015. *See* Capital Market Authority, *CMA Announcement to lift the suspension of trading the shares of Etihad Etisalat Co. (Mobily)*, (Aug. 11, 2015), http://www.cma.org.sa/En/News/Pages/CMA_N_1840.aspx.
222. Article 34 (a) of the Listing Rules states that "the issuer must comply with these Rules and must provide to the Authority without delay all information, explanations, books and records that the Authority may require, which must be complete, clear, accurate and not misleading." Listing Rules, Article 34 (a) (2004).
223. Capital Market Authority, *Imposition of a Fine on Al-Baha Investment and Development Co.*, (Aug. 11, 2015), http://www.cma.org.sa/En/News/Pages/CMA_N_1839.aspx.
224. Article 46 (a) of the CML states that "a party who issues Securities must inform the Authority in writing upon becoming aware of any material developments which may affect the prices of the Securities issued by such party. If such party has a Security traded on the Exchange, the Exchange must be informed of such developments in writing."

August 28, 2012 in the amount of SAR 100,000,000 (USD 26,666,666), but did not disclose this activity until April 23, 2014.[225]

- The CMA announced on June 15, 2015 the issuance of a CMA Board resolution to impose a fine of SAR 10,000 (USD 2,666) on Al-Ahlia Insurance Co. "due to its violation of clause (A) of Article (46) of the CML and clause (A) of Article (41) of the LR." The company failed to timely inform CMA and the public about the April 14, 2015 Saudi Monetary Agency's temporary approval on its products. It was later announced on April 20, 2015.[226]

Altogether, the CMA filed and investigated 56 disclosure violations cases in 2013, 244 cases in 2014,[227] and 99 such cases in 2015.[228] Rather curiously, the agency did not refer any matters to the CRSD during the period of 2013 and 2014; all cases were handled internally.[229] The Board of CMA issued decisions on all of the disclosure violations during 2013 and 2014 as administrative decisions. However, in 2015, the CMA referred two disclosure violations cases to the CRSD.[230]

[E] Has the CMA's Enforcement Pattern Effectively Elevated the Disclosure Level in the Market?

One of the standout features in all these cases is that the fines are extremely low; arguably, they are much too low to serve as effective deterrents to wrongful conduct. It is entirely possible that companies may choose to act illegally and to pay the minimal fine, because the profits to be gained from such activity far outweigh the financial penalties.[231] In fact, even at the time these penalties first appeared, some observers maintained that they were "too lenient."[232]

By tracking the disclosure level by listed companies and the role of the CMA since its creation in 2004, one notices that the CMA has lifted the disclosure level among the listed companies in the market, but transparency is not yet at an acceptable level. While there is no doubt that the CMA has worked hard since its creation to improve the disclosure and the transparency in the market, the CMA has more to do in this area.

Generally, most people only comply with laws or instructions that are not in their best interest out of fear of punishment or hope of reward. This idea is commonly called

225. Capital Market Authority, *Imposition of a Fine on Saudi Marketing Co.-Farm Superstores-* (Aug. 11, 2015), http://www.cma.org.sa/En/News/Pages/CMA_N_1830.aspx.
226. Capital Market Authority, *Imposition of a Fine on Al-Ahlia Insurance Co.* (Aug. 11, 2015), http://www.cma.org.sa/En/News/Pages/CMA_N_1813.aspx.
227. Capital Market Authority, *Annual Report 2014*, 95 (2014).
228. Capital Market Authority, *Annual Report 2015*, 88 (2015).
229. Capital Market Authority, *Annual Report 2014*, 98 (2014).
230. Capital Market Authority, *Annual Report 2015*, 90 (2015).
231. *See* Mohammed Suliman Alangari, *Tadeel Alanthmah Llhad Men Almokalafat Bealsoug, "Modifying the Regulations to limit the Violations in the Market"*, Al-Jazirah, May 28, 2014, http://www.al-jazirah.com/2014/20140528/ec5.htm.
232. Mohamed A. Ramady, *The Saudi Arabian Economy, Policies, Achievements, and Challenges* 151 (2d ed. 2010).

the "carrot and the stick"[233] approach. In any free market, even normally law-abiding companies are tempted to cheat and to increase their profits, especially in a highly competitive environment. To be blunt, the "stick" in Saudi Arabia's capital market regulatory laws is too short. Based on the experience in the U.S., and the economic realities of the situation, the CMA should consider increasing the monetary fines in order to deter disclosure violations and to increase the level of the transparency in the market. U.S. SEC Enforcement Chief Andrew Ceresney rightly concluded that "monetary penalties speak very loudly and in a language any potential defendant understands," so "enforcement needs to be aggressive in our use of penalties."[234]

Further complicating the matter, the Board rarely imposes the maximum fine upon disclosure violators. The capital of the listed companies in the Saudi Stock Market amount to hundreds millions of dollars, and a monetary fine of USD 2,666 or even the maximum amount of USD 26,000 does not deter market participants from violating the disclosure requirements. One financial advisor declared that no one fears the CMA monetary penalties because they are "simple" when compared with the disclosure violations committed.[235] As U.S. Senator Chuck Grassley[236] said: "If a fine is just decimal dust for a Wall Street firm, that's not a deterrent ... A penalty should mean something, and it should get the recidivists' attention."[237]

Therefore, the U.S.' federal securities laws "authorize the SEC to obtain monetary penalties in both administrative proceedings and federal court actions." There are two possible methods. First, there is a per-violation calculation, in which the amount varies according to the severity of the alleged misconduct. This amount is capped at USD 150,000 per violation for individuals, and USD 725,000 per violation for entities. The second calculation method, which is typically available only in federal court, sets fines equal to the "gross amount of the pecuniary gain ... as a result of the violation."[238]

The U.S. Government is considering even stiffer fines and penalties in this area. Congress is currently debating the proposed Stronger Enforcement of Civil Penalties Act (SEC Penalties Act) as a way "to strengthen the SEC's ability to crack down on violations of securities laws." This proposal increases the per-violation cap in more serious securities laws violations to USD 1 million for individuals and USD 10 million for entities. It would also triple the penalty cap for repeat securities law violators who have been held civilly or criminally liable within the preceding five years. Additionally,

233. *See generally* Gerrit De Geest & Giuseppe Dari-Mattiacci, *The Rise of Carrots and the Decline of Sticks*, U. Chi. L. Rev. (2013).
234. Jean Eaglesham, *SEC Ramps Up Fine Amounts to Deter Misconduct*, The Wall Street Journal, Oct. 1, 2013, http://www.wsj.com/articles/SB10001424052702303918804579109554149460532.
235. Mohammed Alsmaiel, *La Ahad Iagsha Ogobat Soug Almal, "No One Fears The Capital Market's Sanctions, Alyaum"*, May 10, 2012, http://www.alyaum.com/article/3049621.
236. Chuck Grassley is the senior U.S. Senator from Iowa.
237. Mj Lee, *Pols: Let SEC Hit Wall Street Harder, Politico*, Jul. 23, 2012, http://www.politico.com/story/2012/07/pols-let-sec-hit-wall-street-harder-078844.
238. *See* Securities Act of 1933 20(d)(2); Securities Exchange Act of 1934 21(d)(3)(B); Investment Company Act of 1940 42(e)((2); Investment Advisers Act of 1940 209(e)(2); Commissioner Luis Aguilar, *Taking a No-Nonsense Approach to Enforcing the Federal Securities Laws*, U.S. Securities and Exchange Commission, Oct. 18, 2012, http://www.sec.gov/News/Speech/Detail/Speech/1365171491510#_ednref34.

the agency could assess these enhanced penalties in-house, without having to go to federal court.[239]

In addition to the low fines, some observers point to additional problems inside the CMA. For example, several legal and financial advisers claim that the disclosure level of the CMA is weak, because there is no immediate disclosure by the CMA about its investigations of some violators. Typically, the CMA only releases such information after a delay of several months, and in a somewhat ambiguous fashion that lacks details regarding the investigation.[240]

These same critics insist that the CMA has not fulfilled its duties, in terms of reforms to the laws and regulations that affect level of disclosure and transparency in the market, as well as investors' protection in the market, and this inattention contributed to the 2006 crash. There is no doubt that the transparency and disclosure level of the listed companies in the market is very weak, and that noncompliance with the disclosure rules is due to the absence of CMA monitoring in the market. In fact, for every violator that is caught and punished, there are many others that go undetected and unpunished.[241]

The 2006 Saudi stock market crash was "widely blamed on richer investors' insider trading and market manipulation, and the lack of investor protection and regulation."[242] The government itself also shared much of the blame, at least as far as some were concerned. Indeed, the government did show little initiative in dealing with the 2006 crash and may have even made the situation worse by issuing false assurances, as was previously discussed. One commentator went so far as to say that the government did nothing to stop "this painful economic catastrophe" or "halt the collapse in an effort to save the country and its citizens from its destructive consequences."[243] As a result, the capital market continues to suffer from a lack of investor confidence,[244] and restoring this confidence should be the first priority for the CMA and other regulators.

The impact of the weak disclosure rules is felt every day, and in many different situations. Even though the CMA has promoted and developed a disclosure and transparency-based regime in the market since its creation, many stocks' prices inexplicably move up and down, without any apparent pattern. Only when the listed company releases material information – which may be two or three weeks later – do the reasons for the price fluctuation become apparent. For instance, in 2011, the share

239. Chuck Grassley, *Bill Seeks Tougher Penalties for Wall Street Fraud*, Chuck Grassley, Jul. 9, 2015, http://www.grassley.senate.gov/news/news-releases/bill-seeks-tougher-penalties-wall-street-fraud.
240. Mohammed Alhilali, *Mohalilon: Hiat Soag Almal Be Hajah Ela Eslah, "Analysts: The Capital Market Authority is Needed To Be Reformed"*, Aleqtisadiah, Dec. 3, 2011, http://www.aleqt.com/2011/12/03/article_603590.html.
241. *Id.*
242. Robin Wigglesworth & Camilla Hall, *Saudis Hope Bourse Reform Will Lure Investors*, Financial Times, Jan. 16, 2012, http://www.ft.com/intl/cms/s/0/431a9448-4057-11e1-82f6-00144feab49a.html#axzz1pWMH8xey.
243. Sami Al-Nwaisir, *Saudi Stock Market Needs to Be Reformed*, Arab News, Jan. 11, 2012, http://www.eurasiareview.com/11012012-saudi-stock-market-needs-to-be-reformed-oped/.
244. *Id.*

of Arabian Pipes Company increased by 50% in only three weeks. After that, the company released two announcements that contained material information regarding an award of major contracts. This situation probably means that some investors knew about the material information before others, and took advantage of that knowledge. Nevertheless, the CMA neither investigated the matter nor took any other steps to protect investors. The CMA was essentially a passive authority and did not offer any official explanation for the price increase and possible information leak. Unfortunately, this issue still occurs in the Saudi stock market. Moreover, as previously stated, the disclosure of financial statements of many of the listed companies is unclear. Additionally, financial statements of the listed companies need more transparency and need to be disclosed with more details and explanation.[245]

Transparency and disclosure are present, to some degree, in the Saudi capital market, but at inconsistent and imperfect levels. Many listed companies sometimes announce that they have signed millions of Riyals contracts to implement expansion and development plans. However, their announcements do not address how these contracts will impact profits, revenue, and operations in any meaningful detail.[246]

A World Bank report in 2009 flatly concluded that "the [Saudi] regime governing the review, approval, and disclosure of related party transactions is underdeveloped"[247] and that "compliance with nonfinancial disclosure requirements appears weak."[248] The report went on to say that the CMA's regulations appear to be effective on paper, but they are not put into practice accordingly and are unevenly enforced. For example, while companies must disclose their dividend policies, corporate objectives, and board composition, they are not required to reveal any information concerning beneficial ownership, nomination procedures, and board member qualifications.[249]

To remedy this situation, the CMA should develop a more systematic approach, which uses an escalating approach involving strict adherence to the reporting requirement, warning letters, and fines as appropriate. Any such enforcement action should be made public by the CMA and published on Tadawul's website. Specifically, the CMA should focus on the existing "comply or explain" requirement in the CGR,[250] as well as other financial disclosure rules. The agency should also give more attention to

245. Mohammed Suliman Alangari, *Alafsah Oa Alshafafiah Fi Almezain, "Disclosure and Transparency in Balance"*, Al-Jazirah, Jan. 11, 2011, http://www.al-jazirah.com/2011/20110111/ec7.htm.
246. Aleqtisadiah, *Alajanab Saoajhoon Sera Thgafat Estathmariah Ma Almothareben Fe Alborsah Alsaodiah, "Foreign Investors Will Face Challenges Related to Investment Culture With Traders in The Saudi Bourse"*, Aleqtisadiah, Aug. 15, 2014, https://www.aleqt.com/2014/08/15/article_876846.html; *See* Ahmed Aljomaiah, *Soag Alashom: Motafaelon Rogam Altama Oa Fogdan Alshafafeih, "The Stock Market: Optimistic Despite the Greed and the Lack of Transparency"*, Alriyadh, Dec. 30, 2014, http://www.alriyadh.com/1008467.
247. The World Bank, *Report on the Observance of Standards and Code: Corporate Governance Country Assessment: Kingdom of Saudi Arabia 3* (Aug. 20, 2015), http://www.worldbank.org/ifa/rosc_cg_saudia_arabia.pdf .
248. *Id.*
249. *Id.* at 4.
250. Corporate Governance Regulations, Article 9 (a) (2006).

smaller issuers because some of the most serious compliance problems are found in these areas.[251]

In a subsequent report, the World Bank urged the CMA to be more transparent itself, by publishing a detailed annual report setting out its budget and disbursements, the fees it assess, the amount of revenue these fees generate, its interpretive guidance, advisory statements, and regulatory actions. The CMA should also not be reluctant to publish detailed disciplinary information, including the violator's name, nature of the offense, and the sanction imposed.[252]

§4.05 CONCLUSION

Disclosure in the Saudi capital market has improved significantly since 2003, as the country itself and the capital market strive to be more attractive to foreign and domestic investors. In fact, the regime is in compliance with applicable international standards. However, this movement suffered a serious setback when the stock market crashed in 2006, and the difference between the progress made regarding the legal structure and its apparent breakdown in 2006 highlights an important area that needs improvement.

The CML gives the CMA broad powers to enforce disclosure requirements, much like, in the U.S., the Securities and Exchange Act gives broad powers to the SEC. But unlike its American counterpart, the CMA is hesitant to enforce the CML's regulations, at least on a consistent and evenhanded basis. The reason for this reluctance is open to speculation, but there is no doubt as to its effect. Confidence in the Saudi stock market was shaken by the events of 2006, and ten years later, that confidence level is still low. As long as fines are not at a level to effectively deter possible violations, this situation will remain in place.

Rather than pass new laws or survey the situation, the solution may be to enforce more vigorously the laws that already exist. For the public, prompt and full disclosure, on the part of the CMA and the entities that it oversees, may do much to erase the memories of prior shortcomings and to promote the idea that the market is reasonably fair. In terms of securities issuers, the fine structure needs to be reexamined and vigorously to be enforced. In other words, the rules and the way they are carried out must work together, in order to effectively modernize the Saudi stock market. This is roughly the same method that the SEC follows, and the CMA may be well served by following that example.

251. The World Bank, *Report on the Observance of Standards and Code: Corporate Governance Country Assessment: Kingdom of Saudi Arabia, supra* n. 247, at 6-7.

252. The World Bank, *Saudi Arabia: Financial Sector Assessment* 11-12, SecM2012-0027, May, 2012, http://www-wds.worldbank.org/external/default/WDSContentServer/WDSP/IB/2015/06/10/090224b0828c8eaf/1_0/Rendered/PDF/Saudi0Arabia000al0sector0assessment.pdf .

Bibliography

I. Primary Sources

[A] Saudi Laws and Regulations

Corporate Governance Regulations, the Board of the Capital Market Authority Resolution Number 1-212-2006, dated 21/10/1427 H (November 12, 2006), Amended by the Resolution of the Board of the Capital Market Authority Number 1-10-2010, dated 30/3/1431 H (March 16, 2010).

Disclosure Rules, Ministerial Committee, Minister of Commerce Circular Reference Number 2222/221/9/3340, Dated 8/11/1417, March 17, 1997 (1997).

Glossary of Defined Terms Used in the Regulations and Rules of the Capital Market Authority, the Board of the Capital Market Authority Resolution Number 4-11-2004, dated 20/8/1425 H (October 4, 2004), Amended by the Resolution of the Board of the Capital Market Authority Number 3-58-2014, dated 17/1/1436 H (November 10, 2014).

Instructions for Regulating Announcements of Listed Companies in the Saudi capital Market, the Board of the Capital Market Authority Resolution Number 1-199-2006, dated 18/07/1427 H (August 12, 2006), Amended by the Resolution of the Board of the Capital Market Authority Number 4-38-2008, dated 26/11/1429 H (November 11, 2008).

Law of Companies, Royal Decree No. M/6, dated 22/3/1385 H (1965).

Listing Rules, the Board of the Capital Market Authority Resolution Number 3-11-2004, dated 20/8/1425 H (October 4, 2004), Amended by the Resolution of the Board of the Capital Market Authority Number 1-64-2016, dated 19/8/1437 H (May 26, 2016).

Market Conduct Regulations, the Board of the Capital Market Authority Resolution Number 1-11-2004, dated 20/8/1425 H (October 4, 2004), Amended by the Resolution of the Board of the Capital Market Authority Number 3-3-2016, dated 27/3/1437H (January 7, 2016).

Offers of Securities Regulations, the Board of the Capital Market Authority Resolution Number 3-11-2004, dated 20/8/1425 H (October 4, 2004), Amended by the Resolution of the Board of the Capital Market Authority Number 1-28-2008, dated 17/8/1429 H (August 18, 2008).

The Board of the Capital Market Authority Resolution Number 2-128-2006, dated 22/12/1426 H (January 22, 2006), http://www.cma.org.sa/Ar/News/Pages/CMA_N156.aspx.

The Capital Market Law, Royal Decree No. M/30, dated 2/6/1424 H (2003).

The Executive Rules to Regulate Share Dealing in Company Shares Through Commercial Banks, The Saudi Arabia Monetary Agency, December 1984 (1984).

The Guidelines for the Conversion of Companies to Joint-Stock Companies, The Ministry of Commerce, Circular 495, dated 25/3/1418, 7/29/1997 (1997).

[B] Other Countries' Laws and Regulations

Egyptian Capital Market Law, Law No. 95 of 1992 (1992).
Investment Advisers Act of 1940.
Investment Company Act of 1940.
Regulation FD, Rule 100(a), 17 C.F.R. § 243.100.
Regulation S-K, 17 C.F.R. §229.303 (2011).
Sarbanes-Oxley Act of 2002, Pub. L. No. 107-204, 116 Stat. 745 (2002).
The Executive Regulations of Egyptian Capital Market Law, Article 42, Law No. 95 of 1992.
The United States Securities and Exchange Commission, Form 8-K.
The United States Securities and Exchange Commission, Form 10-k.
U.S. Securities Act of 1933.
U.S. Securities Exchange Act of 1934.

[C] Official/Semi-Official Reports – Government & Nongovernment Bodies

Capital Market Authority, *Annual Report 2014* (2014).
Capital Market Authority, *Annual Report 2015* (2015).
Capital Market Authority, *An Announcement of the Issuance of the Board of the CMA Resolution Number (1-38-2016) Dated 22/6/1437H Corresponding to 31/3/2016G to Adopt the Amended Listing Rules*, (March 31, 2016), http://cma.org.sa/en/News/Pages/CMA_N_1990.aspx.
Capital Market Authority, *CMA Announcement in Regard to the Suspension of Trading the Shares of Al-Ahsa Development Co.* (August 14, 2015), http://www.cma.org.sa/En/News/Pages/CMA_N_1846.aspx.
Capital Market Authority, *CMA Announcement in Regards to the Suspension of Trading the Shares of Etihad Etisalat Co. (Mobily),* (August 11, 2015), http://www.cma.org.sa/En/News/Pages/CMA_N_1801.aspx.
Capital Market Authority, *CMA Announcement to Lift the Suspension of Trading the Shares of Etihad Etisalat Co. (Mobily),* (August 11, 2015), http://www.cma.org.sa/En/News/Pages/CMA_N_1840.aspx.
Capital Market Authority, *CMA: Listed Companies are Obligated to Inform the Public about Any Significant Developments which Are Not Available to the Public,* (May 27, 2015), http://cma.org.sa/Ar/MediaCenter/PK/Pages/Disclosure-Awareness-Report.aspx.
Capital Market Authority, *Disclosure*, December 31, 2015, http://www.cma.org.sa/en/FormsSite/Pages/Disclosure.aspx.
Capital Market Authority, *Imposition of a Fine on Al-Ahlia Insurance Co.* (August 11, 2015), http://www.cma.org.sa/En/News/Pages/CMA_N_1813.aspx.
Capital Market Authority, *Imposition of a Fine on Al-Baha Investment and Development Co.,* (August 11, 2015), http://www.cma.org.sa/En/News/Pages/CMA_N_1839.aspx.

Capital Market Authority, *Imposition of a Fine on Alinma Tokio Marine Co.* (August 11, 2015), http://www.cma.org.sa/En/News/Pages/CMA_N_1841.aspx.

Capital Market Authority, *Imposition of a Fine on Ash-Sharqiyah Development Co.* (August 11, 2015), http://www.cma.org.sa/En/News/Pages/CMA_N_1842.aspx.

Capital Market Authority, *Imposition of a Fine on Jarir Marketing Co.* (August 11, 2015), http://www.cma.org.sa/En/News/Pages/CMA_N_1752.aspx.

Capital Market Authority, *Imposition of a Fine on Saudi Marketing Co.-Farm Superstores-* (August 11, 2015), http://www.cma.org.sa/En/News/Pages/CMA_N_1830.aspx.

Commissioner Luis Aguilar, *Taking a No-Nonsense Approach to Enforcing the Federal Securities Laws*, U.S. Securities and Exchange Commission, October 18, 2012, http://www.sec.gov/News/Speech/Detail/Speech/1365171491510#_ednref34.

International Monetary Fund, *Saudi Arabia: Financial Sector Assessment Program-Detailed Assessment of Observance of the IOSCO Objectives and Principles of Securities Regulation*, IMF Country Report No. 13/212 (July 2013).

Saudi Arabian Monetary Agency, *51st Annual Report* (2015).

Saudi Arabian Monetary Agency, *Historical Preview*, (December 31, 2015), http://www.sama.gov.sa/en-US/About/Pages/SAMAHistory.aspx.

Saudi Stock Exchange "Tadawul", *The Saudi Stock Exchange (Tadawul) Announces Changes to Its Equities and ETF Markets Trading Hours*, (June 9, 2016), https://www.tadawul.com.sa/wps/portal/tadawul/markets/Press-Release/news-details/!ut/p/z1/rVNNc9owEP0tPeTo0cqSPzi6QDCYmDQYEvvCCHshbrDsGKUp-fWVPzLNJTCZVqPDPs3b1du3EknIA0mk-JXvhcpLKQ4ax4m9Cf350AfXDMA3R-DZ4yAYDS0TmE3uW4JpDl064DCfTEMHvB-ev75eRwwmjCT_kg_8Uv6aJCRJparUI4mVyMTry2GD8gqOwuhhG1d1nuJRyCyXGeqoPZT42gWFqJ9QdZBbFm-KVmmekZiD5TiCgWHt0DU4c7gxoGxnDEyHI4XtbgtZ38T0dsLpVKt0I_s7eKvhPByFSwqWfdmEpKWcq9ASzvl8lgC8J8AnywMS6y6cDxrCgIE3pgFw_4YC52TZ1MiEwlus81KbY9DWKLHHsCQxhQYp_K2WKOpUz6PBQsryJS1QquhUIYnNTZd1bDn92XvhWsg9dnnHU7EtD32MqSrraXdjJ_Ovm9FYq79ZzK7vrBldLKCT-YXpzS6NR3-C_Ofzc-Lpl1bKpkHy8P-eWlWsVoXLTsbTnf8W4fbtfbvArMP-2x-8PVON/dz/d5/L0lDUmlTUSEhL3dHa0FKRnNBLzROV3FpQSEhL2Vu/.

The International Organization of Securities Commissions, *Annual Report 2014* (2014).

The International Organization of Securities Commissions, *Growth and Emerging Markets Committee*, (December 31, 2015), https://www.iosco.org/about/?subsection=display_committee&cmtid=8.

The International Organization of Securities Commissions, *IOSCO Board*, (December 31, 2015), https://www.iosco.org/about/?subsection=display_committee&cmtid=11.

The International Organization of Securities Commissions, *Principles for Ongoing Disclosure and Material Development Reporting by Listed Entities* (October 2002).

The International Organization of Securities Commissions, *Principles for Periodic Disclosure By Listed Entities* (February 2010).

The United States Securities and Exchange Commission, *Exchange Act Form 8-K*, (June 1, 2015), https://www.sec.gov/divisions/corpfin/guidance/8-kinterp.htm.

The World Bank, *Report on the Observance of Standards and Code: Corporate Governance Country Assessment: Kingdom of Saudi Arabia* (August 20, 2015), http://www.worldbank.org/ifa/rosc_cg_saudia_arabia.pdf.

The World Bank, *Saudi Arabia: Financial Sector Assessment*, SecM2012-0027, May, 2012, http://www-wds.worldbank.org/external/default/WDSContentServer/WDSP/IB/2015/06/10/090224b0828c8eaf/1_0/Rendered/PDF/Saudi0Arabia00 0al0sector0assessment.pdf.

U.S. Securities & Exchange Commission, *How to Read a 10-K*, December 31, 2015, http://www.sec.gov/answers/reada10k.htm.

II. Secondary Sources

[A] Books

Alhadad, Radi Saleh, *Daorat Alastathmar Fi Alaorag Almaleah: Grarat Ethafeh [Cycle Investment in Securities: Extra Decisions]* (Riyadh Business 1992).

Alhamidi, Abdulrahman Abdullah & Abdulrahman Abdulmohsen Alkalaf, *Alnagood Oa Albonok Oa Alasoag Almalih [Money, Banks, and Capital Markets]*, (Alfarazdak Press Company, 2009).

Alstyne, Debra Van & Stephanie Tsacoumis, *Periodic Reporting Under the Federal Securities Laws*, Corporate Practice Portfolio Series 89-2nd (BNA 2015).

Alsuhaibani, Mohammed Ibrahim, *Aalaiat Almogasah Oa Altasaoih Fi Alasoag Almalih [Clearing and Settlement Mechanisms in Financial Markets]*, (Dar Kanoze Eshbilia Press 2009).

Alsuraiseri, Ahmed Sulaiman, *Saana Alsoag Aldoalih Fi Tadawul Alasahom Almahaleeh, [The Maker of International Market in Trading the Local Stocks]* (King Fahad National Library, Riyadh 2008).

Hammad, Adli Ali, *Mosoat Gaoanin Soag Almal Alsaoadi* [*Laws Encyclopedia of the Saudi Capital Market*], (King Fahad National Library 2013).

Hazen, Thomas Lee, Federal Securities Law (2nd. 2003).

Khdar, Ahmed Ali, *Alefsah Oa Alshafafiah Kaahad Mabada Alhokmah Fi Ganon Alsharekat [Disclosure and Transparency Are One of Corporate Governance Principles in the Companies Law]*, (Dar Alfakar Aljamae 2012).

Ramady, Mohamed A, *The Saudi Arabian Economy, Policies, Achievements, and Challenges* (2nd ed. 2010).

[B] Articles

Aljamal, Hisham, *Financial Markets and Financial Institutions*, Majmaah University (2013).

Beach, Joseph W., *The Saudi Arabian Capital Market Law: A Practical Study of the Creation of Law in Developing Markets*, 41 Stan. J. Int'l L. 307 (2005).

Butler, Kirt C. & S. Jamal Malaikah, *Efficiency and Inefficiency in Thinly Traded Stock Markets: Kuwait and Saudi Arabia*, 16 Journal of Banking & Finance 197 (1992).

Fox, Merritt B., *Civil Liability and Mandatory Disclosure,* 109 Colum. L. Rev. 237 (2009).

Fox, Merritt B., *Securities Disclosure in a Globalizing Market: Who Should Regulate Whom,* 95 Mich. L. Rev. 2498 (1997).

Geest, Gerrit De & Giuseppe Dari-Mattiacci, *The Rise of Carrots and the Decline of Sticks,* U. Chi. L. Rev. (2013).

Hu, Henry T.C., *Disclosure Universes and Modes of Information: Banks, Innovation, and Divergent Regulatory Quests,* 31 Yale J. On Reg 565 (2014).

Sarra, Janis, *Disclosure as a Public Policy Instrument in Global Capital Markets,* 42 Tex. Int'l L. J. 875 (2007).

[C] News

Alangari, Mohammed Suliman, *Alafsah Oa Alshafafiah Fi Almezain, "Disclosure and Transparency in Balance",* Al-Jazirah, January 11, 2011, http://www.al-jazirah.com/2011/20110111/ec7.htm.

Alangari, Mohammed Suliman, *Tadeel Alanthmah Llhad Men Almokalafat Bealsoug, "Modifying the Regulations to Limit the Violations in the Market",* Al-Jazirah, May 28, 2014, http://www.al-jazirah.com/2014/20140528/ec5.htm.

Aleqtisadiah, *Alajanab Saoajhoon Sera Thgafat Estathmariah Ma Almothareben Fe Alborsah Alsaodiah, "Foreign Investors Will Face Challenges Related to Investment Culture With Traders in The Saudi Bourse",* Aleqtisadiah, August 15, 2014, https://www.aleqt.com/2014/08/15/article_876846.html.

Alhilali, Mohammed, *Mohalilon: Hiat Soag Almal Be Hajah Ela Eslah, " Analysts: The Capital Market Authority Is Needed To Be Reformed",* Aleqtisadiah, December 3, 2011, http://www.aleqt.com/2011/12/03/article_603590.html.

Aljomaiah, Ahmed, *Soag Alashom: Motafaelon Rogam Altama Oa Fogdan Alshafafeih, "The Stock Market: Optimistic Despite the Greed and the Lack of Transparency",* Alriyadh, December 30, 2014, http://www.alriyadh.com/1008467.

Al-Nwaisir, *Sami, Saudi Stock Market Needs to Be Reformed,* Arab News, January 11, 2012, http://www.eurasiareview.com/11012012-saudi-stock-market-needs-to-be-reformed-oped/.

Alsmaiel, Mohammed, *La Ahad Iagsha Ogobat Soug Almal, "No One Fears The Capital Market's Sanctions, Alyaum",* May 10, 2012, http://www.alyaum.com/article/3049621.

Eaglesham, Jean, *SEC Ramps Up Fine Amounts to Deter Misconduct,* The Wall Street Journal, October 1, 2013, http://www.wsj.com/articles/SB10001424052702303918804579109554149460532.

Grassley, Chuck, *Bill Seeks Tougher Penalties for Wall Street Fraud,* Chuck Grassley, July 9, 2015.

Lee, Mj, *Pols: Let SEC Hit Wall Street Harder, Politico,* July 23, 2012, http://www.politico.com/story/2012/07/pols-let-sec-hit-wall-street-harder-078844.

Wigglesworth, Robin & Camilla Hall, *Saudis Hope Bourse Reform Will Lure Investors*, Financial Times, January 16, 2012, http://www.ft.com/intl/cms/s/0/431a9448-4057-11e1-82f6-00144feab49a.html#axzz1pWMH8xey.

CHAPTER 5

Insider Trading in the Kingdom of Saudi Arabia

SUMMARY

If the capital market in Saudi Arabia is to further its growth and development, it must deal with the challenge of "insider trading." But, in Saudi society, many people consider helping others, which includes dispensing financial advice, to be a high personal and societal obligation. As such, many investors simply do not believe, or even know, that insider trading is wrong, illegal, and detrimental to the government's efforts to develop a strong modern economy.

Illegal insider trading is broadly defined as unlawful trading securities based on material nonpublic information. In the U.S., there are federal statutes and regulations addressing these matters, and the U.S. Supreme Court has developed a series of judicial guidelines that further define the practice. However, in Saudi Arabia, there is little law or jurisprudence in this area. Largely due to the extensive use of "hidden agreements," or plea bargains, whose terms are never made public, the Committee for Securities Dispute Resolution ("CSDR") has decided only five insider-trading cases as of the end of 2015.

Instead, Saudi law relies on a web of articles from the "CML" and the Market Conduct Regulations ("MCR") to frame insider trading in terms of business, family, and contractual relationships. But these subparts are poorly defined. Moreover, the penalties for violating the insider-trading laws are tepid and sparsely enforced. For example, insider trading in Saudi Arabia carries a maximum five years in prison, but incarceration has only been imposed once and the sentence was a mere three months. These three items - lack of awareness, weak enforcement, and anemic penalties - represent one of the greatest challenges to fairness, accountability, and transparency in the Saudi capital market.

This chapter critically examines the law and procedure of insider trading in Saudi Arabia, and makes some suggestions for improving the processes and laws. One such improvement should come by borrowing the "Whistleblower Program" from the U.S.

§5.01 INTRODUCTION

Saudi Arabia enacted the[1] "CML" in 2003 to regulate, restructure, and develop the capital market in the country. This Law introduced new concepts designed to protect investors, to enhance confidence in the market, and to attract more potential investors. Furthermore, the Law also contributes to an enhanced disclosure process, market fairness, and transparency.[2] The government of Saudi Arabia believed the CML would unify the regulatory structure, establish rules and procedures for all investors to participate in the capital market, and level the playing field in the Saudi financial sector.[3]

Notwithstanding the recent establishment of a regulated Saudi stock market, this market is witnessing many violations such as manipulation and "insider trading." The Saudi stock market largely consists of a small number of listed companies in the market, the small size of the capital of many listed companies, the lack and weakness of the investigation procedures in manipulation and insider-trading cases, the weakness of sanctions in a way to deter offenders, and the high financial capacity of many big traders who may trade in a value exceeding some of the capital of many listed companies.[4]

Insider trading, as defined in the CML, prohibits any person who obtains, through family, business, or contractual relationship, inside information from directly or indirectly trading in the security related to such information, or to disclose such information to another person with the expectation that such person will trade in such security.[5]

Going back to the history of the U.S., the stock market crash of 1929 provided the necessity to enact securities regulations, such as the Securities Exchange Act of 1934.[6] The investigation of the 1929 stock market exchange crash revealed that there were stock market manipulation, insider trading, breaches of fiduciary duty and other abuses engaged in by many respected leaders, directors, major banks, and other

1. In Jul. 31, 2003, the government of Saudi Arabia enacted the Capital Market Law. Capital Market Law, Royal Decree No. M/30, dated 2/6/1424 (2003).
2. Saudi Stock Exchange "Tadawul", *Market Rules*, Nov. 14, 2015, http://www.tadawul.com.sa/wps/portal/!ut/p/c1/04_SB8K8xLLM9MSSzPy8xBz9CP0os3g_A-ewIE8TIwMLf3czA0_vIKegIBN_QwNXQ6B8JJK8e0CYqYGniU-wUXCAl7GBpxEB3X4e-bmp-gW5EeUATNtVlg!!/dl2/d1/L0lDUmlTUSEhL3dHa0FKRnNBL1lCUlp3QSEhL2Vu/.
3. BBC New, *Saudi Stock Exchange Approved*, BBC News, Jun. 17, 2003, http://news.bbc.co.uk/2/hi/business/2998086.stm .
4. Mohammed Ibrahim Alsuhaibani, *Altalaob Fi Alasoag Almaliah: Alboad Aleqtesade* 23-24, [*The Manipulation in the Capital Markets: The Economic Impacts* 23-24], A Papare Presented at the Speculation and Manupulation in the Capital Markets: Their Economic and Legal Impact Conference, Islamic International Foundation for Economics and Finance. (Mar. 5, 2008).
5. Capital Market Law, Article 50(a) (2003).
6. Nasser Arshadi & Thomas Eyssell, *The Law and Finance of Corporate Insider Trading: Theory and Evidence* 19 (Kluwer Academic Publishers 1993).

financial institutions.[7] The Great Depression spurred the improvement and development of federal securities laws and the creation of the "SEC" in 1934.[8] In addition to the U.S.,[9] various other countries such as Canada,[10] Japan,[11] and, very recently, Saudi Arabia[12] have also adopted prohibitions on insider trading.

The lesson learned from the U.S. is that "inside information" that is related to listed (publicly traded) companies is very important in capital markets, since most investors usually base their decisions to buy or to sell stocks on the public information in regards to these stocks.[13] A market that is to have integrity and merit public confidence needs to have a level playing field as the flow of material information.

This chapter will examine the "nonpublic information" and insider-trading provisions of the CML and its regulations and enforcement in the KSA, and its contributions in preventing violations from occurring and protecting investors, the integrity of the Saudi economy and the capital market. Within this chapter, actual insider-trading cases in Saudi Arabia will be analyzed, along with the way the Committee for the Resolution of Securities Disputes ("CRSD")[14] has dealt with these cases. There is a very small sample size as the CRSD has adjudicated only about a half-dozen insider-trading cases in its entire existence.

This chapter also discusses the evolution of insider trading in the specific historical and societal background that makes up modern-day Saudi Arabia, along with its specific legal definition. The primary elements of this definition are "materiality" and nonpublic information. Subsequently, once these cases go to court, the CRSD and American courts employ different ways of evaluating the facts and applying the law, and these items will be discussed in some detail. After the cases are concluded, both the U.S. and Saudi Arabia rely on a system of prison sentences and monetary penalties, including disgorgement and fines, to punish violators.

Furthermore, in support of the enforcement process, the U.S. has rather successfully employed a "Whistleblower Program" that is based on whistleblower confidentiality, large payouts and concrete protections against retaliation.

---

7. Ferdinand Pecora, *Wall Street Under Oath: The Story of Our Modern Money Changers* 283 (A. M. Kelley Publishers 1968).
8. Laura Hughes, *The Impact of Insider Trading Regulations on Stock Market Efficiency: A Critique of The Law and Economics Debate and A cross Country Comparison*, 23 Temp. Int'l & Comp. L.J. 479 (2009).
9. Securities Exchange Act of 1934, § 10(b), 15 U.S.C.A. § 78j (West).
10. Securities Act, R.S.O., ch. XVIII, § 76 (1990) (Can.).
11. Financial Instruments and Exchange Act, Law No. 25 of 1948, Article 166 (as amended 1988) (Japan).
12. Saudi Capital Market Law, Article 50 (2003).
13. Mohammed Ibrahim Mousa, *Haokamat Alsharekat Almogiedah Be Soug Alaorag Almaleih* 52-53 [*The Corporate Governance of Listed Companies in the Capital Market* 52-53], (Dar Aljamiah Aljadidah 2010).
14. A part of Article 25(a) of the CML states that the CML shall establish a committee known as the "Committee for the Resolution of Securities Disputes." Capital Market Law, Article 25(a) (2003).

§5.02 A BRIEF HISTORY OF INSIDER-TRADING REGULATION IN SAUDI ARABIA

A salient feature of Saudi Arabian insider-trading law and procedure is that the Kingdom does not have a long history in regulating insider trading in the stock market. In fact, prior to 1997, directors of listed companies could trade freely and legally on the companies they managed without violating the law because there was no law at all prohibiting them to trade based on inside information. In effect, a "culture" of "instability" prevailed.

The only related law in effect at that time, the 1965 Law of Companies,[15] failed to regulate insider trading in the market. Articles 72[16] and 133[17] of that Law only prohibited directors and auditors from disclosing nonpublic information to shareholders or to third parties. However, the law did not prohibit anyone other than directors and auditors from disclosing such information at will. More importantly, the law did not prohibit directors, auditors or others from trading based on nonpublic information, which is the very essence of insider trading.

In 1990, the Ministerial Committee for Supervising Share Trading[18] issued "Instruction for Central Trading Units" ("CTU"),[19] and the "SAMA" was responsible for reviewing and updating these instructions as deemed necessary.[20] These instructions contained a limited scope of restriction on insider trading. They prohibit only banks' employees who work with buying/selling shares orders to trade stocks based on nonpublic information.[21] Similar to the 1965 Law of Company, this minor limitation did

15. Law of Companies, Royal Decree No. M/6, dated 22/3/1385 H (1965).
16. Article 72 of the Law of Companies stated that "directors might not disclose to the stockholders or to third parties outside a general meeting, such secrets of the company because they are liable for its administration; otherwise, they must be removed and held liable for damages." The Law of Companies, Article 72 (1965).
17. The language of Article 133 of the Law of Companies is as follows: "It is not permissible for the auditor to broadcast to the shareholders in the General Assembly or to others what he knew of the secrets of the company because of doing his job, otherwise he shall be removed as well as requested for compensation. The auditor shall be asked for compensating the damage that occurs to the company, the shareholders or others because of errors made by him in the performance of his work. And if the observers who participated in the error were many, they shall be jointly liable." The Law of Companies, Article 133 (1965).
18. The Ministerial Committee was formed in 1984 by Royal Decree Number 1230/8 to regulate and develop the Saudi Arabian Stock Market. The committee consisted of the Ministry of Finance and National Economy, Ministry of Commerce, and SAMA. For more details, *See* Kirt C. Butler & S. Jamal Malaikah, *Efficiency and Inefficiency in Thinly Traded Stock Markets: Kuwait and Saudi Arabia*, 16 J. Banking & Finance 197 (1992); Abdulrahman Abdullah Alhamidi & Abdulrahman Abdulmohsen Alkalaf, *Alnagood Oa Albonok Oa Alasoag Almalih 348 [Money, Banks, and Capital Markets 348]*, (Alfarazdak Press Company, 2009); Saudi Arabian Monetary Agency, *Historical Preview*, (Nov. 14, 2015), http://www.sama.gov.sa/en-US/About/Pages/SAMAHistory.aspx.
19. Central Trading Units were dealing rooms available in each commercial bank. At that time, stocks brokerage was limited to only commercial banks. All bank branches took orders to sell/buy share from clients and passed the orders to the bank's central unit. Alhamidi, *supra* n. 18, at 351-53.
20. The Electronic Securities Information System Instructions to CTUs 1990, Saudi Arabian Monetary Agency (1990).
21. The Electronic Securities Information System Instructions to CTUs, Article 9(3) (1990).

not cover anyone other than bank employees. In fact, the "Instruction for Central Trading Units" only governed banks and their employees.[22]

Later in 1997, the Saudi government prohibited, for the first time, insider trading to cover all market participants. The Ministerial Committee issued in 1997 the Disclosure Rules[23] to increase the level of transparency and disclosure in the market.[24] Specifically, Article 3(a) of the Disclosure Rules prohibited all boards of directors, managers, and executive employees from dealing or trading before the company announced any major events that were likely to affect the price of the shares.[25] And, in a more general restriction, Article 4(a) of the Disclosure Rules prohibited "any person" from trading based on inside information, which was defined as information not published and freely available to the public, whether it was received directly or indirectly.[26]

However, the 1997 Disclosure Rule did not include sanctions for violations. It only stated that "the creation of an unfair market and/or persons acting on inside information.... is prohibited. Any violation will be punishable according to the regulations within the Kingdom."[27] As a result, sanctions that are mentioned in 1965 Law of Companies would be applied, which are too weak to deter violations since that Law was written over five decades previously. Additionally, historically, Saudi authorities have not been very serious in imposing sanctions against insider-trading violations. "In practice, an offender usually receives a warning for such a violation asking him not to do it again."[28]

The Saudi government enacted the CML in 2003 and established the "CMA" in 2004 in order to increase transparency and disclosure in the market, and to protect investors from abusive conducts such as insider trading.[29] Specifically, Chapter Eight of the CML, titled as "Manipulation and Insider Trading,"[30] indicated that the Saudi government had become more seriously concerned about the integrity of the capital market, as well as its transparency. Further, not long after the establishment of the CMA, the agency[31] issued the "MCR" in 2004 to provide additional details about illegal conduct in the capital market, such as insider trading.[32] However, since insider trading continues to occur in the Saudi capital market, one might question the actual level of

22. *See Id.* Article 1(1).
23. Disclosure Rules, Ministerial Committee, Minister of Commerce Circular Reference Number 2222/221/9/3340, dated 8/11/1417, Mar. 17, 1997 (1997).
24. Alhamidi, *supra* n. 18, at 354.
25. Disclosure Rules, Article 3(a) (1997).
26. *Id.* Article 4(a).
27. *Id.* Article 5.
28. Henry T. Azzam, *The Emerging Arab Capital Markets: Investment Opportunities in Relatively Underplayed Markets* 156 (Kegan Paul International 1997).
29. The Capital Market Authority was established on Jul. 2, 2004, in accordance with Article 4 of the CML, to regulate and to supervise the capital market. Alhamidi, *supra* n. 18, at 361.
30. The Capital Market Law, Chapter Eight (2003).
31. The CMA has the power under the Capital Market Law to issue regulations to enforce the provisions of the CML. The Capital Market Law, Article 6 (2) (2003).
32. Market Conduct Regulations, the Board of the Capital Market Authority Resolution Number 1-11-2004, dated 20/8/1425 H (Oct. 4, 2004), Amended by the Resolution of the Board of the Capital Market Authority Number 3-3-2016, dated 27/3/1437 H (Jan. 7, 2016).

transparency and disclosure in the market, along with the efficiency of legal sanctions to deter insider-trading violations. Part of the issue may be that, while Saudi laws define insider trading well in overarching and general terms, these laws and regulations remain somewhat vague in terms of their applications to specific situations.

§5.03 INSIDE INFORMATION

[A] Overview

As a general rule, insider trading cannot occur without involving material nonpublic information.[33] As a result, it is important to define the meaning of inside information.

The CML defines "material nonpublic information" in Article 50 as information obtained by the insider that has not been officially disclosed, is not available to the general public, and "is of the type that a normal person would realize that in view of the nature and content of this information, its release and availability would have a material effect on the price or value of a Security related to such information, and the insider knows that such information is not generally available and that, if it were available, it would have a material effect on the price or value of such Security."[34]

Article 4(c) of the MCR identifies several elements that must be in place in order to consider information as "material inside information." These elements include information: (1) that relates to a security; (2) that has not been disclosed to the general public and that is not otherwise available to the general public; (3) and that a normal person would realize that, in view of the nature and content of the information, disclosing it or making it available to the public would have a material effect on the price or value of the security.[35]

In Egypt, inside information is defined as "any material information which has not been made public to the dealing/investing public, and which is related to the operations of a company whose securities are negotiable, or to any party or entities related to it."[36] So, in Egypt, there is no requirement of actual or constructive knowledge.

In Jordan, inside information in the capital market is defined as "information relating to one or several issuers or to one or several securities which has not been made public and which, if it were made public, would likely affect the price of any such security. This does not include inferences drawn on the basis of economic and financial studies, research and analysis."[37]

Likewise, the U.S. defines material nonpublic information as any information that has not been disseminated and which a reasonable investor would classify as meaningful to the price or value of the security. Typically, U.S. courts consider

33. Mohammed Nasser Albjad, *Garaim Alsoug Almalih Fi Alnedam Alsaoudi 152 [Stock Market Crimes in Saudi Law 152]*, (King Fahad National Library 2008).
34. Capital Market Law, Article 50(a) (2003).
35. Market Conduct Regulations, Article 4(c) (2004).
36. The Executive Regulations of Egyptian Capital Market Law, Article 319 (C), Law No. 95 (1992).
37. The Securities Law of Jordan, Article 2, Law No. 76 (2002).

information to be "material"[38] if: "(a) there is a substantial likelihood that a reasonable investor could consider the information important in deciding whether to buy, sell or hold the securities in question; or (b) the information, if disclosed, could be viewed by a reasonable investor as having significantly altered the 'total mix' of information available."[39]

[B] The "Materiality of Information"

In general terms, "materiality" is a key element of insider trading. Again, in general, most Middle Eastern and North African ("MENA") states have similar approaches. In Egypt, material information is "a piece, or pieces, of information that have a material effect on the price of an offered or negotiable security, investment decisions of those dealing in it, or trends of dealing in the market."[40] In Jordan, the law defines material information as "any event or datum that, to a reasonable person, would have an effect in making a decision to buy, hold, sell or dispose of a security."[41]

In the U.S., the U.S. Supreme Court in *TSC Industries v. Northway* provided a test to determine the materiality of information. The test is that if there is substantial likelihood that a reasonable shareholder would consider it important in deciding how to vote, the disclosure information is material.[42] Moreover, in the same case, the U.S. Supreme Court explained the test further: "there must be a substantial likelihood that the disclosure of the omitted fact would have been viewed by the reasonable investor as having significantly altered the 'total mix' of information made available."[43] It is well established that materiality is a mixed question of law and fact[44] and that "the determination requires delicate assessments of the inferences a 'reasonable shareholder' would draw from a given set of facts and the significance of those inferences to him...".[45]

However, some have questioned this standard. For example, the U.S. Court of Appeals for the Second Circuit held that "it is well-established that a material fact need not be outcome-determinative; that is, it need not be important enough that it "would have caused the reasonable investor to change his vote."[46] "What the standard does contemplate is a showing of a substantial likelihood that, under all the circumstances,

38. The meaning of material information is addressed in the next section, §5.03 [B].
39. Alan S. Gutterman, *Business Transactions Solutions* § 290:113 (Westlaw 2015); *TSC Indus., Inc. v. Northway, Inc.*, 426 U.S. 438, 449 (1976).
40. The Executive Regulations of Egyptian Capital Market Law, Article 319 (B), Law No. 95 (1992).
41. The Securities Law of Jordan, Article 2, Law No. 76 (2002).
42. *TSC Indus., Inc. v. Northway, Inc.* at 449. Though this is a proxy case, the definition has become generally accepted as the standard under the federal sentencing laws.
43. *Id.*
44. *SEC v. Cuban*, No. 3:08-CV-2050-D, 2013 WL 791405, at *11 (N.D. Tex. Mar. 5, 2013); *SEC v. Mayhew*, 121 F.3d 44, 51 (2d Cir. 1997).
45. *TSC Indus., Inc. v. Northway* at 450.
46. *Folger Adam Co. v. PMI Indus., Inc.*, 938 F.2d 1529, 1533 (2d Cir. 1991).

the omitted fact would have assumed actual significance in the deliberations of the reasonable shareholder."[47]

Nevertheless, in *Basic Inc. v. Levinson*, the U.S. Supreme Court expressly reaffirmed the standard of materiality set forth in *TSC Industries* for Section 10(b) and Rule 10b-5.[48] The Court in *Basic* also pointed out that the materiality of information depends on the significance the reasonable investor would place on the withheld or misrepresented information.[49] The court noted that trading and profit making by insiders could serve as an indication of materiality.[50]

Furthermore, in the matter of contingent or speculative information, such as preliminary merger discussions, "materiality will depend at any given time upon a balancing of both the indicated probability that the event will occur and the anticipated magnitude of the event in light of the totality of the company activity."[51]

The U.S. courts have looked to other factors to determine whether the information in question is material.[52] "Materiality is not judged in the abstract, but in light of the surrounding circumstances."[53] One of these factors is "the importance attached to it by those who knew about it."[54] The Second Circuit in *SEC v. Texas Gulf Sulphur Co.* stated that:

> a major factor in determining whether the K-55-1 discovery [of an area that was rich in minerals] was a material fact is the importance attached to the drilling results by those who knew about it ...... Nevertheless, the timing by those who knew of it of their stock purchases and their purchases of short-term calls–purchases in some cases by individuals who had never before purchased calls or even TGS[55] stock– virtually compels the inference that the insiders were influenced by the drilling results.[56]

Another factor in determining the materiality of information is the reaction of the market when the information becomes available to the public.[57] For instance, in *SEC v. Kirch*, the market priced closed at USD 9.50, but when a public announcement was made related to negative inside information, the stock price dropped precipitously the next day to USD 4 per share.[58] The court held that this kind of information was

47. *TSC Indus., Inc. v. Northway, Inc.* at 449. In *SEC v. Mayhew*, the Second Circuit stated "to be material, the information need not be such that a reasonable investor would necessarily change his investment decision based on the information, as long as a reasonable investor would have viewed it as significantly altering the 'total mix' of information available." *S.E.C. v. Mayhew* at 52.
48. *Basic Inc. v. Levinson*, 485 U.S. 224, 232 (1988).
49. *Id.* at 240; *see SEC v. Tex. Gulf Sulphur Co.*, 401 F.2d 833, 851 (2d Cir. 1968).
50. *Basic Inc. v. Levinson*, at 240 n. 18.
51. *Finnerty v. Stiefel Labs., Inc.*, 756 F.3d 1310, 1321 (11th Cir. 2014); *Basic Inc. v. Levinson*, at 238; *SEC v. Ginsburg*, 362 F.3d 1292, 1302 (11th Cir. 2004).
52. Marc I. Steinberg & William K.S. Wang, *Insider Trading* 111 (Oxford University Press 2010).
53. *SEC v. Cuban*, No. 3:08-CV-2050-D, 2013 WL 791405, at 11 (N.D. Tex. Mar. 5, 2013); *Rosenzweig v. Azurix Corp.*, 332 F.3d 854, 866 (5th Cir.2003).
54. *SEC v. Thrasher*, 152 F. Supp. 2d 291, 300 (S.D.N.Y. 2001); *SEC v. Mayhew*, 121 F.3d 44, 52 (2d Cir. 1997).
55. Texas Gulf Sulphur company.
56. *SEC v. Tex. Gulf Sulphur Co.* at 851.
57. Marc I. Steinberg & William K.S. Wang, *Insider Trading* 113 (Oxford University Press 2010).
58. *SEC v. Kirch*, 263 F. Supp. 2d 1144, 1148 (N.D. Ill. 2003).

"confirmed dramatically" material because of its reaction in the market when the information became public.[59] Moreover, in *SEC v. Farrell*, the court held that the jump of the share price from approximately USD 15 per share to approximately USD 17.75 per share on the day of announcement indicated the materiality of the information.[60] Similarly, in *S.E.C. v. Carroll*, the 60% increase in the company's share price immediately after the public announcement of the company's acquisition by another company provides strong evidence of materiality.[61]

An important factor for determining the materiality of information is its source.[62] In *Burlington Indus. v. Edelman*, the court pointed out that the information came from an executive who worked twenty-three years at Burlington and who was privy to the company's confidential information.[63] These facts heighten "the credence a reasonable shareholder would attach to such information."[64]

Moreover, the specificity of the tip is another factor for determining the materiality of information.[65] In *Elkind v. Liggett & Myers, Inc.*,[66] the Second Circuit held that only the second of two statements made to analysts was material because the second statement specifically addressed that earnings would decline in the quarter; but, the first statement was about some difficulties on various corporate divisions and that a press release would come out soon.[67]

In 2000, the SEC provided guidance about types of information or events that are more likely to be considered "material." The SEC declares that "it is not possible to

59. *Id.* at 1149; another example is *SEC v. Tome*, in which the court discussed the materiality of information regarding an impending tender offer. The court stated that "the significance of this information to investors is highlighted by the temporary halting of trading in St. Joe securities and by the virtually immediate jump in price of St. Joe stock from approximately USD 30 per share to approximately USD 45 per share when the Seagram tender offer was publicly announced." *SEC v. Tome*, 638 F. Supp. 596, 623 (S.D.N.Y. 1986).
60. *SEC v. Farrell*, 1996 WL 788367, at 5 (W.D.N.Y. 1996); *See*, e.g., *SEC v. Geon Industries, Inc.*, 531 F.2d 39, 47-48 (2d Cir. 1976); *SEC v. Shapiro*, 494 F.2d 1301, 1307 (2d Cir. 1974).
61. *SEC v. Carroll*, 9 F. Supp. 3d 761, 768 (W.D. Ky. 2014); *See SEC v. Michel*, 521 F.Supp.2d 795, 825-826 (N.D.Ill.2007) ("Also significant to the materiality analysis is the fact that Blue Rhino's stock price increased by 20% when the merger was publicly announced."); *SEC v. Blackwell*, 291 F.Supp.2d 673, 689 n. 9 (S.D.Ohio 2003) ("After the public announcement ... the price of Worthington stock increased dramatically, giving rise to the clear inference [of materiality."); *United States v. Mylett*, 97 F.3d 663, 667 (2d Cir.1996) ("[T]he sharp jump in NCR's stock price after a formal acquisition announcement was made suffices to support a finding" of materiality.); *SEC v. Talbot*, 530 F.3d 1085, 1097-98 (9th Cir. 2008) (An increase in the stock price after public announcement of the merger is a factor of the materiality of information); *see SEC v. Sekhri*, No. 98 Civ. 2320, 2002 WL 31100823, at 13 (S.D.N.Y. Jul. 22, 2002).
62. Marc I. Steinberg & William K.S. Wang, *Insider Trading* 117 (Oxford University Press 2010).
63. *Burlington Indus., Inc. v. Edelman*, 666 F. Supp. 799, 816 (M.D.N.C. 1987).
64. *Id.* at 816.
65. Marc I. Steinberg & William K.S. Wang, *Insider Trading* 117 (Oxford University Press 2010).
66. *Elkind v. Liggett & Myers, Inc.*, 635 F.2d 156, 167 (2d Cir. 1980).
67. "[T]he disclosure in that conversation consisted of confirmation that J&B sales were slowing due to earlier stockpiling and that Alpo sales were being adversely affected by Campbell's competing product and by the information that a preliminary earnings statement would be coming out in a week. The 'news' about J&B and Alpo was already common knowledge among the analysts; indeed, Liggett had publicly stated that a decline in J&B sales was expected. The confirmation of these facts, which were fairly obvious to all who followed the stock and were not accompanied by any quantification of the downturns, cannot be deemed 'reasonably certain to have a substantial effect on the market price of the security.'" *Elkind v. Liggett & Myers, Inc.* at 166.

create an exhaustive list"; however, "the following items are some types of information or events that should be reviewed carefully to determine whether they are material:[68] (1) earnings information; (2) mergers, acquisitions, tender offers, joint ventures, or changes in assets; (3) new products or discoveries, or developments regarding customers or suppliers (e.g., the acquisition or loss of a contract); (4) changes in control or in management; (5) change in auditors or auditor notification that the issuer may no longer rely on an auditor's audit report; (6) events regarding the issuer's securities - e.g., defaults on senior securities, calls of securities for redemption, repurchase plans, stock splits or changes in dividends, changes to the rights of security holders, public or private sales of additional securities; and (7) bankruptcies or receiverships."[69] Moreover, Form 8-K[70] includes a list of events where disclosure is required.[71]

In Saudi Arabia, Article 50 of the CML describes material information as "the type that a normal person would realize that in view of the nature and content of this information, its release and availability would have a material effect on the price or value of a Security related to such information."[72]

Article 4(c)(3) of the MCR requires that a normal person would realize that, in view of the nature and content of the information, disclosing it or making it available to the public would have a "material effect" on the price or value of the security.[73] Therefore, not all information that is related to an issuer of a security will be considered as inside information; it has to have a material effect on the price or the value of a security. Moreover, it is not necessary that the inside information had actual material effects on the price of the securities when the information becomes public; it is

68. These items are not per se material. U.S. Securities and Exchange Commission, *Selective Disclosure and Insider Trading*, Exchange Act Release No. 33-7881, 34-43154, IC-24599 (Aug. 15, 2000).
69. U.S. Securities and Exchange Commission, *Final Rule: Selective Disclosure and Insider Trading*, 17 CFR Parts 240, 243, and 249, Release No. 33-7881, 34-43154, IC-24599 (Aug. 15, 2000).
70. Form 8-K is the "current report" which public companies must file with the SEC to announce material events that shareholders should know about. The U.S. Securities and Exchange Commission, *Form 8-K*, (Nov. 15, 2015), http://www.sec.gov/answers/form8k.htm.
71. These events include entry into a material definitive agreement, termination of a material definitive agreement, bankruptcy or receivership, completion of acquisition or disposition of assets, results of operations and financial condition, creation of a direct financial obligation or an obligation under an off-balance sheet arrangement of a registrant, triggering events that accelerate or increase a direct financial obligation or an obligation under an off-balance sheet arrangement, costs associated with exit or disposal activities, material impairments, notice of delisting or failure to satisfy a continued listing rule or standard, transfer of listing, unregistered sales of equity securities, material modification to rights of security holders, changes in registrant's certifying accountant, non-reliance on previously issued financial statements or a related audit report or completed interim review, changes in control of registrant, departure of directors or certain officers, election of directors, appointment of certain officers, compensatory arrangements of certain officers, amendments to articles of incorporation or bylaws, change in fiscal year, amendments to the registrant's code of ethics, or waiver of a provision of the code of ethics, and submission of matters to a vote of security holders. *See* The United States Securities and Exchange Commission, *Form 8-K*.
72. Capital Market Law, Article 50(a) (2003).
73. Market Conducts Regulations, Article 4(c)(3).

sufficient to have a "potential" material effect on the security, even though the change did not occur in reality.[74]

Under Saudi law, the standard for determining the "materiality of information" is based on a "normal person."[75] That person is an investor who has an average knowledge and experience in trading in the market.[76] Also, the determination of the materiality of inside information is about what a normal person "realizes," which means that the understanding and inferring of the information by a normal person.[77]

By looking to the Saudi continuous disclosure requirements upon listed companies, the "LR"[78] requires issuers to inform the CMA and the public without delay of any private developments in their sphere of activity that affects the issuer's assets, liabilities, financial position, or course of business, if that development may create movement in the security's price or affect the issuer's abilities in terms of debt servicing.[79] In this regard, the LR provides twelve events where a "material development" occurs.[80] These events can assist in determining the "materiality of information" regarding insider-trading conduct.

---

74. Albjad, *Stock Market Crimes in Saudi Law, supra* n. 33, at 213.
75. Capital Market Law, Article 50(a) (2003).
76. Albjad, *Stock Market Crimes in Saudi Law, supra* n. 33, at 164.
77. Mohammed Nasser Albjad, *Jaremat Alefsah An Almalomat Aldakliah Fi Nedam Alsoag Almaliah Alsaodi [The Crime of Disclosure Inside Information in the Saudi Capital Market Law]*, 47 Periodic Pub. Admin. 557, 571 (2007).
78. Listing Rules, the Board of the Capital Market Authority Resolution Number 3-11-2004, dated 20/8/1425 H (Oct. 4, 2004), Amended by the Resolution of the Board of the Capital Market Authority Number 1-64-2016, dated 19/8/1437 H (May 26, 2016).
79. Listing Rules, Article 41(a) (2004). The language of this provision is as following:

> An issuer must notify the Authority and the public without delay of any material developments in its sphere of activity which are not public knowledge and which may effect the assets and liabilities or financial position or on the general course of business of the issuer or its subsidiaries and which may: 1) lead to movements in the price of the listed securities; or 2) significantly affect an issuer's ability to meet its commitments in respect of debt instruments.

80. Material developments include, but not limit to: (1) any transaction to purchase, sell, lease or mortgage an asset at a price equal to or greater than 10% of the net asset of the issuer according to the latest reviewed interim financial statements or audited annual financial statements, whichever is later; (2) any debt outside the issuer's ordinary course of business, of a value equal to or greater than 10% of the issuer's net assets; according to the latest reviewed interim financial statements or audited annual financial statements, whichever is later; (3) any losses equal to or greater than 10% of the issuer's net assets; according to the latest reviewed interim financial statements or audited annual financial statements, whichever is later; (4) any significant change in the issuer's production environment or activity including but not limited to the availability of resources and the possibility of obtaining them; (5) any changes in the composition of the directors or to CEO's position of the issuer; (6) any dispute including any litigation, arbitration or mediation where the value involved is equal to or greater than 5% of the net assets of the issuer according to the latest reviewed interim financial statements or audited annual financial statements, whichever is later; (7) any judicial decision issued against the board or any of the directors where the subject of the decision involved relates to the business of the board or any of the directors in the issuer; (8) the increase or decrease in the net assets of the issuer equal to or greater than 10% according to the latest reviewed interim financial statements or audited annual financial statements, whichever is later; (9) the increase or decrease in the gross profit of the issuer equal to or greater than 10% according to the latest audited annual financial statements; (10) the entering into, or the unexpected termination of, any contract with

The CMA might do well to consider adopting some of the other factors used by the U.S. in determining the materiality of information, including the significance of the information that those who knew about it attached to it, the reaction of the market when the information becomes available, the source of the information, and the specificity of the tip. These strategies should increase the domination of the CMA over market activities, leading to fairness in the market and the growth in the economy. This evaluation might also be applied to the differing definitions of nonpublic information.

[C] Nonpublic Information

In analyzing the liability of trading based on inside information, it is important to determine whether the information in question is nonpublic information.

In Egypt, the laws explain when material information becomes "public." "A material piece of information becomes public when it is made available to the dealing/investing public at the same time and in the same manner in accordance with rules and procedures governing and regulating disclosure at the securities exchange."[81] So, here is a very straightforward definition.

The U.S., however, employs a more flexible standard that takes into account both market conditions and investor attitudes. Generally speaking, most courts use one of two approaches. Some consider information to be public not at the moment of its release, but rather when the information has been disseminated into, and absorbed by, the investment community. Dissemination, in this context, means that the information is widely available; the information is absorbed following a reasonable waiting period that must take place before investors actually use the information to make informed decisions.

Other courts employ a more objective approach and consider information to be public once it is known in the community at large and affects prices, whether or not an individual investor is aware of the information. A corollary to this approach is that an "insider," or any other person subject to the "disclose or abstain" mandate, cannot use the information to make a profit.[82]

---

revenues equal to or greater than 5% of the gross revenues of the issuer according to the latest audited annual financial statements; (11) any transaction between the issuer and a related party or any arrangement through which the issuer and a related party invest in any project or asset or provide financing therefor if this transaction or arrangement is equal to or greater than 1% of the gross revenues of the issuer according to the latest audited annual financial statements; and (12) any interruption in the principal activities of the issuer or its subsidiaries equal to or greater than 5% of the gross revenues according to the latest audited annual financial statements. Listing Rules, Article 41 (b) (2004).

81. The Executive Regulations of Egyptian Capital Market Law, Article 319 (B), Law No. 95 (1992).
82. Marc I. Steinberg & William K.S. Wang, *Insider Trading* 4-58, 4-59 (Practising Law Institute 2005). Information becomes public when either (1) the information has been disclosed "to achieve a broad dissemination to the investing public generally and without favoring any special person or group," *Dirks v. SEC*, 463 U.S. 646, 653 n. 12 (1983) (citing *In re Faberge, Inc.*, 45 S.E.C. 249, 256 (1973)), or (2) although known only by a few persons, their trading on it "has caused the information to be fully impounded into the price of the particular stock," *United States v. Libera*, 989 F.2d 596, 601 (2d Cir. 1993). *See SEC v. Mayhew*, 121 F.3d 44, 50 (2d Cir. 1997); *SEC v. Sekhri*, 2002 WL 31100823, at 14 (S.D.N.Y. 22 July 2002); *United States v. Royer*, 549 F.3d 886,

The Second Circuit clearly adopted the second approach in *United States v. Libera*. The court states "we agree that information may be considered public for Section 10(b) purposes even though there has been no public announcement and only a small number of people know of it. The issue is not the number of people who possess it but whether their trading has caused the information to be fully impounded into the price of the particular stock. Once the information is fully impounded in price, such information can no longer be misused by trading because no further profit can be made."[83] This approach has been described as "theoretically appealing and sound."[84]

In a related case from the same Circuit, *SEC v. Tex. Gulf Sulphur Co.*, the court held that "before insiders may act upon material information, such information must have been effectively disclosed in a manner sufficient to ensure its availability to the investing public."[85] Merely waiting until a press release has been read to reporters is not enough.[86] The Court emphasized that insiders "should have waited until the news could reasonably have been expected to appear over the media of widest circulation, the Dow Jones broad tape."[87]

U.S. courts have also considered the specificity of the information to be a factor when determining the nonpublic information regarding disclosure.[88] In *SEC v. Lund*, the insider was told that negotiations had largely concluded, a concrete agreement was forthcoming, and a letter of intent would most likely be executed on the following business day. Even though some vague information concerning these developments had been publically available for several months, the court held that such availability did not convert the very specific information into public information.[89]

When inside information is disclosed, "insiders" may not trade or tip on this information until the information is absorbed by investing public. The Second Circuit in *SEC v. Tex. Gulf Sulphur Co.* clarified that "where the news is of a sort which is not readily translatable into investment action, insiders may not take advantage of their advance opportunity to evaluate the information by acting immediately upon dissemination."[90]

The question of how long insiders need to wait to trade after information becomes public has several answers. "A common approach" to defining when information has been assimilated into the market price after the disclosure is to see how long it took the price in market to level off after the disclosure.[91] While the determination of

---

898 (2d Cir. 2008) (stating that when an investor with such information chooses to disclose it, the nonpublic information remains nonpublic for purposes of the insider trading laws until it has been disseminated in a manner sufficient to insure its availability to the investing public or to insure that the market has had an opportunity to "absorb" the disclosed information such that the company's stock price has already adjusted to reflect that information).

83. *United States v. Libera* at 601.
84. Donald C. Langevoort, *Insider Trading Regulation, Enforcement and Prevention* § 5:4 (Westlaw 2015).
85. *SEC v. Tex. Gulf Sulphur Co.* at 854.
86. Stephen M. Bainbridge, *Insider Trading Law and Policy* 69 (Foundation Press 2014).
87. *SEC v. Tex. Gulf Sulphur Co.* at 854.
88. Marc I. Steinberg & William K.S. Wang, *Insider Trading* 4-61 (Practising Law Institute 2005).
89. *SEC v. Lund*, 570 F. Supp. 1397, 1401 (C.D. Cal. 1983).
90. *SEC v. Tex. Gulf Sulphur Co.* at 854 n. 18.
91. Langevoort, *supra* n. 84, at § 5:4.

the reasonable waiting period is a fact-specific inquiry, a common rule of thumb is that absorption occurs twenty-four hours following dissemination.[92] In contrast, the American Law Institute's proposed Federal Securities Code would have set a presumption that absorption occurs one week after dissemination, and the defendant would have had the burden of proof to demonstrate that a shorter period was more appropriate.[93]

To assist in determining the point of adequate dissemination, Professors Steinberg and Wang found that many courts consider the specificity of the release, whether it was local or national, and the clarity of the media involved. All these factors are geared towards determining the "reasonable waiting period" in each situation. They identified several other variables to determine the reasonable waiting period's duration, such as the scope of dissemination, the speed at which the information can be used to make investment decisions, the market's activity level, and analyst activity level.[94]

In Saudi Arabia, Article 50 of the CML characterizes inside information to be nonpublic information that it is not available to the general public and has not been disclosed.[95] Article 4(c) of the MCR describes nonpublic information as information "that has not been disclosed to the general public, and that is not otherwise available to the general public."[96] Inside information is considered nonpublic information even if other people besides insiders know about it, so long as the information is in possession of a limited number of people that cannot be compared to the number of the market participants.[97] Thus, the standard of nonpublic information is the proportionality between the number of people who have received the information and the number of those who have not got it.[98]

Article 50 of the CML and Article 4 of the MCR do not explain the method of disclosing the inside information to the general public. However, Article 45(c) of the CML states all information related to balance sheet, profit and loss account, cash flow statement, and evaluation of the issuing company management's current and future developments is deemed confidential, and issuers must disclose this information to the CMA before disclosing it to anyone who is not bound by a confidentiality obligation to protect this information.[99] Thus, the law requires listed companies to disclose inside information to CMA before disclosing it to the public.

92. *Id.*
93. American Law Institute, Fed. Sec. Code § 202(64)(proposed); Langevoort, *supra* n. 84, at § 5:4.
94. Marc I. Steinberg & William K.S. Wang, *Insider Trading* 4-76 (Practising Law Institute 2005).
95. Capital Market Law, Article 50(a) (2003).
96. Market Conducts Regulations, Article 4(c) (2004).
97. Saleh Ahmed Albrbari, *Soag Alaorag Almaliah Oa Estaglal Almalomat Aldakliah Beoasatat Alalmen Bboatan Alomor 14-15 [The Capital Market and the Abused of Nonpublic Information by Insiders 14-15]*, (United Arab Emirates University 2007); Mohammed Farog Abdalrasool, *Alhemaiah Algenaiah Le Borsah Alaorag Almaleih 137 [The Criminal Protection for the Securities Exchange 137]*, (Dar Aljamiah Aljadidah 2007); Albjad, *Stock Market Crimes in Saudi Law, supra* n. 33, at 158.
98. Albjad, *Stock Market Crimes in Saudi Law, supra* n. 33, at 158; Albrbari, *The Capital Market and the Abused of Nonpublic Information by Insiders, supra* n. 97, at 14-15; Belal Abdulmataleb Badawi, *Aleltazam Bealefasah An Almalumat Fi Soag Alaorag Almaleih 112 [the Obligation of Disclosing Information in the Stock Market 112]*, (Dar Alnahathah Alarabia Press 2006).
99. Capital Market Law, Article 45(c) (2003).

Additionally, Article 46(a) of the CML requires issuers to inform the CMA, in writing, upon becoming aware of any material developments that may affect the prices of the shares. Moreover, in case the security is traded in the stock exchange "Tadawul," the issuer must inform, in writing, both the CMA and Tadawul.[100] In practice, listed companies disclose inside information through both the CMA and Tadawul websites.[101]

Currently, Article 4(c)(2) of the MCR describes nonpublic information as information that has not been disclosed to the general public, and that is not otherwise available to the general public.[102] Nonpublic information loses its status as soon as the information is disclosed to the general public or the information is otherwise made available to the general public by any means. This regulatory condition has been poorly written. For instance, the second phrase, which is "that is not otherwise available to the general public," opens the door for insiders to circumvent and avoid liability. Hypothetically, insiders might conduct a small conference and then buy a huge amount of stocks without liability. Or, insiders might disclose inside information in a small spot in a newspaper and trade in a security legally. Thus, by disclosing the information by any means, insiders could use this loophole to legally trade in a security. The CMA should omit this phrase, in order to close the door on fraudulent insiders and to protect other investors.

At the same time, the CMA should specify the means by which inside information should be disclosed and when inside information becomes public. The CMA should amend Article 4 by adding a new provision to it such as a version of the following:

> Article 4(e): Inside information shall still be considered non-public until it has been published on both the CMA and the Exchange websites.

This clarification would be important not only for protecting the market and maintaining its fairness, but also for knowing when nonpublic information loses its status and becomes public information, for litigation purposes. Since the CML is new and there are no related cases that appear (as far as this author is aware of) to address this issue, it is possible that some cases may arise in the near future. The resolution of the existing ambiguity would directly affect the fairness of the capital market in Saudi Arabia.

The CML, MCR, and "LR" do not specify how long insiders should wait after announcing the material nonpublic information. However, LR requires listed companies to disclose and to report material developments at least half an hour prior to the start of the trading period that takes place immediately after the material development occurs.[103] If any such material development occurs less than half an hour prior to the start of the trading period, or during trading, the issuer must wait until the end of the

100. Capital Market Law, Article 46(a) (2003).
101. Albjad, *Stock Market Crimes in Saudi Law, supra* n. 33, at 160.
102. Market Conducts Regulations, Article 4(c)(2) (2004).
103. Listing Rules, Article 40(b) (2004); Capital Market Authority, *CMA: Listed Companies are Obligated to Inform the Public about Any Significant Developments Which Are Not Available to the Public*, (Feb. 2, 2015), http://cma.org.sa/Ar/MediaCenter/PK/Pages/Disclosure-Awareness-Report.aspx.

trading period, and then announce the information publically.[104] However, if a listed company violates the half an hour requirement, the CMA will impose and sanction only the listed company; the CMA will not track insiders to see how long the insiders have waited after the announcement because there is no rule that regulates this issue.

Thus, it might be advisable to require insiders to wait at least thirty minutes after the announcement of material nonpublic information. This waiting period allows market participants to learn about the information, to evaluate it, and to employ it to make informed decisions about their investments. Otherwise, insiders will take advantage of the knowledge and the evaluation they have about the nonpublic information prior the announcement.

Once the authorities believe that insider trading has occurred, based on the uses of nonpublic material information, the next step is to prosecute the alleged violators in an appropriate forum. In the U.S., the U.S. Supreme Court has developed several different approaches that guide judges and juries as they evaluate these matters. In addition, the U.S. "SEC" has developed specific regulatory and enforcement approaches respecting these matters.

§5.04 INSIDER TRADING

American jurisprudence has long focused on insider trading based on material nonpublic information, as it is one of the most commonly prohibited conducts in most all capital markets and directly violates the principle of equality among traders in capital markets. As a way to uphold this principle, to maintain protection and fairness in the market, and to raise confidence among investors, insider trading should be prohibited in any market.[105] The U.S. has long prohibited the practice of insider trading, and it has developed several theories through this experience.

[A] Theories under U.S. Laws

Curiously, there is no federal law that defines insider trading in express terms, except in cases of tender offers.[106] Rather, the prohibition arises from federal courts that have applied anti-fraud laws to capital market transactions.[107] Initially, courts applied Section 10(b) of the Securities Exchange Act of 1934, which provides:

---

104. During such a waiting period, the issuer must take all necessary precautions to ensure that the material information does not leak before the disclosure. *See* Capital Market Authority, Instructions for Regulating Announcements of Listed Companies in the Saudi capital Market, the Board of the Capital Market Authority Resolution Number 1-199-2006, dated 18/07/1427 H (Aug. 12, 2006), Amended by the Resolution of the Board of the Capital Market Authority Number 4-38-2008, dated 26/11/1429 H (Nov. 11, 2008). However, in case the issuer cannot maintain the confidentiality of the information until the end of the trading period, the issuer may request a temporary trading halt and immediately inform the CMA about the event. Listing Rules, Article 37 (2004).
105. Abdalrasool, *supra* n. 97, at 136.
106. 17 CFR 240.14e-3.
107. Larry P. Ellsworth & Michael K. Lowman, *Inside Information: Prevention of Abuse A-3*, 15-4th C.P.S. (The Bureau of National Affairs 2014).

> It shall be unlawful for any person, directly or indirectly, by the use of any means or instrumentality of interstate commerce or of the mails, or of any facility of any national securities exchange ... to use or employ, in connection with the purchase or sale of any security registered on a national securities exchange or any security not so registered, or any securities-based swap agreement any manipulative or deceptive device or contrivance in contravention of such rules and regulations as the Commission may prescribe as necessary or appropriate in the public interest or for the protection of investors.[108]

Later in 1942, SEC promulgated Rule 10b-5[109] pursuant to Section 10(b) of the Exchange Act.[110] The U.S. Supreme Court described Rule 10b-5 as "a judicial oak which has grown from little more than an acorn."[111] Rule 10b-5 provides:

> It shall be unlawful for any person, directly or indirectly, by the use of any means or instrumentality of interstate commerce, or of the mails or of any facility of any national securities exchange:
>
> (a) To employ any device, scheme, or artifice to defraud,
> (b) To make any untrue statement of a material fact or to omit to state a material fact necessary in order to make the statements made, in the light of the circumstances under which they were made, not misleading, or
> (c) To engage in any act, practice, or course of business which operates or would operate as a fraud or deceit upon any person, in connection with the purchase or sale of any security.[112]

Essentially, in the absence of any direct Congressional action, the rules on insider trading in U.S. courts have evolved as a mixture of judicial interpretations and SEC regulations. Because "there is no clear statement of the scope of the law," there is the very real possibility of "new applications, sometimes seemingly at the whim of the SEC and federal prosecutors."[113] Consequently, the U.S. Supreme Court has decided three major cases that shaped insider trading liabilities and theories,[114] including: (1) *Chiarella v. United States*;[115] (2) *Dirks v. SEC*;[116] and (3) *United States v.*

108. Securities Exchange Act of 1934, 15 U.S.C. § 78j(b) (2012).
109. 17 C.F.R. § 240.10b-5.
110. Steven Mark Levy, *Regulation of Securities: SEC Answer Book* 11-1 (Aspen Publishers 2004).
111. *Blue Chip Stamps v. Manor Drug Stores*, 421 U.S. 723, 737 (1975).
112. 17 C.F.R. § 240.10b-5.
113. Peter J. Henning, *What's So Bad About Insider Trading Law?*, 70 Bus. Law. 751, 754-55 (2015). "That does not mean courts always accept efforts to push the boundaries of insider trading law. For example, in *SEC v. Bauer*, 723 F.3d 758 (7th Cir. 2012), the Seventh Circuit pointed out that an insider trading claim based on the sale of mutual fund shares was unique because it had never been brought before by the SEC, and the court overturned a grant of summary judgment so that the district court could consider whether the 'misappropriation theory' applied to sales of such securities. *Id.* at 770-71. The district court subsequently dismissed the case because the SEC had not sought to establish a violation based on the 'misappropriation theory' and therefore 'any theory not raised before the district court is considered to be waived or forfeited.'" *SEC v. Bauer*, No. 03-C 1427, 2014 WL 4267412, at *5 (E.D. Wis. Aug. 29, 2014).
114. Marc I. Steinberg, *Understanding Securities Law* 383 (LexisNexis 2014).
115. *Chiarella v. United States*, 445 U.S. 222 (1980).
116. *Dirks v. SEC*, 463 U.S. 646 (1983).

O'Hagan.[117] One more recent case, *SEC v. Newman,*[118] from the Second Circuit, might eventually change some aspects of insider-trading law in the U.S.

[1] Chiarella and the Classical Theory

The facts of the *Chiarella v. United States* case are as follows: Chiarella was an employee of a financial printer. Among the documents that Chiarella handled were five announcements of corporate takeover bids. When these documents were delivered to the printer, the identities of the acquiring and target corporations were concealed by blank spaces or false names until the night of the final printing. However, the employee was able to deduce the names of the target companies from other information contained in the documents. Without disclosing his knowledge, the employee purchased stock in the target companies and sold the shares immediately after the takeover attempts were made public. The employee realized a profit of about USD 30,000.[119]

Chiarella was convicted in the U.S. District Court of violating § 10(b) of the Securities Exchange Act of 1934 and SEC Rule 10b-5. The Second Circuit affirmed the conviction[120] by applying the equality of access theory.[121] The court earlier in *Texas Gulf Sulphur* stated that "Anyone in possession of material inside information must either disclose it to the investing public, or, if he is disabled from disclosing it in order to protect a corporate confidence, or he chooses not to do so, must abstain from trading in or recommending the securities concerned while such inside information remains undisclosed."[122] However, the U.S. Supreme Court in *Chiarella v. United States* reversed the conviction.[123]

The Supreme Court held that when an allegation of fraud is based upon nondisclosure, there could be no fraud absent a duty to speak. It states that a duty to disclose under § 10(b) does not arise from the mere possession of nonpublic market information.[124] Thus, the Court rejected the "equality of access theory" and described it as a broad duty and a departing radically from the established doctrine that required a specific relationship.[125]

117. *United States v. O'Hagan,* 521 U.S. 642 (1997).
118. *United States v. Newman,* 773 F.3d 438, 452 (2d Cir. 2014), *cert. denied,* 136 S. Ct. 242 (Oct. 5, 2015).
119. *Chiarella v. United States* at 224.
120. *Id.* at 225.
121. The Second Circuit states that "the draftsmen of our nation's securities laws, rejecting the philosophy of Caveat emptor, Created a system providing equal access to the information necessary for reasoned and intelligent investment decisions." *United States v. Chiarella,* 588 F.2d 1358, 1362 (2d Cir. 1978) *rev'd,* 445 U.S. 222 (1980).
122. *SEC v. Tex. Gulf Sulphur Co.* at 848.
123. *Chiarella v. United States* at 225. The U.S. Supreme Court explained the Second Circuit's decision and reasoning as follows: the Court of Appeal's decision, as well as the District Court's resolution, "rested solely upon [their] belief that the federal securities laws have 'created a system providing equal access to information necessary for reasoned and intelligent investment decisions.'" *See Chiarella v. United States* at 232.
124. *Chiarella v. United States* at 235.
125. *Id.* at 233.

"One who fails to disclose material information prior to the consummation of a transaction commits fraud only when he is under a duty to do so." The Court reasoned that the duty to disclose arises only when one party has information "that the other [party] is entitled to know because of a fiduciary or other similar relation of trust and confidence between them."[126] This relationship gives rise to a duty to disclose because of the "necessity of preventing a corporate insider from ... tak[ing] unfair advantage of the uninformed minority stockholders."[127] This theory has come to be known as the "traditional" or "classical theory" of insider-trading liability.[128]

Moreover, the Supreme Court extended the liability of insider trading to "tippees" of corporate insiders. The tippees' obligation has been viewed as arising from their role as participants after the fact of the insider's breach of a fiduciary duty.[129]

The Supreme Court concluded that the employee, Chiarella, in this case owed no duty to the target corporations or to their shareholders. The Court declared that "no duty could arise from petitioner's relationship with the sellers of the target company's securities, for petitioner had no prior dealings with them. He was not their agent, he was not a fiduciary, and he was not a person in whom the sellers had placed their trust and confidence."[130]

To conclude, the imposition of liability under Section 10(b) and Rule 10b-5 for trading on material nonpublic information must be premised upon a duty to disclose.[131]

Shortly after *Chiarella*, the SEC promulgated Rule 14e-3 in September 1980.[132] The SEC "acted to close the gap that the Court had created with respect to trading on the basis of information related to a tender offer."[133] The Rule prohibits insider trading and tipping in the special context of information concerning tender offers. Within this context, the prohibition on insider trading is broader than Rule 10b-5 because there is no requirement to prove a breach of a duty of nondisclosure.[134] In 1997, the U.S. Supreme Court in *United States v. O'Hagan* affirmed the validity of Rule 14e-3.[135]

126. *Id.* at 228.
127. *Id.* at 228-29; *Speed v. Transamerica Corp.*, 99 F.Supp. 808, 829 (D.Del.1951).
128. *United States v. O'Hagan* at 651-52.
129. *Chiarella v. United States* at 230 n. 12.
130. *Id.* at 232-33 (1980).
131. Marc I. Steinberg, *Understanding Securities Law* 383 (LexisNexis 2014).
132. 17 C.F.R. § 240.14e-3; Securities Exchange Act Release No. 17120 (1980). Rule 14e-3 (a) states that "if any person has taken a substantial step or steps to commence, or has commenced, a tender offer (the 'offering person'), it shall constitute a fraudulent, deceptive or manipulative act or practice within the meaning of section 14(e) of the Act for any other person who is in possession of material information relating to such tender offer which information he knows or has reason to know is non-public and which he knows or has reason to know has been acquired directly or indirectly from the offering person, the issuer of the securities sought or to be sought by such tender offer, or Any officer, director, partner or employee or any other person acting on behalf of the offering person or such issuer."
133. Langevoort, *supra* n. 84, at § 7:1.
134. Ellsworth, *supra* n. 107, at A-21.
135. *United States v. O'Hagan* at 676.

[2] Dirks and the Liability of Tipper-Tippee

Three years after *Chiarella*, the Supreme Court revisited insider-trading laws, this time in the context of the relationship between "tippers" and "tippees." *Dirks v. SEC* is the second important case that the U.S. Supreme Court has decided. The facts of the case are as follows: Raymond Dirks, an investment analyst, received material nonpublic information from Ronald Secrist who was a former officer of Equity Funding of America.[136] Secrist told Dirks that the assets of Equity Funding were vastly overstated as the result of fraudulent corporate practices. Secrist also told Dirks that various regulatory agencies had failed to act on similar charges made by the company employees. Secrist asked Dirks to verify the fraud and make it public. Dirks investigated the allegations and found the fraud. Throughout his investigation, Dirks disclosed the information to some clients and investors. Some of these people sold their holdings of Equity Funding securities.[137]

The SEC investigated Dirks' role in revealing the fraud and found that Dirks had "aided and abetted" insider trading.[138] However, the SEC only censured Dirks, since he "played an important role in bringing [Equity Funding's] massive fraud to light."[139] The Court of Appeals for the District of Columbia Circuit entered judgment against Dirks "for the reasons stated by the Commission in its opinion."[140] However, the U.S. Supreme Court reversed.[141]

The Court reaffirmed its holding in *Chiarella v. United States* that there is "no duty to disclose where the person who has traded on inside information 'was not [the corporation's] agent, ... was not a fiduciary, [or] was not a person in whom the sellers [of the securities] had placed their trust and confidence.'"[142] The duty to disclose arises from the relationship between parties and not merely from one's ability to acquire information because of his position in the market.[143] The Court was concerned that imposing a broad duty to disclose or abstain only because a person knowingly receives material nonpublic information from an insider and trades on it could have an inhibiting influence on the role of market analysts.[144]

In order to determine whether a tippee is obligated "to disclose or to abstain," it is important to figure out whether the insider's "tip" constituted a breach of the insider's fiduciary duty.[145] This depends in large part on the purpose of, and motivation

136. *Dirks v. SEC* at 648-49.
137. *Id.* at 649.
138. *Id.* at 650. The SEC concluded that where "'tippees – regardless of their motivation or occupation – come into possession of material 'information that they know is confidential and know or should know came from a corporate insider,' they must either publicly disclose that information or refrain from trading." 21 S.E.C. Docket 1401, 1407 (1981) (quoting *Chiarella v. United States* at 230 n. 12). *Dirks v. SEC* at 651.
139. *Dirks v. SEC* at 651-52.
140. *Id.* at 652.
141. *Id.*
142. *Id.* at 654.
143. *Id.* at 657-58.
144. *Id.* at 658.
145. *Id.* at 661.

for, the disclosure.[146] The Court provides "objective criteria" to determine whether there has been a breach of duty by the insider. The test is "whether the insider receives a direct or indirect personal benefit from the disclosure, such as a pecuniary gain or a reputational benefit that will translate into future earnings."[147] The Courts states clearly that absent some "personal gain," there has been no breach of duty to stockholders. And absent a breach by the insider, there is no derivative breach.[148]

The Court also clarified the liability of for tippee's trading under Section 10(b) and Rule 10b-5 to be: (1) the insider breaches of a fiduciary duty; and (2) the tippee's knowledge of the breach. The Court states "a tippee assumes a fiduciary duty to the shareholders of a corporation not to trade on material nonpublic information only when the insider has breached his fiduciary duty to the shareholders by disclosing the information to the tippee and the tippee knows or should know that there has been a breach."[149] In other words, the tippee's duty to disclose or abstain is derived from the insider's duty.[150]

The Court concluded that the former officer, Secrist, and the other employees did not breach their duty to the corporation's shareholders by providing information to Dirks.[151] The tippers did not receive monetary or personal benefit for revealing Equity Funding's secrets, and it was not their purpose to make a gift of valuable information to Dirks. In fact, the tipper's motivation was "a desire to expose the fraud." As a result, the Court held that the insiders did not breach their duty to shareholders, and there was no derivative breach by Dirks.[152]

[3] O'Hagan and the Misappropriation Theory

Roughly a dozen years after *Chiarella* and *Dirks*, the stock trading landscape had somewhat changed. Therefore, while the "traditional theory" is useful in almost all situations, there are some fact patterns that do not involve company insiders. So, many courts now apply a misappropriation theory in these instances. In brief, "[t]he misappropriation theory finds liability generally for outsiders who trade in violation of a duty of trust or confidence owed to the source of the inside information, rather than to the corporation's shareholders." This duty may arise from both business and

146. *Id.* at 662.
147. *Id.* at 663.
148. *Id.* at 662. The Supreme Court provided some illustrations of insider motivations that constitute a breach of fiduciary duty. "For example, there may be a relationship between the insider and the recipient that suggests a *quid pro quo* from the latter, or an intention to benefit the particular recipient. The elements of fiduciary duty and exploitation of non-public information also exist when an insider makes a gift of confidential information to a trading relative or friend. The tip and trade resemble trading by the insider himself followed by a gift of the profits to the recipient." *Dirks v. SEC* at 664.
149. *Dirks v. SEC* at 660.
150. *Id.* at 659.
151. *Id.* at 666.
152. *Id.* at 667.

personal relationships.[153] The misappropriation theory targets "outsiders" of a company who become privy to confidential information but owe no fiduciary duty to that company's shareholders. Therefore, this theory fills the gap left open by traditional insider-trading liability, in that the breach of a duty owed is not to a trader on the other side of the transaction but rather is owed to the source of the information.[154] In fact, one commentator described the misappropriation theory as "the focal point" of insider-trading regulation.[155]

The "misappropriation theory" was first examined by the Supreme Court in *Chiarella v. United States*. In separate opinions, both Chief Justice Warren Burger (dissenting)[156] and Justice John Paul Stevens (concurring)[157] "suggested that in some circumstances, a non-insider like Chiarella could violate Rule 10b-5 by misappropriating non-public information from his or her employer and using that information to trade."[158] Much later, seventeen years after deciding *Chiarella v. United States* in 1980, the U.S. Supreme Court formally endorsed the misappropriation theory in 1997s *United States v. O'Hagan.*[159]

In *United States v. O'Hagan*, James O'Hagan was a partner in a law firm and learned that Grand Metropolitan retained his law firm to represent it in a potential tender offer for the common stock of the Pillsbury Company; O'Hagan did no work on the Grand Metropolitan representation. Prompted by the information he learned, O'Hagan purchased Pillsbury call options and common stock. After Grand Metropolitan publicly announced its tender offer for Pillsbury stock, O'Hagan sold his Pillsbury call options and common stock and made a profit of more than USD 4.3 million.[160]

Among other charges, O'Hagan was convicted of violating Rule 10b-5 and SEC Rule 10b-5.[161] The Court of Appeals for the Eighth Circuit reversed all of O'Hagan's convictions and held that § 10(b) liability could not be based on the misappropriation theory. The Court provided two reasons for its holding: (1) Contrary to § 10(b)'s explicit requirements, the misappropriation theory does not require "deception," and (2), even assuming that it does, it renders nugatory the requirement that the "deception" be "in connection with the purchase or sale of any security."[162]

---

153. Ellsworth, *supra* n. 107, at A-4a.
154. Marc I. Steinberg, *Understanding Securities Law* 388 (LexisNexis 2014).
155. Langevoort, *supra* n. 84, at § 6:1.
156. *Chiarella v. United States* at 239.
157. *Id.* at 237.
158. Ellsworth, *supra* n. 107, at A-4a. After *Chiarella v. United States* case, many courts of appeals followed the misappropriation theory. For example *SEC v. Cherif*, 933 F.2d 403 (7th Cir. 1991); *SEC v. Clark*, 915 F.2d 439 (9th Cir. 1990); *Rothberg v. Rosenbloom*, 771 F.2d 818 (3rd Cir.1985); *United States v. Newman*, 664 F.2d 12 (2nd Cir.1981).
159. *United States v. O'Hagan*, 521 U.S. 642 (1997).
160. *Id.* at 647-48.
161. *United States v. O'Hagan*, 92 F.3d 612, 622 (8th Cir. 1996).
162. *Id.* at 617. The Court of Appeals also held that "the SEC exceeded its rulemaking authority under § 14(e) when it promulgated Rule 14e-3(a) without including a requirement of a breach of a fiduciary obligation." *Id.* at 627.

The U.S. Supreme Court reversed the Eighth Circuit's judgment, declaring its decision to be in conflict with the misappropriation theory under § 10(b) and Rule 10b-5, as well as the legitimacy of Rule 14e-3(a) under § 14(e).[163]

The Supreme Court endorsed the misappropriation theory. Under the theory that the Court set forth, a person commits fraud "in connection with" a securities transaction, and thereby violates § 10(b) and Rule 10b-5, when he misappropriates confidential information for securities trading purposes, in breach of a duty owed to the source of the information. Therefore, the misappropriation theory premises liability on a fiduciary-turned-trader's deception of those who entrusted him with access to confidential information.[164]

The "classical-traditional theory" and the misappropriation theory are complementary, in that each addresses efforts to capitalize on nonpublic information through the purchase or sale of securities. Under the classical theory, it targets a corporate insider's breach of duty to shareholders with whom the insider transacts. However, the misappropriation theory outlaws trading on the basis of nonpublic information by a corporate "outsider" in breach of a duty owed not to a trading party, but to the source of the information. Thus, a breach of duty in the misappropriation theory is related to the source of the information.[165] However, in the case of full disclosure to the source of information, the liability under the misappropriation theory forecloses by such disclosure.[166]

The Supreme Court also upheld the validity of Rule 14e-3 by declaring that, under §14(e), the Commission may prohibit acts, not themselves fraudulent under the common law or §10(b), if the prohibition is "reasonably designed to prevent ... acts and practices [that] are fraudulent."[167] Rule 14e-3(a) creates a duty in those traders who fall within its scope to abstain or to disclose, without regard to whether the trader owes a preexisting fiduciary duty to respect the confidentiality of the information. That prescription is a "means reasonably designed to prevent" fraudulent trading on material, nonpublic information in the tender offer context.[168]

Since the much broader misappropriation theory encompasses all "abstain or disclose" violations, at least in theory, it may very well replace the narrow *Chiarella/Dirks* analysis as the leading theory regarding insider trading.[169] Recent Appeals Court cases further highlight the transitory and evolving nature of securities law in the U.S.

---

163. *United States v. O'Hagan*, 521 U.S. 642, 649 (1997).
164. *Id.* at 652.
165. *Id.* at 652-53. The Court explains that the misappropriation theory is designed to protect the integrity of the securities markets against abuses by outsiders to a corporation who have access to confidential information that will affect the corporation's security price when revealed, but who owe no fiduciary or other duty to that corporation's shareholders. *Id.*
166. Because "the deception essential to the misappropriation theory involves feigning fidelity to the source of information, if the fiduciary discloses to the source that he plans to trade on the nonpublic information, there is no 'deceptive device' and thus no § 10(b) violation–although the fiduciary-turned-trader may remain liable under state law for breach of a duty of loyalty." *United States v. O'Hagan*, 521 U.S. 642, 655 (1997).
167. *Id.* at 673.
168. *Id.* at 669-76.
169. Langevoort, *supra* n. 84, at § 1:9.

[4] The "Personal Benefit" Requirement and the Split in the Circuits

A recent case from the Second Circuit Court of Appeals directly challenged the *Dirks* standard of direct or indirect personal benefit. In *Dirks,* the Justices envisioned a situation whereby an insider might obtain an intangible benefit, such as a *quid pro quo,* in exchange for a securities tip.[170] But *United States v. Newman*[171] employed a much more narrow test.

That case concerned two New York stock traders who were convicted of trading on inside information in Dell and NVIDIA shares, yet they received no money in exchange for the tips. In reversing the convictions, the court held that "the government must prove beyond a reasonable doubt that ... an insider disclosed confidential information ... in exchange for a personal benefit." In the alternative, according to this case, the government must establish the existence of a "meaningfully close personal relationship [which represents] a potential gain of a pecuniary or similarly valuable nature."[172]

Newman has been sharply criticized by some because it seemingly does not take into account the policy considerations of transparency and fairness espoused in *Dirks* and some other cases.[173] In October 2015, the Supreme Court ultimately denied the Solicitor General's petition for *writ of certiorari.*[174]

However, there is clearly a split in the circuits. On July 6, 2015, the Ninth Circuit openly questioned the *Newman* test. It expressly followed the *Dirks* standard that "[t]he elements of fiduciary duty and exploitation of non-public information also exist when an insider makes a gift of confidential information to a trading relative or friend."[175] Clearly, the law on this point is unsettled and the Supreme Court has ultimately chosen to step in and may either reaffirm or revise *Dirks* in the near future.

In contrast, Saudi Arabia has never employed a "personal benefit" requirement, so there is a much broader prohibition on insider trading. Such a blanket prohibition is well suited for a country like Saudi Arabia, where close personal relationships are the norm. Indeed, the nature of these relationships has considerable influence over the more general Saudi laws that prohibit insider trading.

[B] Saudi Arabia Laws Against Insider Trading

The CML prohibits the conduct of insider trading. However, unlike U.S. law, Article 50(a) of the CML states that an insider is "any person who obtains, through family, business or contractual relationship, inside information." Furthermore, such a person

170. *Dirks v. SEC* at 667; *See supra* nn. 147 & 148, and accompanying text.
171. *United States v. Newman,* 773 F.3d 438, 452 (2d Cir. 2014), *cert. denied,* 136 S. Ct. 242 (Oct. 5, 2015).
172. *Id.* at 452-53.
173. Donna M. Nagy, *Beyond Dirks: Gratuitous Tipping and Insider Trading,* Indiana Legal Studies Research Paper No. 327, pp. 27-28 (2015).
174. *United States v. Newman,* 773 F.3d 438 (2d Cir. 2014), *cert. denied,* 136 S. Ct. 242 (Oct. 5, 2015).
175. *United States v. Salman,* 792 F.3d 1087, 1092 (9th Cir. 2015), *cert. granted,* 136 S. Ct. 899 (Jan. 19, 2016).

"is prohibited from directly or indirectly trading in the Security related to such information, or [disclosing] such information to another person with the expectation that such person will trade in such Security."[176] Additionally, Article 50(b) of the CML extends the prohibition to restrict "any person" from trading based on inside information obtained from an insider, while knowing that such person has violated paragraph (a) of Article 50 by such disclosure.[177] However, the specific nature of "insiders," especially when evaluating the facts of individual cases, is much harder to determine.

[1] Who Is an "Insider"?

Article 50(a) of the CML does not clearly define this term. It only states that an insider is a person who obtains inside information through family, business, or contractual relationship.[178] This definition of insider is ambiguous because it does not clearly state what these three relationships mean and what their scopes are. However, fifteen months after enacting the CML, the CMA issued the MCR, based on the authorization of Article 50(c) of the CML, which provides more details about insider trading.[179] This Article grants the CMA the power to establish rules for specifying and defining the terms provided for under paragraphs (a) and (b) of Article 50 of the CML.[180]

Article 50 of the CML provides three classes of people who are insiders; the MCR provides an additional class of people. In other words, the three classes listed in the CML are only examples, and the definition is not strictly limited to only the listed classes.[181] However, the four classes listed in the MCR are determinative, because Article 4 of the MCR states that "insider means any of the following." Thus, anyone who is not among these classes cannot be considered to be an "insider" for the purpose of the insider-trading liability.

According to Article 4(b) of the MCR, "insider" means any of the following:

1) A director, a senior executive or an employee of the issuer of a security related to inside information;
2) A person who obtains inside information through a family relationship, including from any person related to the person who obtains the information;
3) A person who obtains inside information through a business relationship, including obtaining the information:
   - From the issuer of a security related to inside information;
   - From any person who has a business relationship with the person who obtains the information; or

176. Capital Market Law, Article 50(a) (2003).
177. Capital Market Law, Article 50(c) (2003). Most of the functional language of Article 50 of the Capital Market Law was originally adapted from the Australian statute that related to insider trading. *See* Joseph W. Beach, *The Saudi Arabian Capital Market Law: A Practical Study of the Creation of Law in Developing Markets*, 41 Stan. J. Int'l L. 307, 344 (2005).
178. Capital Market Law, Article 50(a) (2003).
179. Market Conduct Regulations (2004).
180. Capital Market Law, Article 50(c) (2003).
181. *See* Albjad, *The Crime of Disclosure Inside Information in the Saudi Capital Market Law*, *supra* n. 77, at 573.

- From any person who is a business associate of the person who obtains the information;

4) A person who obtains inside information through a contractual relationship, including obtaining the information:
   - From the issuer of a security related to inside information; or
   - From any person who has a contractual relationship with the person who obtains the information.[182]

Even though the CMA issued the MCR in order to explain the CML and make it clear, there are some difficulties and ambiguities in the regulation itself. For example, Article 4(b) of the MCR indicates three types of relationships a person may be seen as an insider: family, business, and contractual relationships. The downside of this seemingly clear law is that it does not define the boundaries of these relationships.

[a] Family Relationship

Article 4(b)(2) of the MCR states that a person who obtains inside information through a "family relationship," including from any person related to the person who obtains the information. Unfortunately, the law does not clearly define a family relationship: is it a distant cousin, brother, stepbrother, and/or father?[183]

It is not clear who can be considered to have a family relationship. It is commonly claimed that the term is limited to immediate family members: spouse, children, siblings, parent, and other very close people who are related by blood or marriage.[184]

However, a number of Saudi law professors argue that the language of the CML and the MCR is much broader when defining the family relationships, and the term should mean and cover any and all family relationships.[185]

An interview, which the author conducted with a legal advisor in the CRSD, revealed that the CRSD considers family relationship to mean any family relationship without limitation.[186] This broader approach is better in a culture like Saudi Arabia, because its citizens have large and connected families. In fact, the average number of family members in a single Saudi Arabian household is about seven members.[187]

Nevertheless, the law should be clear as to what the family relationship means. As currently written, it creates uncertainty about the family relationship. Thus, although the purpose of the MCR is to define the terms of Article 50 of the CML and to make the Article understandable to people, there is still ambiguity in Article 4(b)(2) of the MCR. Therefore, the CMA should review Article 4 (b)(2) of the MCR and provide a

182. Market Conduct Regulations, Article 4(b) (2004).
183. Market Conduct Regulations, Article 4(b)(2) (2004).
184. Article 1 of the CML defines "relatives" as husband, wife, and minor children. Capital Market Law, Article 1 (2003).
185. Albjad, *The Crime of Disclosure Inside Information in the Saudi Capital Market Law*, *supra* n. 77, at 578-79.
186. Interview with a legal advisor for the Committees for the Resolution of Securities Disputes, Riyadh, Saudi Arabia (Aug. 12, 2014).
187. King Khalid Bin Abdul Aziz Database, *Alosar, [Families]*, (Nov. 20, 2015), http://www.kingkhalid.org.sa/Gallery/Text/ViewTextSubjects.aspx?View=Page&BookID=106&PageID=7&NodeID=79.

clear and concise definition of the family relationship. The author proposes to add to Article 4(b)(2) the words "any degree of" before the phrase "family relationship." Thus, this provision would read as follows:

> A person who obtains inside information through any degree of family relationship, including from any person related to the person who obtains the information.

In the alternative, the CMA might consider adding a separate definition of the term "family relationship."

Article 4(b)(2) of the MCR adds a new class of insider that the CML does not address. This Article provides that insider means, among others, "a person who obtains inside information through a family relationship, including from any person related to the person who obtains the information."[188] The phrase "including from any person related to the person who obtains the information" adds a new class of insider. For example, if a director of a company discloses inside information to his spouse and then the spouse discloses the information to her friend, the friend is now considered as an insider because the friend receives the inside information from a person who obtains the information by family relationship.[189]

[b] Business Relationship

The second type of relationship is the "business relationship." Once again, neither the CML nor the MCR defines the term. The MCR states that insider means, among others, "a person who obtains inside information through a business relationship, including obtaining the information from the issuer of a security related to inside information, from any person who has a business relationship with the person who obtains the information, or from any person who is a business associate of the person who obtains the information."[190]

Business relationship has been defined as "the relationship that allows a person who is doing a job or a task in or for a company to access inside information of the company."[191] Thus, all persons who do any kind of business with the company are insiders as long as their job allows them to access inside information, whether the company consents to such access or not. Therefore, government employees, including workers at the CMA, the SAMA, and the Ministry of Commerce and Industry, are insiders, if they have access to any nonpublic information. Moreover, employees in the private sector are also insiders when their jobs allow them to access companies' nonpublic information. For instance, employees of banks access inside information in the course of their jobs, such as company loans and funding.[192] The MCR also provides

188. Market Conduct Regulations, Article 4(b)(2) (2004).
189. Albjad, *Stock Market Crimes in Saudi Law*, *supra* n. 33, at 170.
190. Market Conduct Regulations, Article 4(b)(3) (2004).
191. Albjad, *Stock Market Crimes in Saudi Law*, *supra* n. 33, at 171.
192. *Id.* at 171-72.

that any person who obtains inside information from these insiders, who access inside information through business relationship, is considered as an insider.[193]

[c] Contractual Relationship

The third kind of relationship that triggers the status of insider is a relationship that is based on a contract. Again, neither the CML nor the MCR defines this term. The MCR does provide that insider means, among other things, a person who obtains inside information through a "contractual relationship," including obtaining the information either from the issuer of a security with inside information or any person who has a contractual relationship with the person who obtains the information.[194] A contractual relationship is a legal relationship between a person and a company to conduct a job by either parties, and that relationship is evidenced by a contract.[195] Two classes of people exist under a contractual relationship: (1) a "company's employees"; and (2) "contractors."

First, employees of a company have contractual relationships with the company. These employees work for the company, and under its supervision. It does not matter whether the employees have part-time or full-time jobs, or whether they are paid or unpaid. Therefore, all employees of a company are insiders, whether a director, officer, or a security guard. It is because employees of a company work in the company, and as such they have, or can access, inside information. Employees may easily access inside information before other people.[196] Through this method, the MCR protects nonpublic information from abusive conduct by expanding the class of insiders, thus protecting the market and investors from illegal practices.

The second class of contractual relationship is contractors who are independent from the company. A company forms a contract with some people to conduct some tasks. For example, a company can contract with law firms, lawyers, legal advisors, accountants, or engineers to perform particular tasks. These people have contractual relationships with the company that they contract with.[197] Therefore, a person who has a contractual relationship with a company is an insider under both the CML and MCR.[198]

Furthermore, the MCR adds a new category of people under the contractual relationship that is not mentioned in Article 50 of the CML. Any person who has a contractual relationship with the person who obtains the information is an insider.[199]

Though the purpose of the Regulations is to define the terms of Article 50 of the CML and make the Article obvious, just as in Article 4, it is ambiguous. This ambiguity allows the investor to interpret the CMLs and regulations to satisfy his or her needs.

193. Market Conduct Regulations, Article 4(b)(3) (2004).
194. *Id.* Article 4(b)(4).
195. Albjad, *The Crime of Disclosure Inside Information in the Saudi Capital Market Law, supra* n. 77, at 574.
196. Albjad, *Stock Market Crimes in Saudi Law, supra* n. 33, at 174-76.
197. *Id.* at 176-77.
198. Capital Market Law, Article 50 (2003); Market Conduct Regulations, Article 4(b)(4) (2004).
199. Market Conduct Regulations, Article 4(b)(4) (2004).

Such uncertainty sometimes creates problems as the investigation and enforcement process moves forward into the next phase.

[2] The Prohibition of Insider Trading

The CML prohibits insiders from directly or indirectly trading in the "security" related to inside information, or from disclosing such information to another person with the expectation that such person will trade in such security.[200] Also, the MCR prohibits an insider from engaging in insider trading.[201]

The CML sets two requirements that the insider must know for the purpose of an insider-trading violation. The insider must know that such information is not generally available and that, if it were available, it would have a material effect on the price or value of such Security.[202] Otherwise, the insider is not liable under the CML and MCR. "The CML does not, however, explicitly require that there be actual knowledge, so it is possible that the CRSD may choose to impute knowledge in some circumstances."[203]

The MCR expressly states three elements of inside information.[204] Inside information is (1) information that relates to a security, provided that it is; (2) material;[205] and (3) nonpublic.[206] This section will discuss only the first element of inside information because the other elements have been already analyzed above.

The MCR requires inside information to be related to a security. Article 4(a) lists a condition of such security: "A security related to inside information must be a traded security."[207] A regulation issued by CMA defines the term "traded security" to mean a security traded on the Saudi Stock Exchange. In Saudi Arabia, there is only one Exchange, "Tadawul."[208] Therefore, a security related to inside information must be traded and listed in Tadawul.[209] In order for a security to be considered as a "listed security" on the exchange, it must be traded in the secondary market, or offered to the public in an IPO.[210]

Under the CML, securities mean: (a) convertible and tradable shares of companies; (b) tradable debt instruments issued by companies, the government, public

200. Capital Market Law, Article 50(a) (2003).
201. Market Conduct Regulations, Article 6(a) (2004).
202. Capital Market Law, Article 50(a) (2003).
203. Beach, *supra* n. 177, at 344 n. 187.
204. Market Conduct Regulations, Article 4(c) (2004).
205. *See* §5.03 [B], *supra*.
206. *See* §5.03 [C], *supra*.
207. Market Conduct Regulations, Article 4(a)(1) (2004).
208. Article 20 of the CML states the Saudi Stock Exchange shall be the sole entity authorized to carry out trading in Securities in the Kingdom of Saudi Arabia. Capital Market Law, Article 20(a) (2003).
209. Glossary of Defined Terms Used in the Regulations and Rules of the Capital Market Authority, the Board of the Capital Market Authority Resolution Number 4-11-2004, dated 20/8/1425 H (Oct. 4, 2004), Amended by the Resolution of the Board of the Capital Market Authority Number 3-58-2014, dated 17/1/1436 H (Nov. 10, 2014).
210. *See* Diah Majeed, *Alborsat* 20 [*The Exchanges* 20] (Moasasat Shabab Aljameah 2003); Moneer Hindi, *Asasiat Alastathmar Fi Alborsah Almaliah* 70 [*The Principles of Investment in Securities* 70 (Monshat Almaraf 1999); Albjad, *Stock Market Crimes in Saudi Law, supra* n. 33, at 208.

institutions or public organizations; (c) investment units issued by investment funds; (d) any instruments representing profit participation rights and/or any rights in the distribution of assets; and (e) any other rights or instruments which the Board determines should be included or treated as Securities, if the Board believes that this would further the safety of the market or the protection of investors.[211]

Article 1 of the CML defines the term "trading" to mean "buying and selling of securities."[212] Additionally, Article 21 of the CML provides that securities listed on the Exchange shall be traded through transactions among brokers.[213] Therefore, any trading outside the Saudi Exchange "Tadawul" that is based on material nonpublic information is not a violation of the insider-trading law, as long as it is implemented entirely outside Tadawul.[214]

The MCR explains when a person is considered to be directly and indirectly trading in securities under Article 50 of the CML. A person shall be considered trading directly in a security in either of the following two situations: (1) if the person executes a trade in the security for any account in which he/she has an interest; or (2) if the person makes a bid or offer on the Exchange for the security.[215]

In the first situation where a person is considered directly, the person executes, by him/herself, the trade in a security in any account that the trader has an interest in doing so. The account, which is an account for trading securities, can be for the trader's own account or for others as long as the trader has an interest of executing such trade.[216]

The second situation does not require executing a trade in securities. Merely by making a bid or an offer to purchase or to sell a security in Tadawul, a trader commits an insider-trading violation. Therefore, the MCR added a new rule that the CML does not mention. More specifically, the CML defines trading as buying and selling of securities.[217] However, MCR expressly states that trading directly, for the purpose of insider trading, can occur by making an offer to buy or sell a security that is based on inside information, regardless of whether the trade is subsequently executed.[218] In other words, in the second situation, securities do not need to change hands to support a conviction for insider trading.[219]

211. Capital Market Law, Article 2 (2003).
212. Capital Market Law, Article 1 (2003).
213. Capital Market Law, Article 21 (2003).
214. *See* Albjad, *Stock Market Crimes in Saudi Law, supra* n. 33, at 192.
215. Market Conduct Regulations, Article 4(a)(3) (2004).
216. Albjad, *Stock Market Crimes in Saudi Law, supra* n. 33, at 194.
217. Capital Market Law, Article 1 (2003).
218. Market Conduct Regulations, Article 4(a)(3) (2004).
219. By this rule, there should not be any argument in Saudi Arabia about whether insider-trading violations occur by making an offer or until the transaction is executed. Most regulators follow this method by imposing liability when a person makes an offer to buy or sell; few jurisdictions require the execution of the transaction because insider-trading violations are composed of several elements, including the possession of material non-public information, making purchase/sell orders, and executing the orders. *See* Mathaher Fargali Ali Mohammed, *Alhamaiah Aljenaiah Lethagah Fi Soug Almal 396 [Criminal Protection for the Confidence in a Capital Market* 396] (Dar Alnahathah Alarabia 2006).

On the contrary, the MCR provides three situations where a person is considered to be indirectly trading in a security. Persons are considered trading indirectly in a security: (1) if they "execute" a trade as agents for other people; (2) if they "arrange" a trade to which a relative,[220] or person with whom they have a business or a contractual relationship, is a party; or (3) if they arrange for their agents, or any other person acting on their behalf or at their direction, to trade in the relevant securities.[221] In any of these three situations, a person is considered indirectly trading in a security for the purpose of insider trading.

The prohibition of insider trading extends beyond "insiders." Article 50(b) of the CML extends the prohibition to restrict "any person" from trading based on inside information obtained from an "insider" while knowing that such person has violated Article 50(a) by such disclosure.[222] Thus, a tippee must get the inside information from an insider and know that the insider has violated Article 50(a) of the CML by disclosing inside information.[223]

The MCR goes one more step in prohibiting insider trading. Article 6(b) of the MCR states that a persons who are not insiders are prohibited from engaging in insider trading if they obtain the inside information from "another person" and they know, or should have known, that the information is inside information.[224] The CML requires the inside information to come from an "insider." However, the MCR does not require this condition. Instead, all people are prohibited from trading based on inside information if they receive inside information from insiders or outsiders, and they know, or should know, that such information is inside information.

Therefore, the abuse of material nonpublic information restriction is very broad in Saudi Arabia and covers many people. In another way to increase the protections against misuse of inside information, realization of profits, or avoiding losses, are not required under both the CML and MCR to find a person liable of insider trading.[225] For example, when material nonpublic information is released publicly and the share price does not change, a person who trades based on the inside information before the information becomes public is still liable under Saudi laws.[226] Therefore, the main goal of the restriction on insider trading is to prohibit any trading and transaction that breaches the "principle of equality and fairness" among market's participants.[227]

Needless to say, without adequate enforcement, laws accomplish little. The Saudi system is not particularly strong in this area, as it is hampered by anemic sanctions and a procedure that utilizes "hidden agreements" which prevent violations from becoming

220. Article 1 of the CML defines a "relative" to include husband, wife, and minor children. Capital Market Law, Article 1 (2003).
221. Market Conduct Regulations, Article 4(a)(4) (2004).
222. Capital Market Law, Article 50(c) (2003).
223. Article 50(a) prohibits an insider: (1) to trade based on material non-public information, and (2) to disclose such information to another person with the expectation that such person will trade in such Security. Capital Market Law, Article 50(a) (2003).
224. Market Conduct Regulations, Article 6(b) (2004).
225. Albjad, *Stock Market Crimes in Saudi Law*, *supra* n. 33, at 203.
226. Capital Market Law, Article 50 (2003); Market Conduct Regulations, Articles 4, 6 (2004).
227. Mathaher Fargali Ali Mohammed, *Criminal Protection for the Confidence in a Capital Market*, *supra* n. 219, at 398.

part of the public record. These deficiencies significantly weaken the authorities' ability to deter future violators. In contrast, the U.S. employs a multilayer approach that may involve monetary penalties from the SEC, penal sanctions from the Department of Justice ("DOJ"), and private actions brought by aggrieved individuals. Collectively, the possible range of punishments acts as a significant barrier against lack of transparency and unfairness in the capital market.

[C] Sanctions upon Insider-Trading Violation

[1] Sanctions under Saudi Law

The CML provides several kinds of penalties that can be imposed upon anyone who violates this Law and its regulations. There are two types of sanctions in the CML: (1) general sanctions that can be imposed in any kind of violations; and (2) sanctions that can be only imposed on specific violations, such as insider trading.

Article 57(c) of the CML provides that the CRSD may, based on a claim filed by the CMA, punish anyone who commits market manipulation or insider trading with imprisonment terms up to five years.[228] This sanction is limited to violations that involve market manipulation or insider trading. The Committee may impose this penalty only when the Authority intervenes in the case and requests such sanction.[229] The language of this provision chooses the word "may," which gives the CRSD discretion to impose the sentence or not. Thus, the CRSD can choose to impose the punishment or to deny the CMA's request.[230] Also, the provision does not specify the minimum term of the imprisonment, so that the Committee can impose any term of imprisonment as long as it does not exceed five years.

On the contrary, the general sanctions that the CRSD may impose on anyone who commits any violation of the CML and its regulations are stated in Article 59 of the CML. This Article states that the CMA has the right to bring public action before the CRSD to seek an order for the appropriate sanctions whenever it appears to the CMA that a person has engaged, is engaging, or is about to engage in acts or practices that violate the CML, the CMA's regulations and rules, or the regulations and rules of the Exchange, Tadawul.[231] As written, the provision is ambiguous to the extent that it does not specify whether the CRSD or the CMA will determine and choose the appropriate sanctions for a given violation.[232] However, in practice, the CMA files a suit before the CRSD and asks the Committee to impose several sanctions. Then, the CRSD determines the appropriate sanctions in a case-by-case approach.[233]

These sanctions include the following: (1) warning the person concerned; (2) obliging the person concerned to cease or refrain from carrying out the act which is

228. Capital Market Law, Article 57(c) (2003).
229. Beach, *supra* n. 177, at 349.
230. As will be seen in §5.05 *infra*, the CRSD has rarely imposed imprisonment in insider trading cases.
231. Capital Market Law, Article 59(a) (2003).
232. Beach, *supra* n. 177, at 350, n. 222.
233. *See* e.g., *CMA v. S. H.*, Appeal CRSD, Decision No. 229/L.S/2010 (May 29, 2010).

the subject of the suit; (3) obliging the person concerned to take the necessary steps to avert the violation, or to take such necessary corrective steps to address the results of the violation; (4) indemnifying the persons who have suffered damages as a consequence of a violation that has occurred, or obliging the violator to pay to the Authority's account the gains realized as a consequence of such violation; (5) suspending the offender's trading in the Security; (6) barring the violating person from acting as a broker, portfolio manager or investment adviser for such period of time as is necessary for the safety of the market and the protection of investors; (7) seizing and executing on property; (8) imposing a travel ban; and (9) barring from working with companies whose Securities are traded on the Exchange.[234] The CMA has the right to seek an order to impose multiple sanctions, depending on the severity of the violation.[235]

Article 59(a)(4) combines two sanctions: indemnifying affected investors, or paying the gains to the CMA account. The language of this subsection uses the word "or." Thus, the CRSD can impose either the investors indemnify or paying the gains into the Authority's account. The drafters of this Law should have made each of these two sanctions in separate subsections in order to give the CRSD more discretion in applying the Law. Sometime, it is more appropriate and wise to combine both of the sanctions together to punish one violation.

In addition to the sanctions in Article 59(a), the CMA may request the CRSD to impose a financial fine upon persons responsible for an intentional violation of the CML, its regulations, the CMA rules, and the regulations of the Exchange.[236] Alternatively,[237] the Board of the CMA may impose a financial fine upon persons responsible for the violation of the Law, its regulations, the rules of the CMA, and the regulations of the Exchange.[238] The different between the CRSD and the Board in imposing the financial fine is that the Committee can impose the fine only when a person deliberately violates the Law, its regulations, the CMA rules, and the regulations of the Exchange. However, the Board may impose a financial fine when a person is "responsible" for the violation of the Law, its regulations, the CMA rules, and the regulations of the Exchange. Thus, the Law does not require the Board to find a "knowledge" element in order to impose fines upon violators.

Article 59(b) provides monetary penalties upon violators. The CRSD or the Board of the CMA can impose monetary fines which are not less than SAR 10,000 and do not

234. Capital Market Law, Article 59(a) (2003).
235. Albjad, *The Crime of Disclosure Inside Information in the Saudi Capital Market Law, supra* n. 77, at 584.
236. Capital Market Law, Article 59(b) (2003).
237. It is important to state exactly the language of Article 59 (b) of the CML. It provides that the CMA "may, in addition to taking the actions provided for under paragraph (a) of this Article, request the Committee to impose a financial fine upon the persons responsible for an intentional violation of the provisions of this Law, its Implementing Regulations, the rules of the Authority and the regulations of the Exchange. As an alternative to the foregoing, the Board may impose a financial fine upon any person responsible for the violation of this Law, its Implementing Regulations, the rules of the Authority and the regulations of the Exchange. The fine that the Committee or the Board can impose shall not be less than SAR 10,000 and shall not exceed SAR 100,000 for each violation committed by the defendant." Capital Market Law, Article 59(b) (2003).
238. Capital Market Law, Article 59(b) (2003).

exceed SAR 100,000 (USD 2,666-26,666) per violation committed by the defendant.[239] Because the language of this Article used the word "alternative," financial penalties cannot be imposed twice on a violator for the same violation by both the CRSD and the Board.[240]

Article 64 of the CML provides that a person charged with an insider-trading violation may avoid proceedings before the CRSD by reaching an agreement with the CMA pursuant to which he agrees to pay the CMA a sum not exceeding three times the profits he/she has realized, or three times the losses he/she has averted by committing such violation.[241] The arrangement between the CMA and the accused of insider trading shall be without prejudice to any compensation awardable as a result of the violation.[242]

Therefore, investors who violate the CML by insider trading can avoid being prosecuted before the CRSD. An interview conducted by the author with a legal advisor in the CRSD revealed that a number of insider-trading violations have been settled with the CMA.[243] However, these settlements are never published. Thus, such agreements are conducted in a hidden approach, and no one knows about it except the CMA and the specific violator.

However, such "hidden" agreements decrease and weaken public policies behind imposing sanctions upon violators in order to deter other investors from committing insider trading and exposing the capital market to illegal conduct. Only when violators stand before the CRSD and face punishments publicly are they, and other market participants, effectively deterred by these punishments. At the very least, the CMA should publish its settlements and agreements with violators and should make the settlements public.

In so doing, domestic and foreign investors should have increased confidence in the market, since the CMA chases offenders and brings them to justice, instead of making "hidden" settlements with offenders for money that is going into the CMA's account. Therefore, the CMA should announce its settlements to the public in order to make a clear message to market participants that the CMA oversees and regulates the market and seriously punish violators.

On December 31, 2014, the CMA transferred the jurisdiction for investigation and prosecution of criminal offenses to the "BIPP."[244] These offenses, which are violations under Articles 31, 49, and 50 of the CML, consist of: (1) performing brokerage activities

239. Capital Market Law, Article 59(b) (2003).

240. The CML does not specify whether the Board of the CMA's decisions to impose monetary fine according to Article 59 (b) are final. However, the Board's decisions are not final, and these decisions can be appealed to the CRSD. Article 25 (c) of the CML provides that the CRSD has jurisdiction over claims against CMA's decisions and actions. Capital Market Law, Article 25 (c) (2003); *see* Albjad, *Stock Market Crimes in Saudi Law*, *supra* n. 33, at 132.

241. Capital Market Law, Article 64 (2003).

242. *Id.*

243. Interview with a legal advisor for the Committees for the Resolution of Securities Disputes, Riyadh, Saudi Arabia (Aug. 12, 2014).

244. This is in pursuant to the High Order No. (4690) and dated 6/2/1435. Capital Market Authority, *CMA Announces the Start of the Referral of Criminal Offences to the Bureau of Investigation and Public Prosecution*, Dec. 31, 2014, http://www.cma.org.sa/en/News/Pages/CMA_N_1589.aspx.

without a valid license; (2) manipulation activities; and (3) insider trading.[245] Prior to December 2014, the CMA had the jurisdiction to investigate these offenses including insider-trading cases and prosecute them before the CRSD. Now, the BIPP has the jurisdiction to investigate insider-trading conduct and prosecute them before the CRSD. This multi-jurisdictional approach more closely mirrors the American version of securities law enforcement, at least in terms of a jurisdictional approach. In terms of the overall approach, however, there is still a significant gap.

[2] Sanctions under U.S. Law

In the U.S., the SEC, the DOJ, and private parties can bring actions to punish securities law violators in accordance with the federal securities laws. The jurisdiction is divided. "The SEC has authority to enforce the securities laws through either civil or administrative enforcement proceedings, while the DOJ has sole jurisdiction over criminal proceedings."[246]

[a] SEC

The SEC can ask for a variety of sanctions against alleged securities violators, and injunctive relief under Section 21(b) of the 1934 Exchange Act is one of the Agency's most common demands in these situations. This provision allows the SEC to request an injunction against any person who "is engaged or is about to engage" in any violation of the Act or the rules thereunder.[247] This remedy is available if there is "a reasonable likelihood of future violations."[248]

In addition to injunctive relief, disgorgement is another common enforcement tool. "Disgorgement is an equitable remedy, awarded to deprive the wrongdoer of the benefits of the unlawful conduct."[249] Typically, the funds at issue are paid into an escrow account for the purpose of distribution to the victims. Other forms of equitable relief include the reorganization of the corporate board[250] and the appointment of an independent audit committee.[251]

The SEC also has the authority to bring administrative "cease-and-desist" proceedings in any violation of the federal securities laws.[252] Additionally, the SEC can

245. Capital Market Law, Articles 31, 49, 50 (2003).
246. 17 C.F.R. § 202.5(f).
247. Securities Exchange Act of 1934, § 21(d), 15 U.S.C. § 78u- (d).
248. Ellsworth, *supra* n. 107, at A-30.
249. *Id.* at A-29. The determination of the profit gained or loss avoided is based on the difference between the purchase or sale price of the security and the security price at a reasonable period of time after public dissemination of the material non-public information in question. Securities Exchange Act of 1934, § 21A, 15 U.S.C. § 78u-1(e).
250. *SEC v. Mattel, Inc.*, 1974 WL 449, 5 (D.D.C. Oct. 1, 1974).
251. *SEC v. Int'l Sys. & Controls Corp.*, 1979 WL 1267, 1 (D.D.C. Dec. 17, 1979); Ellsworth, *supra* n. 107, at A-29 n. 11.
252. Securities Exchange Act of 1934, § 21C(a), 15 U.S.C. § 78u-3(a).

enter an order requiring accounting and disgorgement with reasonable interest in any cease-and-desist proceedings.[253]

Any and all of these penalties may be levied against any securities dealers, including broker-dealers and investment advisers, for any violation of securities laws.[254] These proceedings may also result in censure, suspension, or disbarment from the industry.[255] A wide range of other penalties, including civil injunctions, is available as well to punish insider trading.[256]

In 1984, Congress enacted the Insider Trading Sanction Act ("ITSA"). It "authorized the SEC to seek a civil penalty of up to three times the amount of profit gained or loss avoided by a person who illegally traded on material nonpublic information."[257] Thereafter, in 1988, Congress amended the Securities Exchange Act of 1938 by adding the Insider Trading and Securities Fraud Enforcement Act ("ITSFEA") to improve the procedures and remedies for prevention of insider trading, and for other purposes.[258]

The ITSFEA authorizes the SEC under § 21A to seek penalties not to exceed three times the profit gained or loss avoided as a result of trading based on nonpublic information.[259] Additionally, the ITSFEA added a new provision for penalties imposed on a "controlling person" who, at the time of the violation, directly or indirectly controlled the person who committed such violation. The penalty shall not exceed the greater of USD 1,000,000 or three times the amount of the profit gained or loss avoided as a result of such controlled person's violation.[260] The penalty amount of USD 1,000,000 has been adjusted to USD 1,525,000 for inflation pursuant to the Debt Collection Improvement Act of 1996.[261]

While violators in Saudi Arabia pay fines and penalties directly to the CMA, Section 21A of the Securities Exchange Act requires these monies to be deposited with the U.S. Treasury, unless the matter relates to securities whistleblowers.[262] Section 308 of the Sarbanes-Oxley Act of 2002 also allows the SEC to request the civil penalties, which are imposed on any person who violates federal securities laws, to "be added to and become part of the disgorgement fund for the benefit of the victims of such violation."[263]

In addition to insider traders, the prohibition in ITSFEA also extends to tippees and, in some instances, the person's employer or other controlling person. Similarly, the civil penalty assessed in these situations "shall not exceed three times the profit

253. *Id.* at § 21C(e).
254. *Id.* at § 15(b)(4); Investment Advisers Act of 1940, § 203(e), 15 U.S.C. § 80b-3(e).
255. Securities Exchange Act of 1934, § 15(b)(6), 15 U.S.C. § 78o(b)(6).
256. Ellsworth, *supra* n. 107, at A-30.
257. Pub. L. No. 98-376, 98 Stat. 1264 (1984); Securities Exchange Act of 1934, § 21A(a)(3), 15 U.S.C. § 78u-1; Ellsworth, *supra* n. 107, at A-30.
258. The Insider Trading and Securities Fraud Enforcement Act of 1988, Pub, L. No. 100-704, 102 Stat. 4677 (1988).
259. Securities Exchange Act of 1934, § 21A(a)(2), 15 U.S.C. § 78u-1 (a)(2).
260. *Id.* at § 21A(a)(3).
261. The Debt Collection Improvement Act of 1996, 17 C.F.R. § 201.1005 (2013).
262. Securities Exchange Act of 1934, § 21A(d)(1), 15 U.S.C. § 78u-1 (d)(1).
263. Sarbanes-Oxley Act of 2002, Pub. L. No. 107-204, §308 (a), 116 Stat. 745 (2002), 15 U.S.C. § 7246(a).

gained or loss avoided as a result of such unlawful purchase, sale or communication."[264] Any disgorgement or other sanctions may also be appropriate, in addition to the civil penalty.[265] Unfortunately for alleged violators, the SEC's assessment of fines and penalties may only be the beginning of their punishment.

[b] Department of Justice

As a procedural matter, the SEC punishments are entirely civil in nature. If the authorities feel as though a criminal action is warranted, the matter must be referred to an appropriate section of the DOJ, which is headed by one of the U.S. Attorneys for the U.S.[266] As a practical matter, many SEC actions give rise to DOJ prosecutions, and the two agencies cooperate closely in these cases.[267] Courts have consistently held that "simultaneous action by the SEC and DOJ does not violate the Constitution's 'due process' or 'double jeopardy' clauses."[268]

The Sarbanes-Oxley Act of 2002 increased the penalties for a vast number of federal securities violations, which may be applied to insider trading. Specifically, the Sarbanes-Oxley Act:

1) amended § 32(a) of the Securities Exchange Act of 1934 to increase the criminal penalties for violations of the Sarbanes-Oxley Act. Any person who willfully violates any provision of the Exchange Act, or the rules thereunder, may be fined up to US$ 5 million (US$ 25 million in the case of defendants other than natural persons) and imprisoned for up to 20 years,[269]
2) increased the maximum jail sentence for violations of the federal mail fraud and wire fraud statutes from five years to 20 years,[270] and
3) created a new crime of knowingly defrauding shareholders of publicly traded companies, carrying the accompanying penalty of a jail sentence of up to 25 years.[271]

Recently, in accordance with the Dodd-Frank Act of 2010,[272] the U.S. Sentencing Commission released guidelines that increased the possible sentences for a number of

264. Securities Exchange Act of 1934, § 21A(a)(2), 15 U.S.C. § 78u-1 (a)(2); Ellsworth, *supra* n. 107, at A-31.
265. Ellsworth, *supra* n. 107, at A-31.
266. 17 C.F.R. § 202.5(f). It provides that "neither the Commission nor its staff has the authority or responsibility for instituting, conducting, settling, or otherwise disposing of criminal proceedings. That authority and responsibility are vested in the Attorney General and representatives of the Department of Justice."
267. Ralph C. Ferrara, et al., *Ferrara on Insider Trading and the Wall* 4-20.13 (Law Journal Press 2015).
268. *See United States v. Stringer*, 535 F.3d 929 (9th Cir. 2008); *SEC v. Palmisano*, 135 F.3d 860, 864-66 (2d Cir. 1998); Ellsworth, *supra* n. 107, at A-33.
269. Sarbanes-Oxley Act of 2002, Pub. L. No. 107-204, §1106, 116 Stat. 745, 810 (2002), 15 U.S.C. § 78ff.
270. *Id.* at §§1341, 1343.
271. *Id.* § 1348; Ellsworth, *supra* n. 107, at A-33.
272. Dodd-Frank Wall Street Reform and Consumer Protection Act, Pub. L. No. 111-203, § 1079A(a), 124 Stat. 1376, 2077-78 (2010).

insider-trading violations.[273] Specifically, these revisions introduced two new categories: persons guilty of an "organized scheme to engage in insider trading"[274] and abuse of a specialized trust, as in the case of lawyers or hedge fund managers.[275]

The DOJ typically brings charges under both SEC Rule 10b-5 and mail/wire fraud laws.[276] A mail fraud or wire fraud conviction is punishably by a prison sentence of up to twenty years.[277]

Allegations of mail or wire fraud often give rise to prosecutions under the Racketeer Influenced Corrupt Organization Act ("RICO"). For purposes of statute, a "pattern of racketeering activity" constitutes wire fraud, mail fraud, and securities fraud.[278] This possibility is significant, because of the severe nature of the sanctions in a RICO case, especially the forfeiture provisions.[279]

[c] *Private Liability*

The U.S.' securities laws also allow financial victims to directly petition the courts for appropriate relief. In 1988, Congress enacted the ITSFEA of 1988. Section 20A of the Act "creates an express right of action against traders, tippers and controlling persons on behalf of certain marketplace traders who bought or sold without the benefit of the insider's information, and leaves open the possibility of suit by other injured persons as well."[280] Section 20A has been described as one of "a variety of measures designed to provide greater deterrence, detection and punishment of violations of insider trading."[281]

The total amount of damages in Section 20A cannot exceed the profit gained or loss avoided,[282] and shall be diminished by the amounts that such person may be required to disgorge.[283] However, "implied actions under Rule 10b-5 may permit

273. Notice of Proposed Amendments to Sentencing Guidelines, 77 Fed. Reg. 2778 (Jan. 19, 2012); Notice of Submission to Congress of Amendment to the Sentencing Guidelines, 77 Fed. Reg. 28226 (May 11, 2012). It took effect on November 11, 2012.
274. U.S. Sentencing Guidelines Manual § 2B1.4(b)(2) (Nov. 1, 2012).
275. *Id.* at § 3B1.3; Ellsworth, *supra* n. 107, at A-33.
276. 18 U.S.C. §§ 1341, 1343. These two sections prohibit the use of mail or by means of wire, radio, or television communication in interstate or foreign commerce as a part of scheme to defraud. *See Carpenter v. United States*, 484 U.S. 19 (1987) (convicting defendants under the mail and wire fraud statues when the defendants used the mail as a part of their scheme); Ellsworth, *supra* n. 107, at A-33.
277. 18 U.S.C. §§ 1341, 1343.
278. The U.S. Racketeer Influenced Corrupt Organization Act, 18 U.S.C. § 1961(1).
279. *Id.* at § 1963(c); Ellsworth, *supra* n. 107, at A-33.
280. Section 20A(a) provides that "[a]ny person who violates any provision of this chapter or the rules or regulations thereunder by purchasing or selling a security while in possession of material, nonpublic information shall be liable in an action in any court of competent jurisdiction to any person who, contemporaneously with the purchase or sale of securities that is the subject of such violation, has purchased (where such violation is based on a sale of securities) or sold (where such violation is based on a purchase of securities) securities of the same class." 15 U.S.C. §78t-1(a); Langevoort, *supra* n. 84, at § 9:1.
281. *Lampf, Pleva, Lipkind, Prupis & Petigrow v. Gilbertson*, 501 U.S. 350, 361(1991) (quoting H.R. Rep. No. 100–910, p. 7 (1988)).
282. Securities Exchange Act of 1934, § 20A (b)(1), 15 U.S.C. § 78t-1 (b)(1).
283. *Id.* § 20A (b)(2), 15 U.S.C. § 78t-1 (b)(2).

plaintiffs to recover the full extent of actual damages. The traditional implied right of action under Rule 10b-5 is therefore critical to a corporation's ability to recover damages caused by insider trading."[284]

The three pillars of SEC civil and administrative sanctions, DOJ criminal penalties, and private civil actions generally might deter insider trading in the U.S. Conversely, the Saudi system gives most enforcement authority to the CMA and BIPP through the CRSD. Such a philosophy places considerable pressure on these entities, especially since the BIPP has less than a year of experience in these matters. To more fully understand the nature of Saudi enforcement proceedings, an extensive examination of insider-trading cases in the Kingdom is appropriate.

§5.05 APPLICATIONS FOR SAUDI INSIDER-TRADING CASES

As mentioned above,[285] many insider-trading violations are settled privately with the CMA and these violations have avoided to be persecuted before the CRSD. There are only five insider-trading cases[286] that the CRSD has decided since its establishment in 2004.[287] Although it may appear that the dearth of cases indicates the presence of a successful system, the opposite is true. In 2012, a former Chairman of the CMA in Saudi Arabia, Dr Abdulrahman Altuwaijri, expressed concern over the increase of violations by investors. Dr Altuwaijri prompted the then-King of Saudi Arabia, Abdullah Bin Abdulaziz, for recommendations that would stem market violations including insider trading. Although the CMA issued a warning at the time to these violators, Dr Altuwaijri indicated that they have not changed their behavior and still committed regular violations with almost reckless disregard for the Law. To his credit, King Abdullah Bin Abdulaziz echoed the former Chairman's concerns that the CML and its Regulations must be enforced, and anyone who violates the law, hypothetically, even a member of the Saudi Royal Family, should be penalized.[288]

---

284. H.R. Rep. No. 100–910, pp. 27-28 (1988); Ferrara, *supra* n. 267, at 3-5.
285. *See supra* n. 243, and accompanying text.
286. The number of cases is based on the author's interviews with the CRSD's Secretary-General, and several legal advisors for the CRSD and for the CMA. Interview with Adel Gabani, Secretary-General of the Committees for the Resolution of Securities Disputes, in Riyadh, Saudi Arabia (Aug. 14, 2014); Interview with a Legal Advisor for the Committees for the Resolution of Securities Disputes, Riyadh, Saudi Arabia (Aug. 12, 2014); Interview with a Legal Advisor for the Committees for the Resolution of Securities Disputes, Riyadh, Saudi Arabia (Jan. 11, 2013); Interview with a Legal Advisor for the Saudi Capital Market Authority, Riyadh, Saudi Arabia (Dec. 29, 2012). Also, the author corresponded with various CMA and CRSD officials throughout the years of 2014-2015.
287. The Capital market Authority, The Resolution of the Board of the Capital Market Authority Number 2-31-2004, dated 7/11/1425 H (Dec. 19, 2004).
288. Ahmed Alabki, Almalik Ela Raeis Hiaat Soug Almal: Tabeego Alganon Ala Kain Mn Kan Bmn Fehim Alomara [*the King to the Capital Market Authority Chairman: Apply the Laws to Whoever Violates the Law Including Princes*], Alsharq (Apr. 9, 2012), http://www.alsharq.net.sa/2012/04/09/209521.

[A] *CMA v. S. H.* (2010)[289]

S.H. was a member of the Board of Directors for "STC."[290] In 2004, the company allocated SAR 150 million for a workforce development program. Each quarter of the year of 2004 was allocated SAR 37.5 million (USD 10 million). In a Board meeting on December 19, 2004, the Board agreed to raise the budget for the program to SAR 700 million (USD 186.6 million) and allocate SAR 467 million (USD 124.5 million) – in the fourth quarter of 2004 instead of SAR 37.5 million (USD 10 million), contradicting what was planned for the year of 2004. As a result of such decision, the financial results of the fourth quarter decreased when comparing with the first three-quarters of the 2004.[291]

S.H. sold 400,968 shares of STC during December 16, 18, 19, and 20, 2014, making over SAR 23 million (USD 6.1 million).[292] S.H. traded in a prohibited period: the LR restricts directors and senior executives from trading during it.[293] On February 6, 2005, the CTS disclosed its financial statement for 2004, which showed poor financial results in the fourth quarter of 2004. On the day of the announcement, the share price dropped 6.8%.[294]

The CRSD held that S.H. was an insider and traded while in possession of material nonpublic information. The information was material because of its effect on the share price.[295] However, the CRSD held that S.H. was only liable for the trading on December 20 because there was no evidence that S.H. knew about the information before the Board meeting on December 19. Therefore, S.H. was not liable for insider trading for transactions executed on December 16, 18, and 19. As a result, the CRSD convicted S.H. for insider-trading violation by violating Article 50 of the CML and Article 6(a) of the MCR.[296]

The CRSD imposed three penalties: (1) requiring S.H. to return the profits he made (SAR 249,365 (USD 1,933,164)) to the CMA's account; (2) imposing a financial penalty of SAR 100,000 (USD 26,666); and (3) restricting S.H. from working for three years in any listed company. On the appeal, the Appeal Committee for the Resolution of Securities Disputes ("ACRSD") confirmed all of CRSD's decisions and reasons.[297] It

289. The author has intentionally abbreviated the names of defendants in these cases because they have not been publically announced. Also, some details of these cases have not been provided to public.
290. *CMA v. S. H.*, Appeal CRSD, Decision No. 229/L.S/2010, p. 5 (May 29, 2010).
291. *Id.*
292. *Id.* at 4.
293. Article 50 of the Listing Rules prohibits directors and senior executives to trade: (1) during the fifteen calendar days preceding the end of the financial quarter and until the date of the announcement of the reviewed interim financial statement of the issuer, and (2) during the thirty calendar days preceding the end of the financial year and until the date of the announcement of the reviewed interim financial statements or the audited annual financial statements of the issuer. Listing Rules, Article 50 (2004). It is worth mentioning that the LR took effect on Dec. 4, 2004, and S.H. started to sell his shares on Dec. 16, 2004. S.H. argued that he had no knowledge about the LR, but the CRSD disagreed.
294. *CMA v. S. H.* at 6.
295. *Id.*
296. *Id.* at 7.
297. *Id.*

is worth mentioning that neither the CRSD nor the ACRSD addressed how they determined the amount of profits that S.H. made.

In this case, the CMA asked both the CRSD and the ACRSD to impose an imprisonment sanction upon S.H. according to Article 57(c) of the CML. However, both the CRSD and the ACRSD refused to grant this request. The ACRSD stated that the CRSD and the ACRSD have the jurisdiction to assess the CMA request according to the power that has been given by Article 25(a) of the CML.[298] The CRSD and the ACRSD are empowered to determine the appropriate sanctions by considering the conditions and the circumstances of each offense. The ACRSD believed that it was not necessary to overturn the CRSD's decision in this regard.[299]

Moreover, the CMA asked the CRSD to consider each of the four trading days (December 16, 18, 19, and 20) as a separate offense. Thus, the CMA asked the CRSD to impose a financial penalty of SAR 400,000 (USD 106,666) as SAR 100,000 (USD 26,666) per day of violation according to Article 59(b) of the CML. However, the CRSD and the ACRSD refused to uphold such request because they considered the four trading days as one violation.[300]

[B] *CMA v. M.R.* (2009)

In this case, M.R. was the Chairman of the Board of Directors for Qassim Agriculture Company ("QAC").[301] In February 2006, QAC and Albandaria Group signed a "MOU" about a potential acquisition. The Board of Directors for QAC authorized M.R. to be in charge of the acquisition negotiation and the agreement. Later, on June 25, 2006, the two companies signed the final agreement of the acquisition. On the next day, QAC announced on Tadawul website its acquisition on Albandaria Group.[302]

M.R. bought 28,700 shares of QAC on June 21. On the same day, M.R.'s brother bought 93,804 shares of QAC. Subsequently, on June 25, 2006, M.R.'s brother bought another 170,914 shares of QAC.[303]

The CMA filed a suit against M.R. and M.R.'s brother. The CMA claimed that M.R. was an insider and traded while in possession of material nonpublic information so that M.R. violated Article 50(a) of the CML and Article 6 of the MCR. Moreover, the CMA claimed that M.R. disclosed inside information to his brother in violation of Article 50(a) of the CML and Article 5 of the MCR.[304]

298. Part of Article 25(a) of the CML provides that the CRSD has all necessary powers to investigate and settle complaints and suits, including the power to issue subpoenas, issue decisions, impose sanctions and order the production of evidence and documents. Capital Market Law, Article 25(a). (2003).
299. *CMA v. S. H.* at 7.
300. *Id.*
301. *CMA v. M.R.*, Appeal CRSD, Decision No. 148/L.S/2009, p. 17 (Jun. 23, 2009).
302. *Id.*
303. *Id.*
304. *Id.* at 1-2.

The CRSD held that M.R. violated Article 50(a) of the CML and Article 6(a) of the MCR by trading based on material nonpublic information while M.R. was the Chairman of the Board of the QAC.[305]

On the contrary, M.R. was not found guilty of tipping his brother in violation of Article 50(a) of the CML and of Article 5 of the MCR, and M.R.'s brother was not guilty of insider trading.[306] Although the CMA introduced evidence of the relationship between the two defendants, and the large quantity of purchase of QAC's shares by M.R.'s brother before the announcement of the acquisition, the CRSD reasoned that there was not enough evidence that proved M.R. had tipped his brother the material information and the M.R.'s brother traded based on such information.[307] The CRSD stated that the relationship between the two defendants could neither prove the occurrence of disclosure nor constitute evidence of accusation unless it was supported by additional evidence based on which the validity of inference could be proved. In other words, a mere family relationship was insufficient. Moreover, the large quantity of stocks purchased by M.R.'s brother was insufficient for the proving of the occurrence of trading that is based on M.R.'s tipping because the CMA failed to exclude alternative possibilities for the purchase.[308] These possibilities included: (1) prices increasing in June 21 by 5.66%, in June 24 by 7.59%, and in June 25 by 7.47%, which prompted some market participants to purchase shares in this company; and (2) M.R.'s brother had traded continuously in QAC's shares during 2006, even though M.R.'s brother trading had significantly increased prior to the announcement.[309] As a result, M.R. was not guilty of disclosing inside information to his brother, and M.R.'s brother was also not guilty of insider trading.[310]

In this case, the CMA asked both the CRSD and the ACRSD to impose an imprisonment sanction upon M.R. according to Article 57(c) of the CML. However, both the CRSD and the ACRSD refused to uphold this request.[311]

The CRSD sanctioned M.R. by: (1) imposing a financial penalty of SAR 100,000 (USD 26,666) – for insider-trading violation; and (2) restricting M.R. from working for three years in any listed company whose shares are traded in the Exchange.[312]

According to the Committee, M.R. did not make any profit so M.R. was not required to return any money. The CRSD determined the profit gained by M.R. was based on the difference between the purchase price of the security – SAR 1,572,200 (USD 419,253) and the selling price - SAR 1,228,647 (USD 327,639). Thus, under this analysis, M.R. lost SAR 343,553 (USD 91,614), and he was not required to pay back anything.[313]

305. *Id.* at 23.
306. *Id.*
307. *Id.*
308. *Id.*
309. *Id.* at 20.
310. *Id.* at 23.
311. *Id.* at 22.
312. *Id.* at 20.
313. *Id.* at 23.

The CRSD explained that the protection of inside information in this case started from the time when M.R. authorized to be in charge for the acquisition negotiation and the agreement until the time of announcement thereof.[314]

On the appeal, the ACRSD confirmed all of CRSD's decisions and reasons.[315]

[C] *CMA v. M.A.* (2009)

In this case, M.A. was a vice chairman of the Board of Directors for the Saudi Hotels Company ("SHC"). The Board of the SHC had reviewed the feasibility study of the possibility of converting some of the subsidiary companies of SHC to public joint companies or integrating these companies with SHC and increasing its capital accordingly.[316]

Since M.A. was a vice chairman of the Board, he learned about the inside information before the Board meeting and bought 249,803 shares in SHC for five of his children and for his wife before and after the board meeting. Then later, SHC published the information on the Tadawul website.[317] The CMA filed a suit against M.A. for committing indirectly insider trading in violating Article 50(a) of the CML.[318]

Similar to the *M.R.* case, the CRSD states that the confidentiality of material nonpublic information starts from the moment when insiders obtain it until the time of its announcement. As the CRSD states, insiders must refrain from trading when they know about material information because of their easy access to such information in order to achieve justice and fairness among all market participants.[319]

However, contrary to *CMA v. M.R.* case, the CRSD introduced another method of determining the profit gained or loss avoided by violators: the difference between the purchase or sale price of the security when the violator starts committing a violation and the security price at the end of the day when the information is made public. M.A. purchased securities based on material nonpublic information for a total of SAR 36,159,215 (USD 9,642,457), and the value of these shares by the end of the announcement day was SAR 39,531,324 (USD 10,541,686). Therefore, the profit that M.A. made was over SAR 3 million (USD 899,229).[320]

The CRSD concluded that M.A. committed indirect insider trading in violating Article 50(a) of the CML. The CRSD imposed three penalties: (1) requiring M.A. to return the profits he made (SAR 3,372,109 (USD 899,229)) to the CMA's account; (2) imposing a financial penalty of SAR 100,000 (USD 26,666); and (3) restricting M.A. from working for three years in any listed company.[321] The CMA did not ask the CRSD to impose an imprisonment sanction upon M.A. according to Article 57(c) of the CML.

314. *Id.* at 21.
315. *Id.* at 24.
316. *CMA v. M.A.*, Appeal CRSD, Decision No. 147/L.S/2009, p. 19 (Jun. 21, 2009).
317. *Id.*
318. *Id.* at 1.
319. *Id.* at 22.
320. *Id.* at 23.
321. *Id.* at 24.

On the appeal, the ACRSD confirmed all of CRSD's decisions and reasons.[322]

[D] *CMA v. S.D.* (2009)

The CMA alleged that on November 11, 2004, S.D. purchased 34,576 shares in the Saudi Arabian Amiantit Company ("Amiantit") based on inside information in violation of Article 50(b) of the CML.[323] In recorded phone conversations, S.D. asked his broker to execute the transaction on his behalf, because S.D. learned that the Vice Minister of the Ministry of Commerce and Industry called someone and told him that a decision to increase Amiantit's capital had been signed, but was awaiting the Minister's approval. S.D. said he was sure that this information would be announced in one or two days, which would cause the current share price to increase by SAR 40 to 50. S.D. informed his broker of his intention to sell these shares after reaching such prices. On the same day, S.D. disclosed this information to his son-in-law in violation of Article 5(b) of the MCR.[324] The son-in-law purchased 4,000 shares in Amiantit on the same day.[325]

To prove this violation, the CRSD pointed out that Article 50(b) of the CML required the nonpublic information be obtained from an "insider" and the trader knows that the insider violated the CML by disclosing such information. In this case, the CMA could not identify the insider from whom S.D. obtained the information. The CRSD concluded that because the CMA failed to identify the insider and there was no evidence to infer whether the source of the inside information which S.D. received was as an "insider," S.D. did not violate Article 50(b) of the CML. The CRSD added that to make S.D. and his son-in-law liable for violating Articles 5(b) and 6(b)[326] of the MCR, the MCR needed to be in force when the violation occurred. MRC took effect in December 4, 2004, and the violation occurred on November 29, 2004. As a result, both S.D. were deemed not guilty of violating the MCR.[327]

In a separate incident, on December 18, 2004, S.D. traded based on material nonpublic information and disclosed this information to his son-in-law, who also traded based on such information. Based on recorded phone conversations, S.D. asked his broker to sell his shares of Amiantit. S.D. revealed to his broker that "people expected the Board of Directors of Amiantit to announce the information. But when I

322. *Id.*
323. Article 50(b) of the CML restricts "any person" from trading based on inside information obtained from an "insider" while knowing that such person has violated Article 50(a) by such disclosure. Capital Market Law, Article 50(b) (2003).
324. Article 5(b) of the MCR states that "[a] person who is not insider is prohibited from disclosing to any other person any inside information obtained from an insider, when he knows or should have known that it is possible that such other person to whom the disclosure has been made may trade in the security related to the inside information." Capital Market Law, Article 50(b) (2003).
325. *CMA v. S.D.*, Appeal CRSD, Decision No. 146/L.S/2009, p. 17 (Jun. 20, 2009).
326. Article 6(b) of the MCR states that "[a] person who is not insider is prohibited from engaging in insider trading if he obtains the inside information from another person and he knows or should have known, that the information is inside information." Market Conduct Regulations, Article 6(b) (2004).
327. *CMA v. S.D.* at 18.

inquired, the Board told me that nothing will be announced. So, I tell you to sell my shares." The information was about Amiantit increasing its capital, and the Board of Amiantit decided not to announce such information. Previously, Amiantit had announced that the Board was considering the proposal of increasing Amiantit's capital and has consulted a specialist firm. As a result, S.D. sold 34,576 shares of Amiantit. Then, on the same day, the son-in-law sold 5,000 shares of Amiantit. The CMA said these activities were violations of Article 50(b) of the CML, in addition to Articles 5(b) and Article 6(b) of the MCR.[328]

In this allegation, the CRSD stated that the nonpublic information had material effects on the share price and a normal person would realize its effect on the price or value of the security. Moreover, through the recorded phone conversations, S.D. demonstrated his knowledge of such a material effect on the price of the Amiantit shares. Therefore, S.D. sold his shares in Amiantit based on material nonpublic information. According to Article 50(b) of the CML, S.D. had to obtain the information from an insider. The CRSD stated that even though the CMA did not know the name of the insider, S.D. obtained the information from someone on the Board of Directors of Amiantit, and all members of the Board are insiders according to Article 4(b) of the MCR. Therefore, S.D. committed insider trading in violation of Article 50(b) of the CML.[329]

Additionally, S.D. violated Article 5(b) of the MCR by disclosing such information to his son-in-law, since S.D. obtained the information from an insider, and S.D. and his son-in-law have a close family relationship. The son-in-law also violated Article 6(b) of the MCR by selling his shares in Amiantit after S.D. sold his shares on the same day, because the son-in-law obtained the information from S.D. The CRSD concluded that S.D. violated Article 50(b) of the CML and Article 5(b) of the MCR.[330]

Third, on February 21, 2005, S.D. and his son-in-law sold all their shares in their portfolio and purchased a large numbers of shares in Amiantit. Three days later, on February 24, Amiantit announced its cooperation with another company to establish a new company. Later, on February 26, Amiantit made another announcement to Tadawul about winning contracts that amounted to SAR 76 million (USD 20 million). The CMA alleged that both S.D. and his son-in-law violated Article 6(b) of the MCR.[331]

In this regard, the CRSD stated that there was not sufficient evidence that S.D. and his son-in-law obtained inside information, and the CMA could not prove which information the two defendants had obtained at the time of trading. There was a probability that may weaken such charge, including the price increasing of the Amiantit shares on February 21, 2005 by 8.52%, which may have prompted participants' desire to purchase shares of the company. As a result, the CRSD held that S.D. and his son-in-law did not commit insider trading on February 21, 2005.[332]

328. *Id.* at 18, 19.
329. *Id.* at 19.
330. *Id.* at 20.
331. *Id.*
332. *Id.* at 21.

In summary:

- S.D. is not guilty of violating Article 50(b) of the CML and Articles 5(b) and 6(b) of the MCR for the first charge (November 29, 2005) and the third charge (February 21, 2005).
- The son-in-law is not guilty of violating Article 6(b) of the MCR for the first charge (November 29, 2005) and the third charge (February 21, 2005).
- S.D. committed insider trading and disclosed nonpublic information to his son-in-law in violating Article 50(b) of the CML and Article 5(b) of the MCR for the second charge (December 18, 2004).
- The son-in-law committed insider trading in violating Article 6(b) of the MCR for the second charge (December 18, 2004).
- The CRSD imposed a financial penalty of SAR 50,000 (USD 13,333) on S.D. and SAR 25,000 (USD 6,666) on the son-in-law and restricted S.D. and his son-in-law from working for three years in any listed company.
- On the appeal, the ACRSD confirmed all of CRSD's decisions and reasons.[333]

The CRSD did not require the two defendants to return the profit gained/loss avoided of the second violation (December 18, 2004). The CRSD stated that the selling of shares by the two defendants on that day did not follow an announcement by Amiantit declaring that Amiantit had stopped considering increasing its capital, which such disclosure would affect the share price. As a result, there was no loss avoided.[334]

In this case, the CMA asked both the CRSD and the ACRSD to imprison S.D. and his son-in-law according to Article 57(c) of the CML. However, both the CRSD and the ACRSD refused to grant the request.[335]

[E] *CMA v. N.D.* (2009)

In this case, the CMA alleged that three brothers committed insider-trading violations. N.D. was the chairman of the Board of Directors of Bishah Agricultural Development Company ("Bishah"). On July 4, 2006, the Board met and discussed the possible acquisition of Ajwa Company ("Ajwa Co."), and the Board agreed initially to the acquisition. The Board authorized N.D. to prepare and to sign an MOU with Ajwa Co. about the potential acquisition. On July 12, 2006, N.D. and Ajwa Co. signed the MOU.[336] Based on recorded phone calls, on July 26, 2006, N.D. asked his broker prior of the end of the day to "purchase shares for me immediately with all the money you have." The broker purchased 2,740 shares of Bishah. Two hours later, after the market had closed, Bishah announced in Tadawul website about the acquisition.[337] On July 30, 2006, N.D. sold his shares in Bishah, making a profit of SAR 52,690 (USD 14,050).[338]

333. *Id.* at 23-24.
334. *Id.* at 22-23.
335. *Id.* at 22.
336. *CMA v. N.D.*, CRSD, Decision No. 535/L./D1/2009, p. 23 (Jun. 2, 2009).
337. *Id.* at 24.
338. *Id.* at 28.

On the same day, N.D.'s brother ("G.D.") called N.D. and asked him "where are you now?" meaning as to which company was N.D. trading. "I will purchase in Bishah," N.D. answered. As a result, G.D. purchased 3,820 shares in Bishah.[339] Then, N.D.'s second brother ("Z.D.") called his brother G.D. and asked him where he should trade. G.D. told Z.D. to purchase Bishah. Z.D. purchased 2,850 shares of Bishah without asking his brother the reasons for his response.[340] The CMA filed a lawsuit against these three brothers for insider trading and disclosing nonpublic information in violation of Article 50 of the CML and Articles 5(a) and 6(a) of the MCR.[341]

In analyzing the case, the CRSD stated that N.D. was an insider and the information he knew was material and nonpublic. N.D. traded in Bishah while in possession of material nonpublic information in violation of Article 50(a) of the CML and Article 6(a) of the MCR.[342] The CRSD explained that the protection of inside information in this case started from the time when N.D. was authorized to sign the acquisition agreement until the time of the announcement thereof.[343]

On the contrary, the CMA's allegation that N.D. disclosed material nonpublic information to G.D. was not proved. When N.D. said he would purchase Bishah stocks, N.D. did not reveal the fact that he had inside information; N.D.'s answer was in the form of "advice." As a result, N.D. did not violate the law by such disclosure. Additionally, both G.D. and Z.D. had not violated the law because the CMA had not proven that G.D. and Z.D. traded while in possession of material nonpublic information.[344]

The CRSD held[345] that N.D. engaged in insider trading in violation of Article 50(a) and Article 5(a) of the MCR. The CRSD imposed several sanctions. For the first and only time in an insider-trading violation in the Kingdom, the CRSD imposed an imprisonment sanction for three months. The CRSD also imposed a financial fine of SAR 100,000 (USD 26,666) on N.D., and restricted him from working for five years in any listed company. The CRSD also required N.D. to return the profits he made (SAR 52,690 (USD 14,050)) to the CMA's account.[346]

Similar to *CMA v. M.R*, but contrary to *CMA v. M.A.*, the CRSD stated that the determination of the profit gained by N.D. was based on the difference between the total purchase price of the shares in July 26, 2006 (SAR 317,208 (USD 84,588)) and the total sale price in July 30, 2006 (SAR 369,900 (USD 98,640)).[347]

339. *Id.* at 4.
340. *Id.* at 6.
341. *Id.* at 1.
342. *Id.* at 25.
343. *Id.* at 26.
344. *Id.*
345. The proceedings against N.D. were conducted *in absentia* because he did not appear at trial, even after the matter had been postponed for more than a year. He has also not appealed the case. *CMA v. N.D.*
346. *CMA v. N.D.* at 29.
347. *Id.* at 28.

[F] Observations and Conclusions

Perhaps the most salient conclusion can be found in the number of cases themselves. The CMA has only prosecuted five insider-trading cases in its entire history. Even assuming that there are a number of cases resolved by "hidden agreement,"[348] there are still few insider-trading prosecutions in Saudi Arabia given the relative size of the market and number of participants.

The cases that do reach the CRSD are decided on an inconsistent basis. Specifically, the Committee has applied different theories as to the determination of profit realized or loss avoided. In *CMA v. M.R.* and *CMA v. N.D.*, the CRSD used a formula that compares the share's purchase price with its sales price. However, in *CMA v. M.A.*, the Members compared the purchase price with the announcement price; i.e., the share price at the close of trading after the announcement was made. In another case, *CMA v. S.H.*, the Committee did not even discuss its rationale for determining profit made or loss avoided. In the fifth case, *CMA v. S.D.*, the Committee did not impose such a sanction.

Even if there is a penalty assessed, the monetary amounts are too low to be an effective deterrent. Indeed, one could speculate that N.D. did not appear at his trial because he did not fear the sanctions that the CRSD might impose; in fact, N.D. received only a three-month sentence out of a five-year maximum. It bears repeating that this case is the only instance in which the CRSD imposed any incarceration for insider-trading violations, despite the fact that the CMA often demands such a penalty. This issue extends beyond just one case: even at the time the maximum financial penalties and prison terms were announced, some observers expressed concern that the punishments were "too lenient."[349] Another commentator labeled the Saudi insider-trading penalty system as "simple," meaning that traders are not afraid of the possible penalties.[350] Even worse, the CRSD only assessed the maximum financial penalty and prison term in one of the cases it considered.[351] In contrast, the SEC is seriously considering an increase in its already stiff penalties for securities laws violations.[352] The CMA should consider doing likewise by increasing the maximum fines to SAR 1,000,000.

Especially in cases like *CMA v. N.D.*, and its ruling that relationship by blood or marriage is insufficient to prove an insider-trading violation without other supporting

348. *See supra* n. 243, and accompanying text.
349. Mohamed A. Ramady, *The Saudi Arabian Economy, Policies, Achievements, and Challenges* 151 (2d ed. 2010).
350. Mohammed Alsmaiel, *La Ahad Iagsha Ogobat Soug Almal, [No One Fears The Capital Market's Sanctions], Alyaum,* May 10, 2012, http://www.alyaum.com/article/3049621.
351. *See CMA v. N.D.*
352. The proposed Stronger Enforcement of Civil Penalties Act (SEC Penalties Act) would "strengthen the SEC's ability to crack down on violations of securities laws" by increasing the per-violation cap to USD 1 million for individuals and USD 10 million for entities, and tripling the penalty cap for some repeat securities law violators. Furthermore, the SEC would not need to file a case in federal court to obtain these sanctions. Chuck Grassley, *Bill Seeks Tougher Penalties for Wall Street Fraud*, Chuck Grassley, Jul. 9, 2015, http://www.grassley.senate.gov/news/news-releases/bill-seeks-tougher-penalties-wall-street-fraud.

evidence, the CRSD may fail to account for the closeness of the people in Saudi Arabia and their intimate connections with one another. Saudi citizens form bonds that are interwoven through the relationship they have within their own families, tribes, neighbors, mosques, cities and provinces. There is a special level of trust and integrity that Saudi Arabians share with one another, especially between family members. Additionally, it is considered an obligation in the Saudi culture for people to help each other in all the matters of life. Some people illegally extend this obligation to include giving information to gain financial profit, which is against *Shari'ah* law and Saudi regulations. As such, many investors simply do not believe, or even know, that insider trading and disclosure of inside information are wrong, illegal, and detrimental to the government's efforts to develop a strong modern economy.[353] In the future, the CRSD should consider giving greater weight to family relationships as it decides whether or not inside information was used and/or passed on.

§5.06 "WHISTLEBLOWER PROGRAM": LESSONS FROM THE U.S. EXPERIENCE

Traditional enforcement tools are sometimes not enough in the area of securities law, which is one reason that the U.S. encourages the use of paid informers. Through ITSFEA in 1988, "Congress authorized the SEC to award a bounty to any person who provided information leading to the imposition of a civil penalty under Section 21A for illegal insider trading or for controlling a person liable for illegal tipping or trading." Section 21A(e) provided that the award could not exceed 10% of the penalty imposed.[354] However, the Program was not as effective as the drafters had hoped. According to an assessment published by the SEC in March 2010, since 1989 when the Program was established, the SEC had paid only USD 159,537 to five claimants.[355] The assessment also pointed out that the bounty Program was not "widely recognized inside or outside" the SEC. Additionally, the report criticized the Program as "not fundamentally well-designed to be successful."[356]

In July 2010, Congress enacted the Dodd-Frank Wall Street Reform and Consumer Protection Act ("Dodd-Frank Act"), which repealed Section 21A(e) and added Section 21F. It provides that the SEC shall award whistleblowers not less than 10% and

353. Mohammed Sultan Alsahali, *Almalomat Aldakeliah Oa Soag Alasahom, [Inside Information and the Stock Market]*, Alriyadh Newspaper, Jan. 14, 2006, http://www.alriyadh.com/8563; Ali Almazid, *Tasreeb Almalomat Aldakaliah Fi Soag Alasahom Yonagath Mafaheem Aladalh Oa Alshafafiah [The Disclosing Inside Information in the Stock Market Is Contrary to the Concepts of Fairness and Transparency]*, Alsharg Alaosad Newspaper, May 20, 2004, http://archive.aawsat.com/details.asp?issueno=9165&article=245750#.VucQhLSrhUQ; Badi Albadrani, *Galag Men Tasareeb Malomat Fi Soag Alasahom Letahagaig Arabah Estethnaiah Oa Qar Masharoah, [Concerns About Illegal Disclosure of Information In the Stock Market to Achieve Substantial Illegal Profits]*, Alriyadh Newspaper, Oct. 22, 2005, http://www.alriyadh.com/102415.

354. 15 U.S.C. § 78u-1(e).

355. U.S. Securities and Exchange Commission, Office of Inspector General Office of Audits, *Assessment of the SEC's Bounty Program*, Report No. 474, p. 5 (Mar. 29, 2010).

356. *Id.* at iii.

not more than 30% of the total amount collected arising from any judicial or administrative action, or related action, brought by SEC under a securities law that results in "monetary sanctions" exceeding USD 1,000,000. Such whistleblowers are those who voluntarily provide "original information" to the Commission that leads to the successful enforcement of the covered judicial or administrative action, or related action.[357] The Whistleblower Program is not limited to illegal insider trading; rather, it covers any violation under the securities law.[358]

Section 21F defines "original information" to mean information that: (1) is derived from the independent knowledge or analysis of a whistleblower; (2) is not known to the Commission from any other source; and (3) is not exclusively derived from an allegation made in a judicial or administrative action.[359] This Section also defines "monetary sanctions" to mean any monies, including penalties, disgorgement, and interest, ordered to be paid. Monetary sanctions also include any monies deposited into a disgorgement fund or other fund pursuant to Section 308(b) of the Sarbanes-Oxley Act of 2002.[360]

Through the expanded power that the Dodd-Frank Act granted to the SEC,[361] the SEC created the Office of the Whistleblower (OWB) to assist and to promote the Program.[362] According to Sean McKessy, the Chief of the "OWB," assistance from a whistleblower is potentially one of the most "powerful weapons" in the SEC's arsenal because they can identify misconduct "much earlier than might otherwise have been possible."[363] Again, according to the Chief, the Program relies on "monetary awards, retaliation protection, and confidentiality protection, each of which is equally important to the continued success of the program."[364]

The difference between the previous Whistleblower Program and the one authorized by the Dodd-Frank Act has been staggering. On November 4, 2015, the SEC announced that "[s]ince its inception in 2011, the SEC's Whistleblower Program has paid more than US$54 million to 22 whistleblowers who provided the SEC with unique and useful information."[365] USD 30 million of this total went to just one person, in September 2014. That whistleblower was actually from a foreign country, "demonstrating the program's international reach."[366]

357. Dodd-Frank Wall Street Reform and Consumer Protection Act, §922; 15 U.S.C. § 78u-6.
358. *Id.* at §922; 15 U.S.C. § 78u-6(a)(1).
359. *Id.* at §922; 15 U.S.C. § 78u-6.
360. *Id.*
361. *Id.* at §922(j); 15 U.S.C. § 78u-6(j).
362. Securities Exchange and Commission, the Office of the Whistleblower, *About Us*, (Nov. 21, 2015), https://www.sec.gov/about/offices/owb/owb-about.shtml.
363. U.S. Securities Exchange and Commission, the Office of the Whistleblower, *Welcome to the Office of the Whistleblower*, (Nov. 21, 2015), https://www.sec.gov/whistleblower.
364. U.S. Securities Exchange and Commission, *2014 Annual Report to Congress on the Dodd-Frank Whistleblower Program*, p. 1 (Nov. 17, 2014).
365. U.S. Securities Exchange and Commission, *SEC Announces Whistleblower Award of More Than $325,000*, Nov. 4, 2015, http://www.sec.gov/news/pressrelease/2015-252.html.
366. U.S. Securities Exchange and Commission, *SEC Announces Largest-Ever Whistleblower Award*, Sep. 22, 2014, https://www.sec.gov/News/PressRelease/Detail/PressRelease/1370543011290.

Additionally, the OWB provides anti-retaliation protection to further encourage individuals to come forward with information.[367] The OWB has also been selective, denying 205 whistleblowing claims (196 by one individual) as of 2014.[368]

Such a Program would be very valuable in Saudi Arabia; currently, there is no such Program. As stated earlier, most citizens feel a need to help each other by passing along inside information. In addition to creating awareness that such a practice is illegal, a Whistleblower Program would create concrete incentives for people to come forward and express what they know without fear of their privacy being breached or retaliation from their employers. Such a Program, which should be part of the CMA, would also increase the number of insider-trading cases that the CRSD considers. Indeed, this one addition to the enforcement system would quite possibly do more good than any other proposal designed to strengthen the insider-trading enforcement process in Saudi Arabia. Additionally, the CMA should also issue an internal policy that provides financial rewards to the CMA's employees who discover insider-trading violations.

The CMA should establish Investor Protection Fund ("IPF"). This entity could be funded by disgorgement and monetary penalties of fraud violations, and used for developing and funding the Whistleblower Program, as well as awarding whistleblowers. Also, the IPF would be used for compensating victims of fraud violations.

§5.07 CONCLUSION

Ironically, the feature of Saudi society that makes it so strong – the close interpersonal relationships between its citizens – creates great difficulty in the area of insider-trading laws. The authorities face a daunting task when they combat insider trading, due to the prolific nature of this offense.

But the task must be accomplished. There is no greater threat to stability, transparency, and fairness in the market than traders who use material nonpublic information to gain an unfair advantage over other traders. This conduct is counter-productive to everything that a healthy capital market should embody.

Although it is a much different country in almost all other ways, the U.S. shares a vision with Saudi Arabia where insider-trading violations are concerned: they must be investigated thoroughly, prosecuted aggressively, and punished severely. At the same time, the rights of the accused must be held sacrosanct. To accomplish these four objectives, American courts primarily rely on a trio of Supreme Court cases to help ensure predictable results when these cases are brought to court.

There is a somewhat similar approach in Saudi Arabia, although the body of jurisprudence is much less developed. Instead of focusing on the details of the transaction itself, Saudi law places more focus on the overall nature of these offenses by attempting to define the business, familial, and contractual relationship between the

367. U.S. Securities Exchange and Commission, *2014 Annual Report to Congress on the Dodd-Frank Whistleblower Program, supra* n. 364, at 8.

368. *Id.* at 15.

parties. However, the law offers little in terms of the specific definitions of these relationships. The weakness in this area may contribute to an even greater deficiency.

Put bluntly, the sanctions provided for in the CML do not deter future violations, which is the primary purpose of such penalties. Issues regarding low fines, unenforced prison sentences, and "hidden agreements" need to be addressed. The addition of an effective Whistleblower Program, like the one currently employed by the SEC, should make the system more effective as well.

Furthermore, in addition to enforcing the laws, the Saudi authorities should increase awareness of illegal insider trading within the investing public. In this context, the CMA should closely supervise and monitor the trading activities of board members at listed companies to discover any securities law violations, and especially insider trading. Such developments would create a strong undercurrent of compliance that makes enforcement less difficult.

In sum, insider trading is a serious problem in Saudi Arabia. Until it is properly addressed, the proper development of a modern capital market inside the Kingdom may remain out of reach.

Bibliography

I. Primary Sources

[A] Saudi Arabia Laws and Regulations

Capital Market Authority, Instructions for Regulating Announcements of Listed Companies in the Saudi Capital Market, the Board of the Capital Market Authority Resolution Number 1-199-2006, dated 18/07/1427 H (August 12, 2006), Amended by the Resolution of the Board of the Capital Market Authority Number 4-38-2008, dated 26/11/1429 H (November 11, 2008).

Capital Market Law, Royal Decree No. M/30, dated 2/6/1424 (2003).

Disclosure Rules, Ministerial Committee, Minister of Commerce Circular Reference Number 2222/221/9/3340, dated 8/11/1417, March 17, 1997 (1997).

Glossary of Defined Terms Used in the Regulations and Rules of the Capital Market Authority, the Board of the Capital Market Authority Resolution Number 4-11-2004, dated 20/8/1425 H (October 4, 2004), Amended by the Resolution of the Board of the Capital Market Authority Number 3-58-2014, dated 17/1/1436 H (November 10, 2014).

Law of Companies, Royal Decree No. M/6, dated 22/3/1385 H (1965).

Listing Rules, the Board of the Capital Market Authority Resolution Number 3-11-2004, dated 20/8/1425 H (October 4, 2004), Amended by the Resolution of the Board of the Capital Market Authority Number 1-64-2016, dated 19/8/1437 H (May 26, 2016).

Market Conduct Regulations, the Board of the Capital Market Authority Resolution Number 1-11-2004, dated 20/8/1425 H (October 4, 2004), Amended by the

Resolution of the Board of the Capital Market Authority Number 3-3-2016, dated 27/3/1437 H (January 7, 2016).
The Electronic Securities Information System Instructions to CTUs 1990, Saudi Arabian Monetary Agency (1990).

[B] Saudi Arabia Cases

CMA v. M.A., Appeal CRSD, Decision No. 147/L.S/2009 (June 21, 2009).
CMA v. M.R., Appeal CRSD, Decision No. 148/L.S/2009 (June 23, 2009).
CMA v. N.D., CRSD, Decision No. 535/L./D1/2009 (June 2, 2009).
CMA v. S.H., Appeal CRSD, Decision No. 229/L.S/2010 (May 29, 2010).
CMA v. S.D., Appeal CRSD, Decision No. 146/L.S/2009 (June 20, 2009).

[C] Foreign Laws and Regulations

American Law Institute, Fed. Sec. Code (proposed).
Financial Instruments and Exchange Act, Law No. 25 of 1948, Article 166 (as amended 1988) (Japan).
Securities Act, R.S.O., ch. XVIII, § 76 (1990) (Can.).
The Executive Regulations of Egyptian Capital Market Law, Law No. 95 (1992).
The Securities Law of Jordan, Law No. 76 (2002).
The U.S. Debt Collection Improvement Act of 1996 (2013).
The U.S. Dodd-Frank Wall Street Reform and Consumer Protection Act, Pub. L. No. 111-203, § 1079A(a), 124 Stat. 1376, 2077-2078 (2010).
The U.S. Insider Trading and Securities Fraud Enforcement Act of 1988, Pub, L. No. 100-704, 102 Stat. 4677 (1988).
The U.S. Investment Advisers Act of 1940.
The U.S. Racketeer Influenced Corrupt Organization Act.
The U.S. Sarbanes-Oxley Act of 2002, Pub. L. No. 107-204, §308 (a), 116 Stat. 745 (2002).
The U.S. Securities and Exchange Commission, *Selective Disclosure and Insider Trading*, Exchange Act Release No. 33-7881, 34-43154, IC-24599 (August 15, 2000).
The U.S. Securities Exchange Act of 1934 (2012).
The U.S. Sentencing Guidelines Manual (November 1, 2012).
The U.S. Racketeer Influenced Corrupt Organization Act.

[D] U.S. Cases

Basic Inc. v. Levinson, 485 U.S. 224 (1988).
Blue Chip Stamps v. Manor Drug Stores, 421 U.S. 723 (1975).
Burlington Indus., Inc. v. Edelman, 666 F. Supp. 799 (M.D.N.C. 1987).
Carpenter v. United States, 484 U.S. 19 (1987).
Chiarella v. United States, 445 U.S. 222 (1980).
Dirks v. SEC, 463 U.S. 646 (1983).

Elkind v. Liggett & Myers, Inc., 635 F.2d 156 (2d Cir. 1980).
Finnerty v. Stiefel Labs., Inc., 756 F.3d 1310 (11th Cir. 2014).
Folger Adam Co. v. PMI Indus., Inc., 938 F.2d 1529 (2d Cir. 1991).
In re Faberge, Inc., 45 S.E.C. 249 (1973).
Lampf, Pleva, Lipkind, Prupis & Petigrow v. Gilbertson, 501 U.S. 350 (1991).
Rosenzweig v. Azurix Corp., 332 F.3d 854 (5th Cir.2003).
Rothberg v. Rosenbloom, 771 F.2d 818 (3rd Cir.1985).
SEC v. Bauer, 723 F.3d 758 (7th Cir. 2012).
SEC v. Bauer, No. 03-C 1427, 2014 WL 4267412 (E.D. Wis. August 29, 2014).
SEC v. Blackwell, 291 F.Supp.2d 673 (S.D.Ohio 2003).
SEC v. Carroll, 9 F. Supp. 3d 761 (W.D. Ky. 2014).
SEC v. Cherif, 933 F.2d 403 (7th Cir. 1991).
SEC v. Clark, 915 F.2d 439 (9th Cir. 1990).
SEC v. Cuban, No. 3:08-CV-2050-D, 2013 WL 791405 (N.D. Tex. March 5, 2013).
SEC v. Farrell, 1996 WL 788367 (W.D.N.Y. 1996).
SEC v. Geon Industries, Inc., 531 F.2d 39 (2d Cir.1976).
SEC v. Ginsburg, 362 F.3d 1292 (11th Cir. 2004).
SEC v. Int'l Sys. & Controls Corp., 1979 WL 1267 (D.D.C. December 17, 1979).
SEC v. Kirch, 263 F. Supp. 2d 1144 (N.D. Ill. 2003).
SEC v. Lund, 570 F. Supp. 1397 (C.D. Cal. 1983).
SEC v. Mattel, Inc., 1974 WL 449 (D.D.C. October 1, 1974).
SEC v. Mayhew, 121 F.3d 44 (2d Cir. 1997).
SEC v. Michel, 521 F.Supp.2d 795 (N.D.Ill.2007).
SEC v. Palmisano, 135 F.3d 860 (2d Cir. 1998).
SEC v. Sekhri, No. 98 Civ. 2320, 2002 WL 31100823 (S.D.N.Y. July 22, 2002).
SEC v. Shapiro, 494 F.2d 1301 (2d Cir.1974).
SEC v. Talbot, 530 F.3d 1085 (9th Cir. 2008).
SEC v. Tex. Gulf Sulphur Co., 401 F.2d 833 (2d Cir. 1968).
SEC v. Thrasher, 152 F. Supp. 2d 291 (S.D.N.Y. 2001).
SEC v. Tome, 638 F. Supp. 596 (S.D.N.Y. 1986).
Speed v. Transamerica Corp., 99 F.Supp. 808 (D.Del.1951).
TSC Indus., Inc. v. Northway, Inc., 426 U.S. 438 (1976).
United States v. Chiarella, 588 F.2d 1358 (2d Cir. 1978) *rev'd*, 445 U.S. 222 (1980).
United States v. Libera, 989 F.2d 596 (2d Cir. 1993).
United States v. Mylett, 97 F.3d 663 (2d Cir.1996).
United States v. Newman, 664 F.2d 12 (2d Cir.1981).
United States v. Newman, 773 F.3d 438 (2d Cir. 2014), *cert. denied*, 136 S. Ct. 242 (October 5, 2015).
United States v. O'Hagan, 521 U.S. 642 (1997).
United States v. O'Hagan, 92 F.3d 612 (8th Cir. 1996).
United States v. Royer, 549 F.3d 886 (2d Cir. 2008).
United States v. Salman, 792 F.3d 1087 (9th Cir. 2015), *cert. granted*, 136 S. Ct. 899 (January 19, 2016).
United States v. Stringer, 535 F.3d 929 (9th Cir. 2008).

[E] Official/Semi-Official Reports – Government & Nongovernment Bodies

Capital Market Authority, *CMA Announces the Start of the Referral of Criminal Offences to the Bureau of Investigation and Public Prosecution*, December 31, 2014, http://www.cma.org.sa/en/News/Pages/CMA_N_1589.aspx.

Capital Market Authority, *CMA: Listed Companies Are Obligated to Inform the Public about Any Significant Developments which Are Not Available to the Public*, (February 2, 2015), http://cma.org.sa/Ar/MediaCenter/PK/Pages/Disclosure-Awareness-Report.aspx.

Chuck Grassley, *Bill Seeks Tougher Penalties for Wall Street Fraud*, Chuck Grassley, July 9, 2015, http://www.grassley.senate.gov/news/news-releases/bill-seeks-tougher-penalties-wall-street-fraud.

King Khalid Bin Abdul Aziz Database, *Alosar, [Families]*, (November 20, 2015), http://www.kingkhalid.org.sa/Gallery/Text/ViewTextSubjects.aspx?View = Page &BookID = 106&PageID = 7&NodeID = 79.

Saudi Arabian Monetary Agency, *Historical Preview*, (November 14, 2015), http://www.sama.gov.sa/en-US/About/Pages/SAMAHistory.aspx.

Saudi Stock Exchange "Tadawul", *Market Rules*, November 14, 2015, http://www.tadawul.com.sa/wps/portal/!ut/p/c1/04_SB8K8xLLM9MSSzPy8xBz9CP0os3g_A-ewIE8TIwMLf3czA0_vIKegIBN_QwNXQ6B8JJK8e0CYqYGniU-wUXCAl7GBpxEB3X4e-bmp-gW5EeUATNtVlg!!/dl2/d1/L0lDUmlTUSEhL3dHa0FKRnNBL1lCUlp3QSEhL2Vu/.

Securities Exchange and Commission, the Office of the Whistleblower, *About Us*, (November 21, 2015), https://www.sec.gov/about/offices/owb/owb-about.shtml.

The U.S. Securities and Exchange Commission, *Form 8-K*, (November 15, 2015), http://www.sec.gov/answers/form8k.htm.

U.S. Securities and Exchange Commission, Office of Inspector General Office of Audits, *Assessment of the SEC's Bounty Program*, Report No. 474 (March 29, 2010).

U.S. Securities Exchange and Commission, *2014 Annual Report to Congress on the Dodd-Frank Whistleblower Program*, (November 17, 2014).

U.S. Securities Exchange and Commission, *SEC Announces Largest-Ever Whistleblower Award*, September 22, 2014, https://www.sec.gov/News/PressRelease/Detail/PressRelease/1370543011290.

U.S. Securities Exchange and Commission, *SEC Announces Whistleblower Award of More Than $325,000*, November 4, 2015, http://www.sec.gov/news/pressrelease/2015-252.html.

U.S. Securities Exchange and Commission, the Office of the Whistleblower, *Welcome to the Office of the Whistleblower*, (November 21, 2015), https://www.sec.gov/whistleblower.

II. Secondary Sources

[A] Books

Abdalrasool, Mohammed Farog, *Alhemaiah Algenaiah Le Borsah Alaorag Almaleih [The Criminal Protection for the Securities Exchange*], (Dar Aljamiah Aljadidah 2007).

Albjad, Mohammed Nasser, *Garaim Alsoug Almalih Fi Alnedam Alsaoudi [Stock Market Crimes in Saudi Law],* (King Fahad National Library 2008).

Albrbari, Saleh Ahmed, *Soag Alaorag Almaliah Oa Estaglal Almalomat Aldakliah Beoasatat Alalmen Bboatan Alomor [The Capital Market and the Abused of Nonpublic Information by Insiders]*, (United Arab Emirates University 2007).

Alhamidi, Abdulrahman Abdullah & Abdulrahman Abdulmohsen Alkalaf, *Alnagood Oa Albonok Oa Alasoag Almalih [Money, Banks, and Capital Markets]*, (Al-farazdak Press Company 2009).

Arshadi, Nasser & Thomas Eyssell, *The Law and Finance of Corporate Insider Trading: Theory and Evidence* (Kluwer Academic Publishers 1993).

Azzam, Henry T, *The Emerging Arab Capital Markets: Investment Opportunities in Relatively Underplayed Markets* (Kegan Paul International London 1997).

Badawi, Belal Abdulmataleb, *Aleltazam Bealefasah An Almalumat Fi Soag Alaorag Almaleih [the Obligation of Disclosing Information in the Stock Market]*, (Dar Alnahathah Alarabia Press 2006).

Bainbridge, Stephen M., *Insider Trading Law and Policy* (Foundation Press 2014).

Ellsworth, Larry P. & Michael K. Lowman, *Inside Information: Prevention of Abuse*, 15-4th C.P.S. (The Bureau of National Affairs 2014).

Ferrara, Ralph C., et al., *Ferrara on Insider Trading and the Wall* (Law Journal Press 2015).

Gutterman, Alan S., *Business Transactions Solutions* (Westlaw 2015).

Hindi, Moneer, *Asasiat Alastathmar Fi Alborsah Almaliah* [*The Principles of Investment in Securities* (Monshat Almaraf 1999).

Langevoort, Donald C., *Insider Trading Regulation, Enforcement and Prevention* (Westlaw 2015).

Levy, Steven Mark, *Regulation of Securities: SEC Answer Book* (Aspen Publishers 2004).

Majeed, Diah, *Alborsat* [*The Exchanges*] (Moasasat Shabab Aljameah 2003).

Mohammed, Mathaher Fargali Ali, *Alhamaiah Aljenaiah Lethagah Fi Soug Almal [Criminal Protection for the Confidence in a Capital Market*] (Dar Alnahathah Alarabia 2006).

Mousa, Mohammed Ibrahim, *Haokamat Alsharekat Almogiedah Be Soug Alaorag Almaleih* [*The Corporate Governance of Listed Companies in the Capital Market*], (Dar Aljamiah Aljadidah 2010).

Pecora, Ferdinand, *Wall Street Under Oath: The Story of Our Modern Money Changers* (A. M. Kelley Publishers 1968).

Ramady, Mohamed A, *The Saudi Arabian Economy, Policies, Achievements, and Challenges* (2d ed. 2010).

Steinberg, Marc I. & William K.S. Wang, *Insider Trading* (Oxford University Press 2010).

Steinberg, Marc I. & William K.S. Wang, *Insider Trading* (Practising Law Institute 2005).

Steinberg, Marc I., *Understanding Securities Law* (LexisNexis 2014).

[B] Articles

Albjad, Mohammed Nasser, *Jaremat Alefsah An Almalomat Aldakliah Fi Nedam Alsoag Almaliah Alsaodi [The Crime of Disclosure Inside Information in the Saudi Capital Market Law]*, 47 Periodic Pub. Admin. 557 (2007).

Alsuhaibani, Mohammed Ibrahim, *Altalaob Fi Alasoag Almaliah: Alboad Aleqtesade* [*The Manipulation in the Capital Markets: The Economic Impacts*], A Paper Presented at the Speculation and Manupulation in the Capital Markets: Their Economic and Legal Impact Conference, Islamic International Foundation for Economics and Finance. (March 5, 2008).

Beach, Joseph W., *The Saudi Arabian Capital Market Law: A Practical Study of the Creation of Law in Developing Markets*, 41 Stan. J. Int'l L. 307 (2005).

Butler, Kirt C & S Jamal Malaikah, *Efficiency and Inefficiency in Thinly Traded Stock Markets: Kuwait and Saudi Arabia*, 16 J. Banking & Fin. 197 (1992).

Henning, Peter J., *What's So Bad About Insider Trading Law?*, 70 Bus. Law. 751 (2015).

Hughes, Laura, *The Impact of Insider Trading Regulations on Stock Market Efficiency: A Critique of The Law and Economics Debate and A cross Country Comparison*, 23 Temp. Int'l & Comp. L.J. 479 (2009).

Nagy, Donna M, *Beyond Dirks: Gratuitous Tipping and Insider Trading*, Indiana Legal Studies Research Paper No. 327 (2015).

[C] News

Alabki, Ahmed, Almalik Ela Raeis Hiaat Soug Almal: Tabeego Alganon Ala Kain Mn Kan Bmn Fehim Alomara [*the King to the Capital Market Authority Chairman: Apply the Laws to Whoever Violates the Law Including Princes*], Alsharq (April 9, 2012), http://www.alsharq.net.sa/2012/04/09/209521.

Albadrani, Badi, *Galag Men Tasareeb Malomat Fi Soag Alasahom Letahagaig Arabah Estethnaiah Oa Qar Masharoah, [Concerns About Illegal Disclosure of Information In the Stock Market to Achieve Substantial Illegal Profits]*, Alriyadh Newspaper, October 22, 2005, http://www.alriyadh.com/102415.

Almazid, Ali, *Tasreeb Almalomat Aldakaliah Fi Soag Alasahom Yonagath Mafaheem Aladalh Oa Alshafafiah [The Disclosing Inside Information in the Stock Market is Contrary to the Concepts of Fairness and Transparency]*, Alsharg Alaosad Newspaper, May 20, 2004, http://archive.aawsat.com/details.asp?issueno=9165&article=245750#.VucQhLSrhUQ.

Alsahali, Mohammed Sultan, *Almalomat Aldakeliah Oa Soag Alasahom, [Inside Information and the Stock Market]*, Alriyadh Newspaper, January 14, 2006, http://www.alriyadh.com/8563.

Alsmaiel, Mohammed, *La Ahad Iagsha Ogobat Soug Almal, [No One Fears The Capital Market's Sanctions]*, *Alyaum*, May 10, 2012, http://www.alyaum.com/article/3049621.

BBC New, *Saudi Stock Exchange Approved*, BBC News, June 17, 2003, http://news.bbc.co.uk/2/hi/business/2998086.stm.

[D] Interviews

Interview with a Legal Advisor for the Committees for the Resolution of Securities Disputes, Riyadh, Saudi Arabia (August 12, 2014).

Interview with a Legal Advisor for the Committees for the Resolution of Securities Disputes, Riyadh, Saudi Arabia (January 1, 2013).

Interview with a Legal Advisor for the Saudi Capital Market Authority, Riyadh, Saudi Arabia (December 29, 2012).

Interview with Adel Gabani, Secretary-General of the Committees for the Resolution of Securities Disputes, in Riyadh, Saudi Arabia (August 14, 2014).

CHAPTER 6

Conclusions and Recommendations

§6.01 CONCLUSIONS AND OBSERVATIONS

As the KSA continues to move forward in the new millennium, one of the largest obstacles to its continued growth and development is how to balance the special "DNA" of the country with the need to diversify and modernize the economy, including its capital market. There are a number of large Muslim countries (e.g., Egypt, Turkey, Malaysia, and Indonesia) in terms of both population and geographic area, and a number of states whose economies are nearly totally dependent on a single commodity. However, there are few, if any, nations that combine both these aspects. Thus, the Kingdom, in developing a robust capital market, will need to adopt and to enforce laws that will serve as a platform for a strong capital market that is based on transparency and fairness while taking into account the Kingdom's unique historical, religious, and economic context.

The first challenge is to move the Kingdom away from a purely energy-based economy. Such transformation will not be easy, as this sector currently accounts for about 90% of Saudi Arabia's GDP. There are signs of progress, however, as that percentage has actually been reduced somewhat in recent years. Several new initiatives, such as privatization and an increased emphasis on foreign investment, appear to be working. But diversification through additional capital investment and private ownership only heightens the need for a strong capital market that is based on a well-educated group of investors and coherent rules that are enforced consistently. Such a market is currently lacking.

One possible solution, which the government has already embraced at least partially, is the use of central planning. The Kingdom's Five-Year Plans serve as effective roadmaps towards increased economic development in the short term and economic sustainability in the long term. But change does not only need to come from inside. By reaching out and embracing membership in both regional and international organizations, such as the GCC, WTO, IOSCO, and G-20, leaders have ready access to other economic models that are successful in other regions and nations. While such systems obviously cannot be copied, or imposed *en masse*, they do offer elements that could enhance the Five-Year Plans and the move towards diversification and globalization.

In a sense, diversification through investment and privatization began in 1935 with the establishment of the first Saudi joint-stock company. But the capital market was completely unregulated until the Law of Companies 1965, and this measure only provided a partial and rudimentary infrastructure for a burgeoning capital market, especially in terms of the secondary market.

Finally, in 1984, the "SAMA," the nation's central bank, received the authority to oversee the capital market's day-to-day functions. SAMA introduced a number of upgrades, such as the creation of a common trading forum. The landmark "CML" followed in 2003. Growth and development continued for several years, highlighted by the creation of the "CMA" in 2004. But the stock market crash of 2006 brought this development to a sudden halt.

Prior to the crash, a large number of new investors entered the market, buoyed by the generous credit policies of major lenders. The increased demand pushed prices upward, creating even higher demand and even higher prices. Unfortunately, the nascent and inexperienced CMA was simply not equipped to deal with this volume. The market bubble burst in February 2006: by the end of the year, TASI had lost over half of its value.

There were many reasons for the crash. The media was all too willing to document high securities prices and the potential for profits. At the same time, some companies inflated their values; for example, a number of companies continued to show profitability even though they had lost a crippling portion of their capitalization. And, rather than questioning the relentless movement towards even higher prices, many uneducated investors continued to participate in the market at that time, unaware that the bubble was due to burst. So, media reporting patterns, investor attitudes, and government inexperience all contributed to the crisis.

To help prevent another crash, or at least minimize its effects, government leaders turned to IOSCO in 2010. Membership led to a "FSAP" review by the IMF, which found the Saudi capital market to be reasonably healthy in a number of respects. However, there were still glaring defects in the areas of dispute resolution, market transparency, disclosure laws, and insider-trading regulations. These challenges remain primary roadblocks between Saudi Arabia and globalization through a modern capital market.

Specifically in the area of dispute resolution, the Kingdom's culture and history again comes into play. Like many other Muslim nations, Saudi Arabia relies on *Shari'ah* law as much more than a moral compass. *Shari'ah* is the very foundation of the country's civil and criminal laws. According to some, judges are prone to overly strict legal interpretations that cause delays and inconsistent results. And, especially with regard to securities transactions, many religious judges simply do not have the necessary training to deal with such issues.

To resolve these specialized disputes, the Kingdom has long relied on quasi-judicial committees. There are a number of technical defects; for example, many of these committees have only one physical location and do not regularly publish their procedures and decisions. Also, these bodies do not fall under the purview of the Ministry of Justice. In fact, the members have no judicial immunity, since they are "members" instead of "judges," and they often fall under the influence of the Ministry that created them. Updates to the Judiciary Law and Board of Grievances in 2007 addressed some of these shortcomings, but the Judiciary Law is still mostly unimplemented. In fact, the Committee for the Resolution of Securities Disputes ("CRSD") is not scheduled for cancellation, and a study by the Supreme Council for the Judiciary to determine its fate has apparently not taken place.

The CML created the CRSD in 2004. It is a two-tier body that has a litigation and appellate division; the appeals members are appointed by the Council of Ministers, and the Board of the CMA appoints the litigation members. In addition to an effective two-tier system, the CRSD is completely free of influence from the CMA in its day-to-day affairs. Nevertheless, there are some identifiable ties between the CMA and CRSD. The two are intertwined on an administrative and financial level. The CMA pays CRSD members and staff, and the monetary penalties that the Committee collects from convicted securities laws violators go to the CMA. These ties compromise the Committee's judicial independence; according to some, this relationship makes the CRSD unconstitutional under Article 46 of the Basic Law of Governance. At the very least, the CRSD is not a wholly independent body and its decisions are therefore tainted.

The CML also set rules and penalties regarding disclosure of information. Prior to 2003, there were essentially no effective regulations in this area, so there was a need for considerable improvement. Specifically, the CML stipulates that disclosure of relevant information must take place in a timely manner. The first of three requirements goes into effect when the security is first offered in an IPO (initial disclosure). Thereafter, information must be disclosed in annual and quarterly reports (periodic disclosure) and at least half an hour before the start of trading on a given day (continuous disclosure). The periodic and continuous disclosure requirements are substantially in full compliance with international standards. The Kingdom should be commended in this area.

While the CMA has worked diligently in recent years and significantly raised the level of transparency in recent years, some challenges remain. For example, the maximum financial penalty for a disclosure violation is only SAR 100,000 (USD 26,666), and the CMA often hesitates to levy the maximum penalty. This lack of enforcement sends the wrong message to potential investors, namely that timely disclosure of critical information is an unimportant matter. Moreover, many of the disclosure cases are handled internally by the CMA and not referred to the CRSD, contain few details, and are not made public for several months, all of which may indicate a reluctance to prosecute these cases to the fullest extent of the law. In fact, the World Bank recently chided the CMA for its lack of transparency in refusing to release an annual budget and a detailed record of enforcement actions.

In contrast, the U.S. aggressively prosecutes these cases in a very public manner and essentially sees the failure to disclose information as a major issue in the markets. Therefore, the penalties are very stiff, and the per-violation caps may increase even further – to USD 1 million for individuals and USD 10 million for entities – for more serious securities law violations.

Regulations alone are clearly not sufficient to ensure a higher level of transparency, disclosure, accountability, and fairness: a strong enforcement regime is also a necessity. If the Saudi capital market is to continue the growth, development, and modernization, it has experienced in the years since the Crash, the CMA should consider enforcing the disclosure rules more vigorously.

Illegal insider trading is perhaps the greatest threat to this growth. In Saudi Arabia, this practice begins in the nature of society itself: people from all walks of life have very close social connections to one another and feel personally obligated to give assistance whenever possible, and this assistance includes the transfer of inside information to help others gain a profit. So, while lack of enforcement is an issue, the matter really begins with a lack of education with regard to the illegal market activities.

In general, this practice is defined as trading securities based on material nonpublic information. The U.S. relies on a trio of Supreme Court cases to define insider trading in everyday terms. A possible fourth case may clarify the personal benefits requirement, but there is no such rule in Saudi Arabia. It is not necessary for a tipper to receive a benefit, since altruism exists as a norm and tippers do not expect to receive a benefit from their tips.

Saudi Arabia uses various regulations to define insider according to family, business, and contractual relationships. The CMA was tasked with developing rules to clarify the meanings of these terms, but the Market Conduct Regulations ("MCR") is poorly drafted in defining these relationships.

Furthermore, in the Kingdom, many insider-trading cases are resolved through "hidden agreements" pursuant to Article 64 of the CML wherein the violators pay to the CMA a sum not to exceed three times the profit realized or loss avoided. The details of the cases and the punishments assessed are never made public, and the matters are not referred to the CRSD. As a result, the CRSD has only decided a handful of insider-trading cases throughout its entire history.

The lack of jurisprudence gives rise to the remaining two challenges in this area. The laws are poorly defined and enforced. Neither the MCR nor the CML defines the three types of relationships mentioned above, and the CRSD does not use a consistent formula to calculate profit made or loss avoided. When these penalties are assessed, the CRSD is very lenient and deterrence is lacking as a result. The maximum fine is not often imposed; imprisonment for insider trading has only been imposed once – for a mere three months – even though the CMA routinely requests such a penalty. In short, lack of awareness, weak enforcement, and anemic penalties all contribute to a lack of transparency and fairness in the capital market.

In contrast, and similarly, to the area of disclosure violations, the U.S. SEC and Justice Department are very assertive in this area. One key feature of its enforcement network is an effective whistleblower program that relies on retaliation protection, monetary awards, and confidentiality protection. There is no such program in Saudi Arabia.

A vigorous and consistent enforcement program is vital to reducing illegal insider trading in Saudi Arabia and to increasing the level of fairness in the capital market.

While such a program should be aggressive in the investigatory, prosecution, and punishment phases, it should also recognize and uphold the rights of accused traders.

This goal could be applied to all aspects of the capital market, and not only to insider trading. By clarifying some vague portions of some laws, establishing a fair and independent dispute resolution system, creating a climate that encourages voluntary compliance with the rules, seriously and thoroughly investigating possible violations at all levels, and punishing violators in a consistent and evenhanded manner with sanctions that have a measurable deterrent effect, a modern capital market can become an important component of globalization in Saudi Arabia in the years to come.

§6.02 RECOMMENDATIONS

In order for Saudi Arabia to have a modern, sustainable, and well-functioning economy, it should have a strong capital market. In doing so, it is important for the government, the CMA, the CRSD, and Saudi law-policy makers to focus on and to develop various approaches: (i) to educate investors and the general public regarding illegal market activities; (ii) to increase the penalties for securities laws violations; and (iii) to take full advantage of the enforcement provisions that are in place.

The following suggested amendments and proposals, which are drawn from discussions made in the preceding chapters, are designed to further these goals.

[A] Amendments to Regulations

[1] Capital Market Law

- Amend Article 4(a) to place the CMA under the authority of the Minister of Commerce as opposed to the President of the Council of Ministers (the King) to facilitate more efficient decision making.[1]
- Amend Article 7 to give the CMA Board members immunity from lawsuits that arise from a bona fide exercise of regulatory powers.[2]
- Amend Article 25 to require that litigation and appeals members of the CRSD be appointed by a Royal Decree based on a recommendation from the Supreme Council for Judiciary (which is the same procedure for judges in the general judiciary).[3]
- Amend the requirements in Article 45(a) to include Management Discussion and Analysis of Financial Conditions and Results of Operations ("MD&A") in quarterly reports as well as annual reports.[4]
- Amend Article 46 to add a new provision: *(d) If the issuer is listed or admitted to trading in multiple jurisdictions, the material periodic and continuous*

1. *See* Chapter 2, §2.02 [C].
2. *See* Chapter 2, §2.03.
3. *See* Chapter 3, §3.06.
4. *See* Chapter 4, §4.03 [C] [1].

information disclosed in one market should be disclosed at the same time in all jurisdictions in which the issuer is listed (new language in italics).[5]

- Amend Article 59(a)(4) to read as follows: Indemnifying the persons who have suffered damage as a consequence of a violation that has occurred, *and/or* obliging the violator to pay to the Authority's account the gains realized as a consequence of such violation (new language in italics).[6]
- Amend Article 59(b) to increase the maximum penalty for securities law violations from SAR 100,000 (USD 26,666) to SAR 1,000,000 (USD 266,666).[7]
- Amend Article 59(b) to increase the minimum penalty for securities law violations from SAR 10,000 (USD 2,666) to SAR 100,000 (USD 26,666).[8]
- Amend Article 64 to require the "hidden agreements" to include a specific disclosure of the misconduct which took place and the penalty assessed therefor, and require the publication of these agreements.[9]

[2] Market Conduct Regulations

- Amend Article 4(a) to include the definitions of "business relationship," "family relationship," and "contractual relationship," as these terms are used in 4(b).[10]
- Amend Article 4(b)(2) to read as follows: a person who obtains inside information through a family relationship *of any degree*, including from any person related to the person who obtains the information (new language in italics).[11]
- Amend Article 4(c)(2) to delete the phrase "and that is not otherwise available to the general public."[12]
- Amend Article 4 to add a new provision: *(d) Some factors to be used in the determination of materiality of information include but are not limited to (1) the significance of the information that those who knew about it attached to it; (2) the reaction of the market when the information became available; (3) the source of the information; and (4) the specificity of the tip* (new language in italics).[13]
- Amend Article 4 to add a new provision: *(e) Inside information shall still be considered non-public until it has been published on both the Capital Market Authority and Exchange websites* (new language in italics).[14]

5. *See* Chapter 4, §4.03 [C].
6. *See* Chapter 5, §5.04 [C] [1].
7. *See* Chapter 4, §4.04 [E]; Chapter 5, §5.05 [F]; Chapter 2, §2.03.
8. *See* Chapter 4, §4.04 [E]; Chapter 5, §5.05 [F]; Chapter 2, §2.03.
9. *See* Chapter 5, §5.04 [C] [1].
10. *See* Chapter 5, §5.04 [B] [1].
11. *See* Chapter 5, §5.04 [B] [1].
12. *See* Chapter 5, §5.03 [C].
13. *See* Chapter 5, §5.03 [B].
14. *See* Chapter 5, §5.03 [C].

- Amend Article 4 to add a new provision: *(f) An insider shall not trade on inside information until 30 minutes have elapsed from the time of the publication of such information* (new language in italics).[15]
- Amend Article 4 to add a new provision: *(g) A family member as defined in this Article is presumed to be an insider under Articles 5 and 6 of this law* (new language in italics).[16]

[3] Listing Rules

- Amend Article 42(d) and (e) to include a consideration of business size in the filing deadlines for annual and quarterly reports.[17]

[4] Foreign Investment Law

- Eliminate the restriction in Article 3 that prohibits foreigners from investing in publishing, fishing, and insurance and replace it with a case-by-case review mechanism.[18]

[B] Governmental Bodies

[1] Capital Market Authority

- Establish a procedure for administrative actions, such as license revocation or denial that includes notice to the applicant and an opportunity to be heard.[19]
- Publish adverse regulatory actions, a report of market conditions, detailed board decisions, trading volume, and price indices to increase deterrence and transparency.[20]
- Publish an annual report that details budget and distributions, fees assessed, amount of revenue generated, and advisory statements.[21]
- Publish detailed disciplinary information, including the violator's name, nature of the offense, and the penalty imposed.[22]
- Contract with a specialized publisher to release information on multiple platforms, such as email, print, and website.[23]

15. *See* Chapter 5, §5.03 [C].
16. *See* Chapter 5, §5.04 [B] [1] & §5.05 [F].
17. *See* Chapter 4, §4.03 [C] [1].
18. *See* Chapter 1, §1.03 [C].
19. *See* Chapter 2, §2.03.
20. *See* Chapter 2, §2.03; Chapter 4, §4.04 [E].
21. *See* Chapter 2, §2.03; Chapter 4, §4.04 [E]; Chapter 5, §5.04 [C] [1].
22. *See* Chapter 2, §2.03; Chapter 4, §4.04 [E]; Chapter 5, §5.04 [C] [1].
23. *See* Chapter 2, §2.03.

- Increase awareness of securities laws and investment strategies through television programs, webinars, free university and college classes, conferences, radio programs, magazines, and so on (these initiatives should be offered in both English and Arabic).[24]
- Closely supervise and monitor the trading activities of board members at listed companies to discover any securities law violations, and especially insider trading.[25]
- Issue an internal policy that provides financial rewards to the CMA's employees who discover insider-trading violations.[26]

[2] The Committee for the Resolution of Securities Disputes

- When a commercial court is established, designate the CRSD as a special division of that court.[27]
- Appoint the members of both the litigation and appeal committees by a Royal Decree based on a Supreme Council for Judiciary's recommendation.[28]
- Place the CRSD under the supervision of the Ministry of Justice.[29]

[C] New Entities

[1] Whistleblower Program

This initiative should be modeled after the Dodd-Frank whistleblower program in the U.S. and based on monetary payments, confidentiality protection, and retaliation protection. Such a program should be part of the CMA.[30]

[2] Investor Protection Fund ("IPF")

The IPF would be funded by disgorgement and monetary penalties of fraud violations, and used for developing and funding the whistleblower program, as well as awarding whistleblowers. Also, the IPF would be used for compensating victims of fraud violations.[31]

24. *See* Chapter 2, §2.03; Chapter 5, §5.06 & §5.07.
25. *See* Chapter 5, §5.07.
26. *See* Chapter 5, §5.06.
27. *See* Chapter 3, §3.06.
28. *See* Chapter 3, §3.06.
29. *See* Chapter 3, §3.06.
30. *See* Chapter 5, §5.06.
31. *See* Chapter 5, §5.06.

[D] Gulf Cooperation Council ("GCC")

- Prioritize the creation of a common currency.[32]
- Focus on economic development by avoiding distractions.[33]
- Develop a Five-Year Plan.[34]

32. *See* Chapter 1, §1.04.
33. *See* Chapter 1, §1.04.
34. *See* Chapter 1, §1.04.

Appendices

APPENDIX I

Saudi Capital Market Law

Chapter One

Definitions

Article One

Unless the context otherwise indicates, the following words and phrases, wherever they appear in this Law, shall have the meaning herein specified:

- **Kingdom:** the Kingdom of Saudi Arabia.
- **The Authority:** the Capital Market Authority.
- **The Board:** the Board of the Capital Market Authority.
- **The Chairman:** the Chairman of the Board of the Capital Market Authority.
- **Person:** any natural or legal person that is recognized as such under the laws of the Kingdom.
- **The Exchange:** the Saudi Stock Exchange.
- **Trading:** buying and selling of securities.
- **Issuer:** a person who is issuing or intending to issue securities.
- **Affiliate:** a person who controls another person or is controlled by that other person, or who is jointly being controlled with that person by a third person.
- **Control:** the direct or indirect ability or power to exercise effective influence over the actions and decisions of another person.
- **Underwriter:** a person who buys securities from the issuer or an affiliate of the issuer for the purpose of offering, placing and marketing such securities to the public, or a person who sells securities on behalf of the issuer or an affiliate of the issuer for the purpose of making a public offering and placement of such securities.
- **Relatives:** husband, wife and minor children.

- **Placement or offering of securities:** issuing securities, inviting the public to subscribe therefor or the direct or indirect marketing thereof; or any statement, announcement or communication that has the effect of selling, issuing or offering securities, but does not include preliminary negotiations or contracts entered into with or among underwriters.
- **Investment Adviser:** an adviser who provides, offers or agrees to provide, advice to others in their capacity as investors or potential investors, in relation to purchasing, selling, subscribing or underwriting a security, or exercising any right conferred by a security to acquire, dispose of, underwrite or convert a security.
- **The Center:** the Securities Depositary Center.
- **The Committee:** the Committee for the Resolution of Securities Disputes.
- **The Implementing Regulations:** the rules, instructions and procedures issued by the Authority for the implementation of the provisions of this Law.
- **Internal Regulations:** the regulations issued by the Authority in relation to the Authority's administrative and financial affairs and its personnel and staff affairs.

Article Two

Subject to the provisions of Article three hereof, for the purposes of this Law, the term "Securities" shall mean:

a. convertible and tradeable shares of companies;
b. Tradeable debt instruments issued by companies, the government, public institutions or public organisations;
c. investment units issued by investment funds;
d. any instruments representing profit participation rights, any rights in the distribution of assets; or either or the foregoing;
e. any other rights or instruments which the Board determines should be included or treated as Securities if the Board believes that this would further the safety of the market or the protection of investors. The Board can exercise its power to exempt from the definition of Securities rights or instruments that otherwise would be treated as Securities under paragraphs (a, b, c, d) of this Article if it believes that it is not necessary to treat them as Securities, based on the requirements of the safety of the market and the protection of investors.

Article Three

Commercial bills such as cheques, bills of exchange, order notes, documentary credits, money transfers, instruments exclusively traded among banks, and insurance policies shall not be considered Securities.

Chapter Two

The Capital Market Authority

Article Four

a. An Authority to be named "The Capital Market Authority" is hereby established in the Kingdom and shall directly report to the President of the Council of Ministers. It shall have a legal personality and financial and administrative autonomy. It shall be vested with all authorities as may be necessary to discharge its responsibilities and functions under this Law. The Authority shall enjoy exemptions and facilities enjoyed by public organisations. Its personnel shall be subject to the Labour Law.
b. The Authority shall not have the right to engage in any commercial activities, to have a special interest in any project intended for profit, to borrow or lend any funds, or to acquire, own or issue any Securities.

Article Five

a. The Authority shall be the agency responsible for issuing regulations, rules and instructions, and for applying the provisions of this Law.
   To achieve these objectives, the Authority shall:

   1. Regulate and develop the Exchange, seek to develop and improve methods of systems and entities trading in Securities, and develop the procedures that would reduce the risks related to Securities transactions.
   2. Regulate the issuance of Securities and monitor Securities and dealing in Securities.
   3. Regulate and monitor the works and activities of parties subject to the control and supervision of the Authority.
   4. Protect citizens and investors in Securities from unfair and unsound practices or practices involving fraud, deceit, cheating or manipulation.
   5. Seek to achieve fairness, efficiency and transparency in Securities transactions.
   6. Regulate and monitor the full disclosure of information regarding Securities and their issuers, the dealings of informed persons and major shareholders and investors, and define and make available information which the participants in the market should provide and disclose to shareholders and the public.
   7. Regulate proxy and purchase requests and public offers of shares.
   8. license the establishment of special purposes entity, and regulate and control its business, uses, issuance of securities, the registration in its registry established by the Authority and the provisions of its articles of incorporation, and regulate the provisions of the registration of funds

transferred to it, including documentation of the rights thereof and its legal standing against others, and the issuance of rules governing thereof.

b. The Authority may publish a draft of regulations and rules before issuing or amending them. The regulations, rules and instructions issued by the Authority shall be effective in the manner prescribed under their provisions.
c. For the purpose of conducting all investigations which, in the opinion of the Board, are necessary for the enforcement of the provisions of this Law and other regulations and rules issued pursuant to this Law, the members of the Authority and its employees designated by the Board are empowered to subpoena witnesses, take evidence, and require the production of any books, papers, or other documents which the Authority deems relevant or material to its investigation.
   The Authority shall have the power to carry out inspections of the records or any other materials, whoever the holder may be, to determine whether the person concerned has violated, or is about to violate any provision of this Law, the Implementing Regulations or the rules issued by the Authority.
d. The special purposes entity shall have legal personality and financial autonomy, and it shall cease to exist with the end of the purpose for which it was established for in accordance with the rules and regulations issued by the Authority.

Article Six

a. The Authority shall have the power to carry out its functions under this Law as well as the regulations, rules and instructions issued pursuant thereto including, but not limited the power to:

   1. Set forth policies and plans, conduct studies and issue necessary rules to achieve the Authority's objectives.
   2. Issue and amend the Implementing Regulations as may be necessary to enforce the provisions of this Law.
   3. Approve the offering of Securities.
   4. Give advice and make recommendations to government authorities in respect of matters that would contribute to the development of the Exchange and the protection of investors in Securities.
   5. Suspend the Exchange's activities for a period of not more than one day; and in cases where the Authority or the Minister of Finance deems it necessary to suspend the Exchange's activity for more than one day, the approval of this decision must be issued by the Minister of Finance.
   6. Approve the listing, cancel or suspend the listing, of any Saudi Security traded on the Exchange of any Saudi issuer, on any stock exchange outside the Kingdom.
   7. Prohibit any Security or suspend the issuance or trading of any Securities on the Exchange, as the Authority may deem necessary.

8. Determine the maximum or the minimum commissions to be charged by brokers to their clients if the Board deems it appropriate, and approve the fees and other commissions to be charged by the Exchange and the Depositary Center.
9. In addition to other provisions of relevant regulations, the Authority shall have the right to establish standards and conditions required for the auditors who audit the books and records of the Exchange, the Depositary Center, brokerage companies, investment funds and joint stock companies listed on the Exchange. The Authority, subject to its supervisory responsibilities, shall have the right to delegate this responsibility to the Saudi Organization for Certified Public Accountants.
10. Determine the contents of annual and periodical financial statements, reports and documents that should be submitted by issuers offering Securities for public subscription or the issuers whose Securities are listed on the Exchange.
11. Define and explain the terms and provisions set out in this Law.
12. Issue decisions, instructions and set the procedure as deemed necessary for the implementation of the provisions of this Law and the Implementing Regulations, and conduct inquiries and investigations regarding violations of the provisions of this Law and the Implementing Regulations.
13. Set Internal Regulations and issue instructions and set the procedures as necessary for the management of the Authority.
14. Approve the regulations, rales and policies of the Exchange and the Depositary Center.
15. Prepare the regulations and rules for the surveillance and supervision of entities subject to the provisions of this Law.
16. Approve the establishment, merger and liquidation of investment funds and their related operating rules in accordance with the provisions of Article Thirty-nine of this Law.
17. Appoint a licensed auditor to audit the Authority's financial statements and final accounts.
18. Grant the necessary licenses to be issued in accordance with the provisions of this Law and its Implementing Regulations, including the licensing of rating companies and agencies and the conditions thereof.
19. Prepare the Authority's annual budget.

b. Upon starting to exercise its powers in accordance with this Law and its Implementing Regulations, the Authority shall coordinate with the Saudi Arabian Monetary Agency in connection with the procedures that it intends to undertake and which may have an impact on the monetary situation.

Article Seven

a. The Authority shall have a board known as the "Board of the Capital Market Authority" comprising five members, who shall be natural Saudi Arabian persons working on a full time basis, and shall be professionally qualified. The Board members shall be appointed, and their salaries and financial benefits determined, by Royal Order. The Royal Order shall specify from the Board members the chairman and deputy chairman who will replace the chairman in his absence.
b. The term of membership of the Board shall be five years, renewable once. The member shall remain in his office on the termination of his membership term until a successor is appointed.
c. The Board shall set forth the Internal Regulations of the Authority and the manner in which the personnel, advisors, auditors and any other experts shall be appointed as may be necessary for carrying out the responsibilities and functions entrusted to the Authority. The Board shall determine their salaries and remunerations.
d. The Board shall exercise all authorities entrusted to the Authority in accordance with the provisions of this Law. The Board will specify how the Authority's functions, responsibilities and operations will be organized among its divisions and departments. The Internal Regulations of the Authority will set forth the requirements for the operation of these departments and divisions. Except for the powers conferred by this Law exclusively upon the Board, the Board may delegate, by a published resolution, any of its functions. The Board shall, however, at its discretion, retain the power to review the actions and decisions made by those who had been delegated with such powers. Such a review will be made at the Board's initiative, upon the request of one of its members, or upon the request of a party to a lawsuit arising under the provisions of this Law and in compliance with the rules issued by the Authority.

Article Eight

Any person who becomes an employee or a member of the Board of the Authority must, immediately upon accepting its functions, disclose to the Authority, in the manner set forth in the regulations of the Authority, the Securities he owns or has at his disposal or the disposal of one of his relatives, and thereafter declare any change thereon, within three days of becoming aware of such change. Any of those who become agents for the Authority must also make this disclosure in connection to what is related to the work entrusted to them, in the manner specified in the regulations of the Authority.

Article Nine

The members of the Board and the employees of the Authority shall not engage in any other profession or job, including occupying a position or a post in any company, in the government, or public or private institutions. Furthermore, they shall not provide advice to companies and private institutions.

Article Ten

a. The Board shall hold its meetings at the request of its chairman. Meetings should be attended by at least three of its members including the chairman or vice chairman. Its decisions shall be made upon a vote of a majority of the members attending the meeting. In case of equal votes, the chairman of the meeting will have a casting vote.
b. The Internal Regulations will set forth the conditions and requirements with respect to convening meetings of the Board, including the notice for a meeting. The rules issued by the Authority may provide that it is permitted to vote for resolutions to be passed by the Board in emergency situations by telephone or by any other means of communication.

Article Eleven

The chairman of the Board shall be the Authority's chief executive officer who shall implement the Authority's policy and shall be responsible for the management of its affairs, including the following:

a. Implementing the decisions taken by the Board.
b. Signing, alone or jointly with others, reports, accounting statements, financial statements, correspondence and the Authority's documents.
c. The Authority's administrative and financial affairs.

Article Twelve

a. The vice chairman shall carry out the tasks and duties of the chairman if the chairman is absent, is unable to carry out his duties, or if his position becomes vacant.
b. The chairman may delegate to another member of the Board or to any employee of the Authority some of the powers entrusted to him provided that such delegation shall be specific and in writing.

Article Thirteen

a. The financial resources of the Authority shall consist of the following:

   1. Fees for services and commissions charged by the Authority in accordance with the provisions of this Law and the regulations and instructions issued in pursuance thereof.
   2. Charges against using its facilities, return on its funds, and proceeds of the sale of its assets.
   3. Fines and financial penalties imposed on violators of the provisions of this Law.
   4. Funds provided by the government to the Authority.
   5. Any other resources determined by the Board.

b. The Board shall determine the fees to be paid to the Authority for the following matters:

   1. Registration of Securities with the Authority.
   2. Listing of Securities on the Exchange.
   3. Trading of Securities.
   4. Licensing and renewal of licenses of brokerage companies or investment advisers.
   5. Registration of investment funds.

Article Fourteen

The Authority shall have a separate annual budget that will be submitted to the Minister of Finance and will be approved in accordance with applicable regulations. Surplus funds collected by the Authority under Article 13 of this Law and under the provisions, rules and instructions issued thereunder, shall be remitted to the Ministry of Finance after deducting all current and capital expenses or other expenses needed by the Authority. However, the Authority shall maintain a general reserve equal to the double of its expenditures as reported in its previous annual budget.

Article Fifteen

Any sums owed to the Authority by third parties shall be considered as public funds and enjoy the same treatment as debts owed to the Public Treasury and shall be collected in accordance with the procedures for the collection of debts due to the Public Treasury.

Article Sixteen

The chairman of the Board shall present to the President of the Council of Ministers an annual report on the Authority's activities and its financial position during the preceding year within ninety days from the end of the year.

Article Seventeen

Any undisclosed information obtained by the Authority is considered confidential. The Authority may disclose any part of this information as the Board deems necessary for the protection of investors.

Article Eighteen

Government agencies and other persons must provide the Authority with the documents and information it requires for the purposes of carrying out its duties in accordance with the provisions of this Law.

Article Nineteen

The internal regulations issued pursuant to this Law will define the rules, instructions and procedures relating to the Authority's administrative and financial affairs and the Authority's personnel affairs, including rules of professional conduct and the means of development of the Authority's operations, realization of its objectives and the enhancement of the performance and professional and academic standards of its staff.

Chapter Three

The Stock Exchange

Article Twenty

a. A market shall be established in the Kingdom for the trading in Securities which shall be known as the "Saudi Stock Exchange", and will have the legal status of a joint stock company in accordance with the provisions of this Law. This Exchange shall be the sole entity authorized to carry out trading in Securities in the Kingdom.
b. Securities listed or traded in a regulated market outside the Kingdom are not subject to the provisions of this Law even though trading in such a market originates by orders transmitted telephonically or electronically from within the Kingdom, with the exception of what may be agreed upon by the Authority with other foreign authorities.
c. The objectives of the Exchange include the following:

    1. Ensuring fair, efficient and transparent listing requirements, trading rules and technical mechanisms and information for Securities listed on the Exchange;
    2. Providing sound and rapid settlement and clearance rules and procedures through its Securities Depositary Center;
    3. Establishing and enforcing professional standards for brokers and their agents;
    4. Ensuring the financial strength and soundness of brokers through the periodic review of their compliance with capital adequacy requirements, and setting such arrangements to protect the funds and Securities in the custody of brokerage companies.

d. The Exchange shall not distribute to its members any cash or in kind distributions by way of a dividend without the approval of the Board.

Article Twenty One

Securities listed on the Exchange shall be traded through transactions among brokers, each on behalf of its client, and shall be evidenced by entries in the Exchange records, in accordance with the provisions of Chapter Four of this Law, unless such transactions are excluded from trading pursuant to the rules and instructions issued by the Authority.

Article Twenty Two

a. The regulations and rules of the Exchange shall specify the terms and requirements of the membership of the Exchange.

b. The Exchange shall be managed by a Board of Directors comprising nine members who shall be appointed by a Council of Ministers Resolution upon nomination by the chairman of the Board of the Authority and who will choose from among them a chairman and a vice chairman. The membership will be as follows:

   1. A representative of the Ministry of Finance.
   2. A representative of the Ministry of Commerce and Industry.
   3. A representative of the Saudi Arabian Monetary Agency.
   4. Four members representing licensed brokerage companies.
   5. Two members representing the joint stock companies listed on the Exchange.

c. The term of the membership at the board of directors of the Exchange shall be three years renewable one or more times.
d. The regulations and instructions issued by the Board of the Authority shall specify the procedures related to convening the meetings of the Board of Directors of the Exchange, the decisions making process at the board of directors, the plans for conducting the affairs of the board of directors, the powers and responsibilities entrusted to each of the board of directors and the executive manager and all other related administrative and financial affairs.
e. The board of directors of the Exchange shall appoint an executive manager with the approval of the Board of the Authority. The manager appointed shall not have the right to perform any other governmental or commercial work or to have any interest or ownership in any brokerage company on the Exchange. The executive manager may be removed from his position by decision of the board of directors of the Exchange.

Article Twenty Three

a. The Board of Directors of the Exchange shall propose the necessary regulations, rules and instructions for the operation of the Exchange including the following matters:

   1. Conditions for the listing of and the trading in Securities.
   2. The minimum capital required for brokerage companies and the financial assurances required from such companies or their employees.
   3. The immediate and timely publication of information regarding transactions executed in Securities traded on the Exchange, and the obligations of issuers of Securities, shareholders and members to disclose such information to the Exchange as the Exchange deems necessary.
   4. Standards of professional conduct applicable to the Exchange's members and their employees, the members of the board of directors, the Exchange's executive manager and employees, including the procedures and disciplinary sanctions applicable against those who violate such standards or any

other conditions or requirements set forth in the regulations and instructions.

5. Settling disputes among members of the Exchange and between the members and their clients.
6. Conditions and requirements for membership of the Exchange and the appropriate limitations and procedures that permit licensed brokerage companies but not members of the Exchange to execute their transactions on the Exchange.
7. The determination of the fees and commissions that brokers charge for their services.
8. Any other rules and instructions that the Exchange deems necessary for the protection of investors through ensuring fairness, efficiency and transparency in all of the Exchange's related affairs.

b. The Exchange shall submit to the Authority the regulations, rules and instructions for the operation of the Exchange and the amendments thereof for approval by the Board.

Article Twenty Four

The Exchange may charge fees on its members, on issuers of Securities listed on the Exchange and others for services it provides to them.

Article Twenty Five

a. The Authority shall establish a committee known as the "Committee for the Resolution of Securities
Disputes" which shall have jurisdiction over the disputes falling under the provisions of this Law, its Implementing Regulations, and the regulations, rules and instructions issued by the Authority and the Exchange, with respect to the public and private actions. The Committee shall have all necessary powers to investigate and settle complaints and suits, including the power to issue subpoenas, issue decisions, impose sanctions and order the production of evidence and documents.
b. The Committee will consist of legal advisors specialized in the doctrine of transactions and capital markets, and experts in commercial and financial affairs and Securities. The members of the Committee shall be appointed by a Board decision for a three-year term renewable. The members of the Committee must not have any direct or indirect financial or commercial interest or have a family relationship up to the fourth degree with the parties to the complaint or the suit brought before the Committee. The Committee must start considering the complaint or the suit within a period not to exceed fourteen days from the date of filing of the complaint or the suit with the Committee.

c. The Committee's jurisdiction shall include claims against decisions and actions taken by the Authority or the Exchange and the Committee shall have the right to issue a decision awarding damages and request to revert to the original status or issue another decision as appropriate and that would guarantee the rights of the aggrieved.
d. The regulations and rules of the Authority shall specify the procedures that the Committee must follow regarding the complaints and the suits presented to it.
e. No complaint or statement of claim may be filed with the Committee without being filed first with the Authority and a 90 day period has passed from the filing date, unless the Authority notifies the grievant otherwise of the permissibility of submitting before the expiration of this period.
f. The Committee's decision may be appealed before the Appeal Panel within thirty days from their notification date.
g. An Appeal Panel is to be formed by a Council of Ministers' decision, and it shall have three members representing the Ministry of Finance, the Ministry of Commerce and Industry and the Bureau of Experts at the Council of Ministers. The members of the Appeal Panel shall be appointed for a three-year term renewable. The Appeal Panel shall have the discretion to refuse to review the decisions of the Committee for the Resolution of Securities Disputes, to affirm such decisions, to undertake a de novo review of the complaint or suit based on the record developed at the hearing before the Committee and to issue such decision as it deems appropriate in relation to the complaint or the suit. The decisions of the Appeal Panel shall be final.
h. At the Authority or the Exchange's request, final decisions shall be enforced through the government agency responsible for the enforcement of judicial judgments. Decisions issued in favor of the parties pursuant to Articles 55, 56 and 57 of Chapter 10 of this Law shall be enforced by such parties in accordance with the procedure for enforcement of judicial judgment in civil proceedings.
i. Evidence in Securities cases shall be admissible in all forms including electronic or computer data, telephone recordings, facsimile messages and electronic mail.

Chapter Four

The Securities Depositary Center

Article Twenty Six

a. The Board of Directors of the Exchange shall establish a department to be known as the "Securities Depositary Center" which shall be the sole entity in the Kingdom authorized to practice the operations of deposit, transfer, settlement, clearing and registering ownership of Saudi Securities traded on the Exchange. The Exchange's Board of Directors may convert the Securities Depositary Center into a company after obtaining the approval of the Authority's Board for the conversion. The Board may give its approval indicating the requirements of the company's structure and its operations, as it deems appropriate and necessary for the safety of the market and the protection of investors.
b. The Depositary Center's operating rules shall specify the sound and efficient procedures which shall ensure the efficient operations for registration, settlement and clearance of Securities traded on the Exchange in a regulatory manner, including the procedures to be followed for the disbursement of funds to investors following settlement. The Depositary Center may maintain cash accounts for settlement and clearance purposes of transactions in the context of its operations. The Authority has the power to adopt, amend, repeal or suspend any of the Depositary Center's operating regulations or rules if it deems appropriate.

Article Twenty Seven

a. The registration of ownership of Securities traded on the Exchange and the settlement and clearance of Securities shall be made by entries in the Depositary Center's records. Ownership of Securities traded on the Exchange must be registered with the Depositary Center in order to be protected against third party claims. The Depositary Center's records will also report pledges or other claims related to the Securities traded on the Exchange.
b. The Depositary Center shall be the sole entity to register all property rights in Securities traded on the Exchange. The final mentions reported in the records of the Depositary Center shall serve as conclusive evidence and proof of ownership of the Securities indicated therein together with the encumbrances and rights associated therewith, subject to the provisions of paragraph (d) of this Article.
c. Registration of ownership of Securities shall be effective from the time of final verification by the Depositary Center of the authenticity of the ownership documents. The Depositary Center shall promptly register all transactions effected upon being reported to and received by the Depositary Center with no

delay. If the Depositary Center has reason to doubt actual or legal facts or consequences related to the registration of ownership or if the Depositary Center receives any notice that registration will cause damages to third parties, the Depositary Center may make a preliminary registration and, if it does so, it shall immediately commence an appropriate process to decide how the final registration for such Security shall be effected.

d. A person who believes that there is an error in the information entered into the registry so that the registry needs to be corrected or otherwise amended should make a written request to the manager of the Depositary Center or the person appointed by the manager to receive such requests. The Depositary Center shall correct or amend the registry after confirming the validity of the comments and information that are requested to be corrected or amended in the registry. Such correction or amendment can only be effected after notice and opportunity to comment by the person or persons the registry identifies as owning the Security, and giving them a reasonable opportunity to comment on the required correction or amendment.
e. The Depositary Center shall issue a certificate of registration upon request by the investor. The operating rules of the Depositary Center will specify the manner in which periodic reports to all the owners of Securities registered on the Depositary Center's records on the Securities owned by each owner and which are recorded with the Depositary Center's records.
f. Complaints about decisions with respect to the registration of Securities listed on the Exchange shall be brought before the Committee.
g. The Depositary Center shall be liable for any monetary damage suffered by an investor and resulting from the proven negligence or misconduct of the Depositary Center's employees that causes an error in the registration process.
h. The compensation due for the damage under paragraph (g) of this Article may be reduced or even eliminated if the claimant has contributed to causing the error in registration or if the error could have been avoided.

Article Twenty Eight

The employees of the Depositary Center and the Exchange and their independent auditors, advisors and consultants may not disclose any information about owners of Securities registered in the records except as set forth in the operating rules issued by the Depositary Center in this regard.

Article Twenty Nine

The Board of Directors of the Exchange, with the approval of Board of the Authority, shall establish the necessary instructions for managing the Depositary Center's affairs, including the standards of professional conduct applicable to the Depositary Center's manager and personnel, to assure efficient and trustworthy operations of the Depositary Center.

Article Thirty

The Depositary Center may charge fees and commissions for the provision of its services as may be provided for in the Implementing Regulations and the Depositary Center's operating rules.

Chapter Five

Brokers Regulation

Article Thirty One

Brokerage business is restricted to a person holding a valid license and who is an agent of a joint stock company that is licensed to perform brokerage activities, unless such person is exempt from these requirements in accordance with paragraph (c) of Article 32.

Article Thirty Two

a. Broker means a joint stock company that carries on brokerage activities and the broker agent who is working at the brokerage company and carries out all or part the following activities:

   1. acts in a commercial capacity as an intermediary in the trading of Securities, other than persons working on the basis of a contractual arrangement as defined in paragraph (b) of this Article, including any person who commercially acts as a custodian for Securities;
   2. presents in a commercial capacity an offer to others for obtaining financial assets in the form of Securities by opening an account through which transactions in Securities may be effected;
   3. effects in a commercial capacity Securities transactions for its own account other than by way of issuing Securities, in order to create a market in Securities and make a profit out of the difference between offer prices for Securities and demand;
   4. acquires or places Securities in a commercial capacity for an issuer or a person who controls an issuer;
   5. acts as an intermediary in a commercial capacity - other than persons who act on the basis of a contractual arrangement as defined in paragraph (b) of this Article - including in arranging currency or Securities swaps.

b. A portfolio manager means:

   1. Any person acting in a commercial capacity who, on the basis of a contractual arrangement or otherwise, manages either Securities owned by a person or investment funds owned by a natural or judicial person which are intended for investment in Securities, and whose activities may include transactions in Securities or ordering Securities transactions to be effected for the account of the person with whom the contractual arrangements have been made;
   2. Any person acting in a commercial capacity who, on the basis of a contractual arrangement, carries on the works mentioned in paragraph (a.5) of this Article.

c. The Authority may specify, in the rules that it issues, such exemptions from the provisions of paragraphs (a) and (b) of this Article as it considers will achieve the safety of the market and the protection of the investor.

Article Thirty Three

a. The Authority shall grant the license referred to under Article 31 within thirty days of receiving from the Exchange the information and documents that are required by the rules issued by the Authority and which demonstrate that the applicant satisfies the conditions and requirements necessary for obtaining a license for working as a broker or a broker's agent. The term of validity of the licenses must be defined and their holder must be subject to periodic qualification examination as set forth by the Implementing Regulations.
b. The regulations and rules of the Exchange shall set forth the requirements and conditions that must be met by applicants for obtaining a brokerage license. In addition to the requirements under the Exchange's regulations, the conditions for licensing or renewal of a license must include the following:

   1. Criteria pertaining to an applicant's competence to act as a broker or a broker's agent;
   2. Criteria of integrity or suitability for persons to conduct brokerage activities;
   3. Minimum capital requirements that brokerage companies must continually meet, which must not be less than SR 50 million.

Article Thirty Four

A broker and a broker's agent must observe the Exchange's regulations and rules pertaining to the regulation of brokers' business.

Article Thirty Five

The Exchange may carry out investigations and inspections in connection with any licensed broker or broker's agent to verify whether that person or another person has violated, is violating or there is evidence substantiating that it is about to violate the regulations and instructions of the Exchange. The Exchange's investigation and inspection powers shall include the power to require the production of any person's testimony, papers, books and documents which the Exchange deems necessary or relevant to its inquiry. The Exchange may require the attendance of witnesses or the submission of documents and evidence. Inspection may take place wherever the records are situated. The Exchange can exercise its power to carry out such investigations and inspections by obtaining a subpoena or an order for interrogation or inspection or such other order from the Committee for Resolution of Securities

Disputes. The Committee shall accept the Exchange's request for a subpoena or other order unless it is established to the Committee that the Exchange's request is arbitrary or involves abuse of power.

Article Thirty Six

Any broker or broker's agent may relinquish its license by filing a written notice of withdrawal with the Authority in accordance with such terms and conditions as the Authority may deem necessary or appropriate for the safety of the market or the protection of the investor.

Article Thirty Seven

Licensed brokers or broker's agents must file with the Authority and the Exchange such reports as required by the regulations and rules of the Authority and the Exchange.

Article Thirty Eight

The Authority shall supervise the compulsory and voluntary liquidation of the broker's business.

Chapter Six

Investment Funds and Collective Investment Schemes

Article Thirty Nine

a. An investment fund is a collective investment scheme aimed at providing investors therein with an opportunity to participate collectively in the profits of the scheme which is managed by a portfolio manager for specified fees.
b. The Authority shall assume the power to regulate the activities of investment funds managed by banks within two years from the enactment of this Law.
c. The Authority shall regulate portfolio managers and investment advisers and supervise them. This shall include setting the regulations, rules and instructions that pertain to the following:

    1. The organizational structure;
    2. Accounting systems and operational rules;
    3. Investment fund governance and decision making;
    4. Securities custody procedures and efficient provision of services to clients;
    5. Services fees and commissions and management remuneration;
    6. Entering into transactions with related parties;
    7. Performance reports and the calculation of asset values and unit prices and advertisement;
    8. Conditions and requirements for the approval of establishing new funds;
    9. Financial and periodic reporting requirements of funds;
    10. Liquidity requirements and risk limits;
    11. Professional qualifications, personal suitability, financial responsibility and licensing requirements.

Chapter Seven

Disclosure

Article Forty

a. The contents of the prospectus set forth under Article 42 of this Law, or portions thereof, shall be published in such a manner and for such duration as required by the regulations and rules of the Authority.
b. An issuer or an affiliate of an issuer or an underwriter may not offer Securities of the issuer or the issuer's affiliate unless he has submitted a prospectus to the Authority, published the prospectus in the manner set forth in paragraph (a) of this Article, and has paid the requisite fees. The Authority may exempt the issuer from some requirements based on the manner of the offering, the amount of the offering, the number of investors and their characteristics, or the characteristic of the issuer of the Security or the Security itself.
c. Upon satisfying the requirements of paragraphs (a) and (b) of this Article, offers may be made in any of the forms listed below:

   1. Verbally;
   2. Through a prospectus satisfying the conditions of Article 42 of this Law;
   3. Through an announcement containing a summary of the prospectus and any other information required by the Authority or authorized by it in accordance with the rules specified by the Authority;
   4. Through other means, including electronic media, provided that such mean has been approved by the Authority.

Article Forty One

An issuer, an affiliate of the issuer or an underwriter may not sell any Security owned by that issuer before the prospectus is approved by the Authority and becomes effective, provided that the approved prospectus shall be sent to the buyer prior to the sale date in accordance with such rules as the Authority may issue.

Article Forty Two

The prospectus must contain the following information and statements:

a. Information required by the Authority's rules which give an adequate description of the issuer, the nature of its business, the individuals in charge of its management such as members of the board of directors, executive officers, senior staff and its major shareholders.
b. Information required by the Authority's rules which give an adequate description of the Securities to be issued, their number, price, and related rights, preferences or privileges of the issuer's other Securities, if any. The description

will set forth how the issue proceeds will be disbursed, and the commissions levied by persons connected with the issue.

c. A clear statement of the financial position of the issuer and any significant financial data including the audited financial balance sheet, profit and loss account and cash flow statement as the rules of the Authority may require.
d. Any other information required or authorized by the Authority in accordance with rules issued by the Authority which it deems necessary to assist investors and their advisers in making decisions about investing in the Securities to be issued.

Article Forty Three

a. After its review of the prospectus, the Authority shall announce its approval or rejection of the prospectus. If it approves the prospectus, the Authority may define a period of time during which the prospectus remains valid.
b. Every issuer offering Securities to the public through a prospectus must notify the Authority in writing of any material change to the statements set forth in the prospectus immediately upon becoming aware of such change provided such change may affect the price or value of the Security. The issuer should also prepare and publish a press release to disclose such change. The Authority's regulations and rules shall set forth the information to be disclosed and the conditions applicable regarding the press release.

Article Forty Four

The Board of the Authority may reject a prospectus in any of the following cases:

a. If the prospectus does not contain the information required by Article 42 of this Law.
b. If the prospectus contains incorrect information pertaining to material matters, false or misleading statements or omits to state material information or statements that would under the circumstances render the prospectus misleading or incorrect.
c. The prospectus issuance fees have not been paid in full to the Authority.
d. The issuer has failed to provide any of the reports stipulated in Article 45 of this Law.

Article Forty Five

a. Every issuer offering Securities to the public or whose Securities are traded on the Exchange must submit to the Authority quarterly and annual reports. Annual reports must be audited as required by the rules of the Authority. These reports shall contain the following:

1. The balance sheet;
2. The profit and loss account;
3. The cash flow statement; and
4. Any other information as required by the rules of the Authority.

b. In addition to the information required in paragraph (a) of this Article, the annual report must contain the following:

   1. An adequate description of the issuing company, the nature of its business and its activities as required under the rules of the Authority;
   2. Information regarding the members of its board of directors, executive officers, senior staff and major investors or shareholders as required under the rules of the Authority;
   3. An evaluation of the issuing company management of current and future developments and any future possibilities that may have significant effect on the business results or financial position of the company as required under the rules of the Authority.
   4. Any other information as may be required by the rules of the Authority as it deems necessary to assist investors and their advisers in making a decision to invest in the issuer's Securities.

c. All information and data described in paragraphs (a - 1, 2, 3) and (b.3) of this Article shall be deemed confidential. Before providing and disclosing such information and data to the Authority, the issuing company shall be prohibited from disclosing such information to parties not bound by a confidentiality obligation and an obligation to protect such information.

Article Forty Six

a. A party who issues Securities must inform the Authority in writing upon becoming aware of any material developments which may affect the prices of the Securities issued by such party. If such party has a Security traded on the Exchange, the Exchange must be informed of such developments in writing.
b. The Authority or the Exchange may request the party issuing Securities to provide any information or data pertaining to such party and the issuing party shall provide the same within the period of time specified in the request.
c. The Board of the Authority or the Exchange may, after reviewing the facts, require the issuing party to disclose any information or data related to that party. The Board or the Exchange shall also have the right to publish such information and data at the expense of the issuing party.

Article Forty Seven

The public shall be allowed, in return for fees to be determined by the Authority, to review and make copies of the prospectuses, periodical reports, and information and data which have been filed with the Authority, made public and obtained.

Article Forty Eight

a. The Authority shall specify the disclosure forms and instructions, including the information which must be included in the prospectuses and periodical reports which must be provided to the Authority by the parties that are subject to its control and supervision or which must be announced to the public, as the case may be.
b. The Authority shall have no responsibility for the omission in prospectuses, periodical reports, advertisements, or any other document filed with it by any party of any important information or data or for including misleading information or data.
c. The publisher of the advertisement shall be responsible for any errors committed by it in publishing the contents of the advertisement pursuant to the regulations applicable in the Kingdom.

Chapter Eight

Manipulation and Insider Trading

Article Forty Nine

a. Any person shall be considered in violation of this Law if he intentionally does any act or engages in any action which creates a false or misleading impression as to the market, the prices or the value of any Security for the purpose of creating that impression or thereby inducing third parties to buy, sell or subscribe for such Security or to refrain from doing so or to induce them to exercise, or refrain from exercising, any rights conferred by such Security.

b. The Authority shall set out rules determining the acts and practices which shall constitute violations of paragraph (a) of this Article. These rules shall specify the acts and practices excluded from the application of the provisions of paragraph (a) of this Article. The powers of the Authority provided for in this paragraph shall include the power to set forth the rules, define the circumstances and procedures aiming at stabilizing the prices of Securities offered to the public, and the manner in which and the period during which these actions must be taken.

c. The following acts and practices shall be among those which shall be considered types of manipulation that are prohibited by paragraph (a) of this Article:

   1. To perform any act or practice aiming at creating a false or misleading impression of an existing active trading in a Security as may be contrary to the reality. These acts and practices shall include, but not be limited to the following:
      a. Undertaking transactions in Securities which do not involve a true transfer of ownership thereof.
      b. Entering an order or orders for the purchase of a particular Security with prior knowledge that an order or orders of substantially the same size, price and timing for the sale of the same Security has been or will be entered by a different party or parties.
      c. Entering an order or orders for the sale of a particular Security with prior knowledge that an order or orders of substantially the same size, price and timing for the purchase of the same Security has been or will be entered by the same party or different parties.
   2. To affect, alone or with others, the price of a particular Security or Securities traded on the Exchange through executing a series of transactions in such Security or Securities creating actual or apparent active trading or causing an increase or decrease in the prices of such Securities, for the purpose of inducing third parties to buy or sell such Securities as the case may be.

3. To affect, alone or with others through any series of transactions such as buying or selling or buying and selling a Security traded on the Exchange for the purpose of pegging or stabilizing the price of such Security in violation of the rules set forth by the Authority for the safety of the market and the protection of investors.

Article Fifty

a. Any person who obtains, through family, business or contractual relationship, inside information (hereinafter an "insider") is prohibited from directly or indirectly trading in the Security related to such information, or to disclose such information to another person with the expectation that such person will trade in such Security.
   Insider information means information obtained by the insider and which is not available to the general public, has not been disclosed, and such information is of the type that a normal person would realize that in view of the nature and content of this information, its release and availability would have a material effect on the price or value of a Security related to such information, and the insider knows that such information is not generally available and that, if it were available, it would have a material effect on the price or value of such Security.
b. No person may purchase or sell a Security based on information obtained from an insider while knowing that such person, by disclosing such insider information related to the Security, has violated paragraph (a) of this Article.
c. The Authority has the power to establish the rules for specifying and defining the terms provided for under paragraphs (a) and (b) of this Article, and such acts or practices which the Authority deems appropriate to exempt them from their application, as may be required for the safety of the market and the protection of investors.

Chapter Nine

Regulation of Proxy Solicitations, Restricted Purchase and Restricted Offer for Shares

Article Fifty One

The Authority shall issue rules for the regulation of disclosure of information and other practices in connection with the solicitation of proxies if such solicitation pertains to any Security listed on the Exchange.

Article Fifty Two

The Authority shall issue rules for the regulation of restricted purchase of shares transactions and restricted offer for shares transactions. For the purpose of application of the provisions of this Law, these two terms mean the following:

a. A restricted purchase of shares is the purchase of voting shares listed on the Exchange when as a consequence of such purchase ten percent (10%) or more of such class of the relevant company shares is owned by, or under control of, the purchaser or those acting in concert with the purchaser.
b. A restricted offer for shares is making a public announcement by which the announcer offers to purchase voting shares of a particular class of shares listed on the Exchange if the amount of shares sought to be acquired by the offering party would increase its ownership or the ownership of those acting in concert with the offering party, or the shares under their control, to ten percent (10%) or more of the shares of the relevant company.

Article Fifty Three

The Authority's powers to issue rules for the regulation of restricted purchases of shares and restricted offers for shares shall include, without limitation, the power to issue rules in connection with the following:

a. Amending the percentages prescribed under Article 52 of this Law and approving exceptions to the definitions of restricted purchases of shares and restricted offers for shares;
b. Specifying the timing, form and manner for announcements in connection with restricted purchases of shares and restricted offers for shares;
c. Setting forth the information which party purchasing the shares or offering party must disclose, and the manner for its disclosure, including any requirements for the continuous disclosure with respect to changes in share ownership;

d. Imposing any conditions or requirements on the company the shares of which are subject or target of a restricted purchase of shares or a restricted offer for shares that it announces its position or viewpoint regarding such restricted purchase or restricted offer;
e. Any other rules pertaining to restricted purchases of shares or restricted offers for shares as may be necessary for the safety of the market and the protection of investors.

Article Fifty Four

If any person increases its ownership of shares in a given company through a restricted purchase of shares or restricted offer for shares so that such person or those with whom such person is acting in concert become the owner of (50%) fifty percent or more of a given class of voting shares listed on the Exchange, the Board shall have the right, within sixty (60) days, if it believes it would achieve the safety of the market and the protection of shareholders, to order such person to offer to purchase the shares of the same class it does not own on such terms and conditions as the Board shall determine. In no case will the prospective purchaser be compelled to offer to purchase the remaining shares at a price exceeding the highest price he paid to purchase any of the shares of that company during the 12 months preceding the date of the Board order.

Chapter Ten

Sanctions and Penalties for Violations

Article Fifty Five

a. In case a prospectus, when approved by the Authority, contained incorrect statements of material matters or omitted material facts required to be stated in the prospectus, the person purchasing the Security that was the subject of such prospectus shall be entitled to compensation for the damages incurred by him as a result thereof. A statement or omission shall be considered material for the purposes of this paragraph if it is proven to the Committee that had the investor been aware of the truth when making such purchase it would have affected the purchase price.
b. The following persons shall be liable under paragraph (a) of this Article:
    1. The party issuing the Security. The issuer shall be liable irrespective of whether it had acted reasonably, or it was not aware of the incorrect statements in connection with material matters, or of the omission of material facts that should have been disclosed in the prospectus.
    2. The senior officers of the issuing party of the Security in accordance with the definition provided in the rules issued by the Authority. Such liability could be relieved according to paragraph (c.l and 2) of this Article.
    3. The members of the board of directors of the issuing party, or persons performing similar functions, as of the date on which the prospectus was approved by the Authority. Such liability could be relieved in accordance with paragraph (c.l and 2) of this Article.
    4. The underwriters who have undertaken to offer on behalf of the issuer the Security for sale to the public, provided that an underwriter shall not be liable for more than the total price of the Securities underwritten or amount of Securities distributed by him (whichever amount is greater).
    5. The accountant, engineer or appraiser and others identified in the prospectus, who have consented in writing to be so identified, as having certified the accuracy and truthfulness of the information stated in the prospectus; however, such person's liability shall not extend to information in parts of the prospectus which are not so certified by him. That person shall be responsible for any part of the prospectus understood to have been prepared according to his statement and approval in his capacity defined under this paragraph, unless he proves that he was convinced after conducting reasonable investigations and on the basis of reasonable grounds, that that part of the prospectus is not in violation of paragraph (a) of this Article.

c. Any of the persons mentioned in paragraph (b.2, 3 and 4) of this Article shall be liable as provided for in the provisions of paragraph (a) of this Article unless it is proven that:

   1. As to any part of the prospectus not certified by the person described in paragraph (b.5) of this Article that, after reasonable investigation, and on the basis of reasonable grounds, he was convinced that such part of the prospectus was not in violation of paragraph (a) of this Article;
   2. As to any part of the prospectus purporting to have been made based on the statement of a person set forth in paragraph (b.5) of this Article, and the person invoking the defense is identified in paragraphs (b.2, 3, 4) of this Article, he had no reasonable ground at that time to believe that such part of the prospectus contained what could be deemed a violation of paragraph (a) of this Article.

d. In determining that investigation shall be deemed reasonable or what shall constitute reasonable ground for belief for the purposes of paragraph (c) of this Article, the standard of reasonableness for the purpose of this Article shall be that of the prudent man in the management of his property.
e. Damages may be obtained through a claim brought on the basis of paragraph (a) of this Article, which damages shall represent the difference between the price actually paid for purchasing the Security (not to exceed the price at which it was offered to the public) and the value thereof as of the date of bringing the legal action or the price which such Security could have been disposed of on the Exchange prior to filing the complaint with the Committee, provided that if the defendant proves that any portion in the decline in value of the Security is due to causes which are not related to the omission or the incorrect statement which is the substance of the suit, such portion shall be excluded from the damages for which the defendant is responsible. The defendants are individually and jointly and severally liable for damages for which they are responsible under this Article. The amount of indemnification shall be subject to the provisions of the contract or agreement entered into between the parties identified in paragraph (b) of this Article or as the Committee believes is equitable and does not harm the interest of investors or otherwise contravene the spirit of this Law.

Article Fifty Six

a. Any person who makes, or is responsible for another making, orally or in writing an untrue statement of material fact or omits to state that material fact, if it causes another person to be misled in relation to the sale or the purchase of a Security, shall be liable for compensation of the damages. For establishing responsibility for damages in pursuance of the provisions of this Article, it is not required that a relationship exists between the claimant and the defendant and the claimant should prove:

1. That he was not aware that the statement was omitted or untrue.
2. That either he would not have purchased or sold the Security in question had he known that information was omitted or untrue, or that he would not have purchased or sold such Security at the price at which such Security was purchased or sold.
3. That the person responsible for the disclosure of the statements or the giving of such incorrect information knew of the said untruthfulness or was aware that there was a substantial likelihood that the information disclosed omitted or misstated a material fact.

b. The damages recoverable under this Article from any defendant, and the rights of indemnity and contribution among the persons responsible shall be as provided in paragraph (e) of Article 55 of this Law.
c. For the purpose of this Article, a statement or omission shall be considered related to an important material fact in accordance with the standard provided for in paragraph (a) of Article 55 of this Law.

Article Fifty Seven

a. Any person who violates Article 49 of this Law or any of the regulations or the rules issued by the Authority pursuant to the said Article by engaging in an act or transaction for the purpose of intentionally manipulating the price of a Security, or participating in such act or transaction, or is responsible for a person who undertakes such act or transaction shall be liable for damages to any person who purchases or sells the Security whose price has been significantly adversely affected by such manipulation for the amount such person's purchase or sale price was so affected.
b. The damages recoverable under this Article from any defendant, and the rights of indemnity and contribution among the persons responsible shall be measured in a manner that is consistent with the provisions of paragraph (e) of Article 55 of this Law.
c. In addition to the penalties and financial compensation provided for under this Law, the Committee may, based on a claim filed by the Authority, punish the persons who violate Articles 49 and 50 with imprisonment terms not exceeding five years.

Article Fifty Eight

A suit under Articles 55, 56 and 57 of this Law shall not be heard if the complaint is filed with the Authority after the elapse of one year from the date when the claimant should reasonably have been aware of facts causing him to believe he had been the victim of a violation, and in no case may such complaint be heard by the Committee after five years from the occurrence of the violation subject of the claim.

Article Fifty Nine

a. If it appears to the Authority that any person has engaged, is engaging, or is about to engage in acts or practices constituting a violation of any provisions of this Law, or the regulations or rules issued by the Authority, or the regulations of the Exchange, the Authority shall have the right to bring a legal action before the Committee to seek an order for the appropriate sanction. The sanctions include the following:

   1. Warning the person concerned.
   2. Obliging the person concerned to cease or refrain from carrying out the act which is the subject of the suit.
   3. Obliging the person concerned to take the necessary steps to avert the violation, or to take such necessary corrective steps to address the results of the violation.
   4. Indemnifying the persons who have suffered damages as a consequence of a violation that has occurred, or obliging the violator to pay to the Authority's account the gains realized as a consequence of such violation.
   5. Suspending the trading in the Security.
   6. Barring the violating person from acting as a broker, portfolio manager or investment adviser for such period of time as is necessary for the safety of the market and the protection of investors.
   7. Seizing and executing on property.
   8. Travel ban.
   9. Barring from working with companies whose Securities are traded on the Exchange.

b. The Authority may, in addition to taking the actions provided for under paragraph (a) of this Article, request the Committee to impose a financial fine upon the persons responsible for an intentional violation of the provisions of this Law, its Implementing Regulations, the rules of the Authority and the regulations of the Exchange. As an alternative to the foregoing, the Board may impose a financial fine upon any person responsible for the violation of this Law, its Implementing Regulations, the rules of the Authority and the regulations of the Exchange. The fine that the Committee or the Board can impose shall not be less than SR 10,000 and shall not exceed SR 100,000 for each violation committed by the defendant.

Article Sixty

a. Any person who carries on, or purports to carry on, brokerage activities without a license shall be considered violating the provisions of Article 31 of this Law and shall be subject to any of the two following sanctions or both:

   1. A fine of not less than SR 10,000 and not to exceed SR 100,000 for each violation.
   2. Imprisonment for a term not to exceed nine (9) months.

b. Any agreement or contract which is entered into in relation to a Security related transaction that is in violation of Article 31 of this Law shall be void and the violating broker may not complain on basis of such agreement or contract against the other party and that party shall be entitled to request the rescission of the agreement or contract and the recovery of any money or other property paid or transferred by him under the agreement or contract, provided the rescinding party restitutes any money or other property received through such agreement or contract. The Committee shall have jurisdiction over the suits brought pursuant to this provision.

Article Sixty One

a. The failure of a licensed broker or his agent to comply with any regulations and rules of the Exchange pertaining to the regulation of the work of brokers can give rise to disciplinary proceedings pursuant to the procedures established in the regulations of the Exchange. Upon discovering a violation of its regulations, the Exchange may file a claim with the Committee to impose a suitable sanction against the violator which may include the revocation of the license granted to it, suspension of said license, the imposition of a financial fine or obliging the broker to restitute the sums due to clients. A broker or his agent sanctioned may request the review of the decision by the Appeal Panel of the Committee.
b. The Authority may, pursuant to its powers under Article 59 of Chapter 10 of this Law, take necessary actions against brokers or their agents who fail to comply with the rules of operation of the Exchange.

Article Sixty Two

a. The Board may issue a decision providing for a reprimand to the violator broker or broker's agent, or may, pursuant to the decision, place restrictions on the licensed activities, functions or operations of the broker or the broker's agent, suspend those activities for a period not exceeding twelve months, or revoke the license of any broker or his agent if the Board finds, after giving notice to the concerned broker or the broker's agent and giving it an opportunity for a hearing, that such broker or the broker's agent, whether prior or subsequent to obtaining a license has committed any of the following:

1. he deliberately gave or caused to be given materially false or misleading statements in the broker's or the broker agent's application to obtain a license, in any document or report submitted to the Exchange or to the Authority.
2. he deliberately violated, or assisted another person to violate any provision of this Law and its regulations.
3. the broker or the broker's agent violated a judgment or decision issued by any court of the Kingdom or by the Committee for Resolution of Securities Disputes prohibiting him permanently or temporarily from carrying on brokerage or portfolio manager business.
4. the Authority has formally been notified by a Securities regulator in another country that the broker or his agent willfully violated the Securities laws of that country or provided false and misleading information in the reports required to be submitted in such foreign jurisdiction.

b. The Board may issue a decision suspending the brokerage license pending the issuance of a final determination in relation to the revocation of the license, if such suspension appears to the Board, after giving the broker or the broker's agent concerned notice and an opportunity to be heard on an urgent basis, to be necessary for the safety of the market and the protection of investors.
c. The Board may, in urgent cases, and without prior notice or hearing being granted to the concerned party to the decision, issue a decision suspending the license of a broker or barring the broker from performing such functions as a broker for a period not to exceed 60 days. Issuing such a decision does not prevent the Authority or the Exchange from taking such other actions against the broker or his agent as provided by this Law.

Article Sixty Three

The license of the broker or the broker's agent may be suspended by order of the Board upon discovering that the broker ceases to exist or has for a period of twelve months ceased to carry out brokerage activities.

Article Sixty Four

A person charged with violation of Article 50 of this Law may avoid proceedings before the Committee by reaching an agreement with the Authority pursuant to which he agrees to pay the Authority a sum not exceeding three times the profits he has realized, or three times the losses he has averted by committing the violation. Such arrangement shall be without prejudice to any compensation awardable as a result of the violation.

Article Sixty Five

This Law shall repeal all provisions that are contrary hereto.

Article Sixty Six

The Implementing Regulations to this Law shall be issued 150 days after the publication of the date of publication of the Law and shall come into effect with the Law.

Article Sixty Seven

This Law shall be published in the Official Gazette and shall be effective 180 days after the date of the publication thereof.

APPENDIX II

Saudi Market Conduct Regulations

TABLE OF CONTENTS

PART 1: PRELIMINARY PROVISIONS

Article 1: Definitions

a. Any reference to the "Capital Market Law" in these Regulations shall mean the Capital Market Law issued by Royal Decree No. M/30 dated 2/6/1424H.
b. Expressions and terms in these Regulations have the meaning which they bear in the Capital Market Law and in the Glossary of defined terms used in the Regulations and Rules of the Capital Market Authority, unless the contrary intention appears.

PART 2: PROHIBITION OF MARKET MANIPULATION

Article 2: Prohibition of manipulative and deceptive acts or practices

a. It is prohibited for any person to engage in or participate in any manipulative or deceptive acts or practices in connection with an order or transaction in a security, if the person knows or has reasonable grounds to know the nature of the act or practice.
b. It is prohibited for any person to, directly or indirectly, enter an order or execute a trade in a security for the purpose of creating any of the following:

    1) a false or misleading impression of trading activity or interest in the purchase or sale of the security; or
    2) an artificial bid price, ask price or trade price for the security or any related security.

Article 3: Manipulative and deceptive acts or practices

a. The following actions shall be among those considered as manipulative or deceptive acts or practices:

    1) making a fictitious trade; or
    2) effecting a trade in a security that involves no change in its beneficial ownership.

b. The following acts shall be among those considered as manipulative or deceptive acts or practices when committed for the purpose of creating a false or misleading impression of trading activity in a security or interest in the purchase or sale of the security, or for the purpose of creating an artificial bid price, ask price or trade price for a security:

    1) entering an order or orders for the purchase of a security with the prior knowledge that an order or orders of substantially the same size, time and price for the sale of that security, has been or will be entered;
    2) entering an order or orders for the sale of a security with the prior knowledge that an order or orders of substantially the same size, time and price for the purchase of that security, has been or will be entered;
    3) purchasing or making offers to purchase, a security at successively higher prices or in a pattern of successively higher prices;
    4) selling or making offers to sell a security at successively lower prices or in a pattern of successively lower prices; or
    5) entering an order or orders for the purchase or sale of a security in order to:
        * establish a predetermined sale price, ask price or bid price;
        * effect a high or low closing sale price, ask price or bid price;
        * maintain the sale price, ask price or bid price within a predetermined range; or
        * entering an order or a series of orders for a security that are not intended to be executed.

PART 3: INSIDER TRADING

Article 4: Disclosure of inside information and insider trading defined

a. For purposes of the application of Article 50 of the Capital Market Law and the provisions of this Part:

1) A security related to inside information must be a traded security.
2) A security related to inside information shall mean any security whose price or value would be materially affected if the information was disclosed or made available to the general public.
3) A person shall be considered directly trading in a security in any of the following two situations:
   * if he executes a trade in the security for any account in which he has an interest; or
   * if he makes a bid or offer on the Exchange for the security.
4) A person shall be considered indirectly trading in a security in any of the following situations:
   * if he executes a trade as agent for another person;
   * if he arranges a trade to which a relative or person with whom he has a business or a contractual relationship is party; or
   * if he arranges for his agent or any other person acting on his behalf or at his direction to trade in the relevant securities.
5) Trading shall constitute insider trading, if it is directly or indirectly effected in a security related to inside information.

b. For greater certainty, insider means any of the following:

1) a director, a senior executive or an employee of the issuer of a security related to inside information;
2) a person who obtains inside information through a family relationship, including from any person related to the person who obtains the information;
3) a person who obtains inside information through a business relationship, including obtaining the information:
   * from the issuer of a security related to inside information;
   * from any person who has a business relationship with the person who obtains the information; or
   * from any person who is a business associate of the person who obtains the information;
4) a person who obtains inside information through a contractual relationship, including obtaining the information:
   * from the issuer of a security related to inside information; or
   * from any person who has a contractual relationship with the person who obtains the information.

c. For greater certainty, inside information means information that fulfils the following:

   1) information that relates to a security;
   2) that has not been disclosed to the general public, and that is not otherwise available to the general public; and
   3) that a normal person would realise that, in view of the nature and content of the information, disclosing it or making it available to the public would have a material effect on the price or value of the security.

Article 5: Prohibition of disclosure of inside information

a. An insider is prohibited from disclosing any inside information to any other person when he knows or should have known that it is possible that such other person may trade in the security related to the inside information.
b. A person who is not insider is prohibited from disclosing to any other person any inside information obtained from an insider, when he knows or should have known that it is possible that such other person to whom the disclosure has been made may trade in the security related to the inside information.

Article 6: Prohibition of insider trading

a. An insider is prohibited from engaging in insider trading.
b. A person who is not insider is prohibited from engaging in insider trading if he obtains the inside information from another person and he knows or should have known, that the information is inside information.

PART 4: UNTRUE STATEMENTS

Article 7: Prohibition of untrue statements

A person is prohibited from making an untrue statement of material fact verbally or in writing or from failing to make a statement required to be made under the Capital Market Law, the Implementing Regulations, or the rules of the Exchange or the Depositary Center, if the statement is made, or the person fails to make the required statement, for the purpose of influencing the price or value of a security, inducing another person to purchase or sell a security, or inducing him to exercise or refrain from exercising rights under a security.

Article 8: Rumours

a. A person is prohibited from circulating, directly or indirectly, an untrue statement of material fact or a statement of opinion for the purpose of influencing the price or value of a security or for any manipulative purpose.
b. The prohibition in paragraph (a) applies to a statement made by the person who circulates the statement or to a statement made by another person.

Article 9: Untrue statements defined

a. A person makes an untrue statement of material fact in any of the following circumstances:

   1) if he makes a statement that is false or inaccurate in a material respect;
   2) if he procures another person to make a statement that is false or inaccurate in a material respect;
   3) if he makes a statement that contains a misrepresentation of a material fact;
   4) if he procures another person to make a statement that contains a misrepresentation of a material fact; or
   5) if he omits a material fact when making a statement.

b. A material fact is any information relating to a security which, if the investor knew about, would have materially affected the price or value at which the investor purchased or sold the security.

Article 10: Responsibility for untrue statements

For the purposes of application of Article 56 of the Capital Market Law and the provisions of this part:

a. A person shall be liable for damages to a claimant if he makes an untrue statement of material fact and the statement is made:

1) for the purpose of profit or commercial benefit; and
2) in relation to the purchase or sale of a security.

b. A claimant for damages under paragraph (a) of this Article must establish that:

1) he was not aware that the statement was untrue;
2) he would not have purchased or sold the security in question if he was aware of the untrue statement, or that he would not have purchased or sold the security at the price at which such security was purchased or sold; and
3) the person who made the untrue statement knew, or knew that there was a substantial likelihood, that the statement was untrue in relation to a material fact.

c. A person shall be liable for damages to a claimant, if he is obliged under the Capital Market Law, the Implementing Regulations, or the rules of the Exchange or the Depositary Center to make a statement and fails to do so provided that:

1) the claim for damages is in relation to the purchase or sale of a security; and
2) what has been omitted relates to a material fact.

d. A claimant for damages under paragraph (c) of this Article must establish that:

1) he was not aware of the failure to make the statement; and
2) he would not have purchased or sold the security in question had he known in advance that the statement was omitted, or that he would not have purchased or sold the security at the price at which such security was purchased or sold.

PART 5: AUTHORISED PERSONS' CONDUCT

Article 11: Conduct in case of market manipulation and insider trading by clients

a. An authorised person or a registered person must not accept or execute a client order if any of them has reasonable grounds to believe that the client:

   1) is engaging in market manipulation or insider trading;
   2) would be engaging in market manipulation or insider trading in another market if these Regulations applied to that market; or
   3) would be considered in breach of the law, regulations or rules applicable in the relevant market.

b. Where an authorised person or registered person has decided not to accept or execute an order under paragraph (a) of this Article, he must document the circumstances of and reasons for his decision in writing and the authorised person must notify the Authority of the decision within three days.
c. An authorised person must retain the records in relation to any decision under this Article for ten years from the date of the decision.

Article 12: Clients priority and front running trades

a. An authorised person or a registered person must execute client orders for a security before executing any order on the same security for his own account.
b. An authorised person, a registered person and any associated person are prohibited from dealing in any security for their own benefit, or for the benefit of another client, or for the benefit of an account which they have an interest in, including any account which they have a discretion on, if such dealing is on the basis of prior knowledge that a client order has been or will be entered on the same security.
c. Persons referred to in paragraph (a) of this Article are porhibited from disclosing to any other person any information related to clients orders that have been entered or will be entered, when they know or should have known that it is possible that such other person may trade in the security related to that information .
d. Any person that obtains through an authorised person or a registered person information related to client orders that have been or will be entered is prohibited from dealing in the security related to such information., if such dealing is for the purpose of benefiting from potential material effect of those orders on the price of that security.
e. Any person authorised to deal with the account of a legal person is prohibited from dealing in any particular security for his own benefit, or for the benefit of an account which he has an interest in, if such dealing is for the purpose of benefiting from potential material effect of that legal person's account orders that have been or will be entered on the price of that security.

f. Any person authorised to deal with the account of a legal person is prohibited from disclosing to any other person any information related to that account orders that have been or will be entered, when he knows or should have known that it is possible that such other person may trade in the security related to that information.
g. Any person that obtains from to deal in any particular security on the basis of information obtained from a person authorsied to deal with the account of a legal person related to this account orders that have been or will be entered, if such dealing is for the purpose of benefiting from potential material effect of those orders on the price of that security.
h. For the purposes of this Article:
   1) "Associated person" means in relation to an authorised person:
      - Any director, partner, employee, or any person that is (directly or indirectly) controlled by that person; or controls (directly or indirectly) that person.
      - any company which is its subsidiary or parent or fellow subsidiary of the parent.
      - any company whose directors are accustomed to act in accordance with the authorised person's directions or instructions.
      - any company in the capital of which the authorised person is directly or indirectly interested so that it is able:
         • to exercise or control the exercise of 30% or more of the votes at the general meeting on all, or substantially all matters; or
         • to appoint or remove directors holding a majority of voting rights at board meetings on all, or substantially all matters.
   2) "Associated person" means in relation to a registered person:
      - that person's spouse or minor children (together "members of his family").
      - any company in whose equity shares the registered person or any member or members (taken together) of his family are directly or indirectly interested so that they are able:
         • to exercise or control the exercise of 30% or more of the votes at the general meeting on all, or substantially all matters; or
         • to appoint or remove directors holding a majority of voting rights at board meetings on all, or substantially all matters.

Article 13: Timely execution

If an authorised person accepts a client order or decides in its discretion to execute a client order, it must execute the order as soon as is practical in the circumstances.

Article 14: Best execution

a. Where an authorised person deals with or for a client, it must provide best execution.

b. An authorised person is considered to provide best execution if:

   1) acting as agent, it ensures that the order is executed at the best prevailing price in the relevant market or markets for the size of the order; or
   2) acting as principal, it executes the transaction at a better price for the client than it would have obtained if it executed the order in accordance with the preceding paragraph.

Article 15: Timely allocation

An authorised person who executes a transaction based on a client order must ensure that the transaction is promptly allocated to the account of that client. An authorised person who executes a discretionary transaction must ensure that the transaction is promptly allocated to the account of the client for whom the authorised person decided to transact.

Article 16: Churning

An authorised person must not advise or solicit a client to deal or deal or arrange a deal in the course of managing for a client if the dealing would reasonably be regarded as contrary to the interest of the client, having regard to the number and frequency of trades relative to the client's investment objectives, financial situation and the size and character of his account.

Article 17: Aggregation of client orders

a. An authorised person must not aggregate a client's orders with those of other clients or with the authorised person's own orders if the order is for a security traded on the Saudi Stock Exchange.
b. If the order is for a security that is not traded on the Saudi Stock Exchange, an authorised person may aggregate a client's orders with those of other clients or with the authorised person's own orders if the following is fulfilled:

   1) the authorised person has provided a written explanation to the client of the advantages and disadvantages of aggregation and obtained written consent from the client to aggregate orders;
   2) the authorised person ensures that no client will be disadvantaged by aggregation of his orders; and
   3) all clients' orders that are aggregated receive the average price of execution for all of the orders that are executed.

c. An authorised person must establish a written policy setting out its method of allocating trades to client and principal orders.

Article 18: Dealing ahead of research

a. Where an authorised person intends, or knows that an affiliate intends, to issue to a client or clients an investment recommendation, or a research, study or analysis relating to a security, subject to paragraph (b) below, the authorised person must not knowingly make a trade for its own account in the security concerned or in any related security until the clients for whom the recommendation or research was intended have had a reasonable opportunity to react to it.
b. An authorised person may make a trade for its own account if the recommendation, research, study or analysis could not reasonably be expected to affect the price of the security concerned or any related security.

Article 19: Prohibition of dealing contrary to a recommendation

Where an authorised person or any of its affiliates issues an investment recommendation, research, study or analysis relating to a security it is prohibited from:

1) providing advice to a client or making a trade for a client that is contrary to the recommendation unless the authorised person, prior to providing the advice or making the trade, discloses to the client the recommendation and the potential conflict of interest between the authorised person and the client; or
2) making a trade for its own account in the security that is contrary to the recommendation unless reasonable grounds exist to make the trade.

Article 20: Liability for acts of others

Where a person is found to have violated the provisions of the Capital Market Law or the Implementing Regulations on market manipulation, insider trading or untrue statements while acting on behalf of another person and at the direction of the person on whose behalf the relevant act is carried out, that other person is liable and is subject to any sanctions to which the person carrying out the relevant acts is subject unless the person on whose behalf the act is carried out:

1) took reasonable steps to prevent the violation of the provisions of the Capital Market Law and its Implementing Regulations; and
2) did not authorise the acts in question.

PART 6: PUBLICATION AND ENTRY INTO FORCE

Article 21: Publication and entry into force

These Regulations shall become effective upon their publication.

Index

E

F

G

H

I

INTERNATIONAL BANKING AND FINANCE LAW SERIES

1. Jan Job de Vries Robbe, *Innovations in Securitisation. Yearbook 2006,* 2006 (ISBN 90-11 - 2533-7).
2. Jim Bartos, *United States Securities Law: A Practical Guide,* Third edition, 2006 (ISBN 90-411-2362-8).
3. Hui Huang, *International Securities Markets: Insider Trading Law in China,* 2006 (ISBN 90-411-2557-4).
4. Barth et al., *Financial Restructuring and Reform in Post-WTO China,* 2007 (ISBN 90-411- 2573-6).
5. Zhongfei Zhou, *Banking Laws in China,* 2007 (ISBN 978-90-411-2519-4).
6. Jan Job de Vries Robbe & Paul Ali, *Expansion and Diversification in Securitization Yearbook 2007,* 2007 (ISBN 978-90-411-2661-0).
7. Ross Buckley, *International Financial System. Policy and Regulation,* 2008 (ISBN 978- 90-411-2746-4).
8. Jan Job de Vries Robbe, *Securitization Law and Practice: In the Face of the Credit Crunch,* 2008 (ISBN 978-90-411-2715-0).
9. Phoebus Athanassiou, *Hedge Fund Regulation in the European Union: Current Trends and Future Prospects,* 2009 (ISBN 978-90-411-2856-0).
10. Jan Job de Vries Robbe, *Structured Finance: On from the Credit Crunch: The Road to Recovery,* 2009 (ISBN 978-90-411-2787-7).
11. Gaetane Schaeken Willemaers, *The EU Issuer-Disclosure Regime: Objectives and Proposals for Reform,* 2011 (ISBN 978-90-411-3394-6).
12. Panagiotis Delimatsis & Nils Herger (eds), *Financial Regulation at the Crossroads: Implications for Supervision, Institutional Design and Trade,* 2011 (ISBN 978-90-411-3355-7).
13. Raffaele Scalcione, *The Derivatives Revolution: A Trapped Innovation and a Blueprint for Regulatory Reform,* 2011 (ISBN 978-90-411-3430-1).
14. Douglas Arner & Ross Buckley, *From Crisis to Crisis: The Global Financial System and Regulatory Failure,* 2011 (ISBN 978-90-411-3354-0).
15. Anton P. Trichardt, *Letters of Comfort: A Trans-Systemic Analysis,* 2012 (ISBN 978-90- 411-3600-8).
16. Eddy Wymeersch, *Alternative Investment Fund Regulation,* 2012 (ISBN 978-90-411-3690- 9).
17. Asif H. Qureshi & Xuan Gao (eds), *International Economic Organizations and Law: The Perspective and Role of the Legal Counsel,* 2012 (ISBN 97890-411-3427-1).
18. Rhys Bollen, *The Law and Regulation of Payment Services: A Comparative Study,* 2012 (ISBN 978-90-411-3818-7).
19. Ramandeep Kaur Chhina, *Standby Letters of Credit in International Trade,* 2012 (ISBN 978-90-411-4560-4).

20. Dirk A. Zetzsche (ed.), *The Alternative Investment Fund Managers Directive: European Regulation of Alternative Investment Funds*, 2012 (ISBN 978-90-411-4044-9).
21. Lorenzo Sasso, *Capital Structure and Corporate Governance: The Role of Hybrid Financial Instruments*, 2013 (ISBN 978-90-411-4843-8).
22. Pablo Iglesias-Rodríguez, *The Accountability of Financial Regulators: A European and International Perspective*, 2013 (ISBN 978-90-411-3874-3).
23. Seraina Neva Grünewald, *The Resolution of Cross-Border Banking Crises in the European Union: A Legal Study from the Perspective of Burden Sharing*, 2014 (ISBN 978-90-411-4909-1).
24. Megan Bowman, *Banking on Climate Change: How Finance Actors and Transnational Regulatory Regimes are Responding*, 2015 (ISBN 978-90-411-5223-7).
25. Jin Sheng, *China's Listed Companies: Conflicts, Governance and Regulation*, 2015 (ISBN 978-90-411-5925-0).
26. Sven Schelo, *Bank Recovery and Resolution*, 2015 (ISBN 978-90-411-4959-6).
27. Luis M. Hinojosa-Martínez & José María Beneyto (eds), *European Banking Union: The New Regime*, 2015 (ISBN 978-90-411-5263-3).
28. Gill North, *Effective Company Disclosure in the Digital Age*, 2015 (ISBN 978-90-411-3815-6).
29. Hanneke Wegman, *Investor Protection: Towards Additional EU Regulation of Investment Funds?*, 2016 (ISBN 978-90-411-5252-7).
30. Ruth Plato-Shinar, *Banking Regulation in Israel: Prudential Regulation versus Consumer Protection*, 2016 (ISBN 978-90-411-6791-0).
31. Bader Alkhaldi, *Saudi Capital Market: Developments and Challenges*, 2017 (ISBN 978-90-411-8351-4).

www.ingramcontent.com/pod-product-compliance
Lightning Source LLC
Chambersburg PA
CBHW071240230926
51849CB00001B/170
* 9 7 8 9 0 4 1 1 8 3 5 1 4 *